# Performance Tuning
# in Theory and Practice

# Four Strokes

## A. Graham Bell

**ISBN 0 85429 275 6**

© A. Graham Bell

First Published February 1981

**A FOULIS book**


*Printed in England by the publishers*
**Haynes Publishing Group**
Sparkford, Yeovil, Somerset BA22 7JJ, England


*Distributed in North America by*
**Haynes Publications Inc**
861 Lawrence Drive, Newbury Park, California 91320  USA


*Editor:* **Jeff Clew**
*Cover Design:* **Phill Jennings**
*Layout Design:* **John Martin**

# Contents

# Preface

PRACTICALLY no private owners, and only a few workshops where engines are prepared, possess dynamometers. Consequently experiments in tuning usually must be conducted on a trial and error basis, which may have unfortunate results if the work has been wrongly conceived or executed. This book represents an endeavor to fill the gaps in the enthusiasts' knowledge, or to extend an acquaintance with the subject a little further.

The range of performance equipment available for almost any car or motorcycle is staggering and often the claims made in advertising various items of equipment are equally staggering. Obviously there must be certain principles, applying to almost any engine, that will, if closely followed, bring good results. I believe that this type of information should be available to the tuner, to enable him to choose the best equipment and install it correctly. With this in mind I have attempted to relate these principles in non-technical English and to illustrate them, using many diagrams.

Certainly it is beyond the scope of this book to give detailed step by step instructions on the modification of any one specific engine. However, realising the need for additional information, an extensive Appendix has been prepared.

While I have endeavoured to make this work as complete and as comprehensive as possible, undoubtedly there will be questions that I will have overlooked and left unanswered. On the other hand there are certain to be times when the reader may feel that I have dwelt far too long on a particular point. I apologise for this. However, in spite of these possible failings I am sure this book will be found both instructive and informative.

*A. Graham Bell*

# Chapter 1
# Introduction

FROM THE outset let me caution you on the need to plan your intended modifications carefully. Avoid over-enthusiasm and keep in mind that seldom, if ever, is the biggest or most expensive the best. Compatibility of the intended modifications cannot be over-stressed. Most enthusiasts' realise that it is useless installing a full race cam in a standard motor, yet it is amazing how many will hang hundreds of dollars worth of impressive looking carburettors off that same standard motor. Then we have the enthusiast who plans his performance modifications carefully. He has a head, cam, carbs and exhaust that work nicely together, but in so doing the motor now produces maximum power at 7800 rpm whereas the crankshaft, rods and pistons have a safe limit of 6800 rpm. Less enthusiasm with the cam and carburettor size would have produced a motor that was much nicer to drive, and less likely to blow up.

To get value for money you must first know and accurately assess your engine. Determine what its good and weak points are and estimate what improvements in performance the rectification of each weak point would bring about in relation to the amount of money it is going to cost to rectify that problem area.

Let's just look at an average motorcycle engine for a moment. The bottom end is good and solid. Valve sizes are good and the combustion chamber is hemispherical. There is a fair size carburettor feeding each cylinder. The motor is very flexible, with a wide power band, and the exhaust is arranged through four individual pipes. We are after a 20% increase in power without much loss of flexibility. Certainly we could get the full 20% increase easily by using a hotter cam; however this would mean fitting stronger valve springs and fly cutting the pistons for valve clearance. A better choice would be to use a cam that will work with the standard springs and won't lift the valves far enough to bang them into the pistons. Such a cam gives us, say a 12% power rise. Furthermore, the exhaust system is a bit of a crumb; it rusts out every twelve or eighteen months because the four individual pipes run too cold. A dandy four-into-one extractor system would pick up power, especially in the mid-range. It's nice and quiet and costs about the same as those forever rusting individual pipes. Obviously a mild cam and a good set of pipes is the way to go.

It is amazing how many performance cars have a good carburettor setup, decent cam, reasonable head etc., all exhausting through a lump of cast-iron. Look at the Lotus Elan; twin sidedraught Webers, twin overhead cams, excellent head, all connected to a cast iron exhaust manifold. A change to a hotter set of cams, even if quite mild, will only result in lost power in an instance like this. However, a good set of exhaust tubes and a pair of mild cams will give an 18-20 hp increase.

Once you begin looking for a power increase in excess of 30%, the choice may not seem quite so obvious, especially if the modifications must be carried out in two, three or four stages due to a limited budget. Keeping in mind that there may be a lapse of many months between each successive stage the need to plan carefully becomes evident.

We have a 2 litre ohc Cortina/Pinto motor and we want around 140 - 145 hp. The following modifications will be required to get a 45% increase reliably over a stock motor:- forged pistons; balanced crank, rods, flywheel and clutch; heavy duty clutch; head port and polish; 7000 rpm valve springs; fairly warm cam; vernier timing gears, twin 40 or 45 DCOE Webers; extractor/header exhaust manifold; modify distributor advance curve. This amount of work obviously will cost a lot of money, so we will break it up into four stages. The motor has done only 17,000 miles so we can forget about the bottom end strengthening for the time being. Firstly, we would buy the extractor exhaust manifold. Next would be the head work including the 7000 rpm valve springs; we should have the twin Weber manifold at this stage too, so that the manifold and head ports can be matched. Then we would fit the twin Webers; the main jets will have to be changed though when the cam is fitted. After the Webers the final stage is to strip the motor and rebuild the bottom end, fit new forged pistons and balance everything, modify the distributor and fit the new cam and vernier timing gears.

When we begin to think about fairly big power increases another aspect of horsepower per dollar must be considered. The situation is this; the more power you are after the more dollars you will spend for each additional horse, so while the first 10 hp may have cost $150, the next 10 hp will possibly cost $250 and the next 10 hp $400. In this example the last 10 hp costs the same amount of money as the first 20 additional hp, so are you really getting value for money? If you are running in competition obviously you are stuck with a particular engine size class limit so there is not much you can do. However, if it's a road car maybe a larger motor of similar external dimensions from a wrecking yard could be the answer. Therefore if you have a 1600 Cortina and you want 130 hp, the cheapest move will be to fit a 2000 Pinto motor, suitably modified, to give 130 hp.

Another area for consideration when you set out to plan engine modifications is always to relate the engine to the vehicle in which it is going to be used, and plan your hot-up accordingly.

The first influence is the size of the motor. Obviously a heavy vehicle with a small motor will require a power curve biased towards low and mid-range power, rather than to all-out power, if it is to remain driveable. A larger engine in the same car could be more extensively modified and it would produce as much, or even more, power at lower engine speeds.

The engine capacity/vehicle weight relationship must also be reckoned along with gear-box ratios, the number of gears and steps between gears, and also the final drive ratio. This is explained more fully later, but it should be clear that it would be useless to modify a motor to produce maximum power at 7500 rpm if the weight of the car, its air resistance, and diff. ratio are such that it could only pull 5500 rpm in top gear. To take this hypothetical case a step further we will assume the gearbox is a three-speed unit and the gear spread is such that the motor will drop 3000 rpm between gears. This motor has a 2000 rpm power band, therefore the motor will bog down between gear changes and be slower than the standard unit.

Throughout the book I make continual reference to an engine's state of tune; standard, sports, semi-race and full race. These terms mean virtually nothing (with the possible exception of the first) without some standard against which to measure. Basically, I would define a sports modification as one that results in a moderate power improvement without much loss of low speed tractability. This is the degree of modification that I would recommend for any road-going vehicle and it would be equivalent to the standard tune of an average production high performance car or motorcycle. (eg. Alfa Romeo Alfetta or Suzuki GS 1000).

Semi-race tune would be recommended only for high speed road or rally work. The engine would have very little low speed power and consequently the gearing and vehicle weight would be an important consideration. An engine in this state of tune would almost always require modifications to strengthen the bottom end.

Full race tune is just that — for competition only. An engine in a lesser degree of full race tune would be used in international rallies, $\frac{1}{4}$ mile dirt speedway and other competition requiring reasonable mid-range power. A less experienced driver or rider, on the lower speed road circuits, would be better able to cope with the power characteristics of an engine in this stage of modification rather than be continually battling to keep within the power band of a more highly modified motor.

However, there are so many degrees of full race tune that it is not possible properly to define them. I might add that modifications of this type must be carefully planned to keep the power band compatable with driver ability, circuit layout, race length, engine endurance level and even fuel consumption.

As you plan your modifications, tend to be conservative. A slightly larger carburettor or a cam with a little more duration may give you 5 - 10 hp more at maximum rpm, but you could be losing something like 25 hp a couple of thousand revs below maximum. I would trade 5 hp at 7000 rpm for an extra 25 hp at 5000 rpm any day. Any vehicle, regardless of whether it is being used on the road or the race track, will spend more time running at 5000 rpm then it will at 7000 rpm. The message is to modify your engine to produce the best power in the range at which you are going to be running it.

It may appear a trifle laughable, especially in a book on four-stroke tuning, to include an explanation of four cycle engine operation. However, I have found many enthusiasts do not really know what happens inside a four-stroke engine or for that matter why it is called a four cycle engine in the first place. Therefore I think it would be appropriate to discuss this, so that there is no misunderstanding when we progress into a consideration of the actual modification of an engine of this design.

The following is the sequence of operations in each cylinder, every two revolutions of the crankshaft. First, as the piston goes down, the inlet valve opens fully and the cylinder is filled with air and vaporised fuel (the induction stroke). On the second stroke (the compression stroke) the piston rises, and part way up the inlet valve closes, allowing the piston to compress the fuel/air mixture. As the piston approaches top dead centre, the spark plug ignites the mixture and drives the piston down on the power stroke. Part way down on the power stroke the exhaust valve begins to open and as the piston rises to TDC again, the burned gases are expelled out of the exhaust port (the exhaust stroke). Before the piston actually reaches TDC, the inlet valve starts to lift off its seat, to allow the fuel/air 11 mixture into the engine when the piston descends on the next induction stroke.

Hopefully the following pages will provide you with the knowledge and know-how to plan and execute successfully any degree of engine modification. As you read on, keep the message of this Chapter at the back of your mind. Ignoring any of the foregoing advice could make the consideration of the following information a wasted effort.

# Chapter 2
# The Cylinder Head

THE CYLINDER head is the most important area to be considered by the serious tuner. Its design has more bearing on the end result, performance-wise, than any other component of the high performance engine. There is no way in which high horsepower can be obtained if the head won't flow efficiently, and in turn burn that air/fuel mixture efficiently.

Many tuners go to extremes, cramming as much air into the cylinder as possible, only to have a combustion chamber that won't burn the mixture efficiently. Personally, I am unimpressed by air flow figures; they tell very little about how well a head has been modified. There is no point in getting a lot of mixture into an engine unless you can manage to burn it at the right time, and if you try too hard to get high flow figures, you can easily end up with a combustion chamber that won't burn effectively. While I believe a gas flow rig is an aid in head development, I also believe that it is possible to look at a port and decide whether or not air would like to flow through it. A port that is nice and straight and has no projections will generally flow well. Most engines start with a head design so horrible that to create an improvement should be very simple.

It has been always thought that there is a direct relationship between high air flow numbers and high power output. In principle this theory sounds correct, but in practice it doesn't always work out that way. At one time a factory racing department picked the best high performance heads off the production line for modification. After being ported, each head was flow checked. The heads which recorded the best results were kept for the factory racing team, and the supposedly inferior heads were sold to selected privateers. The interesting thing is that on the dyno, the engines with the heads that produced the best air flow figures actually recorded power outputs no better than engines with average flow heads. After this discovery the factory tested all their heads for power output, before any were released to the private teams, and they found that some of the 'average' heads they had been selling produced the best power.

If the valves are enlarged and the ports are hogged out to the limit, then you will get big power. It is amazing how many people are trapped by this fallacy. TABLES 2.1a and 2.1b 13 indicate the valve sizes that you should be aiming for. Valves of this size in an engine in racing tune will yield maximum power at 7000 to 8000 rpm. Some motors can, because of their oversquare design, benefit from the bigger valves listed and on these maximum power will be gained at 8500 to 9000 rpm.

$$\text{Using the formula } RPM = \frac{GS \times 5900 \times Va}{CV}$$

we can estimate at what speed maximum power will occur for a given inlet valve area, where GS is gas speed in ft/sec, Va is valve area in sq in and CV is cylinder volume in cc. From TABLE 2.2 you will be able to determine the approximate gas speed by estimating whether the camshaft is standard, sports, semi-race or full race. Keep in mind that many standard factory high performance road motors employ sports cams. Valve area is found using the formula $Va = \pi r^2$ where $\pi = 3.1416$ and r is half the valve diameter in inches.

The next area to look at, having established the correct valve sizes, is the inlet port. A round port will flow best and should be 0.81 to 0.83 of the valve head diameter for best performance on the road or the track. I have found this figure to give the best compromise for high air flow and high gas velocity, which is important to give an acceptable power band and good fuel vaporisation at low revs.

There are a few exceptions to this, however. Take the Hillman Imp as an example. In 998 cc form it is possible to fit up to 1.37 inch inlet valves, which according to TABLE 2.1a should be about right for a racing engine spinning at 9000 rpm. Now herein lies the problem; the Imp has very small inlet ports, which can be taken out to only 1.0 inch in diameter because of the closeness of the water jacket. So what is the solution; do you fit 1.22 inch inlet valves to keep the valve to port ratio 100 : 82? No, the valve is always the major restriction; the small port can flow more air than the valve will allow to pass, but only up to a point. In this instance I have found on the dyno that a 1.34 inch valve will give the best hp.

More and more motors are turning to the use of oval, rectangular and square ports. Obviously these will not flow as well as the round port, due to increased surface drag and turbulence. I have obtained the best results by using a valve-to-port ratio of 100 : 72 or 73, with a nice oval port, while rectangular and square ports work best at a 100 : 75 to 76 ratio, the higher figure being for ports with no radius in the corners at all.

Some of our friends in Detroit have gone absolutely wild with big ports. In 1969 Ford,

### TABLE 2.1a    Valve sizes for two valve motors

| Cylinder volume (cc) | Inlet valve diameter (in) | Exhaust valve diameter (in) |
|---|---|---|
| 125 | 1.16 | 1.0 |
| 200 | 1.25 - 1.31 | 1.06 - 1.12 |
| 250 | 1.31 - 1.37 | 1.16 - 1.20 |
| 275 | 1.37 - 1.45 | 1.20 - 1.25 |
| 325 | 1.45 - 1.53 | 1.25 - 1.32 |
| 375 | 1.56 - 1.60 | 1.32 - 1.37 |
| 400 | 1.62 - 1.68 | 1.37 - 1.42 |
| 450 | 1.70 - 1.75 | 1.42 - 1.50 |
| 500 | 1.75 - 1.85 | 1.50 - 1.56 |
| 600 | 2.00 | 1.65 |
| 700 | 2.10 | 1.75 |
| 800 | 2.25 | 1.85 |
| 900 | 2.40 | 1.93 |

## TABLE 2.1b    Valve sizes for four valve motors

| Cylinder volume (cc) | Inlet valve diameter (in) | Exhaust valve diameter (in) |
|---|---|---|
| 250 | 1.16 | 1.00 |
| 325 | 1.25 | 1.06 |
| 400 | 1.31 | 1.12 |
| 450 | 1.35 | 1.16 |
| 500 | 1.38 | 1.20 |
| 600 | 1.50 | 1.28 |
| 700 | 1.60 | 1.35 |
| 800 | 1.65 | 1.40 |

chasing the Trans-Am Championship, introduced the Boss 302 with inlet ports all of 2.5 in tall and 1.75 in wide. They must have realized their mistake, that you just can't get acceptable gas velocities through ports that big, by reducing the inlet valve size from 2.23 to 2.19 in the next year. These same heads are used on the Boss 351 and they are still useless, but they do have a very nice combustion chamber which almost makes up for the horrible big inlet ports.

On the Super Cobra Jet 429 Ford made a similar error but as the combustion chamber in this head has very little going for it, it is best to fit this motor with the standard small port 429 heads, having Super Cobra Jet 2.25 in inlet and 1.75 in exhaust valves.

A fairly uncommon head layout these days is the siamesed port, where one port serves two cylinders. This is the arrangement used by BMC or British Leyland as they prefer now. This type of head has come in for much criticism over the years, but if carefully modified it will yield very good power considering how the undersquare design of these motors restricts the use of large valves. For this type of port the valve to port ratio to look for is 100 : 103.

With round ports it is not necessary to use complicated mathematics to work out the port size; it is just a matter of working to the ratios stated. Therefore a head with 1.5 in inlet valves will use a 1.23 in inlet port or a 1.55 in port if siamesed.

Heads using oval, square or rectangular ports are a different kettle of fish. First, the area of the inlet valve must be calculated. With a 2.1 in inlet valve,

$$\text{area} = \pi \, r^2$$
$$= 3.1416 \times 1.05^2$$
$$= 3.46 \text{ in}^2$$

Therefore a 2.1 in valve will require a port area of 2.63 in² using the ratio of 100 : 76.

The size of the exhaust valve and port is currently being scrutinised by engine tuners all around the world. For many years it was believed that racing engines required an exhaust valve at least 85% of the inlet valve diameter for optimum gas flow. A valve of this size enables the exhaust valve and port to flow around 80 - 85% as much air, on a flow bench as the inlet tract.

Now it is being questioned if the exhaust flow really has to be so high to make good horsepower. A few years ago it didn't really matter if the exhaust valve was too large, but presently we are finding ways of keeping racing machines reliable at higher and higher engine speeds, which makes the use of very large inlet valves a necessity. When all the available combustion chamber space is already taken up, the only way larger inlets can be accommodated is by reducing the exhaust valve size. This move does not appear to choke the motor with unscavenged exhaust gases; in fact it could be beneficial to use smaller 15 exhaust valves than usually recommended as some engines have actually shown an increase in mid-range power as a result.

Some tuners maintain there is no power improvement when the exhaust flow is increased to more than 60% of intake flow, others claim a loss in power occurs when exhaust flow drops to 80 - 83%. I take a middle of the road position. I prefer about 65 - 68% flow for road and rally engines, and 70 - 73% for racing motors.

To get this sort of flow balance between exhaust and intake, the exhaust valve need only be 0.78 to 0.82 times the inlet valve diameter in wedge and bath-tub heads. Hemi and pent roof heads with steeply inclined inlet ports (eg. Cosworth BDA and Lotus Twin Cam) require a valve 0.81 to 0.85 times the inlet size because the flat exhaust port does not flow as well, comparatively, as the inclined inlet port. Motorcycles with either hemi or pent roof heads, and all wedge and bath-tub chambered heads with semi-downdraught inlet ports (see FIGURE 2.12) should use an exhaust valve 0.79 to 0.83 of the inlet valve size.

Generally, exhaust ports should be 95% to 100% of the exhaust valve diameter or area. Siamesed ports need to be considerably larger, but in most instances there just isn't enough metal in the port to achieve this.

When the exhaust port area is being enlarged, gas flow increases dramatically if the port roof is raised, as this serves to reduce flow restriction. It has been proved that 'D' shape exhaust ports outflow round ports of the same area. Therefore square and rectangular ports can be left with a flat floor, and the port roof should be ground round to give the finished shape of a 'D' turned onto its flat.

I must point out that it is an incorrect practice to match the exhaust port to the header pipe. This is definitely one sure way of losing power, particularly in the mid-range. There

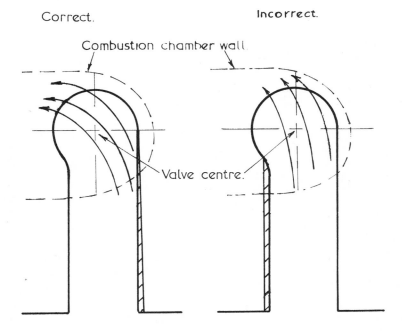

Fig. 2.1  Correctly modified port promotes swirl.

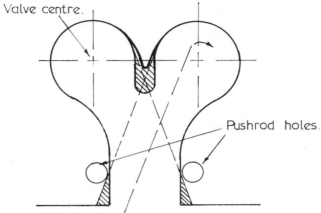

Fig. 2.2  Modified siamese inlet port improves gas flow but deters charge robbing.

must be a sharp step between the exhaust port and the entrance to the header pipe, to reduce exhaust gas backflow into the cylinder. Exhaust backflow is always a problem at lower engine speeds and unfortunately long duration camshafts just worsen the situation.

How much power you will pick up because of the mismatch between the port and header pipe will depend on how large the step is, but it seems the larger the difference in sizes, the greater the power gain. This is not to say you should choke the engine with an exhaust port which is too small or build the header with a pipe size that is larger than required, merely to create a big step, but on the other hand don't enlarge the exhaust port to match the header.

For instance, you may have a 1600 cc racing engine with 1.43 in exhaust valves and ports of the same diameter. The header pipes for this particular unit will have an inside diameter of 1.654 in, which gives quite a good step to impede the backflow of gases. From my testing I have determined a mismatch of this degree can increase maximum power as much as 2 - 3%, and mid-range power by around 5%.

It seems the best arrangement is to have the headers built such that the bottom of the pipe almost lines up with the exhaust port floor, leaving most of the mismatch to occur at the port roof. I'm not sure exactly why this is so, but it could be that concentrating the obstruction on one side of the pipe creates a strong pulse wave to bounce back down the headers and reduce backflow, whereas a small lip right the way around the pipe may act as a constriction and not produce a pulse wave of any magnitude.

## TABLE 2.2   Estimated gas speed at inlet valve (ft/sec)

| Camshaft Profile | Combustion chamber type | | |
|---|---|---|---|
| | *Pent roof & hemi* | *Wedge* | *Bath tub* |
| Standard | 200 | 190 | 175 |
| Sports | 215 | 210 | 210 |
| Semi-race | 235 | 225 | 220 |
| Full race | 260 - 280 | 240 - 255 | 230 - 240 |

*Note – in most motorcycles with pent roof & hemi chambers flow is very similar to wedge chamber figures.*

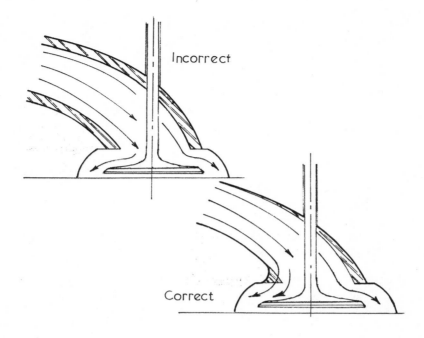

Fig. 2.3    Inlet port should be modified to improve gas flow
around back of valve.

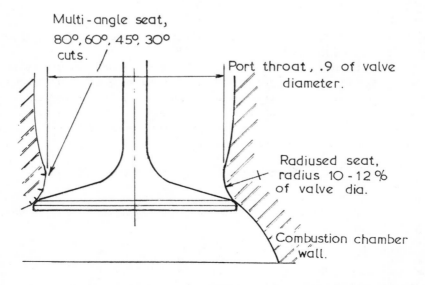

Fig. 2.4    Inlet valve seat profiles.

The next aspect of the cylinder head that we wish to take a look at is swirl. Swirl is defined as the directional effect imparted to the inflowing gas by the shape of the inlet port or its angle of entry into the combustion chamber. Swirl assists eventual combustion by causing the mixture to be evenly and homogenously distributed in the cylinder. At the end of every exhaust cycle there is always a certain amount of exhaust gas which is left unscavenged in the cylinder. If this exhaust gas is allowed to collect into a pocket, it will retard the ignition flame travel, even preventing quite an amount of the fuel/air mixture from burning. Good swirl will prevent this pocket of exhaust gas from forming by evenly mixing the fresh mixture coming into the cylinder with the unscavenged exhaust gas.

Generally, swirl is created by the engine manufacturer offsetting the port from the valve centre. FIGURE 2.1 illustrates an inlet port in plan view. Any tendency of the port to curve and produce swirl should be encouraged, as shown by the port on the left. The port on the right shows a common mistake made by turners, who grind away metal at the easiest place. The port straightening reduces swirl, causing poor mixture distribution, with poor combustion being the end result.

Offsetting the inlet port improves gas flow by causing the mixture to turn as it flows past the valve. This assists in directing flow along the combustion chamber wall and into the cylinder (FIGURE 2.7). Also the section of valve which is completely unshrouded (ie. on the side adjacent to the exhaust valve) will flow more mixture. If you take a look at FIGURE 2.8, you will note that this extreme example of port offset is the reason why the siamese port BMC Mini head flows so well.

To improve flow and discourage charge robbing, the Mini inlet port is modified as in FIGURE 2.2. The port cannot be made much wider because of the location of the pushrod holes, but this restriction has little effect on gas flow, providing the peak between the two inlet pockets is cut back to open up the flow path. The peak deters charge robbing, therefore it should not be cut back further than the port wall alignment, as shown.

Looking at FIGURE 2.3, you can see that there will be better flow on one side of the valve because of the bend in the inlet port. This is another aspect of flow that we must consider, as gas flow along the floor of the port, and around the short radius into the combustion chamber, can be as little as 25% of the flow on the other side of the valve. The majority of mixture flows along the roof of the port and around the more gentle radius into the engine.

The initial flow into the cylinder at low valve lifts is along the floor of the port. As the inertia generated by this initial flow contributes much toward the total flow of the port at full lift, the lower side of the port must be very carefully modified to assist in cylinder filling.

Obviously the mixture must be encouraged to flow better on the lower side of the inlet tract. Sure enough, the improperly modified port in FIGURE 2.3 will flow more air, but not with the valve fitted. The mixture flowing down the inside wall merely bangs into the valve and having lost much of its energy relies on the underhead shape of the valve to direct it into the combustion chamber.

It is an interesting phenomenon, but an improperly modified port will usually flow more air with the valve removed, while a correctly shaped port actually flows slightly less air when the valve is removed. This is assuming that a valve with the correct underhead shape is fitted. If a valve of the wrong shape is used, air flow will always increase when the valve is removed completely out of the head.

The correct thing to do is to remove metal in such a way that a progressive radius is retained on the inside wall. This will cause the air mixture to progressively turn as it remains attached to the port wall. Little energy will be lost as the mixture spills into the cylinder. This contributes to more mixture being introduced.

The blend from the valve throat to the seat and from the seat into the combustion chamber should be a continuous radius, as shown on the right half of FIGURE 2.4. A safe inlet seat width is from 0.035 to 0.050 in. The valve seat itself requires a radius of 10 - 12% of the valve head diameter. The port throat is 0.9 of the valve diameter and blends into an enlarged throat section which is equal to the valve diameter. The inlet port in turn blends into the enlarged throat. These changes in the inlet port cross section are intended to produce a venturi effect to aid gas flow.

For longer valve seat life in endurance racing and road use, or where very heavy valve spring pressures are used, a multi-angle seat is more practical. Air flow is almost as good as with a radiused seat, and the seat will last longer, to provide a good seal right to the end of the race (see left half of FIGURE 2.4).

When a multi-angle seat is used, the actual seat angle should be $45^0$, and 0.050 in wide. The outside diameter of the seat is cut 0.015 - 0.025 in less than the valve head diameter. The top cut to blend the seat into the combustion chamber is at a $30^0$ angle, and a $60^0$ throat cut blends the seat into the inlet port. In racing applications, an additional $15^0$ hand-blended chamber cut, and a further $80^0$ hand-blended throat cut, is used to improve flow.

The exhaust valve seat is the exhaust valve's main point of contact with the engine coolant. In this instance the seat should be cut at $45^0$ and be of 0.070 in width. The exhaust valve reaches a temperature of $1500^0$ to $1800^0$F each ignition cycle, consequently adequate cooling must be maintained through the valve seat and valve guide. The overall diameter of the seat should be the same as or up to 0.010 in less than the valve head diameter. (The heat will normally cause the exhaust valve to grow 0.010 - 0.020 in). To finish the seat, a narrow 0.025 in, $30^0$ chamber cut, and a $55^0$ throat cut should be used.

The inlet valves in many motors are tulip shape. This is the preferred valve shape in motors with symetrical port flow. However, very few motors lend themselves to this type of flow. The few that do are purposely designed high performance motors such as the Ford

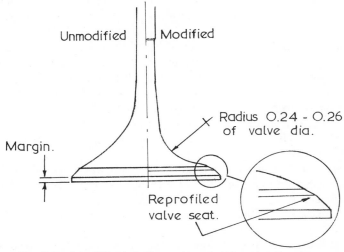

Unmodified | Modified

Radius 0.24 - 0.26 of valve dia.

Margin.

Reprofiled valve seat.

Fig. 2.5 Modified tulip valve for hemi chamber.

Lotus Twin Cam and Cosworth 4 valve motors. These are in the happy position of having the right relationship between port, valve and combustion chamber angle, to eliminate any sharp bend by the port into the combustion chamber. This promotes good gas flow around the entire face of the inlet valve. As shown in FIGURE 2.5, the underhead radius is 0.24-0.26 of the valve diameter.

The majority of motors have the valve/port arrangement shown in FIGURE 2.3, which lends itself to a valve shape with an underhead radius 0.19-0.21 of the valve diameter. Flow on the lower side of the port is improved with this valve shape and this is what we are aiming for. Comparison of the two valves in FIGURE 2.6 shows the improved flow path. You will notice with all inlet valve designs the improvement brought about by recontouring the valve seating area to eliminate any projections.

The inlet valve face seat should be cut at $45^0$ and be 0.065 in wide. Often a $25^0$ - $35^0$ backcut is used to reduce the seat width to the required 0.065 in. The backcut angle will vary from engine to engine, as the angle chosen is the one that best blends the valve head contour into the $45^0$ seat cut. The valve margin should be 0.040 in wide, with a sharp edge to discourage backflow of the mixture into the inlet port.

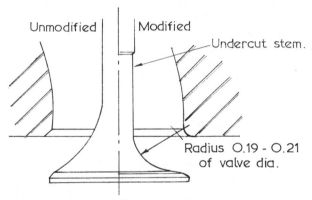

Fig. 2.6 Valve modified for flat roof chamber.

The valve stem should be undercut to reduce its diameter by 0.035 in, immediately below the valve head. This improves the flow by about 10% at valve lifts up to 0.360 in. As the valve opens further, and the thicker section of stem enters deeper into the port, the improvement in flow tapers off. The valve stem is undercut in the area between the head of the valve and the end of the valve guide, with the valve on the seat.

Exhaust valves can also do with some reshaping to improve flow out of the cylinder. The valve face seat should be 0.085 in wide, and radiused back to the stem. The margin width for best flow is 0.060 - 0.085 in, depending on the valve diameter. The lower edge of the margin should be lightly radiused into the valve face, as a square edge disrupts flow out of the motor. The stem is undercut 0.035 in, as for the inlet valve.

A popular fad in American drag racing circles is to modify the back of the exhaust valve by cutting a ditch into it, hence the term ditch cutting. The ditch is usually cut to a depth of 0.050 in all the way around the valve tulip, from the valve stem right to the back of the valve seat. This creates a lip 0.050 in high which is intended to impede exhaust backflow. In theory it sounds good, and on the air flow bench there was a reduction in backflow of about 20% at 0.100 in valve lift, but in practice I have never been able to pick up any power on the dyno. It is probably just as well that this modification doesn't work, because I don't really think a valve weakened by ditching would stay in shape for too long in a road race or rally engine.

The combustion chamber in most overhead valve motors is either bath tub or wedge shape. FIGURE 2.7 shows a Ford Anglia 105E bath tub chamber with the swirl condition described earlier. It is not possible to get the intake mixture to curl around more than a certain amount, so the first obvious modification is to cut away the chamber wall opposite the port. The correct way to achieve this unshrouding is to grind the chamber wall in a concave curve. This will allow the mixture to flow unimpeded outward from the valve and down the cylinder, still swirling. This is essential to maintain a homogenous mixture in the cylinder.

The flat head surface between the wall of the combustion chamber and the cylinder wall is the squish area, which plays a very important part in the combustion process. As the piston travels up to top dead centre it comes into close proximity with the squish area of the head. This squish action actually drives mixture from this area towards the spark plug, for ignition. Obviously the squish area is important for good combustion so a compromise has to be made when cutting away the chamber wall to improve gas flow. I always strive to relieve the chamber wall so that the passage between the valve edge and chamber wall is equal to the valve lift. Therefore if full lift is, say, 0.420 in, we should aim for a chamber wall with a radius of 0.420 in from the valve head (FIGURE 2.7). It is not always possible to cut the chamber wall this amount so we have to be satisfied with less gas flow.

The squish area is also called the quench area, or quench band, as it increases the surface area of the combustion chamber and actually cools or quenches the burning

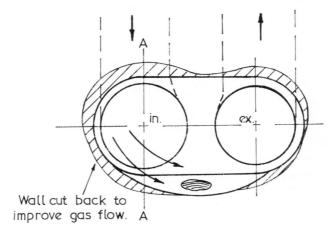

Wall cut back to improve gas flow.

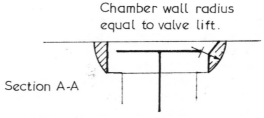

Chamber wall radius equal to valve lift.

Section A-A

Fig. 2.7   Bath-tub chamber modifications.

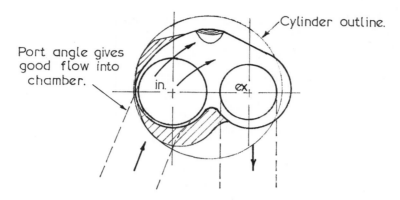

Fig. 2.8. BMC Mini chamber modifications.

mixture around the edges of the combustion chamber. This assists in maintaining a steady (not violent) burn rate, and offsets any tendency for high speed detonation or pre-ignition to occur.

Under certain conditions it is possible for the combustion flame to pre-heat the fuel charge directly in front of the flame to the point of self ignition. When this flame collides with the spark ignited combustion flame, explosion-like combustion results (detonation). The quench area normally prevents this by removing excess heat from the outer gases. With the temperature lowered, the end gases do not self-ignite, to initiate a dangerous detonation condition.

The quench area also lowers the piston crown temperature by momentarily restricting the combustion flame to just the area of the combustion chamber. This increases piston and ring life, and helps prevent the piston becoming a hot spot, able to pre-ignite the fuel/air charge.

The exhaust valve requires very little unshrouding at all. I generally work to a figure of 60% of valve lift for the radius between the valve head and chamber wall. It is a mistake to exceed this figure as the exhaust valve flows very well partially shrouded; in fact it seems to enjoy being shrouded. I well remember an occasion where I was able to pick up 6 hp on a VW 1600 by shrouding the exhaust valve a little. Power went up from 163 to 169 hp which represents a 4% gain.

The heart-shape chamber of the Mini (FIGURE 2.8) is an easy one to modify. It yields high power due to the inlet port offset producing a good swirl effect. The valves should be unshrouded as with a bath tub chamber.

The wedge chamber common to almost every American V8, the Hillman Imp and a few others, is just a bath tub chamber inclined, usually at around 15⁰. This is a more difficult chamber to modify as the wall opposite the inlet port requires so much grinding to unshroud the inlet valve that high top pistons must be fitted to restore compression.

FIGURE 2.9 shows three high performance wedge chamber heads. The first head, from the 427 Chevy L-88, has a very closed chamber design. In 1969, the ZL-1 chambers were opened up to improve breathing. The third head, from the Ford Boss 302/351, also has very open chambers. You will note that the Boss chambers are not opened right out to the edge of the bore as on the ZL-1 head. This is done for a very good reason, so learn from it.

Remember we were talking before about squish and its importance in the combustion 23

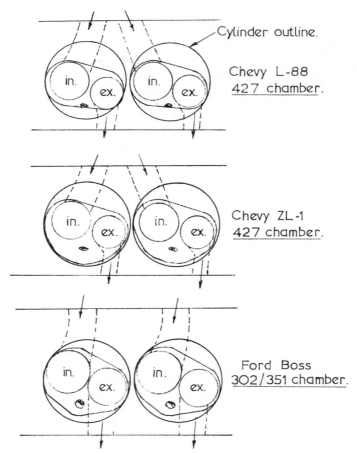

Fig. 2.9   Three high performance wedge chambers.

process. The primary or major squish area should be somewhere about opposite the spark plug, to squish the bulk of the fuel/air mixture over into the combustion area. Now behind the spark plug we have a secondary squish area (see Boss 302/351 head). Its effect too is to squish and create a pressure wave. As the spark plug ignites the mixture, this wave assists the flame front to travel through and ignite the mixture that the major squish area has pushed towards the spark plug.

If the combustion chamber is cut back right to the bore wall, what is the result? Gas flow will improve, but remember I said right at the outset that gas flow has to be balanced against good combustion. With no secondary squish to assist the flame front and impede the mixture rushing across from the major squish area, you must lose power. This is what happens; the mixture being purged across to the spark plug bangs into the chamber wall and spark plug and devaporises, wetting the chamber wall and possibly the spark plug too, depending on its temperature. Try holding your hand in front of an aerosol spray pack when you are spraying and you will see what I am getting at.

At the very least, a head modified in this way will waste fuel and dilute your engine oil.

Some of that lovely fuel mixture you have managed to cram into the cylinder will end up going out of the exhaust or at low revs and/or with a cold motor it will end up in the sump, wrecking your super-good oil.

This same problem can exist if bath tub or heart shape chambers are not modified properly but it seems to be more common to the wedge chamber because of the desire of tuners to carve away at that high chamber wall opposite the inlet port to improve gas flow.

Why use the wedge chamber then, you may ask? FIGURE 2.10 illustrates the most obvious benefit from this design, namely to reduce the bend in the inlet port, allowing the valve to flow better, particularly on the lower side. A straight (non-inclined) port flowing into a bath tub chamber flows only about 20% of the mixture on the lower or 'dead' side of the valve, but the wedge chamber can flow 25 to 30% of the mixture on this side.

The other obvious benefit is the concentration of fuel/air mixture close to the spark plug in the deepest part of the chamber. This effectively shortens the flame travel, allowing for complete combustion if a flat top piston is used. All those lumpy pistons alter the shape of the combustion chamber, so high top pistons have to be matched to the combustion chamber and vice versa.

Remember at all times that high top pistons can cause serious combustion problems. They mask the spark plug in many instances and always cause a longer flame travel path. Often, stale pockets are created, where no combustion takes place. Many high top 12.5:1 compression pistons are of such poor design that I am sure the same motor running flat tops at 10:1 would produce as much power, more smoothly. Hopefully, advances in piston design will overcome, if not completely eliminate, these problems in the near future.

This leads us to what I regard as the most horrible design of all time, the Heron head. It works just fine on 2000 rpm diesels, but used on a petrol engine it is nothing like so good. The design utilises a flat face head without a combustion chamber. Instead, combustion takes

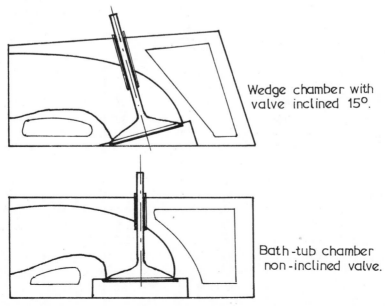

Wedge chamber with valve inclined 15°.

Bath-tub chamber non-inclined valve.

Fig. 2.10 Wedge chamber decreases port entry angle.

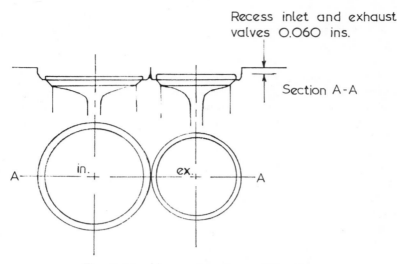

Recess inlet and exhaust
valves 0.060 ins.

Section A-A

A — in. — ex. — A

Fig. 2.11   Heron head modification.

place in a combustion chamber cast into the piston crown. Ford use this design in their so-called 'Crossflow' Escort and Cortina and 3 litre V6 Capri motor. Chrysler also use it in their Avenger motors.

Having no effective squish area, this design suffers chronic ignition problems. The Avenger, for example, is only happy with $46 - 47^0$ spark advance. If you must stick with this design rather than using a head with combustion chambers machined into it (very expensive), there are a few principles to keep in mind. The first is to keep the inlet system on the small side. Use a small bore carburettor venturi and port diameter to keep gas speed high. Profile grind the inlet port but leave it reasonably rough. Machine the top of the cylinder block to bring the pistons to around 0.005 to 0.007 in from the deck. This will induce some squish effect. I have found that recessing the valves into the head (FIGURE 2.11) about 0.060 in improves not only the gas flow but also, I suspect, the combustion. The shrouding of the valves possibly causes some sort of venturi effect, which aids vaporisation and homogenisation of the mixture. The early Ford 1600GT had small combustion chambers machined into the head. This head is best pensioned off and replaced with a counter-bored flat head, which will improve the compression as well.

Besides the combustion problem, a basic mechanical problem exists with the Heron design. Because the combustion chamber is in the crown of the piston, the heat path is made longer. This increases the piston crown temperature. With thermal distortion thrown in for good measure, piston seizure is commonplace.

Now I don't deny that Cosworth used this design on their very successful 1 litre SCA engine, finally extracting 140 hp from it with a $49^0$ spark advance. However, keep this in mind; a 250 cc cylinder running a 12.5:1 compression ratio has a very small combustion chamber and as half of the combustion chamber on this motor is in the head, the heat path across the piston crown is not much longer than that across a flat top piston. Furthermore, a racing engine can be run with very big piston clearances and rattle all it likes, so piston distortion and/or seizure would not be such a problem.

Decreasing the valve to port angle is really what high power outputs are all about. By

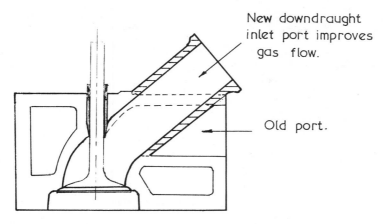

New downdraught
inlet port improves
gas flow.

Old port.

Fig. 2.12    Downdraught conversion.

coaxing the 'dead' side of the port and valve to flow better, we can cram more mixture into the cylinder in any given time. FIGURE 2.12 shows the Ford Anglia 105E head modified with downdraught inlet ports. On the 1300 cc Ford Escort, I have seen 143 hp with this head on carburettors, which is all of 15 hp or 12% more power than the same motor would produce on a 105E sidedraught head.

Today, many European performance engines use what is known as the hemispherical chamber for this very reason. The inlet tract is straightened out and a large valve area is possible. This design too has had its problems. Back in the early '50s, the hemispherical chamber was being pioneered by such manufacturers as Jaguar, Chrysler, and Norton. The design suffered a basic mixture burn problem so $50^0$ spark advance was commonplace. In FIGURE 2.13 you will note the valve angle (usually around 70 - $90^0$ included angle), creating a huge combustion chamber. This large chamber surface area allows heat loss from the compressed mixture, reducing efficiency. Also, because of the large chamber area, the ignition flame must travel an extreme distance. Consequently two spark plugs were used in

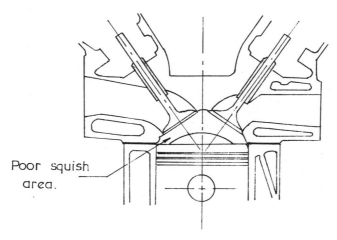

Poor squish
area.

Fig. 2.13   Early  Jaguar  head  design.

27

racing engines, to aid combustion. Even today, after 20 years of development, the Chrysler hemi still works better with two plugs.

Remember our friend squish, well he is lacking too with this design. Referring back to FIGURE 2.13 you will notice that some squish does occur due to the radius of the combustion chamber being smaller than that of the piston dome, but this isn't enough to promote good combustion.

Later, the piston dome design was changed to that shown in FIGURE 2.14. This design is still used by Chrysler and Jaguar today. The piston dome in this design is supplemented by a flat section running right round the crown, which comes into close contact with the lower reaches of the combustion chamber. Squish is improved, bringing an improvement in combustion. This has resulted in higher power outputs and a reduction in spark advance.

1963 saw the introduction of the Lotus/Ford Twin Cam. Not a true hemi but a semi-hemi, this motor set the pace in head design, in the car world at any rate, for many years. In 1.6 litre form this motor will produce 210 hp on carburettors. It will run quite happily with just a 30 to 34° spark lead. In fact the motor I ran on the road in my Ford Anglia for many years operated with only 25° total advance. It was no slouch either, producing 156 hp at 6800 rpm.

The semi-hemi combustion chamber (FIGURE 2.15) has two distinct squish areas which drive the fuel mixture towards the spark plug. The valve angle has been closed up (54° on Lotus/Ford Twin Cam), allowing the use of a flat top piston. Consequently this design enjoys a more compact combustion chamber than the true hemi, and this feature, combined with good squish control, makes for high power outputs while still allowing a large valve area and a relatively straight inlet port.

You will note too with this design, as with the hemi, that the inlet valve, and also generally the exhaust valve, are completely unshrouded. This allows for fairly even mixture flow right round the valve head. Instead of the valve flowing 80% on one side and 20% on the other, as with the bath tub chamber, it will probably be flowing something more like 57% and 43% in this instance. Therefore the available area is being used more effectively so that air flow and horsepower goes up.

The final development of this type of chamber is what we call the pent roof chamber (FIGURE 2.16.) This design is immediately associated with Cosworth because of the

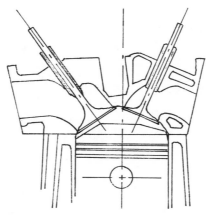

Fig. 2.14 Late Chrysler Hemi has improved squish control.

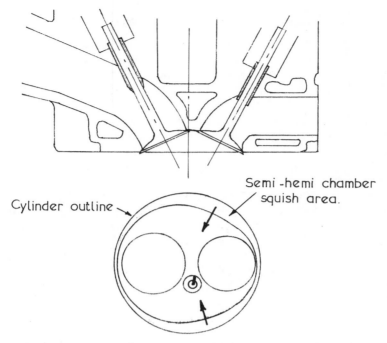

Fig. 2.15    Lotus/Ford twin cam head arrangement.

pioneering done by Keith Duckworth in developing the 1.6 litre 225 hp Ford FVA and later the 3 litre 470 hp Ford DFV Grand Prix engine, proving the advantages of the four valve pent roof chamber. From the outset, the advantages of the design were not so obvious. Both Coventry Climax and BRM had earlier tried this layout but without much improvement over the more conventional semi-hemi. BRM, in its typical enthusiasm, even tried a four valve with diametrically opposed inlet and exhaust valves. Can you imagine designing the intake and exhaust system for a V12 so equipped?

It was the motorcycle world that brought us this design. Back in the early '60s Honda was using the four valve principle on its Grand Prix bikes. At that time they were running a five cylinder 125, a six cylinder 250 and 297 and a four cylinder 500, all with four valve pent roof chambers. The 250 produced 60 hp at 17,000 rpm. Honda then carried the design on to the car Grand Prix circuit with their 160 hp 1 litre Formula 2 engine. The two valve 140 hp Cosworth SCA was no match, so when the Formual 2 capacity limit was lifted to 1.6 litres, Keith Duckworth designed his new motor, the Ford FVA, around the four valve pent roof chamber. He got his maths right; for the first time the FVA rode the dyno it pushed out 202 hp at 9000 rpm.

After the FVA and DFV engines, Cosworth applied this same formula to the Ford Capri, producing a 450 hp 3.5 litre V6. Today, both Ford and Chevy have put the Duckworth design into production; Ford with the BDA 1600 and 1800 RS Escorts, and Chevy with the Cosworth Vega. Lotus too use the four valve arrangement for their production 2 litre motor based on the Vauxhall slant block.

Honda 250 and 350 trail bikes use the four valve arrangement, operated by a single overhead cam, as does the 2 litre Triumph Dolomite Sprint. Weslake produce a four valve 29 conversion for the small block Chevy, the result being an honest 640 hp and 473 ft/lb torque from a 350.

With the pent roof chamber, the valve angle is further closed up to 40° on the Cosworth motors (32° on DFV V8), producing a very shallow combustion chamber which allows the use of a flat top piston. Squish is good and from opposite sides of a single central spark plug. (FIGURE 2.16) The arrangement of two inlet and two exhaust valves in the chamber allows for an increase of over 30% valve area in the case of the Cosworth FVA when compared with the Lotus/Ford Twin Cam. It is this increased air flow, coupled with excellent combustion, that makes this design the way to go. Something to keep in mind is that in spite of the high power and rpm potential of this design, the valve train and valves are relatively unstressed. Because the valves are so small in size and consequently in weight, valve springs can be lighter. The smaller size makes life much more pleasant for the exhaust valve too. As valve diameter increases, valve and seat temperatures increase accordingly.

An interesting development of the four valve pent roof design has been brought to us by Honda in the form of their 400 cc twin. This head offers the same increased inlet valve area and good combustion of the more conventional four valve design, but instead uses one large exhaust valve offset towards the centre of the combustion chamber. The spark plug is still central in the chamber but instead of being vertical it enters at an angle so as to be more easily serviced.

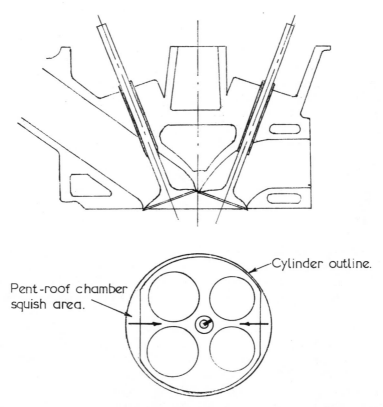

Cylinder outline.

Pent-roof chamber squish area.

Fig. 2.16 Cosworth Chevy Vega four valve head.

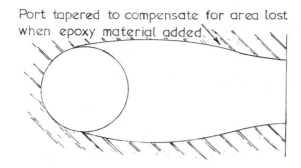

Port tapered to compensate for area lost when epoxy material added.

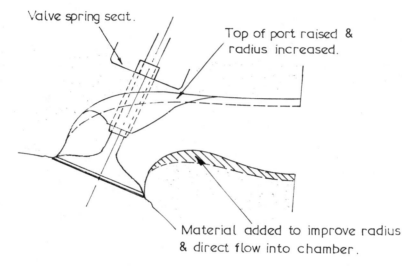

Valve spring seat.

Top of port raised & radius increased.

Material added to improve radius & direct flow into chamber.

Fig. 2.17 Motorcycle inlet port modification.

The design of the semi-hemi (eg. Lotus Twin Cam) and pent root heads is usually so good that not much can be done to improve upon them. The combustion chamber sometimes requires mild reshaping, particularly if larger valves are fitted. The ports too are quite good, needing only the rough cast to be ground off. It is always difficult and expensive to get power increases from a head that is a good design to begin with.

Unfortunately, most motorcycles engines do not gain full benefit from inclined valves and hemi or pent roof chambers, as the inlet port always has a sharp bend in it. On cars it is no problem fitting carburettors on downdraught or semi-downdraught inlet ports, but on bikes the ports have to be kept as low as possible so that the carburettors clear the frame and fuel tank.

This presents quite a problem as the inlet ports can usually be raised no more than about an eighth of an inch, and this small amount does little to straighten out the bend into the combustion chamber. Usually, all that can be done is to increase the radius of the bend. By grinding the top curve of the port, the top radius can be increased, but the amount of 31 grinding is limited by the close proximity of the valve spring seat. The bottom side of the port is built up with epoxy or aluminum weld, and this effectively increases its radius. To further aid air flow, the port should be made gradually wider, so that at the bend the port is no longer round, but oval.

A typical 1.2 in round port would narrow down at the bend to a height of perhaps 0.9 in (due to the small radius being welded up), and widen out to a width of around 1.45 in (FIGURE 2.17).

The next aspect to consider is the compression ratio, which is the relationship between the total volume of the cylinder, head gasket and combustion chamber, with the piston at bottom dead centre (BDC) and the volume contained in the space between the piston crown, head gasket and combustion chamber at top dead centre (TDC). Changes in the compression ratio have a considerable effect on power output, because the higher the ratio, the higher the compression pressure at any given engine speed. As is true at all times, you can't get something for nothing, which applies equally in this instance. An increase in compression ratio brings a corresponding increase in combustion temperature, so will the valves stand it? Bearing loads increase as does the load on the ignition system, so don't rush in without considering the consequences. As a general rule, a road engine running on 98 to 100 octane petrol will be quite happy on a 9.5 - 10.5:1 ratio, while racing engines using 100 octane petrol usually run an 11-12.5:1 ratio and up to 13.5:1 on 115 octane petrol. With methanol, this can be increased to 14:1 or 15:1.

Above a true compression ratio of 14:1 no power is gained. However, if the engine has exceptional anti-detonation characteristics, a theoretical compression ratio of 15:1 may pick up a little power due to the fact that unsupercharged engines seldom, if ever, attain a volumetric efficiency of 100%. Simply stated, volumetric efficiency is the ability of an engine to fill its cylinders with mixture expressed as a percentage of the actual volume of the cylinders. Therefore a motor with cylinders of 100 cc will be operating at 50% volumetric efficiency if it manages to get only 50 cc of mixture into its cylinders. Obviously such a motor, while operating on a theoretical compression ratio of 14:1, will, in actual fact, have a true compression ratio of only 7:1. As the average racing motor operates at approximately 93% volumetric efficiency, the theoretical compression ratio of 15:1 will actually be a true compression ratio of 14:1.

It should be noted at this stage that quoted compression ratio figures are always theoretical compression ratios and are expressed by the following formula :

$$CR = \frac{CV + CCV}{CCV}$$

where   CV = cylinder volume
CCV = combustion chamber volume.

CV is easily found by dividing the engine capacity by the number of cylinders. Therefore a 2000 cc four cylinder motor has a cylinder volume (or swept volume) of 500 cc.

CCV however is not so easy. This volume is made up of the combustion chamber volume, plus the volume that remains above the piston when the piston is at TDC, plus the volume caused by the thickness of the head gasket, plus the volume of the dish if dished pistons are used, or minus the amount displaced if high top pistons are used.

Assuming the pistons are flat tops, the formula for finding the volume of the head

gasket or the volume above the piston is :

$$V = \frac{\pi\ D^2 \times H}{4000}$$

where $\pi = 3.1416$

$D$ = diameter of bore in mm

$H$ = compressed thickness of head gasket or clearance between piston crown and block deck in mm

The volume of the combustion chamber is measured as shown in FIGURE 2.18, using a burette filled with liquid paraffin. If the head has been modified by a tuner, he should have told you the chamber volumes when you purchased the head. Incidently, the combustion chambers should have been equalised in volume so that the volume of the largest is no more than 0.2 cc larger than that of the smallest.

If you are running dished or high top pistons you can find what increase or decrease in combustion chamber volume they are causing by using the method shown in FIGURE 2.19. In this instance the cylinder bore is 102 mm in diameter and the piston crown is 13 mm from the block deck, therefore using the formula

$$V = \frac{\pi\ D^2 \times H}{4000}$$

this volume should be

$$V = \frac{\pi \times 102^2 \times 13}{4000} \qquad 106.2\ cc$$

However, measuring the volume with a burette we find it to be only 74.7 cc. Therefore the lump on top of the piston occupies 106.2 — 74.7 = 31.5 cc. Having found these volumes we must go back to the original formula to calculate the compression ratio.

Today's engine makes extremely taxing demands on the valves. Let's just look at a typical exhaust valve during a single cycle. At the beginning of the intake stroke, during the overlap period, it is subjected to a chilling blast of fuel mixuture. Then it is slammed against the valve seat and blasted with a hot flame that will raise its temperature to perhaps 1800°F, before it is suddenly hit by another chilling intake charge. In an average racing engine this

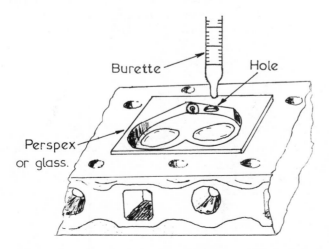

Fig. 2.18  Measuring combustion chamber volume.

can be happening 3000 to 4000 times a minute, during which time it is expected to form a gas seal that successfully contains pressure up around 1500 pounds per square inch.

To exist under such conditions, a valve has to be made of pretty good material, but here we have a problem. Racing valves made of austenitic stainless steel which, while being able to withstand high combustion temperatures, has very poor scuff resistance. Therefore they should be used only with valve guides made of aluminium bronze. This material is more compatible with austenitic steel as far as anti-scuffing is concerned, and of course bronze aids with heat transfer. The type of material we want to use in the valves is something like KE 965, EN54, 21/4N or Nimonic 80a steel.

Most current production valves are of bi-metal or tri-metal construction. By this we mean that the valve head and stem are of different materials, welded together. This is to overcome the scuffing problem mentioned earlier. The result is that we have a head made of quality austenitic steel such as 21/4N and a stem made of something like EN8, which is perfectly happy running in a cast iron valve guide. A valve made of such material is suitable for a high performance or racing engine.

The way to test if the valve is of austenitic steel is to see if it is magnetic. This applies to all valves; if they are magnetic they are no good. If the stem is magnetic and the head is nonmagnetic you have a welded valve, which is alright. Check before you buy any worked-over heads or valves to see that you are getting good valves. Generally, production inlet valves use a head of EN52 steel welded to a stem of EN8, which is not quite good enough, unless you don't plan on more than a 15% power increase. This type of valve has a magnetic head and stem.

A little earlier we mentioned the valve guide's role of transferring heat, from the exhaust valve in particular, to the engine coolant. An equally important aspect of the valve guide we need to consider is its role from the aspect of engine performance. As its name implies, the guide is responsible for guiding the valve accurately onto the seat, to effect a gas seal. A worn guide cannot do this, so power is lost. If the inlet guide is worn, it will allow oil into the engine, upsetting combustion and sometimes causing detonation.

Just as too much clearance between the valve stem and guide is to be avoided, so is too little clearance. In this situation the exhaust valve can seize in the guide and knock a hole in the piston crown. Air-cooled and supercharged engines are prone to this problem, so be sure to measure the clearance; don't just rely upon your sense of feel. Generally, the

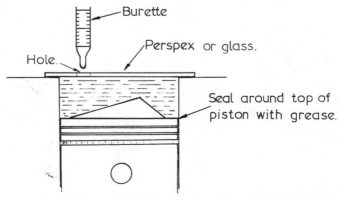

Fig. 2.19 Measuring high-top piston displacement.

clearance should be from 0.0015 - 0.003 in for inlet valves and 0.002 - 0.0045 in in the case of exhaust valves.

I never fit valve stem oil seals to exhaust valves; in fact with some motors I machine the top of the valve guide to encourage lubrication. Beside helping to prevent seizure, this added lubrication will increase valve stem and guide life. On the other hand, while I prefer not to use seals on the inlets, with some motors this is necessary, to prevent excessive oil consumption and carbon build-up on the inlet valve and in the combustion chamber.

Remember with supercharged motors that there is an added load on the inlet valve, due to increased valve temperature, and also inadequate lubrication. While the motor is operating with a positive boost, little or no oil will flow down the valve stem. This can lead to rapid stem and guide wear and even seizure, if the clearance is inadequate.

Armed with all this information on cylinder heads you are in a good position to make a sensible choice when you go shopping for a modified head. There are, however, just a few more points worth mentioning at this time. Don't allow yourself to be tempted by all the dazzle and shine of the ports and chambers. You are wasting money; sure the finish should be good and fine, but it certainly doesn't need polishing. Some cars have such poor carburettors that fuel will actually collect on a polished port wall. Particularly must this point be kept in mind if you are running a competition motor where alcohol fuel is permitted. Alcohol, being less volatile, separates from the air easily, and as the inlet tract is pretty well refrigerated, and especially so when running on alcohol, it remains clinging to the port, causing a flat spot and power loss.

Before you take delivery of the ported head it should be matched to the inlet manifold. At the same time dowels should be fitted so that each time the manifold is removed, it will, on being replaced, be perfectly aligned with the ports in the head. These dowels need only be $\frac{1}{8}$ in diameter silver steel.

While the head porting work is being done, other specialised work should also be caried out such as recutting the valve spring pads. Therefore the head modifier will have to be given specific instructions by you regarding such things as what valve springs, retainers

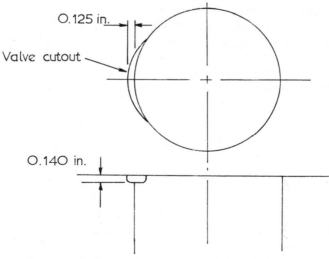

Fig. 2.20 BMC Mini exhaust valve cutout.

and collets to fit, what the valve spring fitted height should be and what rocker stud modifications are required.

At the same time you should find out if you need to do any grinding of the cylinder block so that your nice big valves don't bang into the top of it. FIGURE 2.20 illustrates the modification required on the Mini when oversize exhaust valves are fitted. To prevent any damage being done to the piston, rings or bore while this grinding is being done, I would suggest that plenty of grease be applied to the piston crown to seal it in the bore. The grease will trap all the iron dust and prevent it going down the side of the piston.

Only after the block deck has been prepared properly should the cylinder head be fitted. The face of the block needs to be cleaned perfectly, using a flat scraper and knife. Do not under any circumstances use emery paper or wet and dry paper as the abrasive particles will end up in the cylinders and on the cam and cam followers for sure; compressed air will not budge it. If the block has dowels or head studs still in place, be very very careful to remove any traces of old gasket or rust from around the base of these, using a knife.

The head gasket has the task of sealing the head to the block. It has to be able to withstand a pressure of up to 1800 psi in supercharged racing engines, so choose carefully. On a high performance motor, copper asbestos gaskets are definitely out. I don't like the black composite or corrugated steel gaskets either, although many high power engines still use them. The most inexpensive gasket for high power motors is the steel/copper/asbestos gasket. This type has a steel face and sealing lip on one side, copper sheet on the other face and asbestos in between. I have reused one such gasket four times on a racing motor, to confirm how good they are.

Some motors, however, require something more than this. The Hillman Imp, for example, running above an 11:1 compression ratio, usually has gasket problems. The way to overcome this is to machine a groove 0.040 in wide × 0.015 in deep into the top of the liners and the face of the head, such that it coincides with the centre of the metal lip of the head gasket. Then a double-lipped reinforced gasket should be fitted. An alternative to this is to use Wills rings. These are gas filled rings that take the place of the metal lip around the gasket bore. As combustion pressures increase, so the need to dispense with the head gasket and 'O' ring the block instead increases.

No amount of gasket fiddling will cure some motors. Take the American Motors 390 as an example. The only way to go with this one is to fit extra head studs. On this particular motor the extra stud should be added just outside the combustion chamber and in line with the spark plug hole. The eight studs should be $\frac{3}{8}$ in and torqued to 35 lbf ft.

The gasket manufacturer's instructions should always be followed regarding the use of gasket sealant. I always use Rolls Royce Hylomar SQ32/M sealant on the copper/steel/

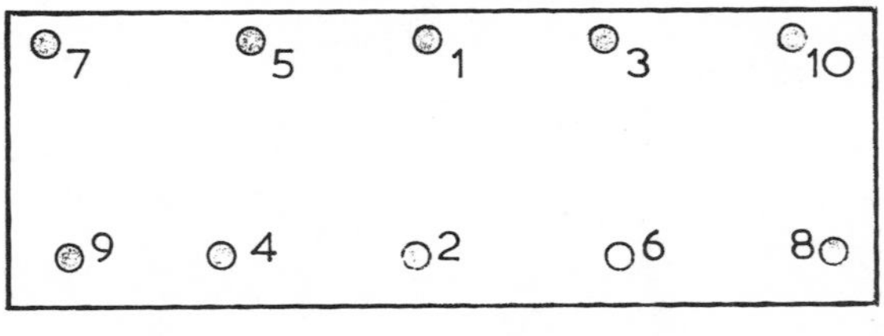

Fig. 2.21  Cylinder head bolt tightening sequence.

asbestos gaskets. Loctite Instant Seal Plastic Gasket is excellent too, especially on motors where the head gasket is not required.

Now that we have sorted out the head gasket/sealant situation it is time to fit the head. The head bolts should have their threads buffed and oiled and be tightened in the sequence recommended by the manufacturer. A typical sequence is shown in FIGURE 2.21. This sequence must be reversed when the bolts are being loosened to remove the head. I always tension the head in four or five progressive steps, to prevent head warpage. Therefore if the head tension is 80 lbf ft you would take it down to 30, 50, 60, 70 and then 80 lbf ft. After the gasket has had time to set (usually 10 - 15 minutes), go over the bolts again. That's about it if the head is alloy. If the head is cast iron, the motor should be started and brought to normal operating temperature and the bolts retensioned. Final gasket set should take place by the time you have done 300 miles, when the head (alloy or cast iron) should be tensioned again.

# Chapter 3
# Carburation

THE FUEL mixing system is looked upon as the most obvious place at which performance modifications should begin. A certain amount of glamour and fascination has always surrounded large or multiple carburettors, and as a result unwary enthusiasts can often be caught out with mixing devices that are either too large or totally unsuited to their particular engine. This results in sluggish performance and excessive fuel consumption.

The basic requirement of a performance carburettor is that it mixes the fuel and air in combustible proportions to produce the best horsepower. Usually the mixture we want is around 1:12 or 1:13, ie. one pound of petrol for every twelve or thirteen pounds of air. However, for other conditions such as starting or light load operation, the fuel-air requirement is different (TABLE 3.1), so the carburettor has to be able to sense the engine's operating conditions and adjust the fuel-air mix accordingly. If the carburettor is not able to do this, flat spots and engine surging will result. For this reason we have to be very selective as to the type and size of carburettor that we choose for our particular engine.

To understand more fully what we should be looking for in a high performance carburettor, we need to go back to the basics and get to know how a carburettor works. Nearly all carburettors employ a fuel inlet system, an idle system, a main running system and also an acceleration-pump system and a power system.

The inlet system consists of the fuel bowl, the float and the needle and seat.

The fuel passing to the other metering systems is stored in the fuel bowl and it is maintained at the correct level by the float and needle and seat. If the fuel is not at the correct level in the fuel bowl, the fuel metering systems will not be able to mix the fuel and air in the correct proportions, particularly when accelerating, cornering and stopping.

A high fuel level will cause high fuel consumption and erratic running. Due to fuel spillover through the carburettor discharge nozzle and/or vent during cornering or braking, it could cause the engine to falter or stop.

A high fuel level may be the result of an incorrectly adjusted float, or a needle and seat which is not seating properly and shutting off the fuel supply when the float reaches the correct level. This may be due to excessive wear of the needle and/or seat or it may be caused by a weak bumper spring (Holley carburettors). High fuel pressure will also raise the fuel level, each 1 psi increase in fuel pressure raising it by about 0.020 in.

A low fuel level causes flat spots because of lean-out in turns and when accelerating. Even more serious is the possibility of a full power lean-out due to reduced fuel flow capacity, resulting in melted pistons.

A low fuel level condition may be due to an improperly adjusted float, low fuel pressure, excessively strong bumper spring (Holley carbs) or a needle and seat too small to flow sufficient fuel to keep the fuel bowl full.

The fuel bowl is always vented so that the fuel is being mixed according to the outside air pressure. Once the fuel passes through the needle and seat it is no longer under pressure. Any fuel vapour is released through the vent, so at all times the metering systems respond to the prevailing atmospheric conditions.

The float is hinged such that it operates the opening and closing of the fuel inlet valve (needle and seat). As the fuel drops, the float drops and opens the valve, allowing fuel to enter the bowl. When the engine is running with a constant load, the float moves the needle to a position where it restricts fuel flow, allowing in only enough fuel to replace that being used.

The float may be made of brass stampings soldered together into an airtight assembly, or of a closed cellular material. Brass floats are resistant to attack from all types of fuel, except nitromethane. Generally, the cellular floats are not damaged by most of the common fuels, but it is always wise to check with the carburettor manufacturer if you are using a fuel which is not petrol or methanol.

The fuel inlet valve or needle and seat controls the flow of fuel into the bowl. The seat is usually steel and the needle may be steel or it may be steel with a Viton coating on the tip. The Viton coated needle provides good sealing but it should not be used with alcohol or nitro fuels.

The needle and seat is usually available in a number of sizes to give the required rate of fuel flow into the bowl. The seat size is selected to allow reasonably quick filling of the bowl so as to be able to meet the demands of wide open throttle and high rpm operation. A seat which is too large is a definite hindrance, as it may give rise to flooding. For this reason use an inlet assembly only marginally larger than the fuel flow requirement of the engine.

How much fuel does your engine need? Remember we said that best power is produced with a fuel-air ratio of one pound of fuel to every twelve and a half pounds of air (only if the fuel is petrol). Therefore if we calculate how much air the engine is pumping we can also work out our engine's maximum fuel flow requirement.

### TABLE 3.1   High performance engine fuel-air requirements

| Running condition | Mixing ratio (by weight) Fuel : Air |
|---|---|
| Starting | 1 : 1 - 3 |
| Idling | 1 : 6 - 10 |
| Low-speed running | 1 : 10 - 13 |
| Light-load ordinary running | 1 : 14 - 16 |
| Heavy-load running | 1 : 12 - 14 |

The formula we use to find the airflow in lb/hr is

$$4.38 \times \frac{D}{32.8} \times \frac{rpm}{1728} \times \frac{VE}{100}$$

Where D = displacement in cc
rpm = engine speed
VE = volumetric efficiency

At maximum torque rpm the volumetric efficiency (VE) would be 90-100% in a racing engine, and this would fall, relative to the engine's torque curve, at higher and lower rpm. If an engine produced maximum torque of 100 lbf ft at 5750 rpm and 74 lbf ft at 6800 rpm (maximum power rpm) the VE at 5750 rpm is, say 95%; therefore the VE at 6500 rpm will be

$$\frac{74 \times 95}{100} = 70.3\%$$

Obviously the engine speed at which the most air is passing through the engine is at maximum horsepower rpm (TABLES 3.2 a, b), so calculate your air flow at this engine speed.

To find the fuel flow (lbs/hr), multiply the air flow by the fuel-air ratio. If the ratio is 1:12.5, multiply by $\frac{1}{12.5}$ or by 0.08. Petrol weighs 7.5 lb per gallon, so to find the fuel flow in gallons per hour (gph) divide by 7.5.

How are you going to know how much fuel a needle and seat will flow? Some manufacturers have published information available, but if you are not able to uncover the particulars from the carburettor maker, you will have to measure the fuel flow yourself.

This may seem to be something of a hassle but it is a very important consideration, particularly in regard to motorcycles, as these seem to be the worst affected by fuel flow restrictions. Actually it is very easy to measure the flow to a bike's fuel bowl as you don't have to worry about fuel pump pressure.

Fill the fuel tank, and after removing the fuel bowl from one carburettor, time how long it takes to drain down to reserve. Now accurately measure how may gallons you have drained off and calculate your fuel flow in gph. Multiply this figure by the number of caburettors on the engine, and compare the answer with the fuel flow requirement for your engine. You are probably in for a surprise; many motorcycles cannot be held wide open for too long on the dyno without fuel starvation problems.

Even if you find that the needle and seat can flow sufficient fuel, you will probably find that the fuel tap will not, so repeat the test with the fuel lines removed from every carburettor, and determine the tap's fuel flow capabilities.

Generally, it is not possible to obtain larger needle and seat assemblies (or fuel taps) for motorcycles, so it will be necessary to modify these by very carefully drilling oversize the fuel delivery holes. I would recommend that you use a pin vice when you drill the fuel inlet seat's fuel discharge holes.

The cold starting system provides mixture enrichment to allow starting when either the engine or the weather is cold. The system used on Weber DCOE, SU and some motorcycle carburettors does not affect the air flow capabilities of the carburettor. However, the choke plate and shaft fitted to most carburettors does reduce air flow and creates unwanted turbulence through the carburettor throat. Racing engines should therefore have the choke assembly removed if the regulations allow this modification.

If you live in a warm climate, the choke assembly can be removed from road machines, but it may be necessary to floor the accelerator a few times to provide a rich starting mixture via the accelerator pump. You will have to allow the engine to warm up before driving off, but this is really a good thing as engine wear and oil dilution will be reduced.

The idle system provides a rich mixture at idle and low speeds, when not enough air is being drawn through the venturi to cause the main system to operate. (FIGURE 3.1).

When the throttle plate (butterfly) is nearly closed, the restriction to air flow causes a high vacuum on the engine side of the throttle plate. This high vacuum provides the pressure differential for the idle system to operate. The normal air pressure (14.7 psi) acts on the fuel in the float bowl, forcing it through the idle jet, and past the idle mixture screw into the manifold.

To emulsify the fuel before it reaches the mixture screw, an air bleed is included in the system. Increasing the size of the air bleed leans the idle mixture, if the size of the idle jet remains constant. Conversely, decreasing the air bleed diameter richens the idle mixture.

The progression or transfer holes are a part of the idle system (FIGURE 3.2) and allow a smooth transition from the idle fuel circuit to the main fuel system without 'flat spots', provided the carburettor size has been correctly matched to the engine displacement.

As the throttle is opened wider, the progression holes are uncovered, and begin to flow fuel metered and emulsified by the idle jet. At this time fuel flow past the mixture screw decreases and gradually tapers off as the next progression hole is opened by the throttle plate.

When the throttle is opened further, the pressure differential between the idle-progression holes and the air pressure acting on the fuel in the fuel bowl decreases, causing fuel flow in the idle system to taper off. Finally, the pressure is not great enough to push the fuel up to the idle jet, and the idle system ceases to supply fuel.

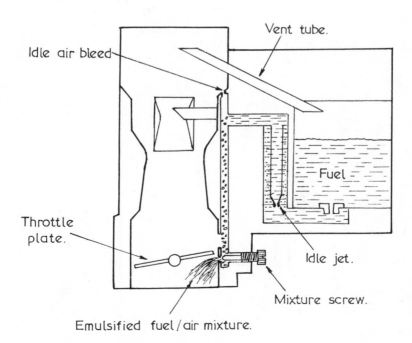

Fig. 3.1    Idle system operation.

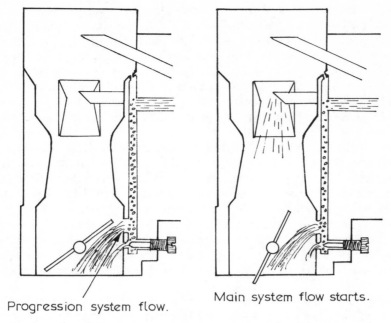

Progression system flow.

Main system flow starts.

Fig. 3.2   Progression system operation.

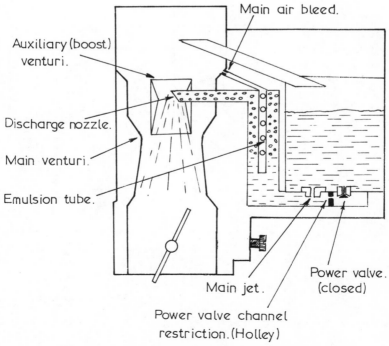

Main air bleed.

Auxiliary (boost)
venturi.

Discharge nozzle.

Main venturi.

Emulsion tube.

Power valve.
(closed)

Main jet.

Power valve channel
restriction.(Holley)

Fig. 3.3  Main & power system operation.

Fuel flow through the main metering system begins before the flow through the idle circuit is reduced, if a carburettor of the right size is being used. The main system meters fuel for cruising and high speed operation.

As the throttle is opened and the engine speed increases, air flow through the venturi is increased so that the main system comes into operation, discharging fuel through the discharge hole in the auxiliary venturi (boost venturi).

The heart of the carburettor is the main venturi, as it causes the pressure differential necessary for the fuel to be pushed from the fuel well, through the main jet, to the discharge nozzle (FIGURE 3.3).

In the internal combustion engine, a partial vacuum is created in the cylinder by the downward stroke of the piston. Because atmospheric pressure is higher than the pressure in the cylinder, air rushes in through the carburettor to equalise the pressure within the cylinder. On its way through the carburettor, the air passes through the venturi, a restriction designed by Italian physicist G. B. Venturi about 200 years ago.

The venturi necks down the inrushing air and then allows it to widen out to the throttle bore. To get through the venturi, the air must speed up, thus reducing the pressure inside the venturi to below atmospheric pressure. This pressure differential allows the main system to discharge fuel, and is commonly referred to as the 'signal' of the main metering system.

No fuel issues from the discharge nozzle until the air flow through the venturi produces a pressure drop or signal sufficiently strong for the atmospheric pressure, acting on the fuel in the fuel bowl, to push the fuel up through the main jet to the discharge nozzle.

Pressure drop (or vacuum) within the venturi varies with the engine speed and throttle opening. Wide open throttle and peak rpm give the highest air flow, and consequently the highest pressure difference between the fuel bowl and the discharge nozzle. This in turn gives the highest fuel flow into the engine.

To compensate for various engine displacements, a range of carburettors with a variety of venturi diameters are available to create the necessary pressure drop to bring the main fuel circuit into operation. A small venturi will provide a higher pressure difference at any given rpm and throttle opening than a large diameter venturi. This is a very important aspect of carburation, which partly explains why the biggest is seldom the best. If the signal being applied by the venturi is too weak (due to the venturi being too large), this could delay fuel discharge in the main system, causing a flat spot. If you must err when buying a carburettor, err on the small side.

The auxiliary venturi acts as a signal amplifier for the main venturi, allowing for more accurate and quicker fuel flow responses. This is important in a performance engine as it allows the use of a larger, less restrictive main venturi than would normally be possible, without sacrificing throttle response.

The tail of the boost venturi discharges at the lowest pressure point in the main venturi. Thus the air flow is accelerated through the boost venturi, and because of this, the air and fuel emerging are travelling faster than the surrounding air passing through the main venturi. This has the effect of assisting fuel atomisation, and subsequently improves combustion.

The actual fuel metering is controlled by the main jet, the air bleed jet, and the emulsion tube.

The main jet controls fuel flow from the fuel well. An increase in diameter richens the mixture, but more is involved. The shape of the jet entry and exit, as well as the bore finish, also affect fuel flow. Carburettor manufacturers measure the flow of every jet, for high 43 performance and low exhaust emission applications, and number the jet according to its flow characteristics, not according to its nominal bore diameter. For this reason jets used to meter petrol should not be drilled to change their size, if you desire accurate fuel metering. An engine burning alcohol does not require such accurate metering, unless fuel consumption is a consideration, so jet drilling may be in order if large jets are not available.

The air bleed reduces the signal from the discharge nozzle, so that there is a less effective pressure difference to cause fuel flow through the main jet. This allows for more fine tuning of the main metering system. A large air bleed leans the mixture, particularly at higher engine rpm.

The air bleed also introduces air into the emulsion tube, to emulsify the fuel into a lighter, frothy mixture of fuel and air. This is done to improve atomisation when the fuel is released from the discharge nozzle. Also it serves to lower the viscosity of the fuel, making it lighter, and able to respond faster to signal changes from the auxiliary venturi. This enables the main system to keep more in step with the fuel requirements of the engine.

The emulsion tube has the task of emulsifying the previously metered air issuing from the air bleed jet with the fuel coming from the main jet. Its influence is more marked at less than full throttle and during acceleration. The diameter of the emulsion tube and the size and location of holes to emulsify the fuel all affect and influence its operation. Usually, a change in emulsion tube will require a change in main jet and air bleed size.

Many carburettors also have a power system for mixture enrichment at heavy load operation. This system supplies additional fuel to complement the main metering system at above normal cruising loads. The added fuel supplied by the power system is controlled by manifold vacuum, which accurately indicates the load on the engine. As the load increases, the throttle must be opened wider to maintain a given speed. This lessens the restriction to air entering the engine, which in turn reduces the manifold vacuum.

The system usually employed (FIGURE 3.3) relies on a high manifold vacuum to hold the power valve closed. As the manifold vacuum drops (usually to around 4 - 6 in of mercury) the power valve spring overcomes manifold vacuum and opens the valve, allowing fuel to flow from the fuel bowl through a power valve jet and into the main metering system. This increases fuel flow in the main system, effectively richening the mixture.

The accelerator pump system complements all of the other systems and fills in for them, so as to eliminate flat spots. It does this by injecting raw fuel for a sufficient length of time to allow the other systems to catch up to the fuel demands of the engine.

If the throttle is opened quickly, the manifold vacuum instantly drops to a pressure approaching atmospheric, allowing the fuel to drop out of vapour and wet the manifold and port walls. (A high manifold vacuum helps to keep the fuel vaporised; remember an increase in altitude, resulting in a lower atmospheric pressure, lowers the boiling point of water; likewise with fuel, lower the atmospheric pressure and it vaporises more easily.) To make up for the lean condition caused by the fuel clinging to the manifold and port walls and to avoid a flat spot, it is necessary instantly to make up the deficiency, by injecting more fuel into the air stream.

The accelerator pump also has to supply fuel if the throttle is opened quickly to a point past the idle-progression system supply period. With gentle acceleration there is an overlap of fuel being supplied by both the idle and the main system, but if the throttle is opened quickly, the main system has not started to supply fuel when the idle system has already shut off supply. To eliminate a lean-out, the accelerator pump injects fuel for a time, to allow the main system flow and metering to be established.

Having discussed the various carburettor systems it should be obvious that not all carburettors are suitable for performance applications. Some are just too small; others do not have metering systems with changeable jets, or if they do, the jets are not readily obtainable; and others have metering systems which allow acceptable performance in stock machines, but are too crude to provide the correct fuel-air mixture in a high performance engine. For these reasons I usually limit myself to the use of Holley, SU and Weber carburettors for cars, and Mikuni carburettors for motorcycles. Don't get me wrong; there are other good carburettors around (eg. Dellorto DHLA sidedraught) but I have found those I have listed to be the most easily obtainable, and there is no problem obtaining jets etc. It's no use using a good carburettor if it can't be tuned correctly due to the unavailability of alternative jets.

Obviously the choice is yours when it comes to selecting a carburettor, but give heed to my advice regarding the size to use. Always remember that the carburettor meters the fuel according to the signal being received in the fuel well. A carburettor too large for the engine produces a weak signal, consequently the metering system cannot function correctly.

To illustrate the problem, let's assume that we are cruising with a light throttle, then we step on the gas. The accelerator pump delivers a shot of fuel to make up for the lag in fuel delivery through the main circuit. At the same time air velocity through the venturis picks up a little because of the reduced resistance to flow. Air velocity only picks up a little because the car has not yet started to gain speed. All we have done is to go from a high manifold vacuum on closed throttle, to a low vacuum when the throttles were cracked wide open.

If the carburettor has huge venturis, there will not be enough air speed to create the depression necessary for the main system to flow fuel, so you will end up with a big flat spot. Conversely, if the venturis are small, the slight increase in air velocity when the throttles are opened will give the necessary pressure differential necessary to get fuel discharging through the main system. This in turn allows the engine to produce more power, which gets the vehicle moving faster. With the vehicle moving faster, air flow through the venturis continues to increase, as does the fuel delivery rate. The result: crisp acceleration and good throttle response.

If you are still not convinced of the need for a strong signal to get the fuel metering systems working, try this simple experiment. Fill a container with water and draw it up through both a straw and a piece of $\frac{5}{8}$ in heater hose. Did you notice the difference; how much more sucking you had to do to get the water flowing up the heater hose? That very same principle applies to fuel flow through a carburettor's metering system. The small venturi being sucked on by the engine (like you sucking on the straw) gets the fuel responding quickly to the needs of the engine.

The other benefit of using a carburettor with venturis of the right size is this. A high air velocity through the venturi lowers the air pressure (creates a partial vacuum), which makes the fuel more volatile and easily atomised. Additionally, the high air speed itself assists in the vaporisation of the fuel. Properly atomised fuel improves fuel distribution from cylinder to cylinder, and power goes up because the quality of combustion is improved, due to the fact that raw fuel will not burn at the correct rate to produce power.

Carburettor engineers have worked with these problems for quite some time, and their solution is simple; use a dual-stage carburettor. One stage (primary) is for low speed and fuel economy operation, and the secondary stage for maximum air flow.

The secondary stage may be opened mechanically by linkages operating from the 45 primary barrel, such that the secondary throttle plate begins to open when the primary throttle plate is about 40⁰ open. This type is said to be a progressive, mechanical secondary carburettor.

The vacuum-operated secondary carburettor does not have a throttle linkage connected to the throttle shaft. Instead, the air demand of the engine at higher engine speeds creates a vacuum which operates on a diaphragm to control the secondary opening. The diaphragm, if correctly adjusted, automatically opens the secondary the correct amount to meet the air flow needs of the engine. Some feel that this feature gives them licence to go ahead and fit the largest vacuum secondary carburettor available. They reason that if the carburettor is too large it does not matter, as the secondary will not open fully anyway. This is false reasoning; maybe the performance won't suffer too much, but fuel consumption could easily increase by 12 - 15%.

Don't be confused into thinking that all two and four barrel carburettors are designed to give a small venturi area with just the primaries open at lower engine speeds and when cruising. This is not so; some have simultaneous throttle action, meaning that all the throttle plates open together. These carburettors are really two, three or four individual carburettors sharing a single carburettor body and a single fuel bowl, in the case of the two barrel versions. Carburettors of this type include the Weber DCOE and IDA, the Dellorto DHLA, the Holley 4500 Dominator (No. 6464 and 6214) and 4160 (No. 4224). Carburettors of this type will give excellent performance on the correct engine and manifold. The Weber and Dellorto carburettors have very special metering systems enabling them to be used even on small high performance road engines, without sacrificing much low speed performance. The Holley carburettors with simultaneous throttle action are for racing use only.

A current fad is the modification of American four barrel carburettors to 'improve' them. The improvements are usually said to improve air flow, due to the throttle bores and the venturi bores being bored out to a larger size. Some may flow more air, but more air is of no value unless fuel has been mixed with it in the correct proportions, to say nothing of throttle response and metering signals. A carburettor modified along these lines would be useless in a vehicle requiring any sort of power range. It would work in a racing boat or in a stick-shift drag car with a 7500 - 9000 rpm power band, but in any other application it would prove a hindrance.

The only type of modification for Holley four barrel carburettors, of which I approve, involves recalibration of the fuel metering circuits to provide more accurate fuel metering. This modification serves to broaden the power range on a racing engine when a large carburettor is being used, by precise fuel metering right from part throttle to wide open throttle.

The problem is that racing engines produce a weaker vacuum signal due to their need for very large carburettors to provide good power at high rpm. Camshaft design also affects fuel metering, because the fuel delivery signal is weakened as the inlet valve is opened earlier and earlier, and as the valve overlap period is increased. As a result the carburettor requires more sensitivily to weaker signals, or it will excessively lean the mixture and reduce the power output at lower engine speeds.

Some feel that this problem can be solved by using a more sensitive booster venturi, but I have found the converse to be true. In a racing engine the carburettor is subject to severe reversion pulses (spit back) and during this reverse flow period more fuel is added to the air, and then again as the air flows back into the engine, the booster senses its flow and further fuel is added. This means that during its three passes through the carburettor, fuel has been added to the air, consequently the mixture becomes extremely rich. A booster that is more sensitive will aggravate this situation at certain engine speeds, and do little to richen the mixture at lower engine speeds where the lean condition is being experienced.

The low speed lean condition is not, in fact, due to any insensitivity in the main metering system, but generally due to the signal being too weak to activate the idle-progression system. Changes to the accelerator pump circuit will help, but the way around the problem is to add an intermediate fuel circuit. This will fill in gaps in the Holley's fuel metering circuits and allow it to perform well at lower engine speeds, to produce a power band almost as wide as that possible when using Weber carburettors.

If you use a Holley carburettor and need a wide power range for road racing or short speedway, take your carburettor to someone who will recalibrate it as outlined; forget about those firms who rebore the venturis.

Regardless of the type of carburettor you use, it should not be modified (except the SU) by boring the venturi or by radiusing the corners at the air entry.

If you take a careful look at the venturi you will find that it has a radiused inlet and diverging tail section. Designers work the venturi shape to create the maximum pressure drop with minimum flow losses. Frequently, when the venturi is rebored, the basic internal shape is not changed to suit the larger internal diameter. Reboring really requires that the entry radius be changed and that the divergant angle of the tail be changed, otherwise the increase in bore size will not increase air flow, but will result in a less effective metering signal.

Radiusing the corners of the air entry can reduce the auxillary venturi signal, since the inflowing air tends to turn into the main venturi sooner and take away flow from the centre of the venturi where the auxillary venturi (booster) is located. This reduces the signal at the booster and results in main circuit fuel lean-out.

Another bad modification involves cutting down the divider wall between the primary and secondary side of four barrel carburettors for clearance under the hood or for improved air flow. Removing just a ¼ in could upset booster sensitivity to the extent that main jets three or four sizes richer would be required, and this will not fully solve the problem.

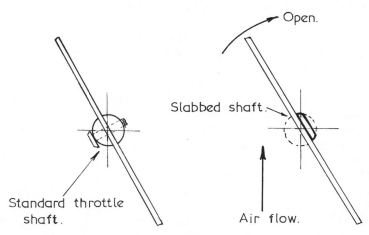

Fig. 3.4  Modified throttle shaft.

The message is; keep your fingers and your files and your grinders right away from the carburettor, particularly its mouth. Any modification in this area will almost always deaden booster sensitivity, which generally will adversely affect fuel flow into the engine.

This is not to say that all modifications to improve the air flow through the carburettor are to be avoided. As I have already pointed out, you should get rid of the choke plate and shaft. That simple modification will improve the flow of a Holley by about 50 cfm.

The next area that you should take a look at is the throttle shaft and throttle plate screws. Most shafts are of $^5\!/_{16}$ - $^3\!/_8$ in diameter and the butterflies are attached by two screws. Some carburettors use countersunk screws, carefully trimmed so that they do not project through the shaft. However, most screws have a flat head and they usually protrude through the shaft by $^1\!/_{16}$ - $^3\!/_{32}$ in. Together, the shaft and screws disrupt air flow by causing turbulence and by partly blocking the carburettor bore.

In racing applications, particularly if the carburettor size is limited by the rules, a useful increase in air flow can be gained (10 - 12%) by removing the screws and cutting down the shaft width. (FIGURE 3.4) One half of the shaft should be cut away completely. The other half of the shaft can be slabbed so that it is no more than $^1\!/_{16}$ in thick, and then ground with a radiused edge. The butterflies are attached by heliarc welding through the existing screw holes.

This modification should be carried out only by a competent machine shop, taking special care not to bend or twist the very thin and weak throttle shaft. If the shaft is twisted, the butterflies will not open together, synchronised. The heliarc welding is a delicate operation; again special care is necessary to ensure that the butterflies are going to open together.

When a carburettor modified as described is being fitted, be sure to attach the throttle return spring to the same end of the throttle shaft as the throttle linkage. If the spring is attached to the opposite end, the shaft will twist due to the opposing forces on each end.

If you race speedway and use a Holley carburettor, you are probably aware of the problem of fuel surge and starvation caused by the constant side forces that push the fuel to the right-hand side of the float chamber, at times at a $45^0$ angle. So steep an angle can easily uncover a main jet and allow air into the main well.

To overcome the problem remove the brass float and replace it with a modified cellular float. By cutting the end of the float at $45^0$ the float can be tricked into staying down and admitting extra fuel to keep the main jets covered. After cutting, it is necessary to re-seal the float using a fuel resistant epoxy, otherwise the float, being porous inside, will sink and flood the engine.

Fuel injection is a fuel mixing system devised to overcome all of the previously mentioned problems: ie. fuel atomisation, metering signal delay and fuel surge.

The carburettor has to rely on the signal produced in its venturi by the inflowing air to meter fuel correctly into the engine. Then it has to wait on the atmospheric pressure to act on the fuel in the fuel bowl to force the fuel through a series of jets and passages, and then into the air stream. This takes time, so the engine's fuel requirements are not instantly meet, resulting in delayed throttle response.

A fuel injection system responds instantaneously to supply the engine's fuel needs; hence there is no throttle lag.

There are two basic types of injection systems. Both types use a mechanical or mechanical and electronic system of metering. The Lucas and Bosch injection is a timed
squirt system operating on a similar principal to the high tension ignition system, so that

each cylinder receives a shot of fuel during the intake stroke.

The constant flow injection system is much less complicated, and as its name suggests, a constant spray of fuel issues from the injectors regardless of whether the inlet valve is open or closed. Injection systems of this type are made by Tecalamit Jackson (England); Crower, Enderle, Hilborn, Jackson (America); McGee (Australia).

The metering system employed on mechanical injection systems (both timed squirt and constant flow) is relatively crude, therefore this type is best suited to racing engines as they are only required to operate in a narrow power band. Engines running on petrol operate more effectively, with a wider power spread, if the timed squirt Lucas system is used. In fact I consider it a waste of time and money to use constant flow injection on a petrol burning engine. An engine on carburettors will produce almost as much peak power and much better mid-range power than one with constant flow injectors. (TABLE 3.3)

Constant flow injectors are suitable only if a methanol or nitro-base fuel is being used. Fuels of this type will be burned quite happily, without a loss of power, even when a grossly over-rich mixture is being supplied.

Fuel injection suitable for road and rally cars is similar in operation to the purely mechanical metering type but intricate electronic circuitry is added so that precise fuel metering is possible at idle and throughout the engine's entire rpm range. Sensors relay to an electronic brain such factors as engine speed, barometric pressure, engine temperature, air temperature, the amount of air travelling to the cylinders and manifold vacuum. The brain decides how much petrol is required and adjusts the fuel supply accordingly.

The fuel metering brain may regulate the fuel flow mechanically, but usually it operates an electromagnet in the injector nozzle. The electromagnet opens and closes the nozzle to start and stop fuel flow. The amount of fuel injected is controlled by the time the electromagnet holds the injector nozzle open.

Enthusiasts often ask how much power increase can be expected if fuel injection is fitted. If Webers are replaced by injectors it is possible to find a 1 - 8% increase in hp, but there may not be any increase at all except in the mid-range.

The real reason for using fuel injection, particularly on road circuit and speedway machines, is the instant throttle response which makes for improved vehicle control and better acceleration out of turns. This type of improvement cannot be measured on the dyno; it is something you feel through the seat of your pants.

Fuel injection is supplied flow regulated to suit the particular engine for which it has been designed. There are some adjustments for fine tuning. The size of the throttle bores (there are no venturis) are determined by the manufacturer, so you won't get into trouble selecting the correct setup.

Carburettor size selection, however, is up to you. The displacement of the engine, the weight of the vehicle, the rear axle ratio and the desired power range all have a big influence on the actual carburettor size and type that will give the best performance. To add a little extra confusion to the issue, one half of the world sizes its carburettors according to the diameter of the throttle bore, while the other half rates its carburettors in accordance with how much air they will flow. Therefore to know what you are actually buying, you need a little background information to understand what all the numbers mean.

All carburettors made in England, Europe and Japan are identified by the diameter of the carburettor bore at the throttle plate. The size may be stated in inches or millimetres. Generally, the stated size tells you very little about the carburettor, as it is the venturi diameter and the throttle bore diameter that determine the air flow capabilities of the 49 carburettor. For example, the Weber 45 DCOE carburettor is a two-barrel, simultaneous throttle action unit, with throttle bores 45 mm in diameter. However, a range of replaceable venturis are available from 30 mm to 40 mm, which allows this carburettor to be used on a wide variety of engines in all stages of tune.

The American system of rating carburettors in cubic feet per minute (cfm) airflow is just as confusing. Enthusiasts have been conditioned to believe that working to the following formula guarantees selection of the correct size of carburettor:

$$cfm = \frac{D \times rpm \times VE}{3456 \times 100}$$

Where D = displacement in cu. in
rpm = engine speed at maximum horsepower
VE = volumetric efficiency at maximum horsepower

Talking as an example the 350 cubic inch Chevy Z - 28 engine in TABLE 3.2 we find its air flow at 5500 rpm, at a volumetric efficiency of 75.1%, to be 418.3 cubic feet per minute. According to the formula, this engine would work best with a carburettor rated to flow 400 - 450 cfm. In actual practice this particular engine will work best using a 600 - 650 cfm carburettor for street use, and a 750 - 780 cfm carburettor for drag racing.

The Chevy racing engine in TABLE 3.2 would have a peak air flow of 640.8 cfm at 7000 rpm with a volumetric efficienty of 90.4%. However, for circle track racing you would use a Holley carburettor of either 850 or 1050 cfm.

### TABLE 3.2a    Theoretical fuel flow 350 cubic inch Chevy Racing Engine
*(1 : 12.5 fuel-air ratio)*

| rpm | hp | Torque (lbf ft) | VE | Air flow (lb/hr) | Fuel flow (lb/hr) |
|-----|------|------|------|--------|-------|
| 4500 | 362 | 423 | 89.1 | 1778.5 | 142.3 |
| 5000 | 415 | 436 | 91.8 | 2036 | 162.9 |
| 5500 | 471 | 450 | 94.8 | 2312.8 | 185 |
| 6000 | 515 | 451 | 95 | 2528.4 | 202.3 |
| 6500 | 547 | 442 | 93.1 | 2684.3 | 214.7 |
| 7000 | 572 | 429 | 90.4 | 2807 | 224.6 |
| 7500 | 570 | 399 | 84 | 2794.5 | 223.6 |

*Note: Actual fuel flow will be approximately 20 - 25% more than theoretical flow due to unequal distribution from cylinder to cylinder and due to accelerator pump operation.*

### TABLE 3.2b    Theoretical fuel flow 350 cubic inch Chevy blue-printed Z-28
*(1 : 12.5 fuel-air ratio)*

| rpm | hp | Torque (lbf ft) | VE | Air flow (lb/hr) | Fuel flow (lb/hr) |
|-----|------|------|------|--------|-------|
| 3000 | 198 | 346 | 81.7 | 1087.2 | 87 |
| 3500 | 237 | 355 | 83.8 | 1301 | 104.1 |
| 4000 | 274 | 360 | 85 | 1508.2 | 120.7 |
| 4500 | 303 | 354 | 83.6 | 1668.7 | 133.5 |
| 5000 | 326 | 342 | 80.8 | 1792 | 143.4 |
| 5500 | 333 | 318 | 75.1 | 1832.2 | 146.6 |
| 6000 | 326 | 285 | 67.3 | 1791.2 | 143.3 |
| 6500 | 295 | 238 | 56.2 | 1620.4 | 129.6 |

*Note: Actual fuel flow will be approximately 20 - 25% more than theoretical flow due to unequal distribution from cylinder to cylinder and due to accelerator pump operation.*

On paper, the air flow formula looks good, but it is of little use as the actual air flow of the engine and the theoretical, laboratory air flow of the carburettor, are worlds apart due to a number of factors.

In the test laboratory, carburettor manufacturers measure the air flow of each type of carburettor at a constant vacuum, usually three inches of Hg (mercury) for one and two barrel carburettors and 1.5 inches of Hg for three and four barrel carburettors. Right away you can see that there is not a true comparison of the theoretical amount of air that two and four barrel carburettors will flow. A carburettor subject to a vacuum of 3 in Hg at wide open throttle will naturally flow more air than one tested at 1.5 in Hg. A two-barrel Holley rated at 650 cfm will not flow as much air as a four barrel Holley rated at 650 cfm.

To relate the two measurements we must use the formula

$$\text{cfm} @ \frac{3 \text{ in Hg}}{1.414} = \text{cfm} @ 1.5 \text{ in Hg}$$

Therefore the 650 cfm two barrel will flow only 460 cfm when tested at 1.5 in Hg.

Taking this principle a step further, it will be found that many racing engines have a manifold vacuum of only 0.5 in Hg at wide open throttle, not 1.5 in Hg vacuum, at which the four barrel carburettors are flow tested. At a depression of 0.5 in Hg the flow will equal the cfm @ 1.5 in Hg, divided by 1.735. Therefore a 1050 cfm carburettor will flow approximately 605 cfm when fitted to a racing engine with a manifold vacuum of 0.5 in Hg.

On the test bench the carburettors are subjected to a constant vacuum for air flow measurement purposes, but in actual practice a carburettor fitted to an engine has to contend with reverse flow (or reversion) pulses, which also cause the air flow capacity of the carburettor to be reduced. Racing engines produce a stronger reversion pulse than stock units, due to the use of wild camshafts which allow more reverse flow in the inlet tract because of early inlet valve opening and lots of valve overlap. Manifold design also influences the intensity of the reverse pulse.

**TABLE 3.3  Power comparison of constant flow fuel injection and carburettors.**
*Hi-performance 396 Chevy burning petrol*

| rpm | Test 1 | Test 2 | Test 3 | Test 4 | Test 5 | Test 6 |
|---|---|---|---|---|---|---|
| 4000 | 300.6 | 342 | 344.1 | 308.8 | 427.7 | 391.5 |
| 4500 | 332.2 | 354.5 | 367.3 | 338.1 | 511.8 | 478.4 |
| 5000 | 355.5 | 376.1 | 390.5 | 371.6 | 573.2 | 557.9 |
| 5500 | 377 | 393.8 | 417 | 400.7 | 622.5 | 616.7 |
| 6000 | 394.3 | 406.9 | 431.4 | 428.5 | 658.6 | 663 |
| 6500 | 407.5 | 420.8 | 439.8 | 441.2 | 682.6 | 686.2 |
| 7000 | 416 | 437.7 | 442.7 | 447.3 | 690.5 | 695.4 |

Test 1 — 1 × Holley 4500 — 1050 cfm.
Test 2 — 2 × Holley 750 cfm.
Test 3 — 4 × 48 IDA Webers
Test 4 — Hilborn constant flow injectors.
Test 5 — GM 6 - 71 supercharger and 2 × Holley 750 cfm.
Test 6 — GM 6 - 71 supercharger and Hilborn constant flow injectors.

*Note: All dyno tests except Test 4 were made using an Offenhauser Turbo Thrust plenum ram manifold with different tops.*

Another aspect of carburettor air flow not considered in the flow room is the on and off type of flow the carburettor actually experiences when the inlet valve opens and then closes. If the inlet valve was held wide open for one minute, carburettor air flow would be constant for that minute, but in use the inlet valve may open and close 4000 times during the entire minute. This serves to reduce air flow. Obviously a tap turned on for a minute will flow more water than one that is turned on then off 4000 times in a minute.

The more cylinders a carburettor venturi is flowing air to, the more constant the air flow through the carburettor will be, so air flow per minute goes up. This partly explains why a small engine with one barrel per cylinder may require a huge carburettor to flow enough air for good power. If you take a look at the RS 1800 Escort rally engine, you will find it breathes through two 48 DCOE Webers, each carburettor capable of flowing around 650 cfm. The motor has a power output of 240 hp from 2000 cc, and a power band compatible with international rally events. Fitted to a V8 Ford Cleveland 351 (5700 cc) racing engine, a pair of Weber 48 DCOE carburettors will flow enough air to produce in excess of 525 hp.

The RS 1800 uses what we call an isolated runner manifold (FIGURE 3.5), with one carburettor throat directly connected to each cylinder. This means that each cylinder is totally independent or isolated from all of the other cylinders. Fuel distribution problems and charge robbing is eliminated, improving fuel economy and power output. An induction arrangement of this type is commonly found on road racing engines, European performance cars and all motorcycles.

From the aspect of horsepower output there is not a lot of difference in the peak power output of V8 engines using four Webers on an isolated runner manifold, or two four barrel Holleys on a plenum ram manifold. If fuel distribution is given proper attention, the Holleys mounted on a plenum ram manifold would produce more power (at times up to 7% more). For this reason Holleys are usually preferred for drag racing, but for road racing, where a wide power band and good throttle response is more important, an isolated runner manifold and Webers are a combination hard to beat.

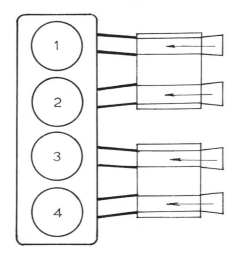

Fig. 3.5   Isolated   runner   manifold.

An important consideration when you go out to buy an isolated runner manifold is to find a design that is not too short; some manifolds are virtually just stubs connecting the carburettor straight onto the head. Particularly in the case of Weber sidedraught carburettors (or Weber downdraught carbs if you are using a downdraught head) can this be bad. If you reduce the manifold bore from 45 mm (1.77 in) at the carburettor to 1.3 in at the head too quickly, this will over-accelerate the fuel mixture after it leaves the carburettor. The resulting turbulance could effectively reduce the area of the inlet port by as much as 40%. By increasing the length of the manifold, the contraction of the intake gases is more gradual, allowing the manifold and port to flow at 100% efficiency.

Most V8 engines in production use a two-plane manifold (FIGURE 3.6). Originally, this type was designed to avoid charge robbing, which resulted when all eight cylinders breathed through a single carburettor. By using a two or four barrel carburettor, the manifold passages are arranged so that cylinders 1, 4, 6, 7 draw through half of the carburettor and one plane of the manifold, and cylinders 8, 3, 5, 2 draw through the other half of the carburettor and the second plane of the manifold, assuming a 1-8-4-3-6-5-7-2 firing order. This separates the induction pulses by 180° and allows reasonably equal cylinder filling if the manifold is of a good design.

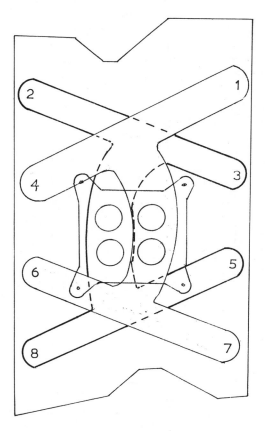

Fig. 3.6   Two plane V8 manifold.

Because there is less air mass to activate on each inlet pulse, throttle response is usually quicker and mid-range power is improved, as compared to a single plane manifold. The division of the manifold into two planes is a mixed blessing as it causes a flow restriction at high rpm because only one half of the carburettor flow capacity is available on any intake stroke.

For this reason the divider can be reduced in height or sometimes removed completely, to make more carburettor flow capacity available. Top end performance is improved but bottom end power is reduced. With the divider cut down, charge robbing can be a problem, but not to the extent of single plane designs.

The two-plane manifolds fitted in normal production are generally of very poor design, with many tortorous corners and restrictive passages that retard air flow. For most V8 road vehicles I recommend the use of either an Edelbrock or Weiand two-plane manifold, but before purchasing any manifold inspect it for casting flaws or core shift that could result in port misalignment.

I like this type of manifold for the good throttle response it is able to produce. This is important on the road, particularly if the vehicle weight to engine displacement is not good. Because the two-plane manifold fosters low and mid-range power, a double pumper mechanical secondary Holley or a pair of 48 DCOE Webers on a Waneford cross-over manifold adapter will work very well. If you use a Holley, pick a 600 - 650 cfm carburettor for a 300 - 350 cubic inch engine and a 700 - 750 cfm unit for engines in the 380 - 450 inch class.

Single plane manifolds (FIGURE 3.7) are found on nearly all in-line engines, and now quite a few V8 manifold manufacturers are marketing replacement high performance single plane (360°) manifolds. This is the very simplest layout with all the cylinders drawing from a single chamber. The manifold may be fitted with any combination of carburettors but in high performance applications it is more usual to fit two single barrel carburettors, or a single two barrel or four barrel carburettor.

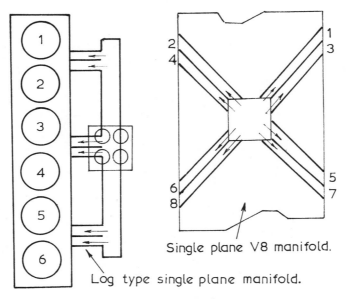

Single plane V8 manifold.

Log type single plane manifold.

Fig. 3.7  Single plane manifolds.

The main problem with the single-plane design is the tendency for one cylinder to rob mixture from another cylinder. By careful design, this deficiency can, and is, being overcome by manifold manufacturers.

In general I prefer to keep well away from single-plane manifolds for in-line engines as these engines are ideal for the isolated runner setup. For sports engines the single-plane manifold will work reasonably well, providing the manifold is of a 'log' design (FIGURE 3.7). To the eye this type may not look as racy as a manifold with nice curves, but it will assist in mixture distribution and it will also help prevent the fuel dropping out of suspension and wetting the manifold and port walls.

The pockets formed at the ends of the log manifold and beneath the carburettor tend to form a soft air cushion that helps keep the mixture atomised as it makes a change in direction. Also, because the shape of the end ports more closely resemble the shape of the inner ports, mixture distribution is equalised. A good rule to keep in mind if you are using a single-plane manifold and you desire reasonably equal mixture distribution is this; where possible, divide the mixture before a change in direction occurs.

There are a number of good, single-plane V8 manifolds available, but in general I stick to the Holley Street Dominator for all engines in sports tune, and engines up to 320 cubic inches in semi-race tune. The Edelbrock Tarantula is suitable for motors larger than 320 in, if in semi-race tune. For race engines, the Holley Strip Dominator and Edelbrock Scorpion are a good choice.

Because throttle response and low end power is not so good, it is best to use a vacuum secondary Holley of around 600 cfm for street engines up to 350 cubic inches and a vacuum secondary 780 cfm for larger engines. Race engines work well with a 750 cfm mechanical secondary double pumper up to 315 in, an 800 cfm up to 350 in, and 1050 cfm above 400 ins.

Offenhauser have tackled the problem by offering a dual port, single-plane manifold. A small and a large passage manifold are stacked one on top of the other in a single casting. The small ports are connected to the primary side of the carburettor, to give a high mixture speed at low rpm; this assists in mixture distribution and gives good throttle response. The larger ports connect to the secondary barrels of the carburettor for high rpm operation.

There are several features that the dual port manifold can boast. The small primary passages, as well as assisting low rpm operation and contributing to good throttle response, also provide a very effective space to keep engine heat away from the secondary passages. This serves to increase the secondary air density, thus improving high speed performance.

The small passages also lift mid-range performance in this way. When the secondary mixture gets to the end of its runner, it is accelerated by the high speed primary fuel/air mixture. This serves to ram the air down the inlet port, and the differences in air speed shears the secondary fuel particles to aid in mixture atomisation.

This is a good manifold for the 3.8 litre Buick V6 and the German Capri 2.8 litre V6. Use a Holley vacuum secondary 390cfm carburettor on the Capri and a 465 cfm on the Buick.

All-out drag cars and racing boats commonly use a plenum ram manifold (FIGURE 3.8) with either one four barrel, or more commonly dual four barrel carburettors. This manifold is very similar to the isolated runner manifold, with a plenum chamber added between the carburettor base and the manifold runners. The plenum helps to dissipate the strong pulsing, common to the isolated runner design, so less pulse enters the carburettor to disrupt air flow. Also it allows the cylinders to share the carburettor/s flow capacity for super-high rpm operation ie. 10,000 rpm on a 302 Chevy; 9000 rpm on a 427 cubic inch 55

Chevy. Manifolds of this design are not suitable for use below 5000 - 6000 rpm, and some such as the Edelbrock TR-2Y for the 396 - 427 - 454 Chevy will not work below 7000 rpm.

For Chevrolet engines I prefer the Team G Super Ram manifold. This type has a split plenum, which is a real asset when manifold modifications are being tested. All plenum ram manifolds have a removable plenum, but to get inside the plenum to carry out modifications it is frequently necessary to saw the chamber in half. Then after any grinding and filling it has to be welded together; all very expensive and time consuming.

When you go out to buy a manifold there are several things to look for and to keep in mind. First, you want to buy a manifold that will, if possible, fit the carburettor/s that you wish to use, without an adaptor. Generally, adaptor plates restrict the air flow by creating undue turbulence, because they attempt to change the air flow path too quickly, the plate being only ½ - 1½ in thick.

Many of the adaptors made to mount the large Holley 4500 carburettors (1050 and 1150 cfm) on standard four barrel pattern manifolds restrict the air flow potential of the carburettor by 100 - 250 cfm, which effectively takes away any advantage of the larger carburettor.

Take an inlet manifold gasket with you to check how the manifold ports match up. As most stock gaskets have port holes much larger than necessary, to allow for port misalignment, it will be necessary to make up a gasket with the exact port and stud locations of your cylinder head. If your engine is a V6, V8, flat four etc. you will need two gaskets; be sure to mark each gasket left or right.

Try to find a manifold that matches as closely as possible to the gasket as this will save some work when the manifold and head are matched.

Look at the ports to check their smoothness; high spots (dingle berries) can be ground out but depressions can be a problem if a suitable epoxy filler is not available.

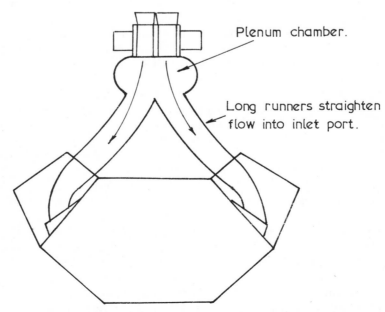

Plenum chamber.

Long runners straighten flow into inlet port.

Fig. 3. 8    V8 plenum ram manifold.

You should note the 'join' in the manifold. This is where the core boxes were joined when the manifold was being cast. At times, the core and core boxes are not correctly aligned, resulting in half of the port being offset from the other half. Choose a manifold with little or no evidence of core shift.

After you have bought your manifold, try fitting it to your engine before you modify it in any way, as you may have to return it if it does not fit. Some V6 and V8 manifolds will not fit with non-standard distributors; on the other hand a couple will not fit with the stock distributor. Due to the large variety of exhaust headers available, a few manifolds will not clear the headers on in-line engines.

When you are sure that the manifold will clear everything, match up the manifold runners with the inlet ports and match the carburettor bore to the manifold entrance. The only exception to this is with Edelbrock Streetmaster manifolds, as these have purposely mismatched runner walls which should not be modified. Edelbrock claim that the mismatch serves to reduce reversion pulses, but as I have not had any experience with this manifold (because it is designed for low performance emission engines), I cannot confirm or deny this.

With the manifold aligned to the ports and the carburettor bore, clean any 'dingle berries' out of the runners with a high-speed grinder, but do not polish the ports. As I have mentioned before, a smooth surface will flow as well as a polished surface, but fuel vaporisation is much better if the ports are left smooth rather than polished. Polished ports can reduce power by 3 - 4%.

Proper fuel distribution always has and probably will be a major problem as long as we use carburettors and non-isolated runner type manifolds. Several factors affect distribution, such as manifold design, carburettor size and type, inlet charge temperature, engine speed and consequently air flow speed. Obviously if port-type fuel injection or an isolated runner manifold is being used, there can not be any variation in the quantity of fuel reaching each cylinder.

Generally, V8 engines using single-plane and low profile cross ram manifolds have the worst distribution. The stock two plane manifold is also affected, but replacement performance manifolds are quite good. So too are the plenum ram manifolds.

In-line engines with one SU (or SU type) carburettor to each pair of cylinders do not have any distribution deficiencies, but single-plane manifolds with a two or four barrel carburettor, or two or three single throat carburettors, may cause serious fuel variations from cylinder to cylinder.

Before we delve into manifold modifications to assist in achieving equal fuel distribution, there are a couple of principles that should be considered.

The purpose of this exercise is to equalise as closely as possible the quantity of fuel entering each cylinder. Equality of air flow is a different consideration and beyond the scope of a tuner without access to an air flow test bench. Therefore you have to assume that the manifold design engineer has done his job and each cylinder is receiving a reasonably equal quantity of air. Fuel distribution variations have a much more serious effect on engine performance than slight air flow differences. Unfortunately many tuners do not realise this.

Because high performance engines (for that matter all engines) operate at less than their ideal engine speed for some of the time, air speed through the carburettor and ports is not high enough to ensure good fuel vaporisation. Some of the fuel separates from the air and falls to the floor of the manifold. When this happens it will be directed partly by the force of gravity to one or more of the inlet ports. If the manifold floor is not horizontal, the 57 wet fuel will flow to cylinders at the low end of the manifold. Therefore the first check should be to ensure that the manifold is horizontal to the ground, not to the angle of the engine. If you have a 'V' or flat engine, the manifold will have to be checked both in-line with the engine and across the engine. Obviously braking, cornering and acceleration, as well as ascending and descending hills, will upset wet flow distribution, but there is no way of overcoming these continually varying forces, except on speedway machines where the cornering force may be reasonably constant.

In production engines, exhaust heat or hot engine coolant is circulated through the manifold floor directly below the carburettor. The heat will cause some fuel to vaporise, but we may want to remove the heat in semi-race and full race engines to improve high rpm air density. In this instance we may have to sacrifice distribution uniformity at lower engine speeds to ensure peak power at maximum rpm.

If hood clearance is not a problem, raising the carburettor using a 1 - 1½ in spacer may assist distribution in two ways. First, because the carburettor is further removed from the floor of the manifold, the fuel/air charge will have less directional effect imparted to it as it leaves the carburettor. This will allow the charge to flow from the carburettor and around the corner of the manifold opening, and into the ports. If the carburettor is mounted very close to the manifold (as is often the case) the fuel/air mixture continues straight on after leaving the carburettor, then the air turns abruptly into the manifold and throws the fuel out of suspension and on to the floor of the manifold. The fuel is much heavier than the air so it

### TABLE 3.4   Checking fuel distribution by spark plug reading

| Spark plug mixture condition | Indications |
| --- | --- |
| Normal — correct mixture | Insulator nose white or very light tan to rust brown. Little or no cement boil where the centre electrode protrudes through the insulator nose. The electrodes are not discoloured or eroded. |
| Fuel fouled — rich mixture | Insulator nose dark grey or black. Steel plug shell end covered with a dry, black soot deposit that will easily rub off. |
| Overheated — lean mixture | Insulator nose chalky white or may have a satin sheen. Excessive cement boil where centre electrode protrudes through the insulator nose. May be milk white or meringue-like. Centre electrode may 'blue' and be rounded off at the edges. Earth electrode may be badly eroded or have a molten appearance. |
| Detonation — lean mixture | Insulator nose covered in tiny pepper specks or maybe tiny beads of aluminium leaving the piston crown. Excessive cement boil where centre electrode protrudes through insulator hose. Specks on the steel plug shell end. |

cannot change direction as quickly, therefore it continues straight on until it hits the manifold floor.

At small throttle openings the spacer also promotes better distribution by reducing the directional effect imparted to the fuel/air mixture by the angle of the throttle plate. This can be a serious problem in the upper plane of two-plane manifolds, causing two cylinders to run very lean. After the spacer (riser) is fitted, distribution will be improved markedly.

After ensuring that the manifold is horizontal, a check must be made on the actual fuel distribution from cylinder to cylinder. The only really accurate way to determine this is by chemically analysing exhaust gas samples from each cylinder. This test will show which cylinders are rich and which are lean.

As a back-up, the exhaust gas temperature measurement system is also used. It is less sensitive than chemical analysis as it does not take into account exhaust temperature variations from cylinder to cylinder, due to differences in exhaust scavenging. However, it is a particularly valuable test in the dyno room, to determine the heat level of a given cylinder, so as to avoid engine damage due to an excessively lean mixture condition.

Obviously at the race track, or on the road, you are not able to use either system. In this case your eyes become the test instrument as you rely on the appearance and colour of the spark plug electrodes and porcelain to tell the story of fuel distribution equality.

At the very best this system is only a rough guide but it will provide us with valuable information if approached correctly. The engine must be in good condition; broken or worn rings and worn valve guides will distort the readings very badly. Also the spark plugs must be of the correct heat range for the engine.

Actually, the colour of the porcelain insulator nose is not as important as some would suppose, as it may not be possible to colour the plugs using certain types of fuel unless the mixture is extremely rich. Added to this it can take many, many miles for the insulator nose to colour so you will appreciate that there is a good deal more to plug reading than merely examining the colour of the insulator.

It takes practice and a proper magnifier of 4x to 6x power to pinpoint fuel distribution equality. The things to look for that indicate certain operating conditions are indicated in TABLE 3.4. You will note that all of the plug end actually exposed to the combustion flame is examined and read, not just the insulator nose.

### TABLE 3.5   Checking fuel distribution by combustion chamber, exhaust valve and piston crown colour

| Mixture condition | Indication |
|---|---|
| Normal | Dry dark hard carbon in combustion chamber and piston crown. Light tan to rust brown exhaust valve. |
| Rich | Dark soft carbon in combustion chamber and on piston crown. Carbon may be wet or have wet stains. Dark exhaust valve. |
| Lean | Gray to white deposit in combustion chamber and on piston crown. Oil may be burned under piston crown a very dark brown. Called 'death ash' if burned to black ash. White chalky colour exhaust valve. |

59

For the plug reading to be accurate it will be necessary to run the engine at full throttle and maximum speed on the track (or road) and then immediately cut the engine dead. If you allow the engine to slow down as you bring the vehicle to a stop, the plug reading will be meaningless.

A tuner must use everything at his disposal to check the distribution from cylinder to cylinder. Usually, race engines are stripped frequently for inspection and periodic replacement of parts. This is an ideal time to read the combustion chamber and also the exhaust valves and the top of the piston. Naturally if the engine is burning a lot of oil because of being overdue for a rebuild, a reliable reading will not be possible (TABLE 3.5).

Having determined which cylinders are rich, normal or lean, we must then set about correcting the problem. Usually, single-plane V8 manifolds cause us the most problems. As this design is very popular in high performance and racing applications, we will concentrate on 'fixes' to overcome distribution deficiencies in manifolds of this type.

The distribution situation can at times be improved by staggered jetting of the carburettor. If you find two adjacent cylinders (ie. 1 and 3, 5 and 7, 2 and 4, 6 and 8; or for Ford engines 1 and 2, 3 and 4, 5 and 6, 7 and 8) that are both either rich or lean, the condition may be corrected by changing the jets in the barrel of the carburettor feeding those cylinders. This will sometimes correct the distribution, but if you find little improvement after several jet changes, you can assume that manifold modifications are necessary.

Before you alter the manifold it is advantageous to determine if the manufacturer has incorporated changes in later versions of that same basic manifold to fix a distribution problem. You will find manifold manufacturers are continually updating their products, so by studying the refinements made by the manufacturer and incorporating these in your manifold, you can save yourself a lot of time experimenting to find a suitable 'fix'.

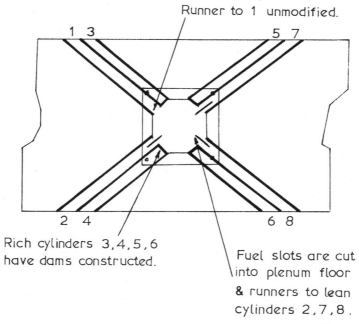

Fig. 3.9 Manifold modified to improve distribution.

Earlier I mentioned that there is always some liquid fuel running around the floor of the manifold. If some of this fuel can be directed into a lean cylinder, or prevented from entering a rich cylinder, the power output of the engine will be improved and the fuel consumption will decrease.

Most racers are after more power but few are concerned about fuel consumption. In reality, many long distance events on road circuits and super speedways have been won and lost on this point. Tuners who work really hard at equalising fuel distribution have been able to get 10 - 15 more laps out of each tank of fuel on the super speedway than their competitors, on the same number of gallons of fuel.

There are two very simple modifications that will correct the majority of distribution deficiencies; fuel dams and fuel slots (FIGURE 3.9).

A dam can be constructed of $\frac{1}{8}$ in rod epoxied to the plenum floor (use a fuel-resistant epoxy). It may be placed across the entry of just one runner or a pair of runners, to reduce the amount of liquid fuel reaching those cylinders. After this modification it is sometimes necessary to fit leaner carburettor jets, as the cylinders without the fuel dams may become too rich.

Fuel slots can be utilised in conjunction with dams or they may be beneficially used just by themselves. Such slots are used to channel liquid fuel to the individual manifold runners that need it. The slots are cut with a high speed $\frac{1}{4}$ in spherical cutter to a depth of $\frac{1}{8}$ -$\frac{3}{16}$ in in the floor of the plenum chamber and runner. To ensure that the fuel reaches the desired cylinder, the slot must extend approximately 1 in past the entry of the runner into the plenum chamber, and $1\frac{1}{4}$ - $1\frac{1}{2}$ in down the throat of the runner itself.

You are probably wondering how directing liquid fuel to a lean cylinder, or preventing it from entering a rich cylinder, will improve power output. It is true that liquid fuel contributes little in the way of actual power because of its very slow burning characteristics, but more is involved.

Normally, to prevent damage in a lean cylinder, it is necessary to increase the carburettor jet sizes so that this cylinder receives sufficient fuel. As a result, the power output of the engine will be reduced as the rest of the engine will no longer be receiving a fuel/air mixture for best power; the other cylinders will now be too rich.

However, by channelling liquid fuel to a lean cylinder, the fuel/air mixture in the other cylinders will be virtually unchanged. The liquid fuel passing into the lean cylinder will not do much to lift its power output to equal that of the other individual cylinders, but it will slow down the burn rate of the combustion flame to deter piston or valve burning and serious detonation. With the lean cylinder taken care of, it is usually possible to fit smaller jets to slightly lean the rest of the engine, such that they are receiving the best fuel/air mix for maximum power. This results in a power increase and a reduction in fuel consumption. The engine will respond more crisply and be less prone to plug fouling.

Restricting the flow of liquid fuel to a rich cylinder raises the engine's power potential. An over-rich mixture burns very slowly, and combustion is usually incomplete, due to the lack of oxygen for proper burning. Consequently less heat is being generated to cause the pressure necessary to force the piston down during the power stroke. The result is a loss of power.

The four cycle engine is really only a specialised air pump. The more air that can be introduced into the cylinders, the higher the power output, providing fuel is mixed with the air in the correct proportions. It is of no value making more fuel available for combustion unless there is a proportional increase in the amount of oxygen drawn into the cylinders. 61

Throughout this book several chapters are devoted to improving the air pumping efficiency of an engine and, of course, the induction system also has an influence in this area.

Beside actually modifying the engine so that it will pump a larger volume of air, we also have to concern ourslves with improving the density of the air inducted. Obviously 2000 cc of cold air will contain more oxygen than 2000 cc of hot air.

To introduce as much oxygen as possible into the engine it is necessary to keep the inlet charge cool. For good low speed performance this is not always desirable, but for race and semi-race engines there are power gains to be made in this way.

There are several areas in the induction system where the inlet charge is being heated. Most inlet manifolds are heated by the engine's exhaust gases or by hot engine coolant. This is done to assist in fuel vaporisation at low rpm. As very high performance engines are operated only in a relatively narrow power band in the higher rpm range, heating of the manifold is not necessary for good atomisation of the fuel. The heating system can be rendered inoperative by blocking the exhaust heat passages, or if water heating is employed, by disconnecting the water hoses.

The inlet manifold may also be heated by radiation from the exhaust headers. Therefore a heat shield made of unpainted aluminium should be fitted between the inlet and the exhaust manifolds. Also, the inlet manifold should be left silver coloured, so that it reflects heat rather than absorbing it.

On 'V-type' engines the inlet manifold is heated by hot oil splashing the valley area. The modification required is to fit a shield to keep the oil, and heat being radiated from the valley, away from the manifold.

Many cars draw in air that has been heated after passing through the radiator. This also reduces the air density. There are several approaches from which this problem can be tackled. The most advantageous system involves sealing the air inlet into the air filter or carburettor so that hot air from around the engine cannot be drawn in. A hole must be cut in the car's bonnet (hood) through which cool air outside the engine bay can enter. Some tuners fit a forward opening air scoop so the air entering at high vehicle speeds is actually rammed into the carburettor. I do not like this type of scoop as most are too low and create undue air turbulence in the mouth of the carburettor, which upsets fuel metering. I prefer a rear opening scoop which allows the carburettor to draw air from the high air pressure area immediately in front of the windscreen.

The other common method is not so successful but a useful power increase is possible without external body modifications. Cold air is ducted from the front of the car to the air filter body through one or more 3 in heater duct tubes. It is usually necessary to cut a suitable hole beside the radiator for the duct to pass through, to pick up cool air at the front of the vehicle. Engines larger than 3.8 litres will require two 3 in ducts.

To prevent the entry of grasshoppers and other flying insects that could quickly block the air filter, a fine fly-screen gauze should be fitted over the duct inlet. This gauze will require frequent and regular cleaning.

The air filter and filter body also reduce the air density, but in this instance by restricting the flow of air into the cylinders. Obviously the restriction can be done away with by removing the air filter. This is acceptable for vehicles racing on sealed tracks but road and rally machines should always be fitted with an effective air filter.

I am constantly shocked at the very poor design of foam type replacement air filters. In general, the foam used is too porous to remove abrasive dust from the air. Added to this, the foam element is often poorly retained by the filter body, which in turn allows a huge volume of abrasive material to be sucked into the motor around the edge of the filter.

For these reasons only paper-type air filters of good design should be used. These restrict air flow but not to the extent that many would suppose. A lot of the restriction is caused by the air filter body itself.

The air filter body (or air box on motorcycles) is designed to comply with certain government-imposed noise regulations. As a result the air flow is badly impeded. TABLE 3.6 indicates the air flow improvement brought about by certain modifications to the filter body, but as you can see, the biggest improvement resulted when two standard air filter elements were stuck together and fitted in place of the single element. This is a practical modification only when a single carburettor is used, but it will require an air scoop in the bonnet to overcome clearance problems.

You will also note the large jump in air flow when the air filter body was cut down so that the filter element is open to draw air around its full 360° circumference. The removal of the inlet snorkel and the addition of a second snorkel had only a marginal effect on air flow. Therefore the filter body should have the entire side cut out so that the filter element is fully exposed.

If you study many air filters fitted as standard, you will find a strap welded to the filter body base that badly impedes the air flow by passing right across the throat of the carburettor. This strap has a stud welded to it for retaining the filter lid, so after its removal other means will have to be found to keep the lid in place and properly sealed.

The air box fitted to most motorcyles has a devastating effect on their performance. Many enthusiasts are fooled into thinking that they have gained many horsepower by fitting larger carburettors to their bikes. Usually the improvement in power is the result of the removal of the air filter and box, as many of these kits will not hook up to the standard factory filter and air box. In fact more often than not, the larger carburettors actually cause a decrease in power if the bike is in otherwise near standard tune.

Many air filter boxes are so restrictive that it is a complete waste of time modifying the engine in any way without first improving the air flow path into the air box. Generally, I have been able to pick up 7 - 12% more power by cutting a few simple holes in the air box. Some boxes also have muffling ribs and baffles inside, which should also be cut out, and if possible a second filtering element should be fitted.

### TABLE 3.6 Air filter air flow comparison
*Holley 850 cfm carburettor tested at 1.5 in Hg*

| Remarks | cfm air flow |
|---|---|
| Carburettor without air filter | 823 |
| Carburettor fitted with air horn | 839 |
| Standard totally enclosed element with single snorkel air intake | 554 |
| As above but with snorkel cut off filter body | 594 |
| Standard totally enclosed element with two snorkel air intakes | 608 |
| As above but with both snorkels cut off filter body | 665 |
| As above but with two filter elements fitted | 796 |
| As above but with filter body cut down flush with base | 818 |
| As above but with one filter element fitted | 743 |
| High performance speed shop foam type air cleaner | 780 |

In standard tune, the Honda Hawk 400 provides adequate but uninspiring performance. It tends to feel as if the timing is badly retarded and it uses a lot of fuel in spite of its small displacement. I haven't done any dyno tests but after removing the plastic muffling device fitted to the air box cover and cutting some holes in the cover, the performance picked up noticeably. The bike's hill climbing ability improved out of sight and as a consequence of no longer needing full throttle over every hill, fuel consumption improved from 46.6 mpg to 59.2 mpg.

There are many 29 mm smooth bore Mikuni carburettor kits being marketed to replace the standard 26 mm Mikunis usually fitted to the Japanese superbikes. These kits will improve top end performance but only if the air filter and air box is removed. A similar improvement is possible (assuming the engine is in standard tune) if the 26 mm carburettors are retained and the air filter and box is removed. TABLE 3.7 shows the dyno test results of a Suzuki 1000/4 with standard and 29 mm carburettors and with and without the air filter and box. You will note the poor low speed performance of the 29 mm smooth bore Mikunis. This is due to the fact that these carburettors are designed for racing only and as such do not have metering circuits conducive to good low speed performance.

### TABLE 3.7   Suzuki 1000/4 dyno test
*(Engine not modified)*

| rpm | Test 1 (hp) | Test 2 (hp) | Test 3 (hp) | Test 4 (hp) | Test 5 (hp) |
|-----|-------------|-------------|-------------|-------------|-------------|
| 3500 | 32.2 | — | — | 29.1 | 30.5 |
| 4000 | 38.7 | 28.7 | — | 34.9 | 37.2 |
| 4500 | 43.3 | 36.2 | 30.8 | 39.7 | 43.4 |
| 5000 | 50.4 | 43.3 | 39.9 | 46.3 | 50.1 |
| 5500 | 56.0 | 52.5 | 49.2 | 53.8 | 56.0 |
| 6000 | 61.8 | 60.3 | 57.5 | 61.2 | 61.9 |
| 6500 | 67.2 | 65.9 | 66.0 | 67.0 | 67.7 |
| 7000 | 70.5 | 70.2 | 73.4 | 71.7 | 72.2 |
| 7500 | 73.9 | 74.1 | 76.6 | 76.8 | 77.4 |
| 8000 | 74.7 | 74.3 | 82.0 | 80.3 | 79.1 |
| 8500 | 71.4 | 73.9 | 77.3 | 75.5 | 74.9 |
| 9000 | 65.8 | 67.4 | 74.5 | 72.6 | 70.7 |

Test 1 —    Standard 26 mm Mikuni carburettors with air filter and air box connected.
Test 2 —    29 mm Mikuni smooth bore carburettors with air filter and air box connected.
Test 3 —    As above but with air filter and air box removed.
Test 4 —    As above but with standard 26 mm carburettors fitted.
Test 5 —    As above but with four K & N air filters fitted.

*Note: Dyno would not hold a steady load below 4500 rpm with the 29 mm carburettors fitted so these figures have been omitted.*

Superbike owners are not the only ones who are being fooled into believing that their machines need large carburettors. There is a lot of speed equipment being produced for the humble Yamaha 500 single, but again in this instance the performance is spoiled when a larger carburettor is fitted (TABLE 3.8). If the engine is bored and stroked to 605 cc and fitted with a wild cam and open exhaust, the large (36 mm) carburettor will work better. The best modification for the standard engine is to remove the obstructions inside the air box

## TABLE 3.8   Yamaha SR500 dyno test
### *(Engine not modified)*

| rpm | Test 1 (hp) | Test 2 (hp) | Test 3 (hp) | Test 4 (hp) |
|-----|-------------|-------------|-------------|-------------|
| 3000 | 14.2 | 13.2 | 12.7 | — |
| 3500 | 16.8 | 16.3 | 16.1 | — |
| 4000 | 19.0 | 18.7 | 18.6 | 18.4 |
| 4500 | 22.3 | 22.6 | 21.6 | 21.6 |
| 5000 | 25.1 | 25.8 | 25.7 | 25.2 |
| 5500 | 26.9 | 28.2 | 28.3 | 28.5 |
| 6000 | 28.3 | 30.3 | 30.4 | 30.0 |
| 6500 | 29.2 | 31.5 | 31.8 | 31.3 |
| 7000 | 28.2 | 31.1 | 31.5 | 31.1 |
| 7500 | 27.1 | 30.1 | 30.7 | 28.8 |

**Test 1 —**  Standard 34 mm Mikuni carburettor with air filter and air box connected.
**Test 2 —**  As above but with two air filters fitted and air box modified to improve air flow.
**Test 3 —**  As above but with air filters and air box removed.
**Test 4 —**  As above with 36mm Mikuni carburettor fitted.

*Note : Dyno would not hold a steady load below 4000 rpm with the 36 mm carburettor fitted so these figures have been omitted.*

and sandwich two filter elements together. This alone will result in a 7 - 12% power rise in the upper power range.

Physically, that is about everything that you can do to the induction system to increase the air density within the cylinders, unless you plan on using a supercharger. However there are other aspects relative to air density that you should know about and make allowance for when you are tuning your carburettors or fuel injection.

You probably already know that air is less dense at 5000 ft than it is at sea level but did you realise that prevailing atmospheric conditions could reduce the air density at sea level to approximately the same density as air at an altitude of 5000 ft?

Since the temperature, humidity and barometric pressure all affect air density, it is obvious that the ratio of fuel and air being introduced into your engine will vary from hour to hour and this will influence the power output of the engine. Under normal circumstances the change in air density from hour to hour is of little or no consequence to the average enthusiast, but the racing engine tuner seeking as much power as possible, or wanting to prevent burned pistons and valves, has to take the present air density into consideration before each and every race or during a rally, where large changes in altitude and climatic conditions are experienced.

When the air density decreases, this reduces the amount of oxygen inducted into the cylinders, therefore the mixture becomes richer. Conversely, an increase in the air density increases the quantity of oxygen entering the motor so there is a corresponding leaning of the fuel/air mixture. To compensate, it will be necessary to fit richer or leaner carburettor main (and at times idle) jets.

Remember when compensating for a change in air density that the change in density also affects the pressure exerted on the fuel in the float bowl. Therefore a decrease in RAD will automatically lean the fuel/air mixture to a degree, because of the lower air pressure. 65

This means that you don't fit 5% smaller jets when the RAD drops by 5%. Usually I reckon that a 12% change in RAD requires a 5% change in fuel jet size.

To make sure that the correct change in jet size is made, you first have to know the relative air density at the time when the carburettor was originally jetted to deliver peak power. If the engine was set up on a dyno, the air density will usually be stated on the dyno sheet, so you can work your calculations from that figure.

If the engine wasn't tuned on the dyno, or the dyno jetting is found to be all wrong (this can happen), you have to set about finding the ideal jet sizes from first principles. When you find what jets give the best performance, make a note in your tuning diary of the jet size and the relative air density, for future reference.

The relative air density can be worked out (FIGURE 3.10) providing you know the air temperature and the uncorrected barometric pressure. Relative air density meters are available and these give a direct percentage density reading.

There is another factor involved and unfortunately this cannot be read off the relative air density graph or meter, but as its influence affects the true air density, we have to take it into account to be completely accurate.

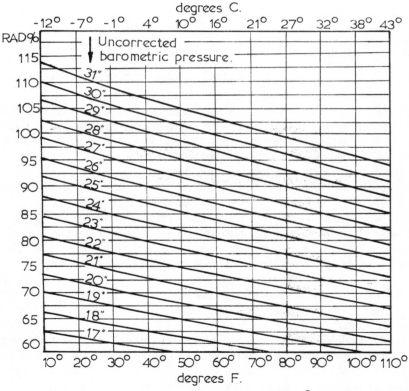

Note - standard sea level pressure at 59°F = 29.92" Hg.
(1013 millibars or 14.706 lb./sq. inch)

Fig. 3.10 Relative air density chart.

The effect of the humidity on the density of the air is small except when both the temperature and the relative humidity are high. Water vapour has weight and as such combines with the weight of the air to distort the true weight or density of the air. Think of it in this way; you are the air and your clothing is water vapour. With clothes on you are going to exert more pressure (weight) on the bathroom scales than your true undressed weight. To find your true weight you have to subtract the weight (or pressure) exerted by your clothes. Similarly, when we want to find the true air density, we have to subtract the pressure exerted by the water vapour.

If you look at TABLE 3.9 you can see that the pressure exerted by water vapour at 100°F is 1.93 in Hg. If the barometric pressure at the time is 30 in Hg, the true air pressure is only 28.07 in Hg or a drop of 6.4%. Therefore the fuel/air ratio will be 6.4% rich if the jets are changed to suit the uncorrected air density.

Usually, the amount of water vapour is less than the amount indicated in the column headed 'Saturation Pressure' as this assumes a relative humidity of 100%. (Relative humidity compares the amount of water vapour present with what the atmosphere is capable of holding).

### TABLE 3.9   Humidity saturation pressure and percentage

| Temperature | | Saturation Pressure | | Saturation percentage of water |
|---|---|---|---|---|
| °F | °C | *in Hg* | *Millibars* | |
| 0 | -17.8 | 0.038 | 1 | 0.12 |
| 20 | -6.7 | 0.103 | 3 | 0.33 |
| 40 | 4.4 | 0.247 | 8 | 0.83 |
| 60 | 15.6 | 0.521 | 18 | 1.7 |
| 70 | 21.1 | 0.739 | 25 | 2.5 |
| 80 | 26.7 | 1.03 | 35 | 3.3 |
| 90 | 32.2 | 1.42 | 48 | 4.7 |
| 100 | 37.8 | 1.93 | 65 | 6.5 |

To find the true air pressure use the formula

$$CAP = UMP - \left(SP \times \frac{RH}{100}\right) \text{ in Hg}$$

CAP = corrected air pressure
UMP = uncorrected barometric pressure
ie. read straight off barometer
SP = saturation pressure (from TABLE 3.9)
RH = relative humidity

Once the corrected air pressure had been calculated, the true relative air density can be read straight off the relative air density graph.

If you are using a relative air density meter, the percentage reading must be corrected using the formula

$$\text{corrected RAD} = \text{RAD reading} - S\% \times \frac{RH}{100}$$

S% = saturation percentage of water (from TABLE 3.9)
RH = relative humidity

The one thing that you must be sure to do if you wish to be successful in tuning your motor according to the relative air density is to keep complete and accurate notes. If you find that the engine works best with 150 main jets and $10^0$ initial spark advance when the air density is 90%, be sure that you make a note of the fact in your tuning diary. Then on each occasion that the air density is again 90%, you will know exactly what size jets and how much spark advance to use to obtain peak performance.

At another location the relative air density might be 98%, so armed with the information in your diary you know that you should try the next size larger main jet. Maybe it will be the correct size, maybe it will not. There are no hard and fast rules here; no two engines respond to air density changes exactly alike. Usually, small displacement, high rpm engines, in a high state of tune, are the most affected by a change in air density.

The mixture ratio is also affected if there are any air leaks, so you must be very careful to seal the manifold to the head, and the carburettor to the manifold, using the correct gasket and the right type of gasket cement. This may seem rather trivial but you would be amazed at the number of tuners who use Silastic to seal the manifold gasket. Silastic is excellent as an oil sealant but it is not petrol resistant, therefore it should not be used anywhere in the induction tract. I recommend the use of Permatex No 3 in this area.

Even when the manifold and carburettor have been correctly installed, this does not guarantee that you do not have an air leak, or that a leak will not start later on. I always check for leaks around the base of the carburettor and along the face of the manifold. The best method is to squirt petrol out of an oil can around the manifold face and carburettor with the engine running. If there is a leak, the engine will run rich or it may even stop. If you use this method of leak detection, always have a fire extinguisher at hand. Usually there are no problems but a backfire could start a serious fire with all that fuel running around.

Some types of carburettor have a tendency to loosen the screws that attach the body to the base. These should be regularly tightened, but do not use Loctite on them as this may cause the soft threads to strip.

Many engines loosen the manifold retaining bolts very quickly, so these should be Loctited. If the same bolts also retain the exhaust manifold, the Loctite will not work too well, so you should tighten them frequently. By paying careful attention to this, most induction air leaks can be avoided.

When you are setting up the carburettors or fuel injection, spend some time sorting out a good throttle linkage. This is not usually a problem when a single carburettor is used but with a multiple unit set-up it is essential that the butterflies open together and that they remain synchronised right through to the full throttle position. If any of the throttle linkages are cranked, it is possible for the butterflies to break open simultaneously, but as full throttle is reached the throttle plates could be opened to differing angles.

While you are attending to the throttle linkage, you should also see that you are indeed getting full throttle. Have someone hold the pedal flat to the floor while you check that the butterflies are opening fully (be sure that the engine is not running!).

Earlier in this chapter we had a look at the fuel flow requirements of modified engines. As well as considering the flow through the needle and seat, we must also check that the fuel pump and fuel lines will flow the required quantity of fuel so that the fuel bowl remains full at sustained high rpm. If the bowl empties slightly, this will immediately lean the fuel/air mixture, reducing power and possibly causing damage to the pistons and valves.

Most fuel pumps are flow rated in gallons per hour. At first glance it would seem very easy to match a given pump to a particular engine. If the engine requires 37 gph of petrol at maximum power rpm then hook up a pump rated at 40 gph.

Unfortunately there is a lot more involved than this. Firstly, the output volume of the pump will drop off as you increase the restriction in the fuel lines and needle valve. Many pumps are rated 'free flow' without any inlet or outlet restriction. For instance, the big Holley 110 gph electric pump will flow not 110 gph but something closer to 65 - 70 gph when used with $\frac{3}{8}$ in i/d fuel lines.

Whenever a liquid flows through a closed pipe there is bound to be a certain amount of restriction due to friction in the pipe, sharp corners and the needle and seat. This restriction causes a drop in pressure from one end of the pipe to the other. The pump may have an output pressure of 5 psi, but at the other end of the pipe the pressure may read only 2 psi due to restriction.

There is always some pressure loss between the fuel tank and the carburettor. It doesn't matter whether you have the fuel pump mounted on the engine, drawing fuel from the tank at the rear of the car, or whether the pump is mounted near the tank at the back of the car, pushing fuel up to the engine. The pressure drop is the same either way, due to line restrictions.

The pressure drop increases as the square of the volume of flow through the pipe, so if you double the gph flow the pressure loss would be multiplied four times. Conversely, the pressure drop is inversely proportional to the square of the internal diameter of the pipe. Thus if you were to use a pipe twice the diameter, a given gph flow rate would only have one quarter the pressure loss. Obviously when large increases in an engine's fuel requirements have been made, larger diameter fuel lines are in order.

The effect of a car's acceleration also effectively causes a flow restriction by tending to pull the fuel back to the tank. This can account for a 2 - 3 psi pressure loss in a drag car.

In view of these factors, the fuel pump selected should be able to flow more than the gph flow requirement of the engine. I use a rule of thumb for a petrol-fired racing engine of 1.75 times the theoretical fuel flow requirement or 0.12 times the maximum horsepower. Because a high performance road engine is not usually held at sustained high rpm, the required flow is considerably less.

When selecting a pump, be sure that you know whether the pump is rated in Imperial gallons or US gallons. If you live outside the US you will run into trouble if you calculate your fuel flow to be say 70 gph and you fit a 70 gph American pump. One US gallon equals 0.8 of an Imperial gallon, so the American pump will actually flow 56 Imperial gph (The above rule of thumb calculates the fuel flow requirement in Imperial gallons per hour when working from the maximum horsepower).

Most high flow American fuel pumps have a very high delivery pressure, which may cause English and European carburettors to flood. Holley carburettors are designed to operate at an idle speed pressure of 6 - 7 psi and 4.5 psi at maximum speed. Weber carburettors should not have a delivery pressure (at the carburettor) of more than 4 - 4½ psi at idle and the pressure at maximum speed should not be less than 3 psi.

To regulate the pressure, you will have to use an in-line pressure regulator or a by-pass line. Holley make a regulator for use with their high pressure pumps which pump at up to 15 psi unregulated. The regulator must be fitted close to the carburettor and then adjusted according to the fuel pressure gauge reading at idle.

Some racers prefer to use a by-pass line from the pump outlet back to the tank, to reduce the pressure. This system will work very well but a lot of time can be spent finding what size restriction plug should be fitted in the by-pass line to get the required fuel pressure. 69

I would recommend that you use a ¼ in line and start off your testing using a restrictor with a ¹/₁₆ in hole.

The front-mounted fuel pump is acceptable in most instances for engines in up to medium semi-race tune. Above this degree of modification an electric pump mounted near the fuel tank should be used.

The main weakness of using a front-mounted pump is that it aggravates vapour lock. A high performance engine requires a lot of fuel so the line from the pump back to the tank will always be subjected to suction or a vacuum. This means that the fuel in the pipe is going to boil at a much lower temperature than it would if at normal atmospheric pressure. The only way around this is to use a rear-mounted electric pump.

In large displacement racing machines it is at times necessary to use two or three electric pumps. When this is done, the pumps must be connected in parallel, so that each pump has an inlet line running to the fuel tank. The outlet lines may be left separate until they reach the front of the car, or they may be connected to a single large bore fuel line.

When installing an electric pump I recommend that a Holley safety switch be included in the electrical circuit, so that the pump will not work unless there is oil pressure. This not only ensures that the engine will not be flooded when the engine is switched off (a simple isolator switch will also do this) but more importantly, in a crash gallons of fuel can be pumped over everything before the pump is switched off, if an ordinary switch is used. With the ever-present risk of fire, this is extremely dangerous.

The fuel line must be protected from possible mechanical damage for the very same reason. Flying stones or abrasions between rubbing parts could puncture the line and allow fuel spillage. To avoid this, the line must be carefully routed and sections exposed to stone damage must be shielded with suitable covering.

The line may also fracture because of vibration . To overcome this a flexible section of line of sufficient length must be used to connect the fuel line to the engine and also the fuel tank. If an electric pump is used, flexible line must be used on the inlet and outlet as these pumps are subject to considerable vibration.

When routing the line, be sure to keep it well away from the engine and the exhaust. This will ensure that the fuel remains cool. If the fuel is heated, it will flash into vapour upon passing into the fuel bowl, creating an under-bonnet fire hazard and upsetting the carburettor fuel metering.

A fuel filter should be fitted in the system to remove dirt and water from the fuel. In racing applications it may be advisable to use two filters in parallel, to reduce flow restriction. A filter should never be fitted on the suction side of the fuel pump.

For competition, fuel of a higher octane rating than that at the local service station can be used. Generally, road racing cars are restricted to 100 octane fuel while motorcycles, go-karts, and certain boat and dragster classes are permitted to use 115 octane fuel.

In most brands the higher octane rating is obtained by adding tetra-ethyl-lead and ethylene dibromide. The decomposition products from these additives may cause severe exhaust valve burning, therefore I recommend the use of racing fuels that contain very little t-e-l. Instead, the higher octane rating should be obtained by the fuel company using additives such as acetone, toluol (methyl benzine), benzole or methanol. Fuels using these additives will not cause any engine damage, but usually they are considerably more expensive than those with an octane rating boosted purely by the addition of t-e-l.

I have found some fuels so loaded with t-e-l. that the spark plug insulator has become covered with small specks of lead that has actually caused the plug to short out and subsequently stop the engine.

Methanol (methyl alcohol) fuel is permitted in most categories of speedway racing, and in some drag car and boat racing classes. This fuel can be used with a compression ratio of up to 15:1 without detonation because of its cooling effect on the internal parts of the engine.

Methanol has a very high latent heat of vaporisation ie. it takes a lot of heat to be converted from liquid into a vapour. Petrol has a latent heat of evaporation of 135 Btu/lb, methanol 472 Btu/lb. This heat required for proper atomisation is removed from the piston crown, combustion chamber and the exhaust valve, resulting in an internally cooler engine.

An engine burning methanol will usually show an 8 - 17 power increase over one running on petrol. Part of that power increase is the result of the higher compression ratio of the alky burner, but where does the majority of the increase come from?

I have already mentioned that the four cycle engine is a heat engine ie. one that burns a fuel to cause the expansion of gas and the subsequent movement of the piston. The more heat produced by the combustion fire, the stronger the pressure exerted on the piston.

Using petrol, the fuel/air ratio for the best power (ie. the strongest force on the piston) is 1:12.5. With alcohol we can increase the fuel/air ratio to 1:4.5 although usually I prefer a ratio of 1:5.5; less than 1:7 is too lean.

One pound of petrol has the energy potential of about 19,000 Btu (one British Thermal Unit is the amount of energy required to raise the temperature of one pound of water one degree Fahrenheit.)

In comparison, methanol delivers arount 9800 Btu/lb, which means that it produces less than 52 of the heat energy of 1 lb of petrol.

However, because we are mixing more methanol with each pound of air (1:5.5) than petrol (1:12.5), we are actually producing more heat energy by burning methanol.

To work out how much more heat energy is produced, we have to divide 12.5 by 5.5, which equals 2.27. Next we multiply 9800 by 2.27, which gives us 22,246. This tells us that methanol in the correct fuel/air proportions will produce 17 more heat energy than petrol in the correct fuel/air ratio.

$$\left( \frac{22,246}{19,000} \times 100 \right) - 100 = 17\%$$

Right away you can see that an engine running straight alky will burn more than twice as much fuel as one burning petrol. Therefore you must be careful to ensure that the needle valve, fuel pump and fuel lines will flow the required amount of fuel.

This can present some problems as many carburettors will not flow the required amount of fuel through the needle and seat, and others do not have main jets large enough. For this reason fuel injection is preferred for alky and nitro burners.

The SU carburettor can be fitted with two or even three fuel bowls if necessary to get proper flow. Holley and Weber have alcohol size needle valves available. If you have a carburettor that you cannot get larger needle valves for, you will have to enlarge the discharge area of the standard needle and seat, but check the fuel flow into a container before you run the engine. If it is not flowing enough fuel you will melt the pistons.

Some carburettor jets are classified with regard to the fuel flow, the number stamped on the jet representing the ccs' of fuel passing through the jet in a given time. For example, the hexagon-head Mikuni carburettor jets follow this pattern. If you are changing from petrol to alky then you will have to start testing with jets 2.2 times as large. eg. change a 200 main jet to a 440.

Other manufacturers rate their jets according to their nominal bore diameter in inches or millimeters. eg. a Holley 66 jet has a nominal aperture of 0.066 in, a Weber 175 jet a nominal aperture of 1.75 mm, a Mikuni 250 round head main jet a nominal aperture of 2.5 mm. When changing from petrol to alcohol you will have to begin testing with jets with an aperture area 2.2 times as large. (Aperture area $= \pi r^2$).

Since most engines are relatively insensitive to rich methanol mixtures, the carburettor jets can be drilled out if large jets are not obtainable. Weber have an excellent set of drills for this purpose, but they are expensive.

There are other problems involved in the change to alcohol, some of which will affect you and some of which will affect your engine.

Since your life is important, we will deal with you first. Methanol is extremely poisonous and as it is accumulative enough can build up and oxidise to form formaldehyde, causing blindness and even insanity. It can be absorbed through the skin and lungs. Inhalation of the exhaust gases is also dangerous as vaporised methanol is usually present, especially when rich mixtures are being used.

Methanol is a very effective paint stripper and it may attack some types of fibreglass resin. It has a scouring effect on tanks and fuel lines so these should be soaked in methanol and then drained so that the residue does not find its way into the carburettor when you switch from petrol to methanol.

Methanol will absorb huge amounts of water out of the air, so it must always be kept in an air-tight container. The fuel will also have to be drained completely from the tank and the carburettor, to prevent the formation of water-induced rust and oxidation. This can be particularly damaging to a carburettor and usually results in blocked metering passages.

Motorcycles using methanol should have only carburettors with chrome plated brass slides fitted, or you could end up a dead rider. Some carburettors use an aluminium or magnesium slide, which is no problem with petrol as petrol tends to lubricate the slide and prevent it sticking. Methanol does not lubricate at all, which may allow the slide to stick, possibly in the wide open position.

In colder climates, starting difficulties may be encountered when pure alcohol is being used. Some use other more volatile fuels blended with the methanol to help overcome this problem. Usually, 5% acetone or a maximum of 3% ether is used. Starting aerosols containing ether should not be used due to the possibility of engine damage being caused by detonation. Personally I feel the best method is to spray either petrol or straight acetone down the throat of the carburettor. Do not attempt to do this while the engine is being cranked over. If the engine backfired you could be badly burned.

Is the ignition system up to the job? Many alky burners use magnetos for a very good reason. Not only does the ignition system have to cope with much higher compression pressures, it may also be called on to fire wet plugs due to the very rich mixtures that are used.

Methanol burns much more slowly than petrol, so it is necessary to advance the ignition accordingly. With some motors $6^0$ more total advance is enough, others may require $15^0$. As a guide you can reckon on requiring $36^0$ advance if you run $30^0$ burning petrol or if your run $40^0$ on petrol you will possibly need close on $50^0$ with alky.

Nitromethane is burned in the most powerful drag machines. Usually 80 - 90% nitro and 10 - 20% methanol is the ratio at which fuel is blended for this purpose.

On the speedway scene nitro is used in smaller percentages (usually 10 - 20%) as a power booster. Methanol is always the base fuel, and acetone may also be added.

Nitromethane is a very special fuel that will lift the power output of an engine quite considerably (70%). This is due to nitro containing approximately 53% by weight oxygen. In itself, nitromethane is a very poor fuel, but because it contains so much oxygen it permits the induction of huge quantities of fuel into the engine for conversion into heat energy.

To deter detonation or other engine damage, it is always necessary to reduce the compression ratio when nitro is used. If you find that your engine is reliable running a 15:1 compression ratio with methanol, then you could use up to 20% nitro by reducing this to a 12:1 ratio. With 60% nitro, the compression ratio would have to be further lowered, to around 9:1, or 7.5:1 if 80 - 90% nitro is used.

At all times the fuel/air mixture must be very rich. With an 80 - 90% blend of nitro it may be as rich as two parts fuel to one part air or as lean as one part fuel to two parts air. Using 20% nitro, this would change to one part fuel to three or four parts air: ie. 1:3-4. TABLE 3.10 indicates the approximate increase necessary in the jet diameter to flow the required amount of fuel.

The safest way to avoid error when blending nitro with other fuels is to mix according to volume. For a 20% nitro fuel blend you would use one gallon of nitro to four gallons of methanol.

## TABLE 3.10    Fuel jet size for nitromethane

| % nitro in methanol (by volume) | * Jet diameter increase over straight methanol |
|:---:|:---:|
| 10 | 1.12 |
| 20 | 1.22 |
| 30 | 1.32 |
| 40 | 1.41 |
| 50 | 1.5 |
| 60 | 1.58 |
| 70 | 1.66 |
| 80 | 1.73 |
| 90 | 1.8 |

Nitro can also be blended using an hydrometer calibrated for this purpose. The problem when using an hydrometer is that it will give only a true nitro content percentage reading when the fuel temperature is 68°F. If you take a look at TABLE 3.11 you can see that with a fuel temperature of 100°F, a fuel with a true nitro content of 80% will read 73% nitro on the hydrometer.

For this reason you should always measure the temperature of the fuels before you attempt any mixing. If, for example, the fuel temperature is 95°F and you want a 70/30 nitro/methanol blend, then you will have to pour enough nitro into the methanol to give a 64% nitro reading on the hydrometer.

There is another item to consider that many people do not realise when mixing is done using an hydrometer. The nitro hydrometer is calibrated to give a true reading only when pure methanol and nitromethane are being blended. If other fuels are also blended, the nitro reading will be inaccuarate.

73

### TABLE 3.11    Nitro hydrometer temperature correction chart

| True Nitro % | Hydrometer reading at fuel temperature °F | | | | | | | | | | |
|---|---|---|---|---|---|---|---|---|---|---|---|
| | *40°* | *50°* | *60°* | *68°* | *75°* | *80°* | *85°* | *90°* | *100°* | *110°* | *120°* |
| 100 | 106 | 104 | 102 | 100 | 98 | 97 | 95 | 94 | 92 | 90 | 87 |
| 90 | 97 | 94 | 92 | 90 | 88 | 87 | 86 | 85 | 83 | 80 | 78 |
| 80 | 86 | 83 | 82 | 80 | 78 | 77 | 76 | 75 | 73 | 70 | 68 |
| 70 | 75 | 73 | 71 | 70 | 69 | 68 | 66 | 65 | 63 | 61 | 59 |
| 60 | 66 | 63 | 61 | 60 | 59 | 58 | 57 | 56 | 54 | 52 | 50 |
| 50 | 55 | 53 | 51 | 50 | 49 | 48 | 47 | 46 | 44 | 42 | 40 |
| 40 | 45 | 43 | 41 | 40 | 38 | 37 | 36 | 35 | 33 | 31 | 30 |
| 30 | 35 | 33 | 31 | 30 | 28 | 27 | 26 | 25 | 23 | 22 | 20 |
| 20 | 27 | 25 | 22 | 20 | 19 | 18 | 17 | 16 | 15 | 13 | 11 |
| 10 | 20 | 16 | 13 | 10 | 9 | 9 | 8 | 7 | 5 | 3 | 1 |

TABLE 3.12 indicates the specific gravity of a number of fuels used for blending. When a methanol/acetone/nitro methane mix is used, the hydrometer will still give a fairly accurate reading, because there is only a very slight difference in the specific gravity of methanol and acetone. However, if any of the other fuels were added, the hydrometer reading would be of no value at all.

As higher percentages of nitro are burned, the combustion rate is reduced (unless a fuel ignition accelerator is blended with the nitro) so the spark advance must be increased. A supercharged Chrysler Hemi burning 80 - 90 nitro runs 55° - 65° advance to compensate for the slow fuel burn rate.

There is a considerable danger to yourself and other drivers associated with the use of nitro. After combustion, relatively large amounts of vaporised nitric acid are exhausted. The higher the nitro percentage, the more acid vapour released.

### TABLE 3.12    Fuel characteristics

| Fuel | Specific Gravity | Weight (lb/gal) | Fuel/air ratio (lb/lb) | Heat energy (Btu/lb) | Latent heat of evaporation |
|---|---|---|---|---|---|
| Acetone (Dimethyl Ketone) | 0.791 | 8 | 1:10.5, 1:9.5 | 12,500 | 225 |
| Benzole (Benzene) | 0.879 | 8.75 | 1:11.5, 1:11 | 17,300 | 169 |
| Ether (Diethyl Ether) | 0.714 | 7 | | 15,000 | 153 |
| Methanol (Methyl Alcohol) | 0.796 | 8 | 1:6.5, 1:4.5 | 9,800 | 472 |
| Nitromethane | 1.13 | 11.25 | 1:2.5, 1:0.5 | 5,000 | 258 |
| Petrol | 0.743 | 7.5 | 1:12.5 | 19,000 | 135 |
| Propylene Oxide | 0.83 | 8.25 | | 14,000 | 220 |

Nitric acid vapours, when inhaled, cause a muscular reaction, making it impossible to breathe. Therefore the use of the correct gas mask is essential if the driver is in a position to inhale the exhaust gases. Certainly mechanics working around the machine, and those in the starting area, will require a gas mask.

Some people feel that nitromethane is explosive, but as already pointed out, it burns much more slowly than petrol or even methanol. There are, however, precautions that must be taken to ensure that it does not become explosive. These are the main causes of nitro becoming shock sensitive:

The addition of hydrazine in fuel blending. This is bannned in many countries because of the danger.

The use of caustic soda or any other alkaline for cleaning the fuel tank or lines.

The use of 'unpickled' anodised aluminium fuel tanks. After anodising, the tank must be allowed to stand for a few days filled with a solution 90% water and 10% vinegar. This serves to remove any deposits remaining in the tank after anodising.

The use of excessive fuel pump pressure. Nitro is liable to become unstable when confined and subjected to shock, therefore the pump pressure must always be less than 100 psi.

When using more than 20% nitro, there is always the danger of a sump fire or explosion due to the large amount of fuel that finds its way past the rings and into the sump. The first signs of such a fire are yellowish flames appearing at any of the breathers. It is important to keep an eye on the engine for at least 2 - 3 minutes after it has been stopped when using over 20% nitro, to check for such fires.

Other fuels can be blended with either petrol, methanol or nitromethane for a variety of reasons.

Propylene oxide is used in high percentage nitro fuel to increase the combustion flame speed. The amount used should never exceed 15% of the amount of nitro in the fuel as the combustion rate could increase to the point of severe detonation. If you were using 80% nitro then you could use 11% propylene oxide

$$15\% \times \frac{80}{100} = 11\%.$$

Propylene oxide can become explosive if allowed to come in contact with copper or copper alloys or rust particles. Therefore it must be stored in aluminium or plastic containers. Once blended with other fuels, it is relatively stable.

Petrol may have its octane rating improved by the addition of methanol, acetone, benzole, or methyl benzine.

Generally, methanol will not mix readily with petrol, particularly if it has absorbed even a small amount of water. The addition of acetone (3-4%) will assist in blending. A blend of 100 octane petrol, 10% methanol and 3% acetone will result in a fuel of about 106 octane.

The addition of 10% acetone or benzole will raise 100 octane petrol 3 and 2 points respectively.

Methyl benzine is a toluol fuel marketed by Shell under that brand name. It may be blended 1 part methyl benzine to 5 parts 100 octane fuel, purely to reduce the quantity of lead per gallon if the 100 octane contains a lot of t-e-l. This will raise the rating to almost 101 octane.

If an increase in octane rating is required, it may be blended 1:3 or 1:2 for a rise of 3 and 5 points respectively.

Methyl benzine should not be blended in larger proportions than 1:2 (ie. $33\frac{1}{2}\%$) as difficulty in starting may result.

When methanol is the base fuel, acetone may be added to accelerate the combustion flame, to improve cold weather starting or to reduce methanol's tendency to pre-ignite when lean mixtures are used. A mixture of 10% acetone/90% methanol may be used.

If high fuel consumption is a concern, benzole may be added in equal proportions with 100 or 115 octane racing fuel. A blend of 60% methanol/20% benzole/20% 115 octane fuel will have very similar anti-knock and cooling properties to straight methanol, but the fuel jets required will need to be about midway in size between those required for petrol and those for methanol.

Water may also be added to methanol (up to 10%), to stop pre-ignition or detonation when lean mixtures are used.

The addition of propylene oxide up to a maximum of 5% in alky will generally result in a power gain, due to accelerated combustion. Be sure that a rich fuel/air mixture of 1:4.5 - 5.5 is used, or mechanical damage may result.

Weber carburettors are known the world over as about the best carburettor that money can buy. Many people do not realise there are Webers and Webers. Some are simply metering devices for use on baby Fiats; others such as the DCOE and IDA series are racing carburettors that can be tuned to work very well, even on mildly modified street engines.

Many people feel that the Weber is difficult to tune; they seem never to be able to get it working correctly. I would say that the Weber is one of the very easiest of carburettors to tune, and that it holds its tune even when subjected to severe banging on a rally car.

The Weber DCOE is a sidedraught unit available with throttle bore diameters of 38 - 40 - 42 - 45 - 48 mm. Because of the large range of venturis (commonly called 'chokes') available, these five basic carburettors can be tuned to suit any engine available.

The downdraught Weber IDA is available in sizes 40 - 44 - 46 - 48 mm. The IDA appears to be a DCOE turned up in the air, but really there is little similarity between the two types.

TABLE 3.13 indicates the carburettor size and choke size recommended for cylinders of various displacements. There will be exceptions to these recommendations but generally you will find them to be very close.

The auxiliary (also called the secondary or booster) venturi is located in the throat of the carburettor, in front of the main venturi (choke). The number stamped on this item indicates the size of the fuel spray hole which connects to the main fuel circuit. Usually, a 4.5 mm auxiliary venturi is the correct size, but at times a 3.5 or 5 mm may be needed. The influence of the flow passage size is felt more markedly at high rpm.

In Weber carburettors the main jet, emulsion tube and air corrector jet are pressed together to form a single assembly. The individual parts may be separated, using a pair of pliers. Never grip the emulsion tube with pliers as it may be damaged.

The main jet is pressed into the bottom of the emulsion tube. It is stamped with a number indicating its nominal bore diameter (eg. a 175 jet has a 1.75 mm bore).

As a starting point, the main jet size can be selected by multiplying the size of the main venturi by 3.9 to 4.3 (eg. a 32 mm choke will usually have a main jet size of 125 to 135. On certain competition engines this rule of thumb can be way off the mark. If you check TABLE 3.14 you will see that this is usually in the case of racing engines with siamesed inlet

### TABLE 3.13a  Weber carburettor and choke size
*Four cylinder engine with siamese inlet ports.*

| Cylinder displacement (cc) | Choke size (mm) | | | | Recommended carburettor |
| --- | --- | --- | --- | --- | --- |
| | | | Full-race | | |
| | *Sports* | *Semi-race* | *7000 rpm* | *8000 rpm* | |
| 200 | 27 | 28 | 30 | 31 | 40 DCOE |
| 250 | | 31 | 32 | 34 | 42 DCOE |
| | 28 | 32 | 33 | 35 | 40 DCOE |
| 325 | 33 | 35 | | | 42 DCOE |
| | 32 | 34 | 36 | 38 | 48 IDA or 45 DCOE |
| 400 | 33 | 35 | 37 | 40 | 48 IDA or 45 DCOE |
| 450 | 34 | 36 | 38 | 40 | 48 IDA or 45 DCOE |
| 500 | 36 | 38 | 40 | | 45 DCOE |
| | | | | 42 | 48 IDA or 48 DCOE |

### TABLE 3.13b  Weber carburettor and choke size
*Four cylinder engine with an inlet port per cylinder*

| Cylinder displacement(cc) | Choke size (mm) | | | | Recommended carburettor |
| --- | --- | --- | --- | --- | --- |
| | | | Full-race | | |
| | *Sports* | *Semi-race* | *7500 rpm* | *8500 rpm* | *9500 rpm* | |
| 200 | | | | 29 | 32 | 2 × 40 DCOE |
| 250 | 27 | 28 | 29 | 32 | 34 | 2 × 40 DCOE |
| 325 | 29 | 32 | 34 | 36 | | 2 × 40 DCOE |
| | | | | 35 | 38 | 2 × 45 DCOE |
| 400 | 32 | 34 | 36 | | | 2 × 40 IDA or 2 × 40 DCOE |
| | | | 36 | 40 | 40 | 2 × 44 IDA or 2 × 45 DCOE |
| | | | | 40 | 42 | 2 × 48 DCOE |
| 450 | 33 | 35 | 36 | | | 2 × 40 IDA or 2 × 40 DCOE |
| | | | 37 | 40 | | 2 × 45 DCOE |
| | | | | 40 | 42 | 2 × 48 DCOE |
| 500 | 34 | 36 | 38 | 40 | | 2 × 45 DCOE |
| | | | 38 | 42 | 45 | 2 × 48 IDA or 2 × 48 DCOE |
| 550 | 35 | 37 | 40 | | | 2 × 45 DCOE |
| | 32 | 35 | 39 | 42 | | 2 × 48 IDA or 2 × 48 DCOE |
| 600 | 34 | 36 | 40 | 43 | | 2 × 48 IDA or 2 × 48 DCOE |

### TABLE 3.13c  Weber carburettor and choke size
*Six cylinder engine with an inlet port per cylinder*

| Cylinder Displacement (cc) | Choke size (mm) | | | | Recommended carburettor |
| --- | --- | --- | --- | --- | --- |
| | | | Full race | | |
| | Sports | Semi-race | 6500 rpm | 7500 rpm | |
| 330 | 27 | 29 | 30 | 32 | 3 × 40 DCOE |
| 400 | 28 | 30 | 33 | 36 | 3 × 40 DCOE |
| 450 | 30 | 31 | 34 | 37 | 3 × 45 DCOE |
| 500 | 31 | 32 | 36 | 40 | 3 × 45 DCOE |
| | | | | 38 | 3 × 48 DCOE |
| 600 | 33 | 34 | 38 | 40 | 3 × 45 DCOE |
| | | | 37 | 40 | 3 × 48 DCOE |
| 700 | 36 | 38 | 40 | | 3 × 45 DCOE |
| | 35 | 37 | 39 | 42 | 3 × 48 DCOE |
| 800 | 36 | 38 | 42 | | 3 × 48 DCOE |

### TABLE 3.13d  Weber carburettor and choke size
*V8 engine with an inlet port per cylinder*

| Cylinder displacement (cc) | Choke size (mm) | | | | | Recommended carburettor |
| --- | --- | --- | --- | --- | --- | --- |
| | | | Full-race | | | |
| | Sports | Semi-race | 7000 rpm | 8000 rpm | 9000 rpm | |
| 500 | | | 38 | 39 | 42 | 4 × 48 DCOE or 4 × 48 IDA |
| | 36 | 38 | 42 | 44 | | 2 × 48 DCOE |
| 600 | | 36 | 38 | 40 | 43 | 4 × 48 DCOE or 4 × 48 IDA |
| | 36 | 38 | 42 | 44 | | 2 × 48 DCOE |
| 700 | 36 | 38 | 42 | 44 | | 4 × 48 DCOE or 4 × 48 IDA |
| | 38 | 40 | 43 | 45 | | 2 × 48 DCOE |
| 800 | 38 | 42 | 44 | 45 | | 4 × 48 DCOE or 4 × 48 IDA |
| | 38 | 42 | 45 | | | 2 × 48 DCOE |
| 900 | 40 | 42 | 45 | | | 4 × 48 DCOE or 4 × 48 IDA |
| | 40 | 42 | 45 | | | 2 × 48 DCOE |
| 1000 | 42 | 42 | 45 | | | 4 × 48 DCOE or 4 × 48 IDA |
| | 40 | 42 | 45 | | | 2 × 48 DCOE |

*Note: the twin 48 DCOE setup uses a Waneford cross-over manifold mounted on a single or two plane manifold.*

ports. In this instance the multiplying factor is 4.6 to 5.0.

The air corrector (or air bleed) jet is pressed into the top of the emulsion tube. Air corrector jets from 1.50 mm to 2.00 mm are more commonly used.

By increasing the diameter of this jet, the fuel mixture is weakened more at high rpm than at lower rpm. A change in the size of the main jet changes the mixture strength uniformly at both high and low rpm.

With DCOE carburettors, the air corrector jet will usually be 0.30 to 0.50 mm larger than the main jet size, eg. with a 125 main jet try a 155 to 175 air corrector. In general, road engines will use the larger jets and racing engines the smaller jets.

Engines using IDA carburettors will generally require an air corrector jet around the same size as the main jet. Racing vehicles may need jets 0.20 mm, and at times up to 0.50 mm, smaller than the main jet.

The emulsion tube emulsifies the fuel previously metered by the main jet. It affects engine performance more at small throttle opening angles and during acceleration.

The fuel well that the emulsion tube fits into in the carburetor is of a fixed size but the tubes themselves are available with a large variety of air holes and in varying diameters. The F2 and F15 tubes have the same number, size and disposition of holes but the tubes are of a different diameter.

The amount of fuel available to be drawn into the air stream is governed by the diameter of the emulsion tube and the air hole pattern. This is why the emulsion tube has such an effect on throttle response and mid-range running.

Once we have selected main and air corrector jets to meet the engine's high rpm fuel requirements, then we have to set about finding an emulsion tube of the correct diameter, and with suitable air drillings, to satisfy the engine's mid-range fuel needs.

A rich tube is one that is thin and with just a row of air holes at the top. A lean tube is thicker, with holes all the way down.

For most applications F2, F15 and F16 tubes are used. F11, F9 and F7 tubes are used in a smaller number of applications.

For the majority of engines with DCOE carburettors using chokes smaller than 36 mm, and one barrel per cylinder, either F16 or F15 tubes will be correct.

Engines with larger chokes (36 - 40 mm) and using DCOE carburettors with one barrel per cylinder usually require an F2 emulsion tube.

Engines with siamesed inlet ports or four cylinder engines using one DCOE carburettor generally use an F2 tube; however some may need an F9.

When IDA carburettors are fitted, an F2 or F7 will be correct in the majority of applications.

As in every carburettor, the accelerator pump circuit in the Weber supplies a shot of fuel to assist in smooth, no lag acceleration. Additionally, this circuit also serves as a power circuit to supply additional fuel at high speeds.

The size of the pump jet and the pump bleed jet (or exhaust jet), and the length of the pump rod all affect the amount of fuel supplied during acceleration.

The size of the pump jet alone determines the fuel metering when the pump circuit serves as a high speed power circuit. Therefore the pump jet size is selected to supply the correct fuel/air mixture for high speed operation.

Once the correct pump jet has been chosen, then you have to determine if the mixture is too rich or lean during acceleration.

If too much fuel is supplied, then it may be necessary to use an open pump bleed jet. This jet is situated in the bottom of the fuel bowl, under the float/s. Usually a closed jet (ie. one without a bleed hole) is used in semi-race and racing motors. However, if the mixture is too rich during acceleration, a pump bleed jet will be required. These are available with a bleed hole from 0.35 to 1.5 mm. If a bleed jet is required, usually a 40, 45 or 50 will be the correct size. To remove or replace this jet you will need a special screwdriver with a 'screw-grip' attachment.

## TABLE 3.14  Weber carburettor settings

| Engine | Capacity (cc) | Tune | Carburettors | Choke | Main | Air | Emulsion | Pump | Pump bleed | Idle | Auxiliary venturi |
|---|---|---|---|---|---|---|---|---|---|---|---|
| Alfa Romeo T/C | 1300 | Sports | 2×40 DCOE | 29 | 110 | 200 | F16 | 35 | 70 | 50F11 | 4.5 |
| T/C | 1600 | Sports | 2×40 DCOE | 30 | 125 | 220 | F16 | 35 | 50 | 50F11 | 4.5 |
| Abarth T/C | 1000 | Full race | 2×40 DCOE | 33 | 135 | 250 | F11 | 40 | 45 | 50F8 | 4.5 |
| Austin Healey | 3000 | Full race | 3×45 DCOE | 34 | 130 | 160 | F2 | 45 | closed | 50F2 | 3.5 |
| | 3000 | Sports | 3×45 DCOE | 32 | 135 | 180 | F2 | 45 | closed | 50F2 | 4.5 |
| Avenger | 1600 | Full race | 2×40 DCOE | 34 | 130 | 170 | F16 | 40 | closed | 45F8 | 4.5 |
| | 1800 | Rally | 2×40 DCOE | 33 | 135 | 170 | F15 | 40 | closed | 45F8 | 4.5 |
| Aston Martin T/C | 3670 | Sports | 3×45 DCOE | 40 | 155 | 150 | F2 | 55 | closed | 50F6 | 4.5 |
| BMW ohc | 2000 | Sports | 2×45 DCOE | 38 | 125 | 170 | F9 | 40 | 70 | 45F8 | 5.0 |
| BMC | 998 | Sports | 1×45 DCOE | 32 | 130 | 165 | F9 | 50 | 50 | 45F9 | 5.0 |
| | 1098 | Sports | 1×45 DCOE | 32 | 140 | 180 | F16 | 40 | 50 | 45F6 | 5.0 |
| | 1098 | Full race | 1×45 DCOE | 37 | 180 | 200 | F2 | 50 | 50 | 50F9 | 3.5 |
| | 1275 | Sports | 1×45 DCOE | 34 | 130 | 175 | F2 | 50 | 50 | 50F9 | 3.5 |
| | 1310 | Full race | 1×45 DCOE | 40 | 195 | 200 | F2 | 50 | 50 | 50F9 | 3.5 |
| | 1366 | Full race | 1×48 IDA | 40 | 195 | 170 | F2 | 50 | closed | 120 & 60F10 | 4.5 |
| Chrysler Slant | 3687 | Sports | 3×45 DCOE | 36 | 145 | 150 | F2 | 40 | closed | 50F8 | 3.5 |
| | 3687 | Full race | 3×45 DCOE | 38 | 145 | 155 | F2 | 40 | closed | 50F8 | 3.5 |
| Chrysler Hemi 6 | 4342 | Sports | 3×45 DCOE | 38 | 135 | 180 | F2 | 50 | closed | 55F9 | 4.5 |
| | 4342 | Semi-race | 3×45 DCOE | 40 | 145 | 180 | F2 | 50 | closed | 55F9 | 4.5 |
| Chevrolet | 4949 | Full race | 4×48 DCOE | 40 | 165 | 160 | F2 | 50 | closed | 55F8 | 4.5 |
| | 5735 | Semi-race | 2×48 DCOE | 42 | 185 | 165 | F2 | 60 | closed | 60F9 | 4.5 |
| | 6096 | Full race | 4×58 DCO | 44 | 190 | 200 | F15 | 55 | closed | 55F9 | 4.5 |
| | 5350 | Sports | 2×48 DCOE | 38 | 170 | 185 | F2 | 60 | closed | 60F8 | 4.5 |
| | 6490 | Semi-race | 4×48 IDA | 42 | 160 | 140 | F7 | 50 | closed | 100 & 65F10 | 4.5 |
| Coventry Climax T/C | 2495 | Full race | 2×58 DCO | 47 | 190 | 200 | F15 | 55 | closed | 70F6 | 4.5 |
| Chevette T/C 4V | 2279 | Rally | 2×48 DCOE | 42 | 170 | 190 | F2 | 50 | closed | 55F9 | 4.5 |
| Datsun | 1300 | Semi-race | 2×40 DCOE | 30 | 115 | 160 | F16 | 40 | closed | 45F6 | 4.5 |
| ohc | 1600 | Sports | 2×40 DCOE | 33 | 135 | 160 | F15 | 40 | closed | 50F8 | 4.5 |
| ohc | 1800 | Rally | 2×45 DCOE | 34 | 145 | 170 | F15 | 40 | closed | 50F8 | 4.5 |
| T/C 4V | 2200 | Rally | 2×48 DCOE | 40 | 165 | 180 | F15 | 50 | closed | 55F9 | 4.5 |

| | | | | | | | | | | | |
|---|---|---|---|---|---|---|---|---|---|---|---|
| Ford | 997 | Full race | 2 × 40 DCOE | 33 | 125 | 175 | F16 | 35 | closed | 40F9 | 4.5 |
| | 1594 | Semi-race | 2 × 40 DCOE | 33 | 125 | 175 | F16 | 40 | closed | 45F9 | 4.5 |
| | 1762 | Semi-race | 2 × 45 DCOE | 34 | 135 | 170 | F16 | 40 | closed | 45F9 | 4.5 |
| | 1298 | Semi-race | 2 × 40 DCOE | 32 | 125 | 180 | F16 | 40 | closed | 45F9 | 4.5 |
| x | 1594 | Sports | 2 × 40 DCOE | 33 | 120 | 160 | F11 | 45 | closed | 45F8 | 4.5 |
| T/C | 1594 | Full race | 2 × 45 DCOE | 39 | 170 | 180 | F9 | 40 | closed | 50F8 | 4.5 |
| T/C | 1720 | Semi-race | 2 × 42 DCOE | 34 | 135 | 170 | F15 | 50 | closed | 45F8 | 4.5 |
| T/C | 1977 | Rally | 2 × 48 DCOE | 42 | 180 | 175 | F9 | 45 | closed | 50F9 | 4.5 |
| T/C 4V | 1993 | Sports | 2 × 45 DCOE | 34 | 135 | 170 | F16 | 40 | closed | 45F9 | 4.5 |
| ohc | 1298 | Full race | 2 × 45 DCOE | 37 | 140 | 165 | F16 | 60 | closed | 60F9 | 4.5 |
| T/C 4V | 4949 | Semi-race | 2 × 48 DCOE | 38 | 165 | 150 | F2 | 60 | closed | 60F9 | 4.5 |
| | 5752 | Semi-race | 2 × 48 DCOE | 42 | 190 | 155 | F2 | 55 | closed | 120 & 55F10 | 4.5 |
| | 5752 | Full race | 4 × 48 DIA | 43 | 170 | 180 | F2 | | closed | | |
| Hillman ohc | 4736 | Sports | 2 × 48 DCOE | 36 | 155 | 175 | F2 | 55 | closed | 60F8 | 4.5 |
| | 998 | Rally | 2 × 40 DCOE | 32 | 120 | 180 | F11 | 35 | closed | 45F9 | 4.5 |
| | 1725 | Sports | 2 × 40 DCOE | 33 | 135 | 170 | F15 | 40 | closed | 45F8 | 4.5 |
| Jaguar T/C | 4200 | Sports | 3 × 45 DCOE | 38 | 165 | 190 | F2 | 40 | closed | 65F8 | 3.5 |
| MG | 1800 | Sports | 1 × 45 DCOE | 34 | 145 | 165 | F2 | 50 | 50 | 50F9 | 3.5 |
| | 1800 | Full race | 1 × 45 DCOE | 36 | 165 | 160 | F16 | 60 | 50 | 50F9 | 5.0 |
| Porsche ohc | 2000 | Sports | 2 × 40 IDA | 30 | 125 | 180 | F26 | 50 | closed | 55 | 4.5 |
| ohc | 2000 | Semi-race | 2 × 40 IDA | 32 | 130 | 180 | F3 | 50 | closed | 55 | 4.5 |
| ohc | 2800 | Full race | 2 × 46 IDA | 42 | 170 | 145 | F24 | 50 | closed | 70 | 4.5 |
| Renault x | 1255 | Semi-race | 2 × 40 DCOE | 32 | 125 | 200 | F15 | 35 | 40 | 45F8 | 4.5 |
| x | 1296 | Rally | 2 × 40 DCOE | 34 | 125 | 160 | F15 | 40 | closed | 45F8 | 4.5 |
| Triumph | 2500 | Semi-race | 3 × 45 DCOE | 33 | 130 | 175 | F15 | 40 | closed | 45F9 | 4.5 |
| | 2188 | Sports | 2 × 45 DCOE | 34 | 140 | 150 | F15 | 50 | closed | 50F8 | 4.5 |
| 4V | 1998 | Full race | 2 × 48 DCOE | 40 | 165 | 175 | F15 | 50 | closed | 50F9 | 4.5 |
| Volvo | 2198 | Full race | 2 × 45 DCOE | 35 | 155 | 170 | F15 | 50 | 50 | 50F8 | 4.5 |
| VW | 2180 | Full race | 2 × 48 IDA | 40 | 155 | 150 | F2 | 50 | closed | 120 & 55F10 | 4.5 |
| | 1850 | Semi-race | 2 × 44 IDA | 35 | 145 | 170 | F11 | 45 | closed | 100 & 50F10 | 4.5 |
| | 1750 | Sports | 2 × 40 IDA | 32 | 120 | 160 | F11 | 40 | closed | 100 & 50F10 | 4.5 |

*Note: Rally tune indicates an engine tuned for international class rallies.*
*T/C – Twin cam, T/C 4V – Twin cam four valve, 4V – ohc four valve, x – pushrod crossflow.*

The length of the pump rod governs the amount of fuel in the pump well; the longer the rod, the bigger the shot of fuel available. Rods of varying lengths are available for the DCOE model carburettor but with the IDA the pump stroke can be shortened by the use of a collar.

The promptness of fuel delivery is controlled partly by the bleed jet and partly by the strength of the pump spring. A closed bleed jet and a strong spring gives a quick shot of fuel of short duration. If a weaker spring is used, there will still be a quick initial delivery of fuel, but the duration of the delivery will be longer. The use of an open bleed jet delays the delivery of the fuel, and reduces the amount delivered.

Seldom is it necessary to change either the length of the pump rod or the strength of the pump spring. However, at times I have found it advantageous to use a strong spring and a 59.5 mm rod when a single 45 DCOE is used on the 1300 Mini Cooper 'S' and 1800 MG 'B' engines.

Both the DCOE and IDA model carburettors have an idle jet assembly which meters fuel and air into the idle circuit. When the correct jet has been chosen, the mixture adjustment screw should be one quarter to one and one quarter turns open to obtain the correct idle mixture.

In DCOE carburettors the idle jet has a fuel hole and an air bleed hole. The fuel hole size is the first number stamped on the jet. eg. if the jet is a 45 F9 then the fuel hole is 0.45 mm. The F9 is a code referring to the air bleed hole size. TABLE 3.15 sets out the 'F' code, from rich to lean. Some jets have two air bleed holes but this has been taken into consideration when working out the table.

All IDA idle jets are coded F10. The F10 jet does not have an air bleed hole; instead air correction is handled by the idle jet holder. The 1366 cc Mini, for example, uses a 60 F10 idle jet and a 120 jet holder. This indicates that the jet holder has a 1.20 mm air bleed. A 100 or 120 jet holder is used in the majority of applications. A larger air bleed hole leans the idle mixture.

To determine the approximately correct idle jet refer to TABLE 3.16. This sets out the size of the fuel metering hole. If, for example, the cylinder capacity is 400 cc then you will require a 50 F8 or 50 F9 jet with which to begin testing. I have arbitarily selected an F8 or F9 air bleed hole in this instance as either size is correct about 80% of the time. The other 20% use an F2 or F6 air bleed.

### TABLE 3.15
### Weber idle jet air bleed characteristics

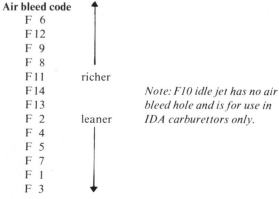

| Air bleed code | |
|---|---|
| F 6 | |
| F 12 | |
| F 9 | |
| F 8 | |
| F 11 | richer |
| F 14 | *Note: F10 idle jet has no air* |
| F 13 | *bleed hole and is for use in* |
| F 2 | leaner *IDA carburettors only.* |
| F 4 | |
| F 5 | |
| F 7 | |
| F 1 | |
| F 3 | |

## TABLE 3.16  Weber idle jet fuel hole selection

| Cylinder displacement (cc) | Fuel jet size |
|---|---|
| 200 | 35 |
| 250 | 40 |
| 325 | 45 |
| 400 | 45 - 50 |
| 450 | 50 |
| 500 | 50 |
| 550 | 50 - 55 |
| 600 | 55 - 60 |
| 700 | 65 - 70 |
| 800 | 70 - 75 |
| 900 | 75 |
| 1000 | 80 |

*Note: Where two cylinders share one carburettor barrel or where the engine has siamesed inlet ports the idle jet size should be increased one size larger than indicated. Engines with wild camshafts may require jets two sizes larger due to poor fuel distribution at low rpm when two cylinders share one carburettor barrel.*

If you were using an IDA carburettor you would select a 50 F10 idle jet in the above example, and you would use either a 100 or 120 jet holder.

After having made your idle jet selection, start the engine and bring it up to normal operating temperature (at this time the float level should have been correctly adjusted). Then carefully adjust the idle mixture and idle speed screws to get the smoothest idle. Remember that if the correct idle jets have been selected, the mixture screws should be $\frac{1}{4}$ - $1\frac{1}{4}$ turns open.

When the mixture has been adjusted, open the throttle to bring the idle speed up to 2000 - 2500 rpm (at this speed the main circuit should not be discharging fuel). If the engine is too lean, it will be backfiring or popping through the carburettors. On the other hand if it is too rich, it will be backfiring through the exhaust. If you have access to an exhaust gas analyser, the fuel/air ratio should be 1:11.5 or 12.5 (Note that many analysers read the other way around to give the air/fuel ratio ie. 11.5 or 12.5:1).

The starting jets in Webers I never worry about as I have never found it necessary to use the choke to get a Weberised engine started, even when the car has been covered in snow. A few pumps on the accelerator to operate the accelerator pump is all that is required.

Usually, you have more trouble starting a Weber-equipped engine when it is hot, due to flooding. If it will not start first hit, slowly push the accelerator right to the floor and turn the motor over until it starts. In most cases the engine will start on the first or second try, but keep the accelerator pedal down until it does. If you pump the pedal you will end up with a real problem.

The float level adjustment is critical on all carburettors and especially so on sidedraught Webers, as engine vibration can cause fuel frothing and flooding. Webers have an additional adjustment to ensure that the float drops enough to open the needle valve completely when fuel demand is high.

To adjust the float level and float stroke on the DCOE carburettor it is necessary to remove the top of the carburettor. The jet inspection cover also has to be removed before the top becomes free. Take care not to damage the floats as they are very delicate, being made of sheet 0.16 - 0.20 mm thick. Do not blow the floats with compressed air.

With the top removed, ensure that the needle valve is tightly screwed into its housing and check that the spring-loaded ball incorporated in the valve is not jammed.

When checking the float level, hold the carburettor top in the vertical position as shown in FIGURE 3.11. With the carburettor top in the vertical position and the float tongue just contacting the spring loaded needle ball, check the distance between both floats and the carburettor top gasket (measurement A). If the float level is not correct, push out the float pivot pin and remove the float. Then carefully bend the float tongue to obtain the correct dimension.

After the float level has been checked and adjusted, hold the float fully open and measure the float stroke (measurement B). If the stroke requires adjustment, bend the tongue to increase or decrease the stroke.

To measure the distances A and B, Weber make a special float gauge, but as these are often difficult to obtain I make my own set of gauges out of steel or aluminium bar. The gauge should be about 8 ins long, dimension A thick and dimension B wide. Be sure to machine four grooves in the bar, (two grooves in two faces of the bar) so that the gauge clears the soldered joining band of the float halves. Without the clearance grooves you will not be able to adjust the float accurately as you will be measuring between the soldered join and the carburettor top gasket, and not between the floats proper and the gasket.

The actual measurements A and B will vary from one application to another, depending primarily on the angle at which the carburettor is mounted. Weber DCOE carburettors are designed to be mounted at $0^0$ - $5^0$ from horizontal and usually at that angle dimension A is 8.5 mm and dimension B is 15 mm.

In some applications the manifold manufacturer finds it necessary to change the mounting angle, so that the carburettor will clear some part of the body or exhaust system. When this is done, a special float level setting is required. The manifold manufacturer should tell you what setting is required when you buy his manifold.

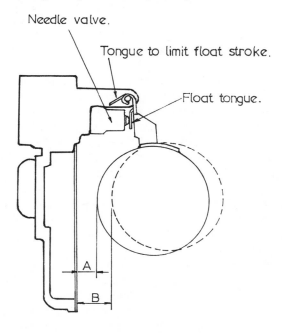

Fig. 3.11   Weber DCOE float levelling.

The majority of BMC Mini manifolds have the Weber mounted at an angle of $7^0$-$7\frac{1}{2}^0$. In this instance dimension A is 7 mm and dimension B 15 mm.

Some manufacturers (eg. Aston Martin DB4, Alfa Romeo 2600) use a high float level with dimension A 5 mm and B 13.5 mm.

To check the float level of IDA model carburettors you will need to make a set of gauges or use Weber gauges No. 9620.175.1839, No. 9620.175.1840, No. 9620.175.2411 and spring No. 9620.175.1329.

Following along with the aid of FIGURE 3.12, the check is carried out as follows:-

Remove the carburettor top and the gasket and insert the spring (No. 9620.175.1329) between the float and the side of the bowl.

Position gauge No. 9620.175.1840 on the carburettor body and manipulate the float so that the tongue just contacts the tip of the gauge (Note the gauge must be first adjusted to 24.2 mm as shown).

With the float in this position check using gauge No. 9620. 175. 1839 that the float is 5.5 - 6 mm above the carburettor body. Ensure that the gasket is removed when this is being checked. Should the level be incorrect, bend the float tongue to obtain the correct level.

Finally, using gauge No. 9620.175.2411 check that the needle valve ball is 25 mm from

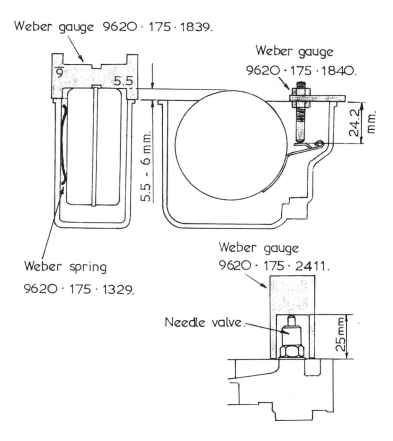

Fig. 3.12   Weber IDA float levelling.

the surface of the carburettor top. When carrying out this check, the top must be inverted and the needle valve ball must not be depressed.

Cars equipped with three barrel IDA, IDAP, IDL, IDS, IDT and IDTP model carburettors have a float level adjustment very similar to the two barrel IDA.

The main change is that gauge No. 9620.175.1840 is adjusted to 18 mm and that a different float level gauge (No. 9620.175.2849 instead of No. 9620.175.1839) is used so that the float level is 12.5 to 13 mm. On Lamborgini Miura cars equipped with IDL carburettors float level gauge No. 9620.175.3071 is used and in this case the float level is 14-14.5 mm. All of these three barrel carburettors have a needle-ball to carburettor-top dimension of 18 mm.

There are just a few points to keep in mind when Weber carburettors are fitted. First, I would suggest that you obtain a copy of the Weber Technical Introduction 2nd edition (or later) and follow very carefully their installation instructions. Pay careful attention to what they have to say about throttle linkage arrangements so that all the butterflies open together.

DCOE carburettors must never be mounted solidly but must always have a neoprene insulator block or a light alloy plate with an 'O' ring in both faces fitted between the carburettor and the manifold. This is necessary to reduce the vibration reaching the carburettor. Excess vibration causes fuel frothing, flooding and inaccurate metering.

When tightening the carburettor mounting bolts, ensure that they are tensioned just enough to effect a good seal, but not enough to squash the 'O' rings or insulator block. Selflocking nuts, and if possible light double wound spring washers should be used, as fitted on the Twin Cam Ford Escort. The special spring washers used on the Weber-equipped Twin Cam Ford are designed to be tightened until there is a gap of 0.040 in between the coils.

Various screws on some model Webers are safety wired and those parts must always be rewired whenever the wire is removed or broken. The wire is there for a very good reason, for if a screw were to drop out, the engine would stop or run badly.

For example, the IDA has the float pivot pin wired; if the pin falls out, the engine floods. The 45 and 48 DCOE have safety wired grub screws that hold the auxiliary venturis in place. If a grub screw comes out, the auxiliary venturi can rotate and cut off fuel to the discharge nozzle.

Before attempting to tune and synchronise the carburettors, the ignition timing, spark plugs, points and float level etc. should have been adjusted. Check that the carburettor choke control levers are all back against their stops. Then bring the engine up to normal operating temperature and switch it off.

Carefully screw in each idle mixture adjusting screw until it just contacts its seat and then unscrew it $\frac{3}{4}$ of a turn (Note — if you find that you need more or less than $\frac{3}{4}$ of a turn to get your engine running, adjust all the mixture screws the same amount).

Synchronising the throttle plates in the majority of twin DCOE applications is very easy when an interconnector linkage, as fitted to the Twin Cam Lotus Fords, four cylinder Alfa Romeos, Renault Gordinis etc, is used.

In these instances start the engine and turn in the idle speed screw until the idle speed reaches 1200 rpm (may be higher if a lumpy cam is used).

For the actual synchronising of the throttle plates you will need either a carburettor synchroniser or a length of $\frac{1}{4}$ in rubber hose and a good ear.

Press the synchroniser over one throat of the carburettor (check the carburettor with the idle speed adjusting screw first). Turn the synchroniser ring so that the indicator float dwells at mid-height in the indicating column.

Shift the synchroniser onto the next carburettor and turn the interconnector linkage screw in or out so that the float again dwells at mid-height.

The second carburettor can also be synchronised with the first by listening to the intensity of the hiss of the first carburettor and then adjusting the other carburettor to produce a hiss of equal intensity.

After synchronisation, screw out the idle speed screw slightly to reduce the idle speed to 800 - 1000 rpm.

At this point it may be necessary to slightly adjust each mixture screw to obtain the smoothest idle. It should not be necessary to adjust any screw more than $\frac{1}{8}$ of a turn, either in or out.

On other installations where throttle control rods operate the carburettor shafts, a similar tuning procedure to that outlined is used. However, in this instance the throttle control rods should generally all be disconnected and each carburettor must be synchronised to the first carburettor, using the idle speed adjustment screw fitted to each one.

After the throttles have been synchronised, reconnect and adjust the length of each throttle control rod.

After this is completed, back off all of the idle speed screws and then adjust the speed screw on the first carburettor to give the desired idle speed. Now carefully screw in all of the other idle speed screws so that they just contact the throttle stop lug on the throttle lever.

To complete the job it may be necessary to adjust each mixture screw to smooth out the idle.

Some Weber models incorporate an adjustable idle air bleed passage to equalise the idle air flow in every barrel. These carburettors can be identified by the idle air bleed screw with lock nut, located on the opposite side of the barrel to the idle mixture screw on some IDA models, and located close to the accelerator pump jet on some DCOE models.

Before accurate synchronisation of these models is possible, the air bleed lock nuts must be slackened and the air bleed screws very carefully screwed in until seated. Be careful not to use too much pressure or the seats could be damaged.

With the air bleeds closed, the butterflies of the carburettors can be synchronised as earlier outlined, using a carburettor synchroniser. When this is being carried out ensure that the idle speed is 1200 - 1500 rpm.

Once the throttle plates are synchronised, the idle speed should be reduced to normal (800 - 1000 rpm). Then use the carburettor synchroniser to find which barrel causes the float indicator to rise the highest in the tube and adjust the air bleed screws on all the barrels, by screwing them out, to cause the float to rise to the same level. While this is being done, it will usually be necessary to lower the idle speed, as the engine will tend to speed up. When the float rises to the same level on every barrel, the air compensation is correct and the lock nuts should be tightened.

After the carburettors have been synchronised, it will be necessary to determine if the main and air corrector jets, and the pump jets, are correct. This check is best done on the dyno, but follow up with a road or track test to confirm that the correct jets have been chosen. It is not possible to accurately determine the accelerator pump metering on the dyno, so this will have to be checked on the road.

When the most suitable jets are fitted, there should be no hesitation during acceleration or when the throttle is suddenly flattened, nor should there be any black smoke 87 (indicating richness) from the exhaust. After a run at sustained high rpm, the spark plugs should be checked against the indications in TABLE 3.3.

The SU constant depression carburettor has been around for many years and it still has something to offer those interested in better performance. It is a very simple carburettor but one that can be exceedingly difficult to tune with precision.

The majority of SU carburettors are type H and type HS. A few of the type HD 'diaphragm' carburettors are still around but these are used only in $1\frac{3}{4}$ and 2 in sizes.

The type H and HD can be identified by having a solidly-mounted float chamber. The type HS has an external nylon tube connecting the float chamber to the jet. TABLE 3.17 indicates the throttle bore diameters of these models.

In TABLE 3.18 I have outlined the size of the carburettor recommended for various engine displacements. You will note that the SU must always be connected to at least two cylinders, otherwise its constant vacuum principles of operation are upset.

SU carburettors are supplied with either a 0.090, a 0.100 or a 0.125 in jet. These rarely need to be changed except for methanol, when 0.187 or 0.250 jets may be necessary.

The volume of fuel introduced into the air stream is controlled by the taper of the needle. There are approximately three hundred different needles listed for 0.090 jets alone. Needles are made to suit 0.090, 0.100 and 0.125 jets. When the 0.187 or 0.250 alcohol jets are fitted, needles intended for use with 0.125 jets may be used. At times these will be too rich at lower rpm. In this instance you will have to make your own needles from $\frac{1}{8}$ in bronze welding wire.

### TABLE 3.17   SU carburettor types

| Type | Throttle bore |
|------|---------------|
| H2, HS2 | $1\frac{1}{4}$ in |
| H4, HS4 | $1\frac{1}{2}$ in |
| H6, HS6, HD6 | $1\frac{3}{4}$ in |
| H8, HD8 | 2 in |

### TABLE 3.18   Recommended SU carburettor sizes

| Displacement (cc) | Tune | |
|-------------------|------|---|
| **Four cylinder engine** | *Sports* | *Semi or full race* |
| 850 | $2 \times 1\frac{1}{4}$ in | $2 \times 1\frac{1}{4}$ in |
| 1000 | $2 \times 1\frac{1}{4}$ in | $2 \times 1\frac{1}{2}$ in |
| 1300 | $2 \times 1\frac{1}{4}$ in | $2 \times 1\frac{1}{2}$ in |
| 1600 | $2 \times 1\frac{1}{2}$ in | $2 \times 1\frac{3}{4}$ in |
| 1800 | $2 \times \frac{3}{4}$ in | $2 \times 1\frac{3}{4}$ in |
| 2000 | $2 \times 1\frac{3}{4}$ in | $2 \times 2$ in |
| 2200 plus | $2 \times 2$ in | $2 \times 2$ in |
| | | |
| **Six cylinder engine** | | |
| 2000 | $2 \times 1\frac{3}{4}$ in or $3 \times 1\frac{1}{2}$ in | $3 \times 1\frac{1}{2}$ in |
| 2500 | $2 \times 2$ in or $3 \times 1\frac{1}{2}$ in | $3 \times 1\frac{3}{4}$ in |
| 3000 | $2 \times 2$ in or $3 \times 1\frac{3}{4}$ in | $3 \times 2$ in |
| 3500 plus | $2 \times 2$ in or $3 \times 2$ in | $3 \times 2$ in |

TABLE 3.19 lists just a few 0.090 jet needles. The numbers refer to the diameter of the needle at twelve or thirteen different points along its length, commencing at the shoulder at the top of the needle and then continuing every eighth of an inch.

## TABLE 3.19    SU carburettor needles

| MME | CZ | BG | 3 | H4 |
|-----|-----|-----|-----|-----|
| 0.089 | 0.089 | 0.089 | 0.089 | 0.089 |
| 0.085 | 0.085 | 0.085 | 0.085 | 0.085 |
| 0.0813 | 0.0827 | 0.0815 | 0.0814 | 0.081 |
| 0.078 | 0.0806 | 0.0782 | 0.0785 | 0.0778 |
| 0.074 | 0.0785 | 0.0745 | 0.0765 | 0.076 |
| 0.0707 | 0.0745 | 0.0695 | 0.0744 | 0.0741 |
| 0.0673 | 0.0727 | 0.0647 | 0.0723 | 0.072 |
| 0.0636 | 0.071 | 0.060 | 0.0703 | 0.0702 |
| 0.060 | 0.0693 | 0.0557 | 0.0683 | 0.0683 |
| 0.0563 | 0.0675 | 0.0515 | 0.0661 | 0.0663 |
| 0.053 | 0.0657 | 0.0474 | 0.064 | 0.064 |
| 0.0495 | 0.064 | 0.043 | 0.063 | 0.062 |
| 0.046 | 0.0625 | 0.039 | 0.062 | |

There are no rules to determine which needle to try first; about all that you can do is refer to the listing I have given in TABLE 3.20 (and any other lists you can find) and choose a needle for an engine that is similar to yours.

After that, it is a matter of testing to find at what point the needle is rich or lean. Then you will have to consult the complete SU needle tables and find a needle that is richer or leaner at the point where you want it to be.

When going from a weak needle to a richer one, it is better to try one about 0.002 thinner at a time, but when changing from a rich needle to a weaker one try a needle 0.001 thicker, unless there are signs of excessive richness.

The mixture strength is also controlled to a degree by the carburettor piston spring and the type of oil in the dash pot. I have seen all grades of oil used in SU carburettors but for best results I recommend the use of automatic transmission fluid. Unfortunately, the dash-pot seldom remains full for long, so check the level frequently as a low level will result in hesitation or spit back when accelerating, due to a lean mixture condition.

The correct oil level for carburettors with a vent hole in the damper piston is $\frac{1}{2}$ in above the top of the hollow carburettor piston rod. Carburettors with a non-vented damper cap should be filled to $\frac{1}{2}$ in below the carburettor piston rod.

The effect of the oil (and the spring) is to slow down the rate of rise of the carburettor piston and so momentarily enrich the mixture immediately following a snap opening of the throttle. This serves the same purpose as an accelerator pump.

Piston springs are identified by a colour code painted on the end coils. The range for carburettors up to and including the $1\frac{3}{4}$ in SU is:- $2\frac{1}{2}$ oz blue, $4\frac{1}{2}$ oz red, 8 oz yellow and 12 oz green.

The correct strength of spring is one which allows the piston to reach its maximum lift at maximum power rpm. This is assuming that carburettors of the correct size are being used.

## TABLE 3.20   SU tuning specification

| Engine | | Displacement (cc) | Tune | Carburettors | Needle | Spring |
|---|---|---|---|---|---|---|
| Austin Healey | | 2912 | full-race | 3×2in | UH | Blue/Black |
| | | 2912 | sports | 3×2in | UH | Red/Green |
| | | 2912 | sports | 3×1¾in | BC | Green |
| | | 2912 | sports | 2×1¾in | CV | Yellow |
| BMC | | 997 | sports | 2×1¼in | GZ | Red |
| | | 998 | sports | 2×1¼in | GY | Blue |
| | | 970 | sports | 2×1¼in | AN | Red |
| | | 1070 | sports | 2×1¼ | H6 | Red |
| | | 1275 | sports | 2×1¼in | M | Red |
| | | 970 | full-race | 2×1½in | CP4 | Blue |
| | | 1070 | full-race | 2×1½in | MME | Blue |
| | | 1275 | full-race | 2×1½in | BG | Blue |
| | | 1098 | sports | 2×1½in | AM | Blue |
| | | 998 | semi-race | 2×1¼in | M | Blue |
| Ford | | 997 | sports | 2×1¼in | A5 | Blue |
| | | 1198 | sports | 2×1¼in | H6 | Red |
| | | 1500 | sports | 2×1½in | CZ | Red |
| | | 2553 | sports | 3×1½in | 3 | Red |
| | | 2553 | sports | 3×1¼in | ES | Red |
| | | 2553 | sports | 2×1½in | 7 | Yellow |
| | | 997 | full-race | 2×1½in | AM | Blue |
| Hillman | ohc | 875 | sports | 2×1¼in | H4 | Blue |
| | | 1600 | sports | 2×1½in | QA | Red |
| Jaguar | T/C | 3441 | sports | 2×1¾in | TL | Red |
| | T/C | 3781 | sports | 2×1¾in | TU | Red |
| | T/C | 3781 | sports | 3×2  in | UM | Blue/Black |
| | T/C | 4235 | sports | 3×2  in | UM | Blue/Black |
| | T/C | 3441 | sports | 3×2  in | UE | Blue/Black |
| MG | T/C | 1588 | sports | 2×1¾in | OA6 | Red |
| | | 1800 | sports | 2×1½in | MB | Red |
| | | 1800 | full-race | 2×2  in | UVD | Blue/Black |
| | | 1098 | sports | 2×1¼in | AN | Blue |
| | | 1800 | semi-race | 2×1¾in | KP | Red |
| Triumph | | 1147 | sports | 2×1¼in | MO | Red |
| | | 1147 | full-race | 2×1½in | DB | Blue |

Normally, a red spring is used, but if the carburettors are the size recommended in TABLE 3.18 for semi and full race engines, a blue spring may be required. Conversely, if a pair of carburettors are fitted to a six cylinder engine or if carburettors smaller than indicated are used (eg. $2 \times 1\frac{1}{2}$ in on a 2000 cc four cylinder) then a stronger yellow or green spring will probably be required, to allow for a richer acceleration.

Float chambers are made in three sizes as indicated in TABLE 3.21. When the carburettor is mounted at an angle (do not exceed $30^0$), it is necessary to machine the attachment lug to keep the chamber vertical at all times.

Whenever SU carburettors are used on high performance vehicles, the float chamber must always be mounted ahead of the carburettor so that the fuel does not surge away from the jet, when accelerating.

The float level should be checked using the appropriate size test bar shown in TABLE 3.21. With the float chamber lid inverted, and the hinged float lever resting on the needle, it should be possible to slide the test bar between the radius of the hinged lever and the chamber lid lip.

The procedure is a little different on the later model HS series carburettors, which have the float attached to the lid. With the lid inverted and the needle valve held in the closed position by the weight of the float only, it should be possible to slide a $\frac{1}{8}$ - $\frac{3}{16}$ in test bar between the float lever and the rim of the lid.

Before attempting to tune and synchronise SU carburettors, several checks are in order, but be very careful not to mismatch any parts from one carburettor to another when these checks are being carried out.

### TABLE 3.21    SU float level settings

**H and HD series carburettors**
T1 float chamber ($1\frac{7}{8}$ in diameter) - use $\frac{7}{16}$ in test bar.
T2 float chamber ($2\frac{1}{4}$ in diameter) - use $\frac{7}{16}$ in test bar.
T3 float chamber (3 in diameter)    - use $\frac{5}{8}$ in test bar.

**HS series carburettors**
Brass float - use $\frac{5}{16}$ in test bar.
Nylon float - use $\frac{1}{8}$ - $\frac{3}{16}$ in test bar.
Delrin needle and new type float - use $\frac{1}{8}$ - $\frac{3}{16}$ in test bar.

Attempt to wriggle the throttle shaft. If there is more than minimal play, new bearings and shaft will be required, as the carburettor will suck air here and make it impossible to synchronise the butterflies or adjust the idle.

Next, mark the relative location of the suction chamber with the main body of the carburettor and then remove the fixing screws and carefully lift the chamber off (If you drop or dent the chamber, it could be ruined). Then lift the piston from the body, taking care not to bend the needle.

When removed, check that the needle is not bent or worn on any side (this indicates that the jet is not centred). Make sure that the shoulder of the needle is flush with the bottom of the piston. If the needle is not flush, you will not be able to get the mixture strength right. Now determine that the needle locking screw is tight.

Using clean petrol (or a non-oily solvent), thoroughly clean the piston (particularly the surface that bears on the wall of the suction chamber) and the inside of the suction chamber. Never use any abrasive or metal polish on these parts.

After being cleaned, the piston and suction chamber may be refitted to the carburetor body but do not oil the inside of the suction chamber or the piston bearing surface. These should remain dry. Be sure to line up the mark that you put on the carburettor body and fully tighten the retaining screws.

Next, lift the piston about $\frac{1}{4}$ in and let it drop. There should be a definate click as it hits the carburettor bridge. If it does not click, the jet is not central and is binding on the needle (Note that this check must be done with the jet screwed into the fully up position. Be sure that the piston is fully raised when the jet is being screwed up).

To centralise the jet you must slacken the jet locking nut. Then insert a thin screwdriver or a pencil through the damper hole in the top of the carburettor and hold the piston down 91 firmly. Retighten the jet locking nut while you hold the jet up hard against the adjusting nut. Finally, check that the piston falls freely and that it clicks as it hits the bridge.

After these checks have been carried out, the carburettors are ready to be tuned and synchronised. First bring the engine up to normal operating temperature. Then loosen the clamps connecting the carburettor shafts together and back the idle speed screws off such that they just contact the stops when the throttles are fully closed. Next, turn each idle speed screw $\frac{3}{4}$ of a turn in, to open the throttle plates.

Screw all the jets fully up and then turn each jet adjusting nut down two complete turns. If the choke is connected to more than one carburettor, be sure to loosen the choke connecting clamps before adjusting the jets.

Restart the engine and using the carburettor synchroniser adjust all of the idle speed screws in turn, to raise the indicator float to mid-height in the indicator column (see the Weber tuning section for more information). Retighten the throttle shaft interconnecting clamps.

Turn up the jet adjusting nuts the same amount on all carburettors to weaken the mixture or down to richen the mixture, until the fastest idle speed consistent with even running is obtained. Then re-adjust the idle speed screws to give the correct idle speed.

Check for the correct mixture by gently pushing up the piston lifting pin of the front carburettor $\frac{1}{32}$ in (after the free travel has been taken up). If the mixture is lean, the engine speed will drop or the engine may even stop. If rich, the engine will speed up and hold that speed. When the mixture is correct, the engine may speed up for just an instant and then slow down to just about normal.

Repeat this operation on all the other carburettors and then make a recheck as they are all interdependent, being connected via the manifold balance pipe.

With the throttle plates synchronised and the mixture adjusted, you can check the suitability of the needles fitted. TABLE 3.22 indicates which segments control which part of the mixture range. You will note that in the smaller carburettors, the tip of the needle does not affect the fuel metering. eg. with the $1\frac{1}{4}$ in SU the last four segments do not do any metering.

A single four barrel Holley is the simplest performance set-up, from the aspect of carburation, for any V6 or V8 engine. Unless class regulations require the use of a two barrel carburettor, forget about using the two barrel Holley on any V8.

The triple two barrel arrangement used on some of the V8 muscle cars a few years ago is also a waste of time. A good four barrel will work better and it is no trouble to tune. The triple two barrel system is all pose, nothing else.

Some enthusiasts like a pair of four barrel Holleys mounted on a low profile ram manifold, for hot street cars. This is a very nice set-up if you can sort out the grave fuel distribution problems usually associated with manifolds of this design.

### TABLE 3.22   SU needle metering range

| Carburettor | | Metering Segments | |
|---|---|---|---|
| *Size* | *Idle* | *Acceleration and cruising* | *Top speed* |
| $1\frac{1}{4}$in | 1st, 2nd | 3rd, 4th, 5th, 6th | 7th, 8th, 9th |
| $1\frac{1}{2}$in | 1st, 2nd | 3rd, 4th, 5th, 6th | 7th, 8th, 9th, 10th |
| $1\frac{3}{4}$in | 1st, 2nd, 3rd | 4th, 5th, 6th, 7th | 8th, 9th, 10th, 11th |
| 2  in | 1st, 2nd, 3rd | 4th, 5th, 6th, 7th, 8th | 9th, 10th, 11th, 12th |

In TABLE 3.23 the Holley carburettors recommend for engines in varying states of tune are listed. Generally, the engines referred to are fitted in the lightest bodies available eg. the Chevy motors listed are tuned for use in Nova, Camaro or Corvette bodies. Engines in semi-race tune would use four-speed manual tranmission and a 3.5:1 rear axle.

When you fit your Holley you will usually find the 'out of the box' jetting to be reasonably close to what you want for a road machine. Even on fairly wild racing engines the jetting should be such that you will be able to get the engine running. Once the engine is working then you can decide what to do to get the jetting right.

## TABLE 3.23  Holley carburettor recommendations

| Engine | Cubic in | Tune | Manifold type | Carb No | Size CFM |
|--------|----------|------|---------------|---------|----------|
| Buick | 455 | sports | Edelbrock B-4BQJ | R-6979 | 600 |
| | | semi-race | as above | R-4780* | 800 |
| | 231 V6 | semi-race | Offenhauser Dual Port | R-1849 | 550 |
| Chevrolet | 283-302 | sports | Edelbrock C-3BX or Torker | R-6979 | 600 |
| | | semi-race | as above | R-4776* | 600 |
| | 327-350 | sports | Edelbrock C-3BX or Torker | R-6979 | 600 |
| | | semi-race | as above | R-4778* | 700 |
| | | semi-race | Edelbrock Tarantula | R-4778* | 700 |
| | | full-race | Edelbrock Scorpion 1 | R-4780* | 800 |
| | | sports | Holley Street Dominator | R-1850 | 600 |
| | 396-427 | sports | Edelbrock Torker | R-6979 | 600 |
| | | semi-race | as above | R-4781* | 850 |
| | | semi-race | Edelbrock C-454 | R-4575* | 1050 |
| | | full-race | Edelbrock Scorpion | R-4781* | 850 |
| | | | | or R-4575* | 1050 |
| Chrysler | 340-360 | sports | Edelbrock Torker | R-7009 | 600 |
| | | semi-race | as above | R-3310 | 780 |
| | | semi-race | Edelbrock LD-340 | R-4778* | 700 |
| | | full-race | Holley Strip Dominator | R-4778* | 700 |
| | 413-440 | sports | Edelbrock Torker | R-7009 | 600 |
| | | semi-race | as above | R-4779* | 750 |
| | | semi-race | Edelbrock Tarantula | R-4779* | 750 |
| | | full-race | as above | R-4780* | 800 |
| Ford | 170 V6 | sports | Offenhauser Dual Port | R-6299 | 390 |
| | 289-302W | sports | Holley Street Dominator | R-1850 | 600 |
| | | semi-race | as above | R-4777* | 650 |
| | 351W | sports | Holley Street Dominator | R-1850 | 600 |
| | | semi-race | as above | R-4777* | 650 |
| | 351C | sports | Edelbrock Torker | R-7010 | 780 |
| | | semi-race | as above | R-6709* | 750 |
| | | full-race | Holley Strip Dominator | R-4781* | 850 |
| | 390-428 | sports | Holley Street Dominator | R-6919 | 600 |
| | | semi-race | as above | R-3310 | 780 |
| | | full-race | as above | R-4780* | 800 |
| Oldsmobile | 400-455 | sports | Edelbrock Torker | R-3310 | 780 |
| Pontiac | 400-455 | sports | Edelbrock Torker | R-3310 | 780 |
| | | semi-race | as above | R-4780* | 800 |

*Note: * indicates double pumper carburettor.*

There are two basic series of Holley main jets. Those with the prefix 22BP-40 followed by the jet size number are the standard jets that have been with us for years. With these jets there is a tolerance of 3% flow difference between jets of the same number. From one size of jet to the next there is an average flow increase or decrease of 4.5%.

A late development by Holley has seen the introduction of a new close limit series of jets. These were developed primarily for pollution control carburettors but they are very useful for fine tuning performance engines. These jets have the prefix 22BP-120 followed by the jet size number.

Following the jet number is a suffix, indicating the jets' flow variation from standard. For example, a 662 jet is a size 66 jet flowing within 1.5% of standard. ie. 0.75% on the rich or lean side of standard. A 663 jet is a 66 jet flowing up to a maximum of 1.5% more than a 662 jet, while a 661 is a lean 66 jet flowing up to 1.5% less than a 662 jet. Therefore there is a maximum of a 1.5% flow difference between any two jets with the same jet number and the same jet suffix.

### TABLE 3.24   Holley main jet nominal bore size

| Jet No | Drill size (in) | Jet No | Drill size (in) |
|--------|-----------------|--------|-----------------|
| 40 | 0.040 | 71 | 0.076 |
| 41 | 0.041 | 72 | 0.079 |
| 42 | 0.042 | 73 | 0.079 |
| 43 | 0.043 | 74 | 0.081 |
| 44 | 0.044 | 75 | 0.082 |
| 45 | 0.045 | 76 | 0.084 |
| 46 | 0.046 | 77 | 0.086 |
| 47 | 0.047 | 78 | 0.089 |
| 48 | 0.048 | 79 | 0.091 |
| 49 | 0.048 | 80 | 0.093 |
| 50 | 0.049 | 81 | 0.093 |
| 51 | 0.050 | 82 | 0.093 |
| 52 | 0.052 | 83 | 0.094 |
| 53 | 0.052 | 84 | 0.099 |
| 54 | 0.053 | 85 | 0.100 |
| 55 | 0.054 | 86 | 0.101 |
| 56 | 0.055 | 87 | 0.103 |
| 57 | 0.056 | 88 | 0.104 |
| 58 | 0.057 | 89 | 0.104 |
| 59 | 0.058 | 90 | 0.104 |
| 60 | 0.060 | 91 | 0.105 |
| 61 | 0.060 | 92 | 0.105 |
| 62 | 0.061 | 93 | 0.105 |
| 63 | 0.062 | 94 | 0.108 |
| 64 | 0.064 | 95 | 0.118 |
| 65 | 0.065 | 96 | 0.118 |
| 66 | 0.066 | 97 | 0.125 |
| 67 | 0.068 | 98 | 0.125 |
| 68 | 0.069 | 99 | 0.125 |
| 69 | 0.070 | 100 | 0.128 |
| 70 | 0.073 | | |

These jets are available from Holley in sizes 35 to 74, so if you have a carburettor with the ordinary jets in this size range fitted it would be well worth the trouble to replace these with a set of close limit jets. At this time only standard jets with a 2 suffix are available, although jets with a 1, 2 or 3 suffix are being fitted to new pollution carburettors at the factory.

All Holley jets are flow rated, but for the benefit of those who may wish to use some exotic fuel blend, I have included TABLE 3.24 so that you have a means of comparing one jet size with another.

All Holley model 4160 and 4175 carburettors have a metering plate with drilled restrictions rather than removable main jets for fuel control in the secondary half of the carburettor. These metering plates also have idle feed restrictions, consequently they are identified by a code number. Unfortunately, this number is just a code and does not relate to the size of the main or idle feed hole. TABLE 3.25 indicates the code number the plate is stamped with and also the main system and idle hole diameters. For example, plate number 10 has a 0.076 in main hole and a 0.026 in idle hole.

The main air bleeds are a fixed size and therefore cannot be altered except by redrilling to a different size. This is not recommended, as it is virtually impossible to drill all four bleeds to exactly the same size.

Holley carburettors employ the power enrichment system mentioned earlier, illustrated in FIGURE 3.3. Many tuners mistakenly believe that this system is a waste of time, so they remove the power valve and fit a plug made by Holley for this purpose. I guess some even feel that as Holley make a plug to stop up the power valve hole, they must propose the removal of the valve in high performance or racing applications. Such could not be further from the truth. Holley make the plug specifically for those engaged in road racing and circle track racing.

In such applications the G forces generated are high enough to move fuel away from the power valve inlet, so air can enter and lean the mixture dangerously. When the secondary power valve is removed, the main jet size must be increased to compensate for the lost fuel flow area of the power valve restriction. Usually, an increase of 4 to 8 numbers in main jet size is about right.

When the power valve is removed, fuel will flood through the main jets and out the discharge nozzles during braking. In fact this can be such a problem, even when the power valve is in place and standard size main jets are used, that some road racers drill out the power valve channel restriction so that smaller main jets can be fitted to reduce the tendency to flood under braking. This is just one problem associated with the use of Holley carburettors on a road racer, which is why I stay well clear of them in this type of application and use Webers instead.

As you can see in FIGURE 3.3 the power valve does not control the volume of fuel entering the main system, the size of the power valve channel restriction does. If you decide to change the size of this restriction, proceed very carefully in steps of 0.002 in. Carburettors using the four and six hole power valves should not have the two restriction holes increased to more than 0.062 in. The newer window type power valves can be used with larger restriction holes, but do not exceed 0.090 in. The number 25 BP-595A power valve is a special type, suitable for two restriction holes of up to 0.122 in.

The power valve is really a vacuum-operated switch, designed to open and allow extra fuel into the main system when the manifold vacuum drops to a predetermined figure. The vacuum at which the valve opens can be determined by the valve suffix number. For 95 example, all the standard window type valves have a prefix 25 BP-591 A, followed by a suffix number from 25 to 105, in increments of 10. A valve with the number 25 BP-591A-45 would open when the manifold vacuum drops to 4.5 in of Hg. A valve numbered 25 BP-591A-105 would open at a vacuum of 10.5 in Hg.

Holley also make two-stage power valves but these should not be used in carburettors fitted to performance vehicles.

To determine what size power valve you need in the primary side of the carburettor, you will have to carry out a series of tests with a vacuum gauge and accurately record the results.

If the engine is fitted with a wild cam, you should note the manifold vacuum at idle. If the gauge reads 6 in Hg at idle then you will have to install a 45 (4.5 in Hg) power valve so that the valve isn't open all of the time. The valve should always open at a lower vacuum pressure than the vacuum at idle.

If the engine has an idle vacuum of more than 10 in Hg, then the vacuum should be checked when the accelerator is floored, as during an overtaking manoeuvre. Note the lowest vacuum reading and then fit a valve that opens at a vacuum 1 to 1.5 in higher. If the

### TABLE 3.25   Holley secondary metering plates - metering restrictions

| Plate No | Main feed (in) | Idle feed (in) | Plate No | Main feed (in) | Idle feed (in) |
|---|---|---|---|---|---|
| 7 | 0.052 | 0.026 | 10 | 0.076 | 0.026 |
| 34 | 0.052 | 0.029 | 22 | 0.076 | 0.028 |
| 3 | 0.055 | 0.026 | 43 | 0.076 | 0.029 |
| 4 | 0.059 | 0.026 | 12 | 0.076 | 0.031 |
| 32 | 0.059 | 0.029 | 3 | 0.076 | 0.035 |
| 40 | 0.059 | 0.035 | 28 | 0.076 | 0.040 |
| 5 | 0.063 | 0.026 | 38 | 0.078 | 0.029 |
| 18 | 0.064 | 0.028 | 11 | 0.079 | 0.031 |
| 30 | 0.064 | 0.029 | 24 | 0.079 | 0.035 |
| 13 | 0.064 | 0.031 | 44 | 0.081 | 0.029 |
| 33 | 0.064 | 0.043 | 21 | 0.081 | 0.040 |
| 8 | 0.067 | 0.026 | 31 | 0.081 | 0.052 |
| 23 | 0.067 | 0.028 | 29 | 0.081 | 0.063 |
| 16 | 0.067 | 0.029 | 46 | 0.082 | 0.031 |
| 9 | 0.067 | 0.031 | 25 | 0.086 | 0.043 |
| 36 | 0.067 | 0.035 | 5 | 0.089 | 0.037 |
| 6 | 0.070 | 0.026 | 27 | 0.089 | 0.040 |
| 19 | 0.070 | 0.028 | 26 | 0.089 | 0.043 |
| 20 | 0.070 | 0.031 | 4 | 0.093 | 0.040 |
| 41 | 0.070 | 0.053 | 15 | 0.094 | 0.070 |
| 35 | 0.071 | 0.029 | 45 | 0.096 | 0.040 |
| 39 | 0.073 | 0.029 | 14 | 0.098 | 0.070 |
| 37 | 0.073 | 0.031 | 42 | 0.113 | 0.026 |
| 17 | 0.073 | 0.040 | 5792 | 0.059 and 0.076 | 0.076 |
| | | | 10 - 3 | 0.063 and 0.073 | 0.070 |
| | | | 5790 | 0.070 and 0.073 | 0.070 |
| | | | 6221 | 0.078 and 0.082 | 0.040 |
| | | | 6217 | 0.089 and 0.093 | 0.040 |
| | | | 4482 | 0.094 and 0.099 | 0.070 |

vacuum is a minimum of 7 in Hg, use power valve number 85, which will open when the vacuum falls to 8.5 in Hg.

As a double check to ensure that you have selected the correct power valve, keep an eye on the vacuum gauge for a few days when you are climbing long hills at close to full throttle. If the gauge regularly reads say 7 - 8 in Hg, then your 85 power valve will provide the needed enrichment in this circumstance. However, if the vacuum stays fairly close to 8 - 9 in Hg, then you will have to replace the 85 valve with a 95 valve.

Anyone involved in drag racing should check the vacuum during the run, and particularly as they approach the traps at the end. If the valve closes toward the end of the run they could very easily hole a piston because of the resulting lean mixture condition. For example, if the manifold vacuum through the traps is 4 in Hg then a 55 or 65 valve should be fitted, but keep in mind that the valve must be closed at idle, as in the first example.

Carburettors with power valves on the secondaries are normally fitted with a valve which opens at a manifold vacuum 2 in lower than the primary valve. Therefore if the primary valve is an 85, a 65 will be used in the secondary. There are exceptions to this general rule. Holley calibrate a small number of their carburettors with the same number primary and secondary valve or even with a primary valve of a lower number than that of the secondary valve.

When it comes to tuning the accelerator pump on the Holley there are a number of factors to consider.

Firstly, Holley offer two different pumps. The standard pump is a 3 cc (or 30 cc per 10 shots) unit. They also have available an optional 5 cc (50 cc per 10 shots) pump which is fitted as standard on the secondaries of all their double pumper mechanical secondary carburettors. The 5 cc pump should be used in all semi and full race applications.

Two other components, the pump cam and the discharge nozzle, actually regulate the pump delivery. The total lift of the cam controls the pump stroke and the profile of the cam affects the phasing of the pump.

The pump cam can be attached in two positions. In the more usual No. 2 position the pump provides a greater initial delivery of fuel and less final volume; the No. 1 position gives a moderate initial delivery and more final volume.

The shape of the pump cam is of little importance in drag racing providing that a cam giving a sufficiently long pump stroke is used. However, on the road or racing circuit the shape of the cam has a great effect on throttle responsiveness. A sharp nose cam gives a quick pump action while a cam with a more gentle shape does not give such quick action. Holley pump cams are colour coded. TABLE 3.26 indicates which cam supplies the most fuel (rich cam) and which cam supplies the least, in both the No. 1 and No. 2 positions. In most instances the richest cam supplies about double the volume of fuel of the leanest cam.

The accelerator pump discharges through the discharge nozzle (shooter) which is available in a number of sizes. The number stamped on the nozzle indicates the bore size in thousandths of an inch, ie. a 28 nozzle has a 0.028 in discharge hole.

A small discharge nozzle lengthens the delivery duration and a large nozzle provides a larger initial volume of fuel. Therefore a car fitted with a large motor in relation to its weight and a numerically large axle ratio will need a large discharge nozzle.

When it comes to tuning, find which nozzle gives the crispest throttle response and then try the different cams to see if the response can be improved. If a better cam is found, then go through the discharge nozzles a second time to be sure that you have found the combination that will give the best performance.

There are a couple of important points to keep an eye on when working with the Holley accelerator pump. Firstly, the pump over-ride spring must never be adjusted so that it is coil bound. The spring must always be compressable to avoid damage to the pump or pump diaphragm.

Also, be sure to check that there is no clearance between the pump actuating lever and the pump cam. Just changing the idle speed can move the cam away from the lever which will delay the discharge of fuel from the pump. When you re-adjust the pump lever adjusting screw to make contact with the cam, be sure to check that at wide open throttle the diaphragm lever can travel an additional 0.015 - 0.020 in by inserting a feeler gauge between the lever and the adjusting screw.

Holleys with vacuum-operated secondary barrels should not be changed over to mechanical operation. Some people feel that this must improve performance because all of the racing Holleys have mechanically-opened secondary throttles, but remember that these are double pumper carburettors and the secondary pump is able to prevent a lean condition when the secondaries are blasted open.

### TABLE 3.26   Holley accelerator pump cams

| | No 2 position | No 1 position |
|---|---|---|
| ↑ | black | white |
| | white | blue |
| leaner | red | red |
| | blue | orange |
| richer | orange | black |
| | green | green |
| ↓ | pink | pink |
| | | brown |

*Note: this chart considers only the volume of fuel delivered not delivery promptness or duration.*

Other people like the 'kick in the pants' feel that you usually get when you change from vacuum control to mechanical. What you are actually feeling is a flat spot followed by a surge of power as the fuel supply catches up with the air flow into the motor.

To allow you to 'tune in' the secondary opening and the rate of opening, Holley provide a selection of diaphragm springs. A light spring will allow the secondaries to open sooner and more quickly than a heavy spring. A light car with a large powerful motor will use a lighter spring than a heavier car with the same motor and rear axle ratio. TABLE 3.27 indicates the range of springs available. Most Holleys have a green, purple or red spring fitted at the factory.

The way to find which spring will give the best performance is to time your acceleration from about 3000 - 3500 rpm to maximum engine speed. Obviously the optimum spring is the one that shows the quickest time. To reduce the number of variables to a minimum, carry out the test in top gear and over the same stretch of road.

As mentioned earlier, there is no other modification that you should do to 'improve' the secondary throttle operation. Change the springs by all means, but leave everything else alone.

At times, vacuum-operated secondary throttles can be slow or sticky in operation, due to the accumulation of gum and carbon on the throttle shaft. Regularly, and before you

## TABLE 3.27  Holley vacuum secondary springs

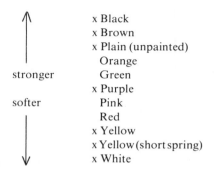

| | |
|---|---|
| | x Black |
| | x Brown |
| | x Plain (unpainted) |
| | Orange |
| stronger | Green |
| | x Purple |
| softer | Pink |
| | Red |
| | x Yellow |
| | x Yellow (short spring) |
| | x White |

*Note: springs marked 'x' are supplied in Holley spring kit No 85BP - 3185*

attempt any tuning, you must hold the primary wide open and manually open the secondaries. There should not be any stiffness encountered and the secondaries should close smoothly, unassisted.

If, after you have manually opened and closed the secondaries several times, resistance is still present, you can be reasonably certain that the binding is due to incorrect or uneven tightening of the carburettor base nuts. This can be a problem when a phenolic heat insulator is used between the carburettor and the manifold. The insulator is necessary to isolate engine heat from the carburettor but take care to tighten each nut a little at a time so that the carb base tightens down evenly, without distortion. The use of thick or multiple base gaskets is to be avoided as this can lead to base distortion and shaft binding.

The idle metering system on Holleys is non-adjustable, except for the mixture screw. There are pressed-in brass air bleeds in the air horn and fuel flow restrictors in the metering blocks. The only way around the problem is drilling the air bleeds (to lean the mixture) or the idle feed restriction (to richen the mixture). This is definitely not a job for the average enthusiast.

In the majority of road applications no changes to the idle system metering will be necessary, but racing engines will require some change. If you do not have the patience or skill to attempt this very fine work, find someone who can do the modifications, or be prepared to spend a lot of money on ruined metering blocks.

If you find that the engine won't idle, first ensure that there is not something else wrong. Air leaks, loose screws, incorrect float or fuel level etc. will all cause you some problem and distort the picture. After you have thoroughly checked everything, and only then, should you modify the carburettor in any way.

Keep an accurate and complete record of every move you make from this point. Remove the carburettor from the manifold and with the throttle lever held against the stop (first wind the screw back to the factory setting) measure the throttle plate to throttle bore clearance in both primary bores, using a feeler gauge.

Refit the carburettor and start the engine. Note how many turns you have to give the idle speed screw to keep the engine running and then attempt to adjust the mixture screws to improve the idle (It is important that you first lightly seat both screws and then turn them out an equal amount). If turning both screws an equal amount does not seem to improve the idle, record that fact.

If you haven't already checked the idle vacuum and fitted a power valve that will stay closed at idle do it now, and check the idle after the change.

Remove the carburettor if there is little or no improvement and turn it upside down. Then measure how much of the transfer slot is visible above the throttle plate. If there is more than 0.040 in visible, drill a $\frac{1}{16}$ in hole in each throttle plate (primary side only) about midway between the throttle shaft and the edge of the throttle plate (Drill the hole on the same side of the plate as the transfer slot).

Some Holleys already have throttle plate holes from the factory so in this instance it will be necessary to enlarge the holes by the equivalent of a $\frac{1}{16}$ in hole in area. ie. if the standard hole is $\frac{1}{16}$, increase the hole size to 0.088 in (or $\frac{3}{32}$ in closest equivalent.)

Before refitting the carburettor, adjust the idle speed screw to obtain the factory set clearance between the throttle plate and throttle bore (This is the first measurement that you recorded).

Refit the carburettor and start the engine. If after adjusting the mixture the idle speed is right, then the holes are of the correct size. If too slow, larger holes are required or if too fast solder over the holes and redrill them a smaller size.

When you are sure that the throttle plate holes are the correct size, check how much change occurs to the idle speed by turning the mixture screws out to richen the mixture (Note on some Holleys you turn the screw in to richen the mixture). If the engine speed drops and the engine runs rough, then the idle feed restriction in the metering block is the correct size.

However, if the mixture screws appear to have little or no control of the idle mixture richness, the idle feed restriction hole will have to be enlarged until turning the mixture screws cause the engine to run rough. The idle feed restriction hole should be enlarged only in steps of 0.002 in, using numbered wire drills and a pin vice.

Once the mixture screws have some control of the idle mixture, very slowly turn the idle speed screw to bring the engine speed up to about 3000 rpm, or below the point where the main system comes into operation. Be certain to increase the engine speed very slowly so that fuel will not issue from the accelerator pump and cover up the lean mixture for which we are looking.

If the engine beat becomes splashy, or it seems to stumble as the speed is increased, a lean mixture condition is indicated. Try to correct the lean condition by tuning out the mixture screws. If the screws have to be backed out more than $\frac{1}{2}$ a turn from the mixture setting previously established, then you will have to continue opening out the idle feed restriction holes 0.002 in at a time until there is no miss up to 3000 rpm.

Once the mixture is correct up to 3000 rpm with no load, you are ready to test the engine at a light load. Accelerate the car as slowly as possible from 15 to 35 mph in the highest gear in which it will run without excessive transmission snatch. If it surges, the mixture is lean. As a cross-check, hold the car on a very light throttle at a steady 20 mph, then a steady 25 mph and so on up to 35 mph, in the highest gear possible, for half a mile at each speed on a smooth and level road. If the engine tends to surge, try turning the mixture screw out a $\frac{1}{2}$ turn. If more than $\frac{1}{2}$ a turn is required to fix the problem then it's back to increasing the idle feed restriction hole size in 0.002 in steps to richen up the idle mixture.

When you are carrying out all of the idle mixture testing and light load running you will have to use fairly warm spark plugs to avoid false results from fuel fouled plugs.

Three types of fuel bowls are used on the four barrel Holley carburettors. Most high performance models use a dual inlet, centre pivot float, with external float level adjustment.

This type of float and bowl is best suited to road circuit and speedway racing where high cornering forces are involved.

Many models use the side hung float and bowl, with external float level adjustment. Usually this design is preferred for drag racing. The other type also uses a side hung float, but it does not have an external float level adjustment. Instead, the float level is set by bending the tongue contacting the needle valve until the proper clearance (this varies with different models) is obtained between the float and the top inside edge of the bowl. This measurement must be taken with the bowl inverted so that the weight of the float closes the needle valve.

The bowls with externally adjustable floats have a sight plug in both the primary and secondary fuel bowls. With the plugs removed, fuel should just be visible along the bottom of the threads when the engine is running. The level is adjusted by loosening the external needle valve locknut and turning the assembly up or down until the fuel level is correct. If the engine idle is very rough, the idle speed will have to be increased when this adjustment is being executed, otherwise the rocking of the engine could give a false fuel level.

As Holley carburettors are used mainly on large displacement engines requiring a high fuel flow, needle valves with sufficient flow capacity must always be used. In TABLE 3.28 I have set out the approximate flow capabilities of the various Holley needle valve assemblies.

Holley market a couple of special devices to aid in fuel control within the float bowl. Some models already incorporate these 'fixes' right from the factory but if your particular carburettor does not have them fitted then you should fit them for improved performance.

A vent 'whistle' (Part No. 59BP-91) should be used in the primary fuel bowl to prevent fuel sloshing into the vent and upsetting the mixture during severe acceleration. The vent whistle extends the bowl vent path over and above the fuel, to provide continuous venting of the primary bowl.

Main jet slosh tubes (Part No. 14BP-505) are used in the secondary main jets for racing and very high performance engines. On maximum acceleration, fuel moves to the rear of the bowl and away from the secondary main jets. When slosh tubes are fitted, fuel starvation is eliminated.

Some model Holley carburettors have stuffers fitted in the float bowls and metering blocks to reduce the fuel bowl capacity. This is purely an emission device which should be removed when these models are used on modified engines. Serious fuel starvation will result if the stuffers are left in place.

When it comes to bolting up a new Holley on your manifold there are few problems

### TABLE 3.28   Holley needle valves - fuel flow

| Valve diameter (in) | Fuel flow at 4 psi (lb/hr) | Fuel flow at 6 psi (lb/hr) |
|---|---|---|
| 0.082 | 155 | 205 |
| 0.097 | 175 | 225 |
| 0.101 | 195 | 255 |
| 0.110 | 230 | 275 |
| x0.110 | 235 | 295 |
| x0.120 | 240 | 305 |

*Note: needle valves marked 'x' have discharge windows and the smaller sizes have discharge holes.*

that you are likely to encounter. However, before you slam the hood closed after fitting the new carburettor, ensure that there is sufficient clearance between the hood and the carburettor. Also check that the accelerator pump lever is not fouling the manifold. When the 50 cc pump is used, it is often necessary to use a $\frac{1}{4}$ in spacer to raise the carburettor. Lastly, have someone hold the accelerator pedal flat while you check that the throttle plates are opening fully.

In the world of motorcycles the Mikuni carburettor reigns the present king. Other carburettors are able to equal or even surpass the Mikuni in certain respects, but overall the Mikuni has much to offer those interested in a good power range and ease of tuning.

Road motorcycles should not have carburettors larger than standard fitted, even when wild camshafts and/or a big bore cylinder kit is used. Larger carburettors will certainly improve high rpm power but the bike will no longer be fun to ride (except on the race track) because of the serious loss of low speed tractability and increased transmission snatch at low speed.

Big bore carburettors are in order on a racing machine but the optimum size will depend more on the layout of the race circuit and rider ability, rather than what is required for peak power.

Mikunis use two types of main jets. The hex-head jets are flow rated in cc per minute. Jets from size 50 to 195 are available in steps of 5, and size 200 to 500 are in steps of 10.

The round head main jets are aperture sized. The largest jet available is a 250, with an aperture size of 2.50 mm.

The needle jet uses a code to identify its size. The first number indicates the jet series. eg. a 159 series jet fits a 30 - 36 mm spigot mount Mikuni (TABLE 3.29). The letter-number combination below the series number shows the fuel hole size. The letter denotes the size in increments of 0.05 mm and the numbers signify size increments of 0.01 mm. eg. a P-4 jet would have a hole size of 2.670 mm. There is one exception to this; the size - 5 needle jet is 0.005 mm larger than the - 4 jet. (TABLE 3.30).

### TABLE 3.29   Mikuni needle jet application

| Series No | Type | Main Jet | Sizes available | Carb type |
|-----------|------|----------|-----------------|-----------|
| 159 | P | Hex | O-O to R-8 | 30 - 36 mm spigot |
| 166 | P | Hex | O-O to R-8 | 38 mm spigot |
| 171 | P | Hex | O-O to Q-8 | 30 mm flange |
| 176 | B | Hex | N-O to Q-8 | 30-36 mm spigot |
| 183 | B | Hex | N-O to Q-8 | 38 mm spigot |
| 188 | P | Hex | O-O to Q-8 | 32 mm flange |
| 193 | P | Hex | N-O to Q-8 | 24 mm flange |
| 196 | P | Round | O-O to Q-8 | 30-36 mm spigot |
| 205 | P | Hex | O-O to Q-8 | 34 mm flange |
| 211 | P | Hex | N-O to Q-8 | 30-36 mm spigot |

*Note: 'P' type needle jets are intended for use primarily in 2 stroke piston port engines.*
*'B' type needle jets have bleed holes and are normally used in 4 stroke and rotary valve 2 stroke engines.*

The needles are identified by a code such as 6DP5. The first number indicates the needle series. The following letter/s indicate the needle taper. If there is one letter, the taper is uniform along the length of the needle, but if there are two letters, this indicates that the

### TABLE 3.30  Mikuni needle jet sizes

| Size | Diameter (mm) | Size | Diameter (mm) |
|------|---------------|------|---------------|
| N-0 | 2.550 | P-5 | 2.675 |
| N-2 | 2.560 | P-6 | 2.680 |
| N-4 | 2.570 | P-8 | 2.690 |
| N-5 | 2.575 | Q-0 | 2.700 |
| N-6 | 2.580 | Q-2 | 2.710 |
| N-8 | 2.590 | Q-4 | 2.720 |
| O-0 | 2.600 | Q-5 | 2.725 |
| O-2 | 2.610 | Q-6 | 2.730 |
| O-4 | 2.620 | Q-8 | 2.740 |
| O-5 | 2.625 | R-0 | 2.750 |
| O-6 | 2.630 | R-2 | 2.760 |
| O-8 | 2.640 | R-4 | 2.770 |
| P-0 | 2.650 | R-5 | 2.775 |
| P-2 | 2.660 | R-6 | 2.780 |
| P-4 | 2.670 | R-8 | 2.790 |

taper changes midway along the tapered section; the first letter indicates the upper taper and the second letter the lower taper.

Starting with letter A, which has a meaning of 15 minutes of arc, each letter in sequence denotes an additional 15 minutes to the angle between the two sides of the needle. Therefore a DP taper has an angle of $1^0\,0'$ on the top and $4^0\,0'$ on the bottom taper (TABLE 3.31).

The number after the letters is a manufacturing code which indicates how far down the needle the taper starts. eg. needles marked 6DP1 and 6DP5 have the same taper, but 6DP1 is the richer needle as the taper starts 28.9 mm from the top of the needle, whereas the taper begins 32.1 mm down with the 6DP5. TABLE 3.32 indicates the dimensions of the more common Mikuni needles.

A final number separated by a dash or in parenthesis indicates the circlip groove position, counting the top groove as number 1. eg. 6DP5-3.

The throttle slide cutaway size is indicated by the number stamped on the slide.eg.2.5 signifies a 2.5 mm cutaway. The cutaway affects off-idle acceleration up to $\frac{1}{2}$ throttle. A large cutaway leans the mixture and a smaller cutaway richens the mixture.

The idle jet (or pilot jet) is available in sizes 15 to 80 in steps of 5. Fine adjustment of the idle mixture is by means of the idle air screw which richens the idle mixture when turned in (clockwise).

### TABLE 3.31  Mikuni needle tapers

| Letter | Taper | Letter | Taper | Letter | Taper |
|--------|-------|--------|-------|--------|-------|
| A | $0^0\,15'$ | J | $2^0\,30'$ | S | $4^0\,45'$ |
| B | $0^0\,30'$ | K | $2^0\,45'$ | T | $5^0\,0'$ |
| C | $0^0\,45'$ | L | $3^0\,0'$ | U | $5^0\,15'$ |
| D | $1^0\,0'$ | M | $3^0\,15'$ | V | $5^0\,30'$ |
| E | $1^0\,15'$ | N | $3^0\,30'$ | W | $5^0\,45'$ |
| F | $1^0\,30'$ | O | $3^0\,45'$ | X | $6^0\,0'$ |
| G | $1^0\,45'$ | P | $4^0\,0'$ | Y | $6^0\,15'$ |
| H | $2^0\,0'$ | Q | $4^0\,15'$ | Z | $6^0\,30'$ |
| I | $2^0\,15'$ | R | $4^0\,30'$ | | |

The float level is adjusted with the fuel bowl removed and the carburettor inverted (FIGURE 3.13). With the float tongue contacting the needle valve the distance 'A' should be equal to the specified float level. Usually, this will be 25 to 35 mm, depending on the carburettor type.

Some Mikuni carburettors have the float level adjusted to dimension 'B'. In this instance the level is usually around 9 to 10 mm; again this varies from model to model.

Many tuners begin tuning the Mikuni by trying to determine the correct main jet size. This procedure is the right one but only if the engine has not been extensively modified and the stock carburettor is being used. If you find that large changes in the size of the main jet do not seem to be having very much influence on the half and full throttle mixture strength, then you can be fairly certain that the needle jet is too small.

When the engine has been extensively modified I prefer to begin testing (after adjusting the float level) with the main jet removed. If the engine will just run at part throttle, but floods as the throttle is opened, then the needle jet is close to the right size. However, if you find that the engine keeps going at $3/4$ to full throttle, then you can be sure that a larger needle jet is required. This test should be done with the needle lowered to the No. 1 (ie. lean) position.

After you have found a needle and needle jet combination that is too rich, you can then try various size main jets until you find one that allows the engine to run reasonably well at full throttle. Don't worry about throttle response or acceleration for the moment. Carry out this test with the needle raised to the middle position.

Next find what size idle jet (pilot jet) is required. Start these adjustments by backing out the idle speed screws until the throttle slides are completely closed and then turn the screws back in until the slides just open.

Having done that, close the idle air screws completely and back each one out 1 to $1\frac{1}{2}$ turns. Start the engine and attempt to obtain a smooth 1000 rpm idle by juggling the idle air

## TABLE 3.32a   Mikuni series 4 needles
### *To fit all 18 mm carburettors and 22 and 24 mm flange mount carburettors*

| Needle | X | Y | 10 | 20 | 30 | 40 | 50 |
|---|---|---|---|---|---|---|---|
| 4D3 | 50.3 | 25.3 | 2.511 | 2.511 | 2.421 | 2.253 | 2.100 |
| 4D8 | 50.3 | 22.8 | 2.519 | 2.519 | 2.381 | 2.211 | 2.000 |
| 4E1 | 50.3 | 28.0 | 2.515 | 2.515 | 2.345 | 2.127 | 1.924 |
| 4DG6 | 50.3 | 24.0 | 2.518 | 2.518 | 2.405 | 2.119 | 1.850 |
| 4DH7 | 50.3 | 23.0 | 2.518 | 2.518 | 2.386 | 2.098 | 1.790 |
| 4F15 | 50.3 | 26.5 | 2.512 | 2.512 | 2.400 | 2.120 | 1.881 |
| 4J13 | 50.2 | 24.0 | 2.513 | 2.513 | 2.230 | 1.800 | 1.400 |
| 4L6 | 50.3 | 24.5 | 2.515 | 2.515 | 2.178 | 1.660 | 1.190 |
| 4F6 | 50.5 | 25.3 | 2.514 | 2.514 | 2.406 | 2.145 | 1.876 |
| 4L13 | 45.1 | 25.0 | 2.518 | 2.516 | 2.339 | 1.842 | |
| 4F10 | 50.2 | 24.5 | 2.513 | 2.513 | 2.385 | 2.135 | 1.877 |
| 4J11 | 41.5 | 21.3 | 2.512 | 2.506 | 2.188 | 1.776 | |
| 4P3 | 50.5 | 25.0 | 2.510 | 2.506 | 2.436 | 2.284 | 2.122 |

*Note: X is the overall length of the needle in mm.*
*Y is the dimension from the top of the needle to the start of the taper.*
*The numbers 10, 20, 30 etc, indicate the needle diameter in mm at a point 10, 20, 30 mm etc from the top of the needle.*

### TABLE 3.32b  Mikuni series 5 needles
*To fit all 26 - 32 mm spigot mount and all 28 - 34 mm flange mount carburettors*

| Needle | X | Y | 10 | 20 | 30 | 40 | 50 | 60 |
|--------|------|------|-------|-------|-------|-------|-------|-------|
| 5D6 | 59.3 | 27.5 | 2.515 | 2.515 | 2.460 | 2.290 | 2.120 | |
| 5FJ9 | 59.2 | 35.0 | 2.517 | 2.517 | 2.517 | 2.364 | 2.021 | |
| 5D120 | 59.1 | 28.2 | 2.520 | 2.520 | 2.479 | 2.311 | 1.980 | |
| 5F3 | 58.0 | 27.4 | 2.519 | 2.519 | 2.419 | 2.135 | 1.863 | |
| 5EH7 | 57.6 | 28.5 | 2.517 | 2.517 | 2.473 | 2.210 | 1.848 | |
| 5E13 | 57.5 | 29.5 | 2.515 | 2.515 | 2.484 | 2.197 | 1.803 | |
| 5EJ13 | 57.8 | 26.5 | 2.519 | 2.519 | 2.431 | 2.210 | 1.766 | |
| 5DL13 | 60.2 | 32.0 | 2.515 | 2.515 | 2.515 | 2.362 | 1.922 | 1.463 |
| 5EJ11 | 60.3 | 28.5 | 2.515 | 2.515 | 2.515 | 2.241 | 1.839 | 1.420 |
| 5EL9 | 60.3 | 27.0 | 2.517 | 2.517 | 2.441 | 2.221 | 1.780 | 1.248 |
| 5FL11 | 60.3 | 28.2 | 2.518 | 2.518 | 2.438 | 2.175 | 1.740 | 1.256 |
| 5EP8 | 60.2 | 33.0 | 2.513 | 2.513 | 2.513 | 2.245 | 1.780 | 1.120 |
| 5FL14 | 58.0 | 28.0 | 2.520 | 2.520 | 2.440 | 2.170 | 1.735 | |
| 5FL7 | 58.0 | 28.0 | 2.518 | 2.518 | 2.440 | 2.170 | 1.735 | |
| 5DP7 | 57.6 | 26.4 | 2.512 | 2.512 | 2.440 | 2.259 | 1.580 | |
| 5J6 | 58.0 | 27.5 | 2.518 | 2.518 | 2.340 | 1.890 | 1.450 | |
| 5L1 | 58.0 | 27.0 | 2.518 | 2.518 | 2.330 | 1.811 | 1.297 | |
| 5C4 | 55.1 | 24.0 | 2.516 | 2.516 | 2.448 | 2.310 | 2.179 | |
| 5F18 | 58.0 | 27.0 | 2.521 | 2.521 | 2.515 | 2.257 | 2.006 | |
| 5J9 | 58.0 | 27.0 | 2.522 | 2.520 | 2.432 | 1.996 | 1.505 | |
| 5F12 | 51.5 | 23.3 | 2.021 | 2.021 | 1.882 | 1.631 | 1.375 | |
| 5D1 | 53.5 | 27.6 | 2.510 | 2.510 | 2.496 | 2.338 | 2.169 | |
| 5DP2 | 60.3 | 32.4 | 2.515 | 2.514 | 2.513 | 2.418 | 2.067 | 1.418 |
| 514 | 60.0 | 27.0 | 2.514 | 2.509 | 2.442 | 2.071 | 1.690 | 1.332 |
| 5D5 | 57.6 | 30.0 | 2.513 | 2.513 | 2.510 | 2.366 | 2.205 | |

*Note:  X is the overall length of the needle in mm.*
*Y is the dimension from the top of the needle to the start of the taper.*
*The numbers 10, 20, 30 etc, indicate the needle diameter in mm at the point 10, 20, 30 mm etc,*
*from the top of the needle.*

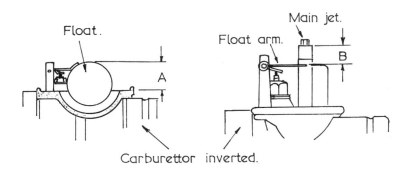

Fig. 3.13   Mikuni float levelling.

### TABLE 3.32 ci   Mikuni series 6 needles
*To fit all 30 - 38 mm spigot mount carburettors*

| Needle | X | Y | 10 | 20 | 30 | 40 | 50 | 60 |
|--------|------|------|-------|-------|-------|-------|-------|-------|
| 6H1    | 62.3 | 37.5 | 2.510 | 2.510 | 2.510 | 2.412 | 2.041 | 1.696 |
| 6DH2   | 62.3 | 28.0 | 2.511 | 2.511 | 2.466 | 2.295 | 2.000 | 1.660 |
| 6F9    | 62.3 | 28.9 | 2.516 | 2.516 | 2.475 | 2.210 | 1.949 | 1.678 |
| 6CF1   | 61.5 | 29.5 | 2.512 | 2.512 | 2.429 | 2.240 | 1.974 | 1.710 |
| 6FJ6   | 62.3 | 35.2 | 2.505 | 2.505 | 2.505 | 2.376 | 2.040 | 1.606 |
| 6DH3   | 62.3 | 22.0 | 2.512 | 2.512 | 2.458 | 2.286 | 1.948 | 1.607 |
| 6J3    | 62.3 | 36.7 | 2.515 | 2.515 | 2.515 | 2.359 | 1.912 | 1.456 |
| 6L1    | 62.3 | 37.0 | 2.512 | 2.512 | 2.512 | 2.335 | 1.826 | 1.313 |
| 6DP5   | 62.3 | 32.1 | 2.518 | 2.518 | 2.518 | 2.372 | 1.834 | 1.141 |
| 6N1    | 62.3 | 37.0 | 2.514 | 2.514 | 2.514 | 2.278 | 1.672 | 1.058 |
| 6DP1   | 62.3 | 28.9 | 2.511 | 2.511 | 2.476 | 2.312 | 1.748 | 1.075 |
| 6F3    | 60.5 | 34.2 | 2.512 | 2.512 | 2.512 | 2.313 | 2.050 |       |
| 6DH4   | 62.3 | 25.5 | 2.520 | 2.520 | 2.440 | 2.258 | 1.915 | 1.575 |
| 6J1    | 64.0 | 36.2 | 2.517 | 2.517 | 2.517 | 2.339 | 1.919 | 1.495 |
| 6DH7   | 62.2 | 28.5 | 2.516 | 2.516 | 2.505 | 2.316 | 2.009 | 1.688 |

*Note: X is the overall length of the needle in mm.*
*Y is the dimension from the top of the needle to the start of the taper.*
*The numbers 10, 20, 30 etc, indicate the needle diameter in mm at a point 10, 20, 30 mm etc from the top of the needle.*

### TABLE 3.32 cii   Mikuni series 6 needles
*To fit all 30 - 38 mm spigot mount carburettors*

| Needle | X | Y | Z | 10 | 20 | 30 | 40 | 50 | 60 |
|--------|------|------|------|-------|-------|-------|-------|-------|-------|
| 6F5    | 62.3 | 38.1 | 19.0 | 2.515 | 2.456 | 2.454 | 2.364 | 2.098 | 1.840 |
| 6F4    | 62.3 | 32.0 | 19.4 | 2.515 | 2.442 | 2.436 | 2.206 | 1.939 | 1.678 |
| 6F8    | 62.3 | 34.0 | 21.5 | 2.512 | 2.512 | 2.386 | 2.214 | 1.945 | 1.688 |
| 6FJ11  | 62.3 | 36.0 | 18.7 | 2.519 | 2.481 | 2.481 | 2.367 | 2.030 | 1.610 |
| 6F16   | 59.1 | 36.7 | 18.5 | 2.519 | 2.489 | 2.489 | 2.372 | 2.104 |       |
| 6DH21  | 52.3 | 30.1 | 16.5 | 2.515 | 2.470 | 2.465 | 2.328 | 2.024 |       |
| 6F16   | 64.6 | 31.2 | 18.4 | 2.520 | 2.404 | 2.400 | 2.201 | 1.941 | 1.679 |

*Note: X is the overall length of the needle in mm.*
*Y is the dimension from the top of the needle to the start of the taper.*
*Z is the dimension in mm from the top of the needle to the pronounced taper point.*
*The numbers 10, 20, 30 etc, indicate the needle diameter in mm at a point 10, 20, 30 mm etc from the top of the needle.*

screws and the idle speed screws in turn. If you can get the engine to settle down to a good idle, then synchronise the throttle slides using a set of vacuum gauges or the multiple column mercury balancer described later.

   If the engine will not idle, it is probable that the idle jets are wrong. Jets that are too small are indicated by an increasing idle speed as the air screws are turned in. Turning the screws in should cause the engine to run rich at some point (usually 1 to 1½ turns from being fully closed) when the idle jets are of the correct size. An idle jet that is too large is indicated by an ever increasing idle speed as the air screws are backed further and further out. The air screw must not be opened more than 3 turns.

When the correct idle jets have been established, then the throttle slides should be synchronised.

Once the slides have been synchronised, you can test that the cutaway is of the correct height. The cutaway influences the mixture most up to one quarter throttle so if the engine tends to cough and die when the throttles are cracked open, change to slides with less cutaway (ie. richer).

When you have settled on the correct slide, recheck the slide synchronisation and determine that the idle jet is still the correct size. Generally, a change in idle jet size is necessary only when a large change in slide cutaway height has been made.

With the idle jets, needle jets and slides finally selected and synchronised, you are ready to begin fine tuning.

First check that the main jet is approximately correct by testing the bike at $\frac{3}{4}$ to full throttle. If the engine runs well and the plugs read a good colour, then the main jet is close enough to begin finding the correct needle profile and/or position.

The needle taper and position controls the fuel/air mixture between $\frac{1}{4}$ and $\frac{3}{4}$ throttle. To determine if a change is required, test the bike on a smooth and level road for at least half a mile at $\frac{1}{4}$ throttle, and then at $\frac{1}{2}$ and $\frac{3}{4}$ throttle. If the engine snatches and surges at a steady throttle opening, the mixture is too rich, so lower the needle one groove at a time until smooth running is realised.

Next, try steady accelerations from $\frac{1}{4}$ to $\frac{1}{2}$ throttle and from $\frac{1}{2}$ to $\frac{3}{4}$ throttle, and note whether the engine appears to be rich or lean. Repeat the test but snap the throttle open each time.

You may find that the mixture is lean at $\frac{1}{4}$ throttle and changes to rich between $\frac{1}{2}$ and $\frac{3}{4}$ throttle. This would indicate that the needle's taper is too steep, so change to a needle with a smaller angle of taper. Obviously a mixture condition the opposite of this would require a needle with more taper (ie. a larger angle).

Once the correct needle has been determined, the bike should be tested at three quarter to full throttle, to find the right main jet diameter.

The tuning procedure for any carburettor using a needle metering system is always slow and tedious. However, by keeping clear notes and by regularly referring to TABLE 3.33 to see what controls the metering at various throttle openings, eventually you will be rewarded with smooth and responsive carburation.

Most workshop manuals recommend the use of vacuum gauges to balance multiple motorcycle carburettors. However, I have found these to give less than perfect synchronisation. As they cost a lot of money, I feel that it is a better plan to make your own mercury column balancer.

The instrument that I will describe is illustrated in FIGURE 3.14. If you own or intend to buy a six cylinder bike then you will need a six, rather than a four, column manometer.

The face board should be 18 in wide and 36 in high, with a matt black background and white scale lines 1 cm apart. The board should be permanently fixed to a wall in your workshop or else mounted solidly on a suitable base, so that it will not fall or be blown over.

The glass U tubes should have an inside diameter of $\frac{5}{32}$ in and be exactly 6 ft long. You could buy the tubes already formed or else buy straight 6 ft lengths of tube and heat each with a gas torch until the glass becomes plastic enough to bend into a U shape around a piece of 2 in pipe.

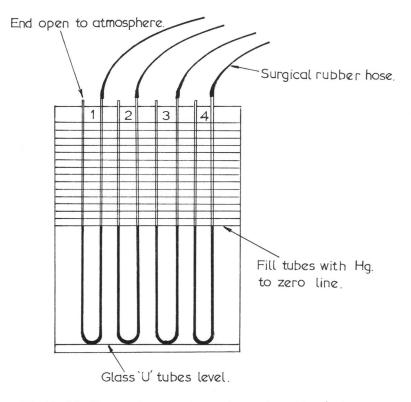

End open to atmosphere.

Surgical rubber hose.

1 2 3 4

Fill tubes with Hg. to zero line.

Glass 'U' tubes level.

Fig. 3 . 14  Four column motorcycle carburettor balancer.

Mount the tubes on the face board with the tops of each tube protruding approximately 1 in past the top of the board. The bottoms of the tubes must be level. The tubes may be mounted by drilling a number of $\frac{1}{16}$ in holes in the board and inserting copper wire through the holes and around each glass tube.

Once the U tubes are secure, they should be filled to the zero line (the halfway point) with mercury. You will require about 10 cc in each column. Mercury is a very dangerous accumulative poison and as such it is not easily obtained in many countries. At times it can be bought from laboratory supply firms but generally you will have to know someone who has the right contacts. ie. a chemistry teacher or an electrician who has access to old mercury switches.

Because mercury is deadly, never handle it or breathe its vapour. It appears to be stable but actually it is very volatile, giving off poisonous vapour continually. Therefore when the balancer is not in use, stop up the ends of the tubes or connect the two ends together with rubber hose, to prevent the escape and buildup of vapour in your workshop. Always keep the balancer locked away from children or pets. Remember the poison is accumulative, which means that it builds up in your body. When the concentration reaches a certain level it will cause blindness, insanity or death.

To connect the U tubes to the inlet manifold you will need 9 ft lengths of $\frac{1}{4}$ in i/d surgical rubber hose. This length and type of hose provides the necessary damping without impairing the accuracy of the readings. Note that the hose is connected to one end of the U tube and the other end is open to the air.

The final connection from the hose to the vacuum test holes in the manifold is made using adaptors produced for this purpose by the manufacturer of your machine, or you may choose to make a set of adaptors yourself.

The balancer is very easy to use. You merely adjust the slide opening of each carburettor to get an even reading in each mercury column. Once the slides have been synchronised, the idle speed and mixture are then adjusted for the best idle.

Bikes with an individual throttle cable to each carburettor can be a problem, so after the initial synchronisation, the carburettors should be checked for balance at several rpm levels. Changes in balance indicate sticky slides or uneven cable pulls.

This balancer is not just for bikes. The triple and quad Weber setups and those carburettors with air screws are also best tuned using this multi-column manometer.

### TABLE 3.33    Mikuni metering guide

| | Throttle opening Position | | | | | |
|---|---|---|---|---|---|---|
| | $\frac{1}{8}$ | $\frac{1}{4}$ | $\frac{3}{8}$ | $\frac{1}{2}$ | $\frac{3}{4}$ | *full* |
| Slide cutaway | A | A | B | B | C | D |
| Pilot or idle jet | A | A | B | C | D | D |
| Pilot air screw | A | A | B | C | D | D |
| Needle jet | B | A | A | C | D | D |
| Needle size | C | B | A | A | C | C |
| Needle position | B | B | A | A | C | D |
| Main jet | D | D | C | C | B | A |

*These letters indicate metering effectiveness at various slide openings.*

*A - most effective*
*B - fairly effective*
*C - small influence*
*D - no influence*

# Chapter 4
# The Exhaust System

IN THE case of the exhaust system appearances can be misleading. It may be visually impressive because of its shape but to many it is still just a bundle of pipes that direct hot gas from the cylinders. Informed modifiers, however, realise full well the importance of tuning the exhaust plumbing to improve performance. As with all other areas of the high performance engine, the exhaust system cannot be regarded as an individual entity; it is influenced by, and in turn affects, other areas, so it must be considered as a part of the whole. What we are aiming for is that the cylinders be completely scavenged of exhaust gas. On all-out racing engines the exhaust system is tuned so that the exhaust gas momentum and pressure waves actually 'suck' the intake charge into the cylinder. In this way the cylinder can actually be overfilled ie. a volumetric efficiency of 101 - 105%. Camshaft valve overlap and the induction system both have a part to play for this to be possible.

Before we discuss the black art of pulse tuning, we will look at what can be done to efficiently scavenge the cylinder of exhaust gas by gas momentum or inertia tuning. The principle of inertia tuning is that exhaust gases have weight so once we get the gas 'rolling' it will continue to flow even after the exhaust valve has closed. This creates a partial vacuum with a resultant suction action which we can use to scavenge the cylinder. As engine speeds increase, the time available for effective cylinder exhausting will decrease, hence the need to use this suction action to empty the cylinder of exhaust gas more quickly.

Obviously if we have a gas pressure of 20 psi in the exhaust manifold when the exhaust valve opens, this will restrict gas flow out of that cylinder. On the other hand if manifold pressure is - 5 to 0 psi the flow restriction will be much less. For this reason we use the extractor type header with individual pipes, rather than a common manifold. The basic idea is to arrange the pipes so the exhaust gas of one cylinder will not pressurise another cylinder. For example, look at what occurs in a four cylinder engine where all cylinders share a common manifold (FIGURE 4.1). The firing order we will assume to be 1 - 3 - 4 - 2. At the end of its exhaust stroke No 2 tends to be pressurised by No 1. No 4 will pressurise No 3 and so on. For this reason modified cams are a waste of time if this type of manifold is retained.

For many years racing engines have used individual pipes for each cylinder, but it is

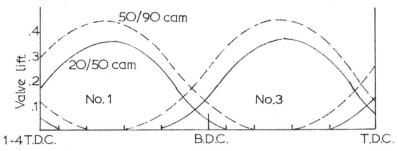

Fig. 4.1 Exhaust valve overlap between cylinders 1 & 3.

now a well established fact that in most instances it is more beneficial to join these individual pipes together, using a collector to which we attach either a straight tailpipe or a megaphone. This arrangement picks up power and as an added bonus it improves the power range. FIGURE 4.2 shows the various header designs for four, six and eight cylinder engines. The six and eight cylinder exhaust should always be split into two separate systems, while the four cylinder engine, whether in line, vee, or flat, works best with the individual pipes collected into one.

Looking at FIGURE 4.2 you will note there are two basic header designs for four cylinder engines. The system giving the best power is the 4 into 1 arrangement, where the four primary pipes collect into one tailpipe. However there are disadvantages; this type weighs more and there are usually clearance problems when trying to fit four exhaust tubes between the side of the motor and steering gear. Another factor to be considered, particularly where four cylinder engines are involved, is the effect of the 4 into 1 system restricting the power band. If good mid-range power is required, then the 4 into 2 into 1 system is the way to go, although maximum power can be down by as much as 5 - 7% in comparison to that obtainable when using a 4 into 1 system.

The other two four cylinder designs are for BMC type engines with a siamese centre port. The header with the long centre branch is the one to use as the increase in volume tends to keep the pulse frequency of the centre pipe in tune with the other two branches. The second design is really only suitable if a mild cam is used.

V8 engines pose a problem in that most use a $90^0$ two-plane crankshaft. $180^0$ crossover headers will give the best power but how you fit them under the hood of the average car is beyond me. For this reason the 4 into 1 system for single-plane $180^0$ cranks is generally used. A balance pipe is necessary. It should be 1.5 times the diameter of the primary pipes and be fitted somewhere close to the collector.

Now that we have had a look at the basic header pipe designs to take advantage of exhaust gas inertia, we next must determine the individual pipe length and diameter. This is where pulse tuning or acoustical tuning enters the scene. The exhaust gas is expelled from the cylinder at a velocity of between 200 and 300 ft per second, but pulses or pressure waves are moving through that gas at around 1500 to 1700 ft per second. By understanding the behaviour of these waves, we can use them to improve cylinder scavenging and to increase cylinder filling with fuel/air mixture.

As the initial charge of burnt gas bursts from the cylinder into the exhaust system, it creates a wave of positive pressure which travels at the speed of sound through the gas to the end of the pipe. As it surges into the atmosphere, the positive wave dissipates and produces

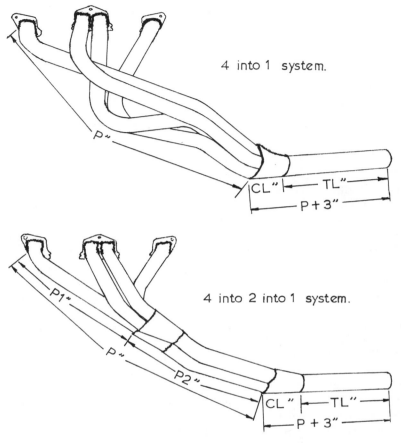

4 into 1 system.

4 into 2 into 1 system.

Fig. 4. 2a   4 cylinder exhaust headers.

a negative pressure wave (suction wave), which returns along the exhaust pipe into the cylinder. It arrives with a certain amount of evacuation power because its pressure is much lower than the cylinder pressure. The art of exhaust tuning is to determine the length and size of the exhaust pipe for this suction wave to arrive back at the cylinder during the valve overlap period.

The formula to work out the primary pipe length is

$$P = \frac{850 \times ED}{rpm} - 3$$

where  rpm = engine speed exhaust is being tuned to

ED = $180°$ plus the number of degrees the exhaust valve opens before BDC

To make the task simpler, I have prepared TABLE 4.1, so that the primary length can be read straight off. Generally, road motors will require a manifold tuned to work at maximum torque rpm. Racing motors on the other hand use a header tuned to work at either maximum horsepower rpm or at a speed midway between maximum torque and maximum hp revs.

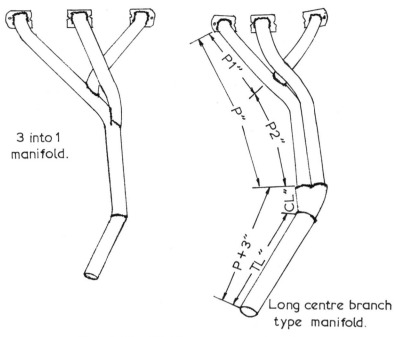

3 into 1 manifold.

Long centre branch type manifold.

Fig. 4.2b B.M.C. 4 cylinder headers.

Once the primary pipe length has been determined, we can then work out the inside diameter using the formula

$$ID = \sqrt{\frac{cc}{(P+3) \times 25}} \times 2.1$$

where cc = cylinder volume in cc

P = primary length in inches

Headers for road engines usually work well enough if the pipes are of the same diameter as the exhaust port. Racing engines demand more exactness than this if we are to achieve ultimate performance. In using the above formula, sizes will have to be worked to suit exhaust tube that is available commercially.

If a 4 into 2 into 1 system is preferred, we use the same formula or TABLE 4.1 to work out the total length (P) of the header pipes, which will be the combined length of the primary (P1) plus the length of the secondary pipe (P2). The inside diameter can then be determined for the four primary pipes (P1) using the same formula

$$ID = \sqrt{\frac{cc}{(P+3) \times 25}} \times 2.1$$

Once the inside diameter of the primary pipes is calculated, we can then work out the inside diameter of the two secondary pipes (P2) by the formula

$$IDS = \sqrt{ID^2 \times 2} \times 0.93$$

where ID = the calculated inside diameter of the primary pipes (P1). 113

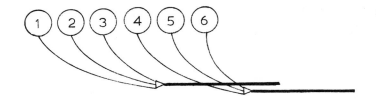

Fig. 4.2c   6 cylinder header.

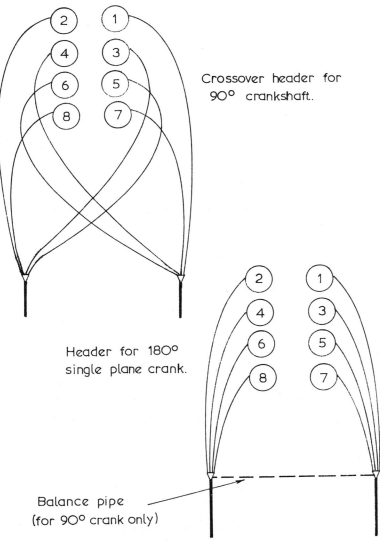

Crossover header for
90° crankshaft.

Header for 180°
single plane crank.

Balance pipe
(for 90° crank only)

Fig. 4.2d   V8 exhaust headers.

## TABLE 4.1   Exhaust primary pipe length (in)

| Tuned rpm | Exhaust valve opening degrees before BDC | | | | | | | | |
|---|---|---|---|---|---|---|---|---|---|
| | *50⁰* | *55⁰* | *60⁰* | *65⁰* | *70⁰* | *75⁰* | *80⁰* | *85⁰* | *90⁰* |
| 4000 | 46.0 | 46.9 | 48.0 | 49.0 | 50.2 | 51.2 | 52.1 | 53.3 | 54.4 |
| 4500 | 40.5 | 41.3 | 42.3 | 43.2 | 44.3 | 45.1 | 46.1 | 47.1 | 48.1 |
| 5000 | 36.2 | 36.9 | 37.7 | 38.6 | 39.5 | 40.4 | 41.1 | 42.0 | 43.0 |
| 5500 | 32.6 | 33.2 | 34.1 | 34.8 | 35.7 | 36.4 | 37.1 | 38.0 | 38.8 |
| 6000 | 29.6 | 30.3 | 31.9 | 31.7 | 32.5 | 33.1 | 33.8 | 34.5 | 35.4 |
| 6500 | 27.2 | 27.7 | 28.4 | 29.0 | 29.8 | 30.4 | 31.0 | 31.7 | 32.4 |
| 7000 | 25.0 | 25.5 | 26.1 | 26.7 | 27.4 | 28.0 | 28.6 | 29.2 | 29.8 |
| 7500 | 23.1 | 23.6 | 24.2 | 24.7 | 25.4 | 25.9 | 26.5 | 27.0 | 27.6 |
| 8000 | 21.5 | 21.9 | 22.5 | 23.0 | 23.6 | 24.1 | 24.6 | 25.2 | 25.8 |
| 8500 | 20.0 | 20.5 | 21.0 | 21.5 | 22.1 | 22.5 | 23.0 | 23.5 | 24.0 |
| 9000 | 18.7 | 19.2 | 19.6 | 20.1 | 20.6 | 21.1 | 21.5 | 22.0 | 22.5 |
| 9500 | 17.6 | 18.0 | 18.4 | 18.9 | 19.4 | 19.8 | 20.2 | 20.7 | 21.2 |
| 10000 | 16.5 | 16.9 | 17.4 | 17.8 | 18.3 | 18.6 | 19.1 | 19.6 | 20.0 |
| 10500 | 15.6 | 16.0 | 16.4 | 16.8 | 17.2 | 17.6 | 18.0 | 18.4 | 18.8 |
| 11000 | 14.8 | 15.1 | 15.5 | 15.9 | 16.3 | 16.7 | 17.0 | 17.4 | 17.8 |
| 11500 | 14.0 | 14.3 | 14.7 | 15.1 | 15.5 | 15.8 | 16.2 | 16.6 | 17.0 |
| 12000 | 13.3 | 13.6 | 14.0 | 14.3 | 14.7 | 15.0 | 15.4 | 15.8 | 16.1 |

The length of the primary pipes (P1) should always be 15 in. The length of the secondary pipes (P2) can be found by simple subtraction: P2 = P - P1.

The calculations for the 4 into 2 into 1 system are also used to determine the pipe sizes for the long centre branch type BMC header. The only difference is that the centre branch is the same diameter as the secondary pipe (IDS) for the full length (P).

In theory it looks very simple to arrive at a header design with pipes of precisely the right length and diameter; unfortunately in practice it doesn't often work out that way. A header constructed to the formulae outlined will work reasonably well and provide a good basis for further experimentation on the dyno or at the race track. However due to variables in the design of cams, inlet manifolds, cylinder head porting etc. the length and diameter of the header pipes will have to be changed about to arrive at the ideal size for your engine.

If you find that the engine's torque peak is at 7000 rpm and you want maximum torque at 6000rpm then reduce the pipe diameter. Generally a reduction in primary pipe diameter of 0.125 in will move the torque peak down by 500 - 600 rpm in larger engines, and by 650 - 800 rpm in motors smaller than 2 litres.

Conversely an increase in the diameter of the headers will raise the engine speed at which maximum torque occurs, by approximately the same rpm for each 0.125 in increase.

Changing the length of the pipes tends to 'rock' the power curve of the engine, around the point of maximum torque. Adding length to the primary pipes will increase low speed and mid-range power, with a corresponding reduction in power at maximum rpm. Shorter primaries give an increase in high speed power, at the expense of a reduction in the midrange. However, there will be little change in peak torque or the engine speed at which it occurs.

FIGURE 4.3 illustrates the way we connect the header pipes, using a collector. The pipes should terminate abruptly at the collector otherwise our tuned pressure wave will carry on into the tailpipe and all our calculations to get the negative wave back to the exhaust valve on time will be amiss. Factory headers leave much to be desired in this respect, but as these are generally used only on street machines the problem is not so serious. Some American competition headers I have seen use a small pyramid shaped airfoil in the collector. A device like this has to be either a gimmick or if it does work there must be some basic design error in the header to begin with.

I have found the best angle of taper for the collector to be $7 - 8^0$ ($14 - 16^0$ included angle); certainly $9 - 10^0$ must be considered the maximum taper and generally I have found this angle to cause a slight power loss. Using the following formula we can work out the required length for the collector:

$$CL = \frac{ID2 - ID3}{2} \times Cot\ A$$

ID2 = diameter of collector inlet

ID3 = diameter of collector outlet

Cot A = cotangent of angle of taper ($7^0 = 8.144, 8^0 = 7.115, 9^0 = 6.314, 10^0 = 5.671$)

Actually, we can't work out the collector size until we calculate the tailpipe size. The combined length of the collector and tailpipe should always be the same length as the primary pipe, plus 3 in (P + 3 in). In the case of a street machine, the tailpipe can be two, three etc. times P + 3 in, providing it is actually two or three times as long. We count the tailpipe as finishing at the front of the muffler. The length of pipe after the muffler does not matter. The tailpipe inside diameter is calculated using the formula

$$ID3 = \sqrt{\frac{cc \times 2}{(P + 3) \times 25}} \times 2$$

where cc = cylinder volume in cc

P = primary length in inches

If a tailpipe two or three times the P + 3 in is being used, ID3 can be reduced, if necessary. Once we have determined the tailpipe diameter (ID3) we can then calculate the collector length (CL). The actual tailpipe length can then be found by subtraction, using the formula TL = (P + 3) - CL.

So much for the straight tailpipe, but what about the tapered tailpipe or megaphone? Firstly, let me point out that a megaphone is not nearly as effective as many believe it to be. In fact I have yet to find a megaphone give consistently higher power when fitted to a multicylinder engine where the primary pipes are joined by a collector to a single megaphone. On the other hand I have found a consistent 5 - 8% power increase if the primary pipes are kept separate, with a megaphone fitted to each primary.

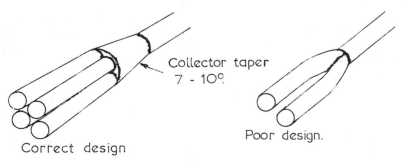

Collector taper 7 - 10°.

Correct design

Poor design.

Fig. 4.3  Primary pipes must terminate as shown.

This increase in power comes about due to the stronger negative pulse (suction wave) created by the megaphone. Due to the megaphone taper controlling the exhaust gas expansion, little pulse energy is lost to the atmosphere. The straight tailpipe loses more pulse energy because of the more rapid gas expansion, so the return negative wave is weaker than the original positive wave.

From the work that I have done with two-stroke motors these past few years, and as you probably know two-strokes live and die by the exhaust, I have found a megaphone taper of $8^0$ ($16^0$ included angle) to give the best return wave for power. A taper of $9^0$ will give slightly more power but cuts down the power range. A smaller taper of $5 - 7^0$ will improve the power band but will restrict the power potential of the engine. A sudden rush of power is very difficult to control, especially on a bike, so a variety of megaphones should be on hand to tune the exhaust to the circuit.

When a megaphone is fitted, the primary pipe length remains unchanged, so in effect the megaphone works as a tailpipe. At times I have seen the primary pipe made 3 - 6 in longer, but usually this is done to improve the midrange power when a megaphone with the wrong taper is being used.

To date I have not been able to arrive at a reliable formula to calculate just how long the megaphone should be. However, for my own testing I use a rule of thumb that states that the outlet diameter of the megaphone should be $3\frac{1}{2}$ - 4 in. From there the length of the megaphone can be worked out using the formula

$$ML = \frac{ID4 - ID}{2} \times Cot\ A$$

ID4 = megaphone outlet inside diameter

ID = primary pipe inside diameter

Note: if a megaphone is attached to a collector ID equals the collector outlet diameter (ID3)

Cot A = cotangent of angle of taper ($3^0 = 19.08, 4^0 = 14.3, 5^0 = 11.43, 6^0 = 9.514, 7^0 = 8.144, 8^0 = 7.115$)

I have been surprised to find just how many megaphones give the type of power band that I am looking for when an outlet of $3\frac{1}{2}$ - 4 in is used. However, I must add that these megaphones have generally been connected to separate primary pipes and the individual cylinder capacity has been 350 - 500 cc. The motors had a rev limit of 7500 - 8500 rpm.

To help restore as much midrange power as possible, it is usually necessary to fit the megaphone outlet with a reverse cone. This suppresses the peak power but the increase in midrange power is of considerable benefit as it results in a much smoother and more easily controlled machine (FIGURE 4.4).

The reverse cone is usually $1\frac{1}{4}$ - $1\frac{3}{4}$ in long, with an outlet $\frac{3}{4}$ - 1 in smaller than the megaphone diameter. The smaller the outlet diameter, the harder the engine will pull in the midrange.

In TABLE 4.2 you can see how the exhaust system with a reverse cone megaphone produced almost identical power from 4500 to 6500 rpm as the straight primary pipe. However at 7000 rpm the megaphone system is giving about 3% more power and this rises to a 7% increase at 7500 rpm. You will also note that there is a corresponding power reduction of 8% at the bottom end of the scale.

In conclusion, let me make one final point that may save you a good deal of money. Whilst we have had an in-depth look at header tuned lengths and sizes, do not get too carried away applying this science to a street machine. Any reasonable header will work well with a 117 road cam as pulse tuning is limited due to the small valve overlap of this type of cam. In fact I have found on the dyno, using cams of up to $290^0$ duration and $70^0$ overlap, that headers 10% 'out of tune' resulted in a power decrease of not more than 3% on the same motor with 'in tune' headers. However, I have also determined that once the valve overlap increased to $100^0$ - $130^0$ the tuned length became very critical, to the point that a slightly out of tune header dropped power by 10 - 12%.

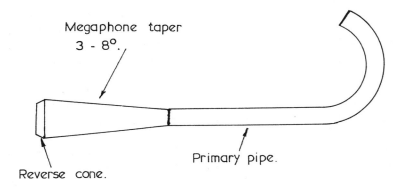

Megaphone taper
3 - 8°.

Primary pipe.

Reverse cone.

Fig. 4.4    Reverse cone megaphone exhaust.

### TABLE 4.2    Standard Yamaha SR500 dyno test

| rpm | Test 1 | Test 2 |
|---|---|---|
| 3500 | 17.2 | 15.8 |
| 4000 | 21.2 | 19.9 |
| 4500 | 24.3 | 24.7 |
| 5000 | 28.5 | 28.5 |
| 5500 | 30.7 | 31.3 |
| 6000 | 32.1 | 32.2 |
| 6500 | 32.9 | 32.6 |
| 7000 | 33.7 | 34.6 |
| 7500 | 32.1 | 34.3 |

**Test 1** - *Standard engine with modified air box and muffler removed.*
**Test 2** - *As above but with a reverse cone megaphone fitted to the engine pipe.*

# Chapter 5
# Camshaft
# and Valve Train

AMONG THE most important components in any performance or racing engine are the camshaft and valve train assembly. Basically, the camshaft is designed to open valves before the piston starts a stroke and to close them after the completion of the stroke, in order to utilise the inertia or momentum of the fast moving gases to fill and empty the cylinder efficiently.

The intake valve is opened before top dead centre (TDC) on the induction stroke, to get the valve moving off the seat before the piston starts down. We keep it open well after bottom dead centre (BDC) to let the inertia of the high velocity fuel/air mixture literally ram additional mixture in while the piston is starting up on the compression stroke.

The exhaust valve we start to open long before the end of the combustion stroke. Most of the effective expansion power of combustion is over by mid-stroke and opening the exhaust valve early lets the cylinder pressure 'blow down' before the piston starts up on the exhaust stroke. By leaving the valve open after TDC we use the momentum of the exhaust gases to scavenge the cylinder efficiently. As the inlet valve is open during this overlap period, the exhaust gas inertia will actually assist cylinder filling by creating a partial vacuum in the cylinder and inlet tract.

However, this theory is not going to work from idle to full engine rpm. At low engine speeds the fuel mixture coming into the cylinder has little velocity and consequently little momentum. In fact the piston will start to push the mixture out of the cylinder back up the inlet port as it comes up on the compression stroke. A similar situation occurs with the late closing of the exhaust valve. When the outgoing exhaust gases have low inertia at low rpm, the piston travelling down on the intake stroke will cause the burned gases to turn around and be sucked back into the cylinder. The other possibility is that of the fuel/air mixture flowing straight past the exhaust valve during the overlap period. This can be particularly troublesome with hemi and pent roof type combustion chambers. It is obvious a compromise must be made to favour either low or high engine speeds. One cam can't give you both, with maximum efficiency.

Today, with the advances that have been made to improve the breathing ability of 119 engines, it is not always necessary or desirable to employ a long duration, high lift cam to improve performance. In fact such a cam can very easily spoil an otherwise well thought out engine modification. As we will discuss later, the valve timing and duration figures tell very little about the power characteristics of a cam. The numbers game is played in the cam grinding industry too, so beware.

The science of camshaft design and operation is very complex, but our understanding the basics will assist us to choose and correctly install a high performance cam. The base circle is the part of the cam that should, at all times, be at a constant radius from the centre of the cam core. The ramp (or clearance ramp) is the part that takes up the valve clearance and begins lifting the valve in a gentle manner. The flank is the part which initiates the valve opening (FIGURE 5.1).

When designing a performance cam, the base circle must remain in the area of $140-160^0$ ($280 - 320$ crankshaft degrees). This is necessary to allow the valves to dissipate heat and to give the whole valve train time to recover from the shock it has just gone through. The ramp will, on a production cam, have $30 - 40^0$ duration. The flank will on average be $60-70^0$. To increase the duration of a cam we increase the flank angle to $70 - 80^0$. To do this we must cut the ramp angle back to $20 - 30^0$.

All production engine designers like to use fairly long ramps in order to lift and seat the valve gently. This has the effect of cutting down on mechanical noise and increasing camshaft life. However, when designing a performance cam we cannot reduce the base circle angle so we have to shorten the ramp.

The average production engine timing is $20^0 - 50^0/50^0 - 20^0$ ie. inlet valve opens $20^0$ before TDC and closes $50^0$ after BDC; exhaust valve opens $50^0$ before BDC and closes $20^0$ after TDC. This type of cam will give good low speed performance. A sports cam of around $25^0 - 65^0/70^0 - 20^0$ will improve performance with little loss in low speed flexibility. The wildest cam I would recommend for a road machine is what I call a semi-race cam. This would have a maximum duration of $290^0$; timing would be $40^0 - 70^0/75^0 - 35^0$. After this we enter the field of full race competition cams. The shorter duration competition cams are more suitable for high speed closed stage rally cars, road circuit cars and $1/4$ mile dirt speedway machines, while the longer duration ($320 -330^0$)cams would be used in one-mile

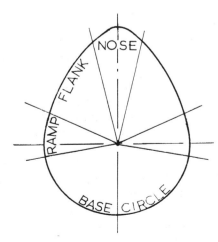

Fig. 5.1    Camshaft lobe

speedway cars and drag machines. TABLE 5.1 indicates the power range of various camshafts.

Many cams have what we call symmetrical timing for ease of manufacture. However, I have found it advantageous to advance the exhaust timing 5 - $10^0$ when grinding cams to improve performance. Top end power is not improved, but the engine will run more smoothly and produce better mid-range power.

The amount the inlet valve is lifted has a large bearing on the performance of an engine. Standard cams normally lift the valve about 23% of its diameter, while racing cams may increase this to 35%. I have found the best air flow to occur with the inlet valve lifted 29 - 31% of its diameter. Why then design a cam to lift the valve 35% of its diameter? A cam designer has to use every trick he can think of to make things work. It may sound silly lifting a valve more than necessary, imposing higher loads on the valve train and making it necessary to use deeper valve cutouts to clear the pistons, but this is how it works. Cam designers have found in recent years that cams with quick opening and closing rates (high acceleration) but with relatively moderate duration and overlap, are a good way to get a broad torque curve. In other words, you pick up top end power without sacrificing so much mid-range power. Now if we accelerate the valve quickly to a high velocity and we want it to maintain that

### TABLE 5.1   Camshaft power range

**Power range rpm (2 and 4 cylinder engines)**

| Timing | 250/twin | 500/twin | 750/twin | 750/4 | 1000/4 | 1300/4 | 1600/4 | 2000/4 |
|---|---|---|---|---|---|---|---|---|
| 25-65 |  |  |  |  | 2500 | 2000 | 2000 | 1500 |
|  |  |  |  |  | -6500 | -6500 | -6000 | -5500 |
| 30-70 | 4500 |  |  | 4000 | 3000 | 2500 | 2500 | 2000 |
|  | -8000 |  |  | -7500 | -7000 | -6800 | -6500 | -6000 |
| 35-75 | 5000 | 4000 | 3000 | 4500 | 4000 | 3000 | 3000 | 2500 |
|  | -8500 | -7500 | -7000 | -8000 | -7200 | -7000 | -6700 | -6500 |
| 40-80 | 6800 | 5000 | 4000 | 5500 | 5000 | 4000 | 4000 | 3000 |
|  | -9500 | -8000 | -7500 | -8500 | -7500 | -7200 | -7000 | -6700 |
| 50-80 | 7500 | 6000 | 4500 | 6500 | 6000 | 5000 | 4500 | 4000 |
|  | -10500 | -8500 | -7800 | -9500 | -8500 | -7500 | -7200 | -7000 |
| 55-85 | 8500 | 6500 | 5000 | 7000 | 6500 | 6000 | 5000 | 5000 |
|  | -11000 | -9000 | -8000 | -10000 | -9500 | -8000 | -7800 | -7200 |
| 60-90 |  | 7500 | 6500 |  |  | 7000 | 6500 | 5500 |
|  |  | -10500 | -9000 |  |  | -9000 | -8700 | -7500 |

**Power range rpm (6 and 8 cylinder engines)**

| Timing | 4000/six | 5000/V8 | 5700/V8 | 7000/V8 |
|---|---|---|---|---|
| 25-65 | 2000-5000 | 2000-5000 | 2000-5000 | 1500-4500 |
| 30-70 | 2500-5500 | 2000-5500 | 2000-5500 | 1700-5000 |
| 35-75 | 3000-5800 | 3000-6500 | 2700-6000 | 2000-5500 |
| 40-80 | 4000-6000 | 4000-7200 | 3500-6700 | 2500-6000 |
| 50-80 | 4500-6500 | 4500-7500 | 4500-7200 | 3000-6500 |
| 55-85 | 4500-7200 | 5500-8500 | 5000-7700 | 3500-7000 |
| 60-90 | 5000-7500 | 6000-9000 | 5500-8500 | 4500-7500 |
| 60-95 |  | 6500-9500 | 6000-9000 | 5000-8000 |

*Note: The above table must be considered as a guide only. Carburation, valve size, porting, valve action (pushrod, ohc, or dohc) and supercharging all influence the power spread.*

velocity up to a certain lift, we have to give the cam extra time to slow the valve train down again, otherwise the tappet will fly off the cam lobe instead of following around the nose. The way we give the cam this extra time is to increase the lift beyond what we require.

This leads us to what we call cam dynamics. FIGURE 5.2 shows a displacement curve,

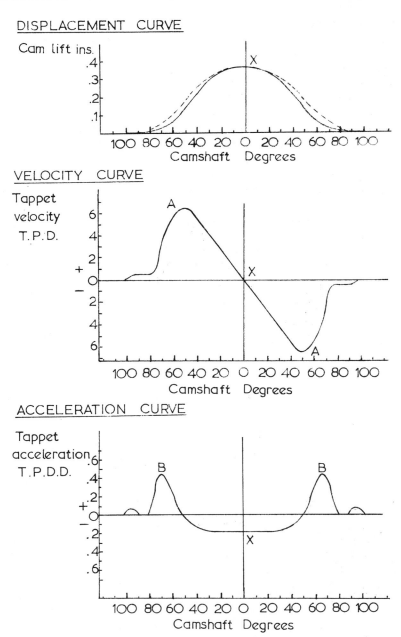

DISPLACEMENT CURVE

VELOCITY CURVE

ACCELERATION CURVE

Fig. 5.2   Camshaft characteristic curves.

a graph of camshaft rotation in degrees relative to the motion of the cam follower. You can readily see that just knowing the duration and lift of a cam will not give a true indication of its performance potential. The dotted line shows a cam of the same timing and lift but with quicker opening and closing times.

The velocity curve is the rate of lift expressed in thousands of an inch per degree of rotation. The most significant parts of this diagram are the maximum velocity points. The maximum velocity of a cam occurs when the cam is contacting the follower nearest its edge. With a given tappet diameter, a maximum practical cam velocity can be used without the cam striking the sharp edge of the cam follower. TABLE 5.2 indicates the maximum velocity for various cam follower diameters. Most high performance cams produce a velocity of 0.007 in per degree (or 7 thousandths of an inch per degree), which is generally within limits, but some racing cams are running 0.009 and up to 0.012 in per degree velocity, which is way above the safe limit for many engines. Once the safe limit is passed, high cam wear and follower breakage is imminent.

The acceleration curve shows us the rate of change of velocity in inches per degree, per degree. As will be explained when we deal with cam 'fingerprinting', this curve is critical in showing factors which affect reliability, as well as information concerning the maximum rpm attainable by the valve train. Negative acceleration determines this maximum rpm. This is the part of the valve train motion which is working against the valve spring, as the lifter is slowing down to go over the nose of the cam. As the engine turns faster and faster, we

## TABLE 5.2   Maximum safe cam and tappet velocity

| Tappet diameter (in) | Cam/tappet velocity (TPD) | Engine application |
|---|---|---|
| 0.780 | 6.63 | |
| 0.800 | 6.8 | Ford Anglia/Cortina |
| 0.812 | 6.9 | B.M.C. 'A' Series |
| 0.842 | 7.16 | Oldsmobile 260/455, Chevy 6 and V8, Holden 6 |
| 0.850 | 7.23 | Cortina/Escort (Kent motor) |
| 0.874 | 7.43 | English Ford 3000 V6, American Ford 6 and V8 |
| 0.904 | 7.68 | American Motors 6 and V8, Chrysler 6 and V8. |
| 0.921 | 7.83 | Oldsmobile 1967 model 400/425 |
| 0.941 | 8.0 | VW Type 4 |
| 0.960 | 8.16 | Replacement Chevy mushroom tappet |
| 0.980 | 8.33 | |
| 1.000 | 8.5 | Replacement Ford V8 mushroom tappet |
| 1.060 | 9.01 | |
| 1.100 | 9.35 | |
| 1.125 | 9.56 | |
| 1.155 | 9.82 | VW |
| 1.186 | 10.08 | Morris 1500 and 1750 ohc |
| 1.200 | 10.2 | |
| 1.300 | 11.05 | |
| 1.375 | 11.69 | Lotus/Ford twin cam Jaguar, Alfa Romeo dohc |
| 1.400 | 11.9 | |

reach a point where the force generated by the mass of the valve train equals that generated by the valve spring in the valve open position. Any further increase in rpm would cause valve float. A cam profile with the lowest negative acceleration (or deceleration) will allow the highest rpm potential or allow the use of softer valve springs if that rpm potential is not going to be used. Ideally, negative acceleration should be less than -0.0002, but up to -0.00028 is tolerable (-0.2 to -0.28 thousandths of an inch per degree, per degree).

The two higher positive acceleration peaks are significant in assessing the durability of a cam, since a heavy valve train combined with high acceleration will cause high cam loading and wear. Valve spring loads in this area are comparatively low, but stresses due to inertia are high. The two smaller positive acceleration peaks are the opening and closing ramps. Maximum positive acceleration may be as high as 0.0006 - 0.0007 in per degree, per degree, (0.6 - 0.7 thousandths of an inch per degree, per degree).

To help you understand what you are looking at, I have marked some points of significance on the three curves. Point 'X' is the nose of the cam, where full lift occurs. Point 'A' is where maximum velocity is reached, and 'B' indicates the point of maximum acceleration. 'A' is also where cam lobe contact is at its farthest from the centre of the tappet. We call this the point of maximum eccentricity.

Quality and grinding accuracy are both very important considerations in buying a high performance camshaft, but unfortunately you don't always get them. An inaccurately ground cam will lose you a lot of power, cause tuning problems, induce early valve float and cause premature lobe and lifter wear. Fortunately there is a way of not only checking out the cam, but also of delving into its actual profile, to produce the curves shown in FIGURE 5.2. All that is needed is to set the cam up in a lathe or rest it on a set of V-blocks. A 0.5 in dial indicator is then attached to one of the lobes and a degree wheel bolted to the cam. I always check my racing cams on the two lobes in the middle and also No 1 intake and exhaust lobe for comparison. If the cam is bent, or if it has been forced against the grinding wheel, this will show up more on the centre lobes. When I find a cam to be outside the tolerances mentioned, I return it to the grinder for replacement.

With the cam set up so that it can rotate between centres, and with the 360° degree wheel bolted up, set a fixed pointer next to the degree wheel and position the dial indicator to read off the desired lobe. It is best to make a fixture to hold the actual lifters you will use with that cam and set the dial indicator up to read off the lifter. For most purposes you can check the cam every 0.005 - 0.010 in of lift.

It is very important to set up the dial indicator accurately and solidly. With this done, and the cam rotated so that the lifter is on the base circle, zero the dial indicator. Rotate the cam to lift and lower the cam follower at least six times to verify that the indicator returns to zero with the follower on the base circle. If it doesn't return to zero either the lifter is sticking or the indicator is not mounted solidly.

The first thing we want to check is base circle runout. This should be around 0.001 in; certainly more than 0.002 in is unacceptable. Next we check the actual timing and lift. The cam grinder should indicate how he arrives at his claimed timing figures. Some measure the duration as starting and finishing when lift is 0.020 in, and others measure a few degrees past the end of the clearance ramp, where lifter acceleration is positive. Many are now specifying a timing figure for 0.050 in lift, which is better as we are well off the ramp at this stage and so the figures are more accurate. I work to a tolerance of ±1° of the stated opening and closing points and ±0.002 in of the rated lift. Remember the cam duration is only half the advertised

124 duration, which is measured off the crankshaft.

After these basic checks we get down to the nitty-gritty of profile curves. As shown in TABLE 5.3, we record the cam angle for every 0.010 in lift. Once we have a full set of figures for that lobe we can set about computing the velocity and acceleration figures. You will note these figures are placed between the basic lift and angle reading. The third column will be the change in degrees for each 0.010 in lift ($\Delta^0$). The fourth column is lift velocity expressed in thousandths of an inch per degree of rotation (TPD). To find the TPD figures simply divide each $\Delta^0$ into 10. The fifth column is the change in TPD ($\Delta$TPD). This tells us the amount the velocity of lift is changing for each 0.010 in of lift. The final column is for acceleration which we call TPDD or thousandths of an inch per degree, per degree and is worked out using the formula

$$TPDD = \frac{\Delta TPD}{\Delta^0}$$

The acceleration figures show us the accuracy of the profile. If the figures jump all over the place this may indicate grinding wheel chatter marks, or it may indicate polydyne correction in the cam design. The machine that grinds cam lobes traces the pattern from a larger master cam. The grinding wheel is controlled by a spring loaded roller that rides on the master cam as it rotates. If the operator feeds the grinding wheel against the cam too rapidly, the roller can be forced off the master cam. This results in a cam profile that does not conform to that of the master cam.

Polydyne correction is a different kettle of fish. It is a designed correction factor that has been planned to correct some valve train problem. It is because most valve trains are not rigid enough (due to pushrod flex, camshaft flex etc) that polydyne correction is used. What this correction really does is to accelerate the lifter, then drop back, and then accelerate again. This is done to give the valve train a chance to 'catch up' so that it is not overstressed. If you find your velocity and acceleration figures are regular and consistent with, say, four or six of these bumps in one full rotation, then you can assume the cam profile has polydyne corrections.

To help in determining this I always draw up an acceleration curve. This will help determine if the 'bumps' are to a set pattern. A golden rule of cam design is that the area

### TABLE 5.3    Cam profile table (in part)

| Cam lift (in) | Angle | $\Delta^0$ | tpd | $\Delta$tpd | tpdd |
|---|---|---|---|---|---|
| 0.010 | 101.6° | | | | |
| | | 7.6 | 1.32 | 0.90 | 0.118 |
| 0.020 | 109.2° | | | | |
| | | 4.5 | 2.22 | 0.72 | 0.160 |
| 0.030 | 113.7° | | | | |
| | | 3.4 | 2.94 | 0.51 | 0.150 |
| 0.040 | 117.1° | | | | |
| | | 2.9 | 3.45 | 0.55 | 0.189 |
| 0.050 | 120.0° | | | | |
| | | 2.5 | 4.00 | 0.76 | 0.304 |
| 0.060 | 122.5° | | | | |
| | | 2.1 | 4.76 | 0.80 | 0.381 |
| 0.070 | 124.6° | | | | |
| | | 1.8 | 5.56 | 0.69 | 0.383 |
| 0.080 | 126.4° | | | | |

inside the acceleration curve on the positive side must always equal the area inside the curve on the negative side. It is quite logical; if you are going to accelerate something a certain amount, the only way you are going to get it back to a standstill is to decelerate it by the same amount. If the cam does not conform to this rule, you are in for valve problems.

The next problem takes some time to check as we must check each lobe to determine correct indexing. If the cam lobes are not phased (or indexed) at exactly the right angle to each other from cylinder to cylinder, the valve timing of the whole engine will be amiss. I have seen cams with lobes out of phase by up to 15⁰. When checking the phasing I also record the maximum lift for each lobe. As mentioned earlier, I would expect the lift to be within ±0.002 in of the cam grinder's quoted figure and all the lobe centres (full lift angle) should be in phase by ± 1⁰.

This means that a four cylinder engine will have all four inlet lobe centres 90⁰ (±1⁰) apart. Therefore if the firing order is 1 - 3 - 4 - 2 and No 1 lobe centre is at say 70⁰ on the 360⁰ degree wheel, and then No 3 should be at 70⁰ + 90⁰ = 160⁰; No 4 at 160⁰ + 90⁰ = 250⁰ and No 2 at 250⁰ + 90⁰ = 340⁰.

The four exhaust lobe centres should also be 90⁰ apart, but to determine at what angle they should be in relation to the No 1 inlet lobe, we have to go back to the cam timing figures and do some calculations. If the cam had symmetrical timing of 30⁰ - 70⁰/70⁰ - 30⁰ this would mean the valve open period would be 30⁰ + 180⁰ + 70⁰ = 280⁰, measured at the crankshaft, or 140⁰ at the cam. Therefore the inlet lobe centre should be at

$$\frac{280}{2} - 30^0 = 110^0 \text{ ATDC (at the crankshaft)}$$

and the exhaust lobe centre should also be at

$$\frac{280}{2} - 30^0 = 110^0 \text{ BTDC (at the crankshaft)}$$

At the camshaft the No 1 exhaust lobe centre should be

$$\frac{110^0 + 110^0}{2} = 110^0 \text{ ahead of the No 1 inlet lobe.}$$

This would mean, using the above example, that the lobe centre for No 1 exhaust would be at 70⁰ - 110⁰ = 320⁰ (±1⁰) on the 360⁰ wheel. No 3 would be at 320⁰ + 90⁰ = 50⁰; No 4 at 50⁰ + 90⁰ = 140⁰ and No 2 at 140⁰ + 90⁰ = 230⁰. It all looks very complicated on paper, but once you sit down to working it out with a cam and a degree wheel in front of you, it is no problem at all.

The next vital link in the valve train is the cam follower, (also called tappet, lifter or bucket). It has the task of changing the rotating motion of the camshaft to up and down motion. The contact point between the tappet and cam lobe is the most heavily loaded spot in any engine. This loading can be a high as 300,000 lb in², which is one reason why cam followers require very special attention in the high performance or racing engine.

Contrary to popular opinion, cam followers are not flat; in fact they are ground with a spherical radius of 37 - 75 in which means they are around 0.003 in high in the centre. This spherical radius, along with a cam lobe angle of 3 - 6⁰, and the tappet offset from the centre of the lobe, causes the tappet to rotate (FIGURE 5.3). The effect is to reduce cam and tappet wear; in fact if the tappets do not rotate, this part of your trick engine is quite likely to self destruct in around 15 minutes. For this reason I always have the cam followers ground to the required spherical radius whether they are new or used. I have found many new followers to be flat which, while not being as bad as old followers worn concave, means they are not up to the task of providing reliable service with a performance cam.

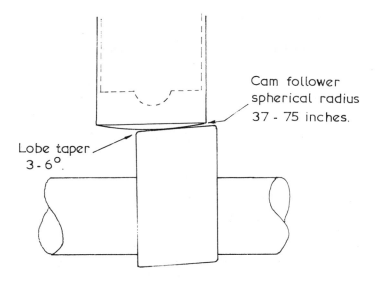

Cam follower
spherical radius
37 - 75 inches.

Lobe taper
3 - 6°.

Fig. 5.3   Cam lobe & tappet design.

Before we take a look at roller tappets it might be as well to examine the basic types of flat tappets. You will note that I do not make mention of the hydraulic lifter because I do not consider it to be a performance set-up. The conventional bucket type flat tappet used in most double overhead cam and a few single overhead cam engines has everything going for it; light weight, large diameter, and small rocking moment. However, manufacturers and service mechanics do not like this simple arrangement because of the tedium of adjusting the valve clearance. The clearance adjustment is made by inserting shims of various thicknesses between the valve stem and bucket. (FIGURE 5.4). This means the cams have to be removed each time valve clearance adjustment is needed and then on being refitted they have to be retimed.

Manufacturers have devised a couple of ways to get around this problem, but in doing this they have created others. The ohc Vauxhall and Chevy Vega both use an adjusting screw with a tapered flat on one side, which does the same job as the adjusting shim. Using an Allen key, the clearance is adjusted by turning the screw in or out. Adjustments must be made in full turns as the screw has a flat only on one side.

The system used by Fiat on its double overhead cam engines and now also by Audi (Fox), Cosworth (Chevy Vega), and virtually every manufacturer of twin cam motorcycles, has a shim recessed in the top of the tappet. To adjust the clearance, a special tool is used to compress the valve spring. The shim can then be flicked out of the recess and another shim of the required thickness fitted.

While both designs have simplified valve adjustment, the weight of the bucket tappet has in some cases been doubled, as compared with the conventional bucket tappet and shim. This is not such a problem on more mundane motors like the Vauxhall and Vega, but the high revving motorcycles and Cosworth Vega are a different matter. The extra weight of the valve train imposes a higher load on the valve springs, and this lowers the valve float rpm drastically. To combat this, valve spring pressures must be increased. An increase in spring pressures soaks up power and increases valve train flex and wear. Another problem is that 127

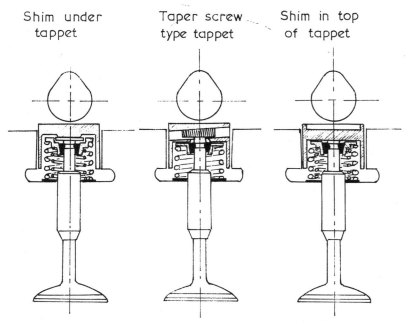

Fig. 5.4  Bucket tappet clearance  adjustment systems.

of valve float, which affects mainly the two-valve-per-cylinder motorcylces, which have the additional problem of heavy valves. Missed gear changes or deceleration over-revving allow the adjusting shims to flick out of the buckets, with disasterous consequences. The only way around the problem, and it should only be a problem in competition engines, is to fit the lighter, conventional bucket tappet and shim. When this is done, special valve spring retainers will be required to keep the shim in position between the valve stem and tappet.

This problem of the adjusting shim jumping out of position can also occur with the conventional bucket tappet and shim, but it is very unusual. In this instance valve float allows the shim to move out of the valve spring retainer recess and become wedged between the top of the spring retainer and the tappet. Instead of the valve closing, it is held open maybe 0.200 in, whereupon the piston bangs into the valve and proceeds to destroy the motor. The more usual problem with the conventional bucket and shim is due to shims which have been ground with faces that are not perfectly parallel. When this happens, the shim rotates in an eccentric path which wears away the top of the valve spring retainer. As a consequence, the retainer collapses and allows the valve to drop into the piston. To ensure this does not happen, measure all adjustment shims of this type with a micrometer, to ensure their faces are parallel within 0.0003 in. Also make sure the shims are of almost the same diameter as the recess in the valve spring retainer.

The conventional flat tappet used in nearly all push-rod type engines is now losing ground to the mushroom tappet, and for obvious reasons. Earlier, we discussed the relationship between cam velocity (and eccentricity) and tappet diameter. We are able to increase the eccentricity of a cam by increasing the tappet diameter. Unfortunately, most blocks cannot be enlarged to accept larger diameter tappets, so the next best thing is to make the face of the tappet larger.

128

**TABLE 5.4    Engine dynomometer results of 350 Chevy using flat tappet, mushroom tappet and roller tappet camshafts.**

Test 1    Flat tappet 0.842 in dia

| rpm | hp | torque (lbf ft) |
|------|------|------|
| 4500 | 346 | 404 |
| 5000 | 401 | 421 |
| 5500 | 462 | 441 |
| 6000 | 506 | 443 |
| 6500 | 541 | 437 |
| 7000 | 569 | 427 |
| 7500 | 567 | 397 |

Test 2    Mushroom tappet 0.960 in dia

| rpm | hp | torque (lbf ft) |
|------|------|------|
| 4500 | 362 | 423 |
| 5000 | 415 | 436 |
| 5500 | 471 | 450 |
| 6000 | 515 | 451 |
| 6500 | 547 | 442 |
| 7000 | 572 | 429 |
| 7500 | 570 | 399 |

Test 3    Roller tappet

| rpm | hp | torque (lbf ft) |
|------|------|------|
| 4500 | 382 | 446 |
| 5000 | 430 | 452 |
| 5500 | 479 | 457 |
| 6000 | 525 | 460 |
| 6500 | 556 | 449 |
| 7000 | 574 | 431 |
| 7500 | 569 | 398 |

Enlarging the tappet diameter means we can increase cam velocity, which results in a gain of around 15% in area under the displacement curve while retaining the same cam duration and lift. This means we can improve performance due to the 15% flow improvement without the disadvantage of a loss of mid-range power if a hotter, long duration, long overlap cam were fitted to give us the same 15% increase. If you take a look at TABLE 5.4 you will see what this means in actual performance. The motor in this instance is a 350 Chevy set up with good mid-range power in mind for road circuit racing. Each cam was chosen to give the best compromise between maximum power and midrange power. The inlet rocker arms were changed to 1.6:1 ratio arms to increase inlet valve acceleration. At 7000 rpm you will note there is very little difference in maximum power between the three cams. However, down at 5000 rpm and below, you can see the power margin widening. This is due to the difference in valve opening rates of each type of cam. All three cams were close to $310^0$ duration and 0.400 in lobe lift. Of course, if we had wanted more top end power, while retaining the same bottom end power as with the flat tappet cam, we could have achieved this too with the mushroom tappet and roller tappet cams. Many cam grinders are producing high velocity cams for use with mushroom tappets, so take a good look at this performance route before resorting to the more expensive roller tappet set-up.    129

If your sport requires the use of over 8500 rpm from a push rod type engine, or super low end power, then roller tappets are the trick set-up. More radical cams can be used as the cam velocity can be increased past that possible with flat or mushroom tappets. Because the roller, by its very nature, rolls over the cam, lobe scuffing is virtually eliminated, which leads to longer cam and lifter life. To gain full benefit from the roller tappet and cams rev potential (10,000 rpm for the small block Chevy V8), greater valve spring pressures are required, so take care to follow the cam manufacturer's recommendations carefully. A 'rev kit' will be required to provide the proper tappet preload for high rpm operation. The rev kit consists of an extra set of springs that fit between the tappet and the head. This loads the tappet during the valve closed period and keeps it in contact with the cam.

Two requirements for an efficient valve train are light weight and rigidity. In the high performance engine you need the light weight to allow an increase in operating rpm and rigid parts to ensure accurate valve operation to attain the desired rpm. Pushrods and rockers require particular attention to both of these important but conflicting ideals. Where possible, I always replace pushrods with those made of aircraft grade seamless 4130 chrome-moly steel tubing, heat treated to 120,000 psi tensile strength. These must be of the correct length to maintain correct rocker arm geometry.

Basically, rocker arm geometry is correct when the centre of the rocker arm tip coincides exactly with the centreline of the valve stem, with the valve lifted 40 - 50% of its total lift. If this is not the case, the valve guide will wear oval very quickly, due to the increased side thrust. This can cause valve seating and valve burning problems. Rocker arm geometry may be upset by the installation of a high lift cam, or high ratio rocker arms, but may also be changed by head and block deck milling.

Also to be considered at this point are pushrod guide plates. If the standard plates have a history of breakage, replace them with plates of a better design or made of better material. Any motor that has ball fulcrum type rockers must be fitted with guide plates if reliability is to be maintained. As well as allowing up and down motion, these rockers unfortunately engage in a side to side motion, which does a great job of wrecking the valve guides. The only way to curtail this sideways twist is to install pushrod guide plates. Generally, I have found standard motors, not fitted with guide plates, to have twice as much valve guide wear in line with the cylinder head (180⁰) rather than across the head. You can imagine how much more the valve is going to be pushed sideways after we fit stiffer valve springs and increase the cam acceleration rate when we have problems with the standard arrangement. Remember when you fit guide plates that hardened pushrods will have to be fitted to prevent rapid pushrod wear.

Next in line for scrutiny are the rocker arms. These transmit the lifter motion to the valve and may be pressed steel or forged items. Generally, forged rocker arms are reasonably rigid and will do a good job in a high performance engine, with some modification. The rocker should be lightened with a view to retaining the vertical section while reducing the horizontal section. The rocker does most of its work directly in line with the pushrod and valve stem centres so in most instances material can be removed without weakening the component. The area over the valve stem must be left wide enough to give full valve stem contact. The shank of the rocker should be left alone except to remove 'dingle berries'. Shot peening is to be recommended in racing applications. Obviously there is no point in removing material close to the rocker shaft as this mass is of no consequence.

Most forged rockers are supported by a light steel rocker shaft and posts of steel or light alloy. The BMC Mini-type shaft and posts are about as rigid as possible in production form.

However, the same cannot be said of the four cylinder English Fords, which leave a lot to be desired in this department. If any modification is intended for one of these, no matter how mild, the alloy rocker posts must be thrown in the garbage can and replaced by more rigid steel posts. The use of a moderately hot cam will also make it necessary to use a heavy duty steel rocker shaft. The ultimate is without doubt the Piper integral rocker box, which supports the outer ends of the shaft very effectively.

The separation springs fitted between the rockers should be replaced by tubular sleeves made of steel. While doing this, pay attention to fitting sleeves of the correct length to centralise the rockers over the valves.

Pressed steel rocker arms are another story. While they have been used with some fairly warm cams, I do not like them, and I would not use them in any motor fitted with anything wilder than a sports cam. The alternative is expensive but well worth it. These are made of aircraft quality, extruded high density aluminium or forged steel, and are fitted with needle roller bearings and a roller tip. Assuming your rocker geometry is correct, these roller rockers will reduce valve guide wear by 'rolling' over the valve stem as it pushes the valve open. The standard rockers scuff the valve to the side, which wears the stem and valve guide. Generally I have found roller rockers reduce the oil temperature of Chevys by up to $20^0$F, due to reduced friction, which means we are picking up power as well.

### TABLE 5.5   Replacement rocker arms

| Engine | Standard ratio | Alternative ratio |
|---|---|---|
| American Motors 290 - 401 | 1.6:1 | 1.7:1 |
| BMC 'A' series | 1.25:1 | 1.4:1 |
| Buick V6 | 1. 5:1 | 1.6:1 (heads modified to fit Chevy arms and studs) |
| Chevy: Small block | 1.5:1 | 1.6:1, 1.65:1, 1.7:1* |
| Chevy: Big block | 1.7:1 | 1.8:1, 1.65:1, 1.6:1, 1.55:1 |
| Ford Cleveland | 1.73:1 | 1.63:1 |
| Ford Big block 332-428 | 1.76:1 | 1.66:1 |
| VW 1200-1500 | 1.23:1 | 1.45:1, 1.5:1, 1.6:1 |

* requires offset studs

Ball type rockers require attention when high lift cams are installed, to ensure adequate working clearance between the end of the slot in the rocker arm and the rocker stud. This clearance should be measured using a wire 0.030 in thick (a paper clip is fine), with the valve closed and also at full lift (FIGURE 5.5).

An absolute must is to replace pressed-in rocker studs with screw-in studs, if a racing cam is going to be fitted. Many push-in studs are marginally stable even with the standard cam and valve springs (eg. English V6 Capri) so if the standard cam is being retained, or if a sports cam is being fitted, at the very least the push-in studs should be pinned. When screw-in studs are being fitted, seal them with gasket sealant, to prevent water seepage if they break into the water jacket.

If possible, $\frac{3}{8}$ in rocker studs should be replaced with $\frac{7}{16}$ in studs, to improve rigidity. A rocker stud girdle is a good investment too as these brace all the rocker studs against each 131 other. This reduces the load on each stud and consequently the amount of flex, as all studs share the load when a valve is opened. With canted valve heads it is not always possible to brace all the studs together, using a single girdle, but generally two studs can be girdled together for load sharing. Some girdles use a single brace bar with 'U' bolts clamping the bar to each stud. This type does a reasonable job but I prefer a double brace bar girdle for added rigidity. With proper setting up, it is possible to make pushrod type valve gear almost as rigid as single ohc valve gear employing rockers. Some ohc motors are, in fact, a joke; their valve train is so poor.

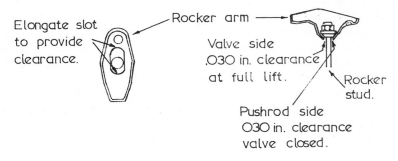

Fig. 5.5   Rocker arm clearance check.

Generally, rocker arms have a ratio of 1.2 - 1.7:1. This means that rocker arms with a 1.5:1 ratio will lift the valve a theoretical 0.600 in if the cam lift is 0.400 in. Many racers get carried away fitting rocker arms of a higher ratio than standard, to increase maximum valve lift. This is not the purpose of the exercise at all. What we are after is to lift the valve off its seat faster in the initial stages of opening, to improve mixture flow and cylinder filling. The actual increase in maximum lift is of little consequence except to cause us more problems with valve spring coil bind, valve to piston clearance etc.

High ratio arms are different from their standard counterparts by having a shorter distance from the pushrod centre to the rocker stud (or shaft). The distance between the rocker stud (or shaft) and valve stem is fixed (unless the rocker studs are repositioned or offset studs are fitted) so the only way we can increase the rocker ratio is decrease the rocker arm length on the pushrod side. For this reason possibly the guide slots in the pushrod guide plates and also the holes in the rev kit bar will require elongation to prevent pushrod fouling.

Before fitting high ratio rocker arms, check with your cam grinder regarding what changes will have to be made in the valve train. Remember the velocity and acceleration characteristics of the cam are being changed when the rocker arm ratio is changed, so will the cam, lifters and valve springs be able to handle the extra forces being imposed on them? Too many tuners, and cam grinders too for that matter, feel you can just go ahead and use any rocker arm ratio you wish. If this were the case, life would indeed be much easier. Unfortunately, today camshaft profiles often are not designed for a specific engine with a specific valve train, so rocker arm ratio can be varied without major problems, but check with the cam grinder first. If all cams were designed as an integral part of one specific motor, with a certain specific amount of valve train flex, as they should be, then a change in rocker arm ratio could mean something as drastic as a cam change as well.

Think carefully before changing the standard rockers for high ratio rockers. If you do not need more low end and mid-range power you will be wasting your time fitting them.

Most performance cams give ample total valve lift without having to worry about rocker ratio fiddling. If your valve train is already marginal in the reliability department, a change to high ratio rockers will worsen the problem, so be careful.

The valve springs have the unenviable task of keeping the whole act together and functioning smoothly. Therefore the cam grinder should be able to give you all the information you need to make that camshaft operate as designed in your engine. This must, of course, include the following vital details:-recommended valve spring, installed height and on-seat pressure, and full lift pressure. Also a safe rpm limit should be stated for a valve train set-up as recommended.

Valve springs have to be heavy enough to keep the lifter in constant contact with the cam lobe and allow a possible over-rev from a missed gear change, yet also be light enough so as not to cause excessive cam and lifter wear and valve train flex.

Valve spring surge can cause erratic valve spring behaviour at certain rpm by vibrations set up in the valve train. These vibrations excite the natural frequency characteristics of the spring. When this happens, surge reduces the available valve spring tension by its force opposing the valve spring tension. This can lead to the tappet losing contact with the cam lobe, the end result being possibly valve float and increased valve train wear.

To help overcome the problem, spring manufacturers have used several approaches to dampen surge. One may take the form of a damper coil of flat spring steel which, because of contact with the inside of the coil spring, produces a friction damping effect. Another is the use of counter wound inner springs, with coils wound in the opposite direction to the outer springs. Variable pitch coil springs with a progressively smaller spacing between coils toward the bottom of the spring have proved successful too. Possibly the most common approach, in production engines at any rate, is to completely close up the coils at the bottom of the spring, and also sometimes at the top as well.

The natural frequency of the valve spring should be five times that of the engine rpm. Therefore if the engine speed is 7500 rpm the valve springs should have a natural frequency of around 37,500 cycles per minute. Interestingly, reducing the number of working coils (ie. those not wound so close as to touch together) increases the natural frequency of the valve spring. This has another benefit to the racing spring manufacturer in that the reduction in working coils will also reduce the solid stack height of the spring. Therefore the spring can be compressed further before coil bind occurs.

Just how much clearance should there be between working coils at full valve lift? That depends on the spring design, but I always work to a minumum of 0.008 in between working coils, although I like to aim for 0.010 - 0.012 in. Some spring manufacturers specify figures as low as 0.005 in and as high as 0.020 in. If they specify a figure higher than my recommendation, follow their instructions. This safe working clearnane between coils must always be maintained, otherwise the valve spring will stack solid with disastrous consequences.

Because of an increase in valve lift, many heads will require modification to prevent this coil bind condition when a high lift cam is installed. Others may not require the valve spring seat to be deepened but may require the valve guides to be slimmed down to permit the installation of inner springs. Either operation can be performed with a counterboring tool of the appropriate dimensions. To determine how much deeper (if at all) the spring seats must be machined, it will be necessary to fit the valve and valve spring retainer and locks. Pull the retainer up tight and measure the distance between the spring seat and 133 bottom face of the retainer. If the measurement is less than the valve open or installed spring height specified by the cam grinder, it will be necessary to deepen the seat. This must be repeated for each valve and must be repeated each time the valves are replaced or refaced, or if the valve seats are recut.

If the valve springs are set up at the on-seat height specified (and they should be otherwise your full lift spring pressures will be all over the place, possibly allowing valve float), then you should not have any problems maintaining the correct clearance between coils. However, check the clearance at full lift, using a feeler guage to be sure, and don't forget to check the inner springs.

On overhead cam motors using bucket type cam followers it is not possible to check for coil bind by using a feeler gauge between the coils. What you must do in this instance is to count the number of working coils and multiply by the required clearance between each coil. If this works out to be, say, 0.036 in, insert a feeler gauge of this thickness between the cam lobe and follower and turn the cam over to full lift. The cam may lock up before full lift, which would indicate insufficient working clearance. To rectify this, the valve spring seat will have to be machined deeper. Just how much the seat will have to be machined can be found by inserting progressively thinner feeler blades until the cam will turn freely. If the cam turned with a 0.023 in blade inserted, this would mean the spring seat must be deepened by 0.036 - 0.023 in = 0.013 in. This procedure should be repeated for each valve spring.

While we are on the subject of bucket tappets there is another very important clearance check which must be made. When high lift cams are installed, it is possible for the tappet to run out of travel and bang into the head. To check for suficient travel it will be necessary to fit just the cams and tappets to the head (leaving out the valves and springs). Turn the cam over by hand until you have a lobe in the full lift position and see if you can fit 0.060 in thickness of feeler strips between the nose of the cam lobe and the face of the cam follower. If you can fit only 0.052 in of feeler strips, you will need to remove 0.008 in from the lower edge of the tappet. Carry out this check on every tappet. Up to 0.015 in can be removed from the tappet. If more material needs to be removed, it is better to machine the head. Put a nice radius on the lower edge of the bucket after any maching is done.

Remember valve springs wear out. On a competition motor this ageing process may cause the spring to break or it may lose tension and become weaker. If you are a racer, check the spring tension each time the head is removed. The pressure at the on-seat and full open lengths should check out within a few pounds of new springs. If not, the spring should be removed.

Many people are rather mystified by any reference to spring rate so it might help to explain just what it is and how we work it out. Firstly, spring rate is defined as the amount of build up in pressure when the spring is compressed. For example, if we had a spring with an on-seat pressure of 100 lbs @ 1.625 ins and in full lift pressure of 300 lbs @ 1.125 in, it would have a spring rate of 400 lb per in, which would mean that we would require a load of 400 lb to compress the spring one inch. In the above example, compressing the spring 0.5 in (1.625 - 1.125 in) resulted in the spring pressure increasing from 100 lb to 300 lb, an increase of 200 lb. Therefore compressing the spring one inch instead of 0.5 in would require a load of 400 lb.

This should help you to appreciate the need to set up valve springs at the precise specified height. If the springs in the case quoted were set too high, this could reduce the on-seat pressure to, say, 70 lb, so the full lift pressure would now be 270 lb, or 10% less than it should have been. In terms of rpm reduction this would reduce valve float rpm to 7115 if the valve float rpm with correctly installed springs had been 7500 rpm.

$$\sqrt{\frac{270}{300}} \times 7500 = 7115 \text{ rpm}$$

When the on-seat height is more than specified, shims of the appropriate thickness must be installed under the valve spring, to compress the spring to the correct height. To measure this height between the valve spring seat and valve cap accurately, a vernier caliper should be used, or you may prefer to use a telescopic gauge and transfer the measurement to a vernier caliper or micrometer.

Sometimes it is possible, and desirable, to increase the rpm at which valve float will occur. Providing the valve train and camshaft are capable of running a higher speed (check with your cam grinder), stronger valve springs will have to be installed. To find the required full lift pressure of the new springs, use the following formula:

$$NP = \frac{Nrpm^2 \times P}{rpm^2}$$

where NP = the new valve spring pressure required.

P = the present valve spring pressure at full lift.

N rpm = new valve float rpm

rpm = the present valve float rpm.

A decrease in effective valve train weight will also increase the valve float rpm limit. We can bring about this decrease by using lightweight, high strength pushrods, by tappet lightening and by fitting light rocker arms or lightening the original rocker arms. Remember though that a decrease in rocker arm weight close to the pivot point does not effectively decrease the valve train weight. The intake and exhaust valves too are effectively lightened when modified to improve flow. However, using a titanium-aluminium-vanadium alloy allows us to lose 35% of the inlet valve's weight. This material is not suitable for exhaust valves, but austenitic stainless steel exhaust valves with hollow stems are around 20% lighter than their counterparts. An effective decrease of 10% would increase the valve float rpm by the factor

$$\sqrt{\frac{100}{90}} = 1.054$$

Therefore if the old valve float speed was 7500 rpm, the new valve float rpm will be 7500 × 1.054 = 7900.

The valve spring retainers and collets (or valve stem locks) require our attention to maintain reliability. A valve stem and collet design that is to be avoided is that used in many BMC engines (FIGURE 5.6). This design is very bad, as the stress concentration at the square shoulder of the collet groove is sure to cause failure. Another problem design is the one where the two collets actually butt together and allow the valve stem to lie loosely and float in the centre of them. This is done to allow the valve more freedom to rotate and clean the valve seat. What has to be done is to grind off the faces of the collets so that they tightly clamp on to the valve stem. When fitted, there must be a gap between both halves of the collet for this to be possible.

Standard spring retainers and stem locks will do a good job, but for ultimate reliability and a weight saving, special pieces should be fitted. Titanium alloy retainers are the lightest/strongest available. Steel retainers of heat-treated 4140 bar stock are the next best, 135

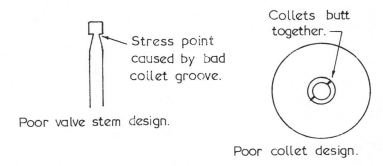

Fig. 5.6    Bad valve & collet designs.

but heavier. I do not like aluminium retainers, and consequently do not recommend their use except in relatively unstressed conditions.

The next check which must be made is for interference between the bottom of the valve spring retainer and the top of the valve guide, in the simulated full valve lift condition. There must be at least 0.060 in clearance at full lift but I always aim for 0.100 in. This clearance check can be done very easily without the heads being fitted to the motor. All that must be done is to set up a telescopic gauge or a snap gauge at the full open valve spring height, then fit the retainers to each valve and check out the clearance between the retainer and valve guide when the snap gauge is fitted in between the retainer and valve spring seat. If there is less than 0.060 in clearance, metal will have to be machined from the valve guide.

Going back to the camshaft, we require some accurate and reliable means of driving it. Several methods are in use, but none are without their problems. For many years cams have been driven by single row chains. These have proved themselves reliable in very high speed racing engines, with open valve spring pressures of 250 lb, but at high engine speeds, chain and sprocket wear is a problem. Double row chains are more up to the job and can successfully handle open valve spring pressures of around 420 lb in excess of 8000 rpm. Note that we are talking about quality roller chains and steel sprockets here, not the silent Morse chain running on fibre or nylon tooth sprockets. With a new chain and sprockets installed, the valve gear will normally retard the cam by $\frac{1}{2}$ - $1^0$, and as wear takes its toll this retarding will increase. Therefore chain drive cams should be initially set up advanced to compensate for this.

The toothed rubber belt seems to be up to the task, but be very careful never to turn the motor over backwards or you could cause the belt to slip and alter the cam and ignition timing. These belts will not last as long as a good chain, and oil is an enemy, so regular inspection is in order. Stretch will allow cam retarding with this type of drive too, so allowances must be made when setting up the cam.

In some ways gear drive is the ideal system, but there are many complications. Align boring (or tunnel boring) the block will allow the crank gear to mesh tighter, so some system to adjust backlash and meshing depth must be provided. If you had the job of setting the gear mesh on a Ford DFV Formula 1 engine you certainly wouldn't consider gear drive to be the ideal set up. If you change from chain drive to gear drive, and use the simple two gear system, it will be necessary to install a reverse ground cam as the cam will now be turning backwards. A reverse distributor gear will also be required, to keep it turning the correct way. However, in spite of all this, gear drive is the best set-up for a competition motor.

Many motors use gears in standard production form, but generally these are useless, and are not capable of reliable service, even if only a sports cam were fitted. Production type gears are designed with silent operation in mind, so are made of such material as compressed fibre, or nylon coated steel and aluminium. If you intend extracting any type of performance at all out of an engine with gear materials such as these, you are in for trouble. The only way around the problem is to use quality steel gears.

Possibly you may not realise this, but accurate ignition timing and performance also has its beginning with a good cam drive arrangement that will keep the spark in step with piston motion. This is one reason why some ignition systems now work directly off the crankshaft and others use sensor-trigger magnets attached to the flywheel or harmonic balancer. As well as driving the distributor or magnets, the cam also looks after the chores of supplying drive for the oil pump, fuel pump and fuel injection too, if fitted.

Now that we have covered the theory of the camshaft and valve train, let's get down to the actual camshaft installation. At this stage we will assume you have already read the chapter on block preparation and the cam is ready to drop in (if the motor is overhead cam the same information covered in block preparation will apply, but in this instance to the head). You will note the cam is covered with a black coating; this should not be removed except from the bearing journals. Freshly ground steel does not have any oil retention ability, and as lubrication of the high performance cam is of utmost importance during the first few minutes of engine operation when running the cam in, we give the cam a special treatment and coating. I also treat the tappet faces in the same way. This treatment is called Lubriting, Parkerising or Parko-Lubriting. Actually the last name describes the treatment best, but in reverse to the way in which we actually apply it. The cam bearing journals are taped and the cam is plunged into a high temperature bath. Phosphoric acid etches open the pores of the cam so that it may retain oil more effectively. This is the Lubriting part of the process. Next the cam receives a phosphate coating to aid break-in.

To assist lubrication even further, I always coat the cams and lifters with a mixture of high pressure Hypoid 90/140 gear oil and moly disulphide or, if the engine will be running on castor oil, I use Castrol R40, as castor oil must not be contaminated by mineral or synthetic oils. The first 10 to 15 minutes is the critical running-in period and during this time engine speed should be maintained at 2000 - 2500 rpm, to ensure adequate oil flow to the cam and lifters. Some engines, notably the pushrod and ohc Cortina/Pinto, require special care, and in their case high performance cams should be run-in for around 25 - 30 minutes and racing cams for 40 - 45 minutes. After this, the racing cam should be given more treatment, a 4000 - 5000 rpm run for 10 - 15 minutes, but taking care not to let the engine overheat.

After the cam has been slid into place, fit the thrust plate (or thrust washers) and measure the end-float. This should be 0.002 in; more than 0.005 in is unacceptable.

If we do not control 'cam walk' within fine limits, we can upset the whole valve train. Remember flat tappet cams have the lobes ground at an angle, which tends to push (or thrust) the camshaft as the lobes open and close the valves. This thrusting backwards and forwards also has a bad influence on the ignition timing as the distributor is usually driven off the camshaft. When mushroom tappets are used, we can have the problem of the tappets overlapping two cam lobes if cam walk is not precisely controlled.

The next thing we must do is time the cam so that the opening and closing of the valves is in a special 'tuned' relationship with the up and down motion of the pistons. Unfortunately, many feel it is just enough to line up the timing marks and leave the valve timing at that. With a sports cam that may be so, but you will not be able to achieve optimum performance. Due to manufacturing tolerances the cam may be several degrees advanced or retarded. This may be the result of timing marks being just slightly out, or a keyway or dowel may be out. Then too, the cam lobes can be out in relation to the cam dowel or keyway, due to grinding error.

Something else which we must take into consideration is this. Even if the cam timing was spot on according to the manufacturers figures, just by lining up the timing marks, would that necessarily be the best position for the cam for best overall performance? In FIGURE 5.7 we have illustrated three timing diagrams which represent one complete cycle (two revolutions or 720$^0$) of the engine. The first diagram indicates the cam has symetric (or split) timing of 30$^0$ - 70$^0$/70$^0$ - 30$^0$. You will also note the inlet valve is fully open (maximum lift) at 110$^0$ after TDC and the exhaust valve is fully open 110$^0$ before TDC. The second diagram shows the cam has been advanced 6$^0$ from the manufacturer's recommendation to produce a timing of 36$^0$ - 64$^0$/76$^0$ - 24$^0$, with full lift occurring at the inlet 104$^0$ after TDC and at the exhaust 116$^0$ before TDC. In the third diagram the cam has been retarded 4$^0$, with a timing of 26$^0$ - 74$^0$/66$^0$ - 34$^0$. Maximum lift will now be at 114$^0$ after TDC at the inlet and 106$^0$ before TDC at the exhaust valve.

You will note in each instance the duration has remained 280$^0$, the overlap 60$^0$, and the lobe centres 220$^0$ apart. This being the case you are probably wondering why bother 'tuning' the cam timing if duration, overlap, lift and lobe centres stay the same? If you think about it, of course these figures must stay the same; we are not altering the physical shape of the cam. All we are doing is changing its position in relation to the crankshaft. There is an exception to this, and that is in the case of twin overhead cams, where we may advance the inlet cam, say 5$^0$, and advance the exhaust cam 9$^0$, but more on that later.

Basically, advancing the cam will improve bottom end and mid-range power; retarding the cam will decrease bottom end and mid-range power but may very slightly increase the top-end. Around 2$^0$ advance will have very little effect, but from 4$^0$ to 8$^0$ it will show a marked improvement in mid-range power, with some decrease in maximum power. The improvement in the mid-range comes about as a result of a decrease in the reverse pumping action, which raises cylinder pressure. Because the inlet valve is being closed earlier, there is less mixture being pushed back up the inlet port as the piston moves up. As the exhaust valve also is being closed earlier there is less chance of the exhaust gas turning around and being drawn back into the cylnder as the piston descends. Generally, I prefer to run all road and rally engines with the cam 6$^0$ or 7$^0$ advanced. For track work, it depends on the nature of the course. If it is a high speed track I run the cam spot on, but for slow circuits again I use 6 - 7$^0$ advance.

I never advise the retarding of a cam except in one circumstance, and that is due to the machine losing traction because of excessive torque in the low or mid-range. This will usually apply only to drag strip or speedway vehicles. On the strip too much low end may cause excessive wheelspin or rear end location problems. At the speedway an excess of power at some particular engine speed may be causing traction problems on the exit of a particular turn. Retarding the cam 4 - 5$^0$ should help with either annoyance.

With twin cam motors we can do a little more cam tuning, but caution is in order to avoid valve to valve fouling with the more radical racing grinds. For instance, we can retard the inlet cam 4$^0$ to give a little more maximum power and then advance the exhaust cam 6$^0$ to restore the lost bottom end power. Again we may decide to leave the inlet on time and advance the exhaust 6 - 10$^0$. This way top end power will stay the same (or it may increase slightly) and bottom end and mid-range power will improve. To pick up the most low end power we will need to advance the inlet 4 - 7⁰ and also advance the exhaust 6 - 10⁰

When you start jiggling twin cam timing, keep in mind the need to maintain a minimum of 0.060 in clearance between the inlet and exhaust valve. I check this by drawing up the cam displacement curves for both the inlet and exhaust cam. But remember when you draw up the curves that the angles (see TABLE 5.3) for each 0.010 in lift will all have to be multiplied

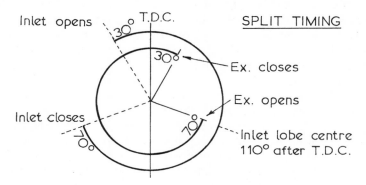

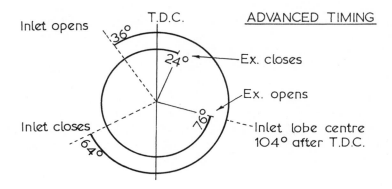

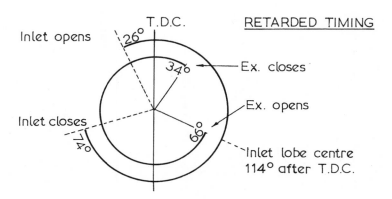

Fig. 5.7   Camshaft timing diagrams.

by two, as the camshaft is turning at half the speed of the crankshaft. Therefore for each revolution (360⁰) the camshaft turns the crankshaft turns twice (720⁰). As we set the cam up in relation to the crankshaft, we now have to know what its valve lift is relative to degrees of crankshaft rotation.

To save time I draw both curves on separate pieces of transparent draughting film, to the same scale. This way I can stick the curves over each other according to whatever lobe centre position I wish to check. To keep things accurate, a third piece of paper is required as a reference or standard, and this piece is placed under the two displacement curves. The reference paper will have just three vertical lines on it. The centre will indicate TDC, the first line will indicate the exhaust lobe centre (full lift position), and the third line will show the inlet lobe centre. These lines will be to the same horizontal scale as the displacement curve horizontal scale. The lobe centre (full lift) positions will be marked in according with cam timing figures given by the cam grinder (FIGURE 5.8).

If the cam grinder has given a lobe centre figure of 102⁰, this means the cams should be set up such that the inlet valve is at full lift 102⁰ after TDC and the exhaust valve is at full lift 102⁰ before TDC. However, if no lobe centre angle is stated, you will have to work it out from the timing figures. Let's say the timing is 53⁰ - 77⁰/82⁰ - 58⁰ for the inlet and exhaust. This would mean the cam had an inlet duration of 53⁰ + 180⁰ + 77⁰ = 310⁰ and an exhaust duration of 52⁰ + 180⁰ = 320⁰. Obviously the lobe centre of the inlet and exhaust has to be 155⁰ (310⁰ ÷ 2) and 160⁰ (320⁰ ÷ 2) respectively after the opening point of each valve. If we subtract the inlet opening angle of 53⁰ from 155⁰, we find the full lift (or lobe centre) position will be 102⁰ after TDC. For the exhaust we subtract the closing angle, 58⁰ from 160⁰, and find the exhaust lobe centre to be 102⁰ before TDC.

Now that you know the lobe centre angles, draw these in as reference lines before and after the TDC line. If you decide to advance the exhaust cam 8⁰, then stick the exhaust displacement curve to the reference sheet with the peak of the curve (see lobe centre) 8⁰ before the exhaust reference line. Similarly, if the inlet is being advanced 4⁰ then stick on the inlet curve with the peak 4⁰ ahead of the inlet reference line. It is only by moving the displacement curves around in relation to the reference lines that the next part of the operation can be accurate.

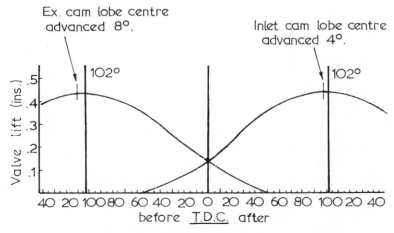

Fig. 5.8 Valve interference checking curves.

Looking at the curves it is obvious the valves will come close to fouling during the overlap period, so what we have to do is make up a list to show us what the inlet and exhaust valve lift will be each $2.5^0$. It is not necessary to record the lift over the entire overlap period; usually $30^0$ on either side of the intersection point of the lift curves is enough. Once the list is made up, then it is necessary physically to measure the clearance between the valves. If at say, $10^0$ after TDC the inlet valve had a lift of 0.180 in and the exhaust had a lift of 0.156 in at the same angle, then accurately set the valves up in the head at those measurements and measure the clearance. As you can see, this involves quite a deal of work, but if you are after that last bit of power and you don't want a wrecked motor, then it is a must.

The procedure just outlined to check twin cam engines for valve fouling can also be used if you are running a pushrod canted valve motor and you wish to increase the rocker arm ratio. Normally, the cam grinder should be able to tell you if you can use that particular cam with say 1.65:1 ratio arms instead of the standard 1.5:1 arms, without risk of the valves coming too close together. However, if he is not able to advise you on this, it will be necessary to draw up a pair of displacement curves for the valve lift with the higher ratio arms and work it all out as for a twin cam.

Now that you know why we advance or retard the cam you are in a good position to set your cam up just where you want it. With the cam fitted, and the timing marks lined up, the next step is to see where the cam is in relation to the crankshaft. In other words, is it advanced or retarded? To check this you will need a degree wheel (8 in is a good size) or a $360^0$ protractor bolted to the nose of the crank. Also you will need a dial gauge to measure the cam lift. You should fix a good solid pointer under a convenient bolt to lap over the face of the degree wheel.

The first thing we must do is accurately find TDC and for this we need another piece of equipment, a positive stop. If you are finding TDC with the heads fitted, the best positive stop is an old spark plug with the insulator removed and a piece of steel rod welded in so that it projects past the thread far enough to stop the piston reaching TDC. An easier way to find TDC is when the head is removed. Then we merely need a piece of steel fixed across the top of the bore to prevent the piston reaching TDC. If the piston does not project out of the top of the bore at TDC it will be necessary to fit a bolt in the middle of the positive stop bar.

With the positive stop fitted, rotate the crank as far as it will go, taking care not to damage the piston as it contacts the stop. Take a note of the angle the pointer is on, and turn the crank in the opposite direction until it stops. Halfway between the two stop angles is TDC so remove the positive stop and rotate the crank to TDC; the halfway point. Now very carefully loosen the degree wheel and turn it around to align the zero mark with the pointer, and lock it in place. To double-check, refit the positive stop and rotate the crank in both directions as before. When the degree wheel is in the correct position, the number of degrees before and after TDC will be identical when the crank stops.

After TDC is found, you can go ahead and check the cam phasing. It is a waste of time trying to set up a cam according to the cam grinder's timing figures. The best way is work out the full lift (or lobe centre) angle and see at what angle you are reaching full lift. If, for instance, the cam had a full lift angle of $110^0$ after TDC, but maximum lift was occuring at $104^0$ after TDC, it would mean the cam in that position is advanced $6^0$.

The cam grinder may supply you checking (or degreeing) timing figures for 0.050 in lift. The cam timing may be $60^0$ - $88^0/96^0$ - $52^0$ and the timing at 0.050 in lift $41^0$ - $69^0/77^0$ - $33^0$. Set up the dial gauge on the lifter or pushrod (not the rocker) and record the angles for 0.050 in lift. Your cam may check out $40^0$ - $70^0/76^0$ - $34^0$, meaning it is retarded $1^0$.

Having determined where the cam is, you may decide to change its phasing, to tune it to your engine. The next problem is just how to do it. With some motors this is easy as they have vernier timing wheels (eg. Jaguar and Alfa-Romeo) or taper fit wheels (Ford BDA). The majority, however, use either dowels or keys to positively locate the cam or crank sprocket.

Dowelled drives will need offset dowels fitted and if more than a central bolt fixes the sprocket to the cam, the bolt holes will require elongation with a round file. The amount of offset required is minute. For example, with the pushrod English Fords and Lotus Twin Cam, 0.006 in offset (at the cam) represents $1^0$ at the crank, so to change the cam position by $6^0$ (at the crank) requires a dowel with 0.036 in offset. Some cam manufacturers, instead of supplying offset dowels, have a range of offset bushes which are fitted to the cam sprocket. Others are able to supply vernier crank sprockets (Pinto) and many American V8s have a range of crank drive sprockets available with three keyways cut to change the cam phasing.

If there is nothing available for your particular engine then you will have to make up the appropriate hardware. Keep in mind that the dowel or key does not require hardening in most instances as it does not actually transmit the driving force. The driving force is taken by the friction between the sprocket and shaft (key located) or by pressure between the sprocket and cam created by the fixing bolts (dowel located). Incidently, these fixing bolts should be locked using Loctite.

With the cam phasing sorted out, the next thing we have to think about is the valve clearance (lash). The cam grinder will supply a clearance for the intake and exhaust valve. Sometimes he will specify a different clearance for different types of valve material. If he gives a 'cold' clearance he means just that; the motor should not have been run in the previous five hours. The 'hot' clearance is for a motor at normal operating temperature; usually 70 - 88$^0$C water temperature, 90 - 100$^0$ oil temperature. It is very important to maintain sufficient valve clearance to allow the valve to seat firmly and to remain on the seat long enough to transfer heat to the cooling medium. Running the valves tight to quieten them is a sure way to get valve burning in a performance engine.

Sometimes we can benefit by changing the valve clearance within reason and according to the type of competition involved. Note we are talking about a competition motor here, not a road or rally motor. We have already pointed out that for serious competition the motor must be set up to suit the track or strip, but our best laid plans can go astray. Say we have set our cam for a particular dirt speedway but as the night progresses the surface begins to break up or the weather turns foul. Obviously you are not going to have time to advance the cam so the only way to pick up some bottom end power in a hurry is to increase the valve lash. This will have the effect of shortening the timing by 3 - 4$^0$ for each 0.001 in the clearance is increased. There is a very definite limit to how far we can go however, as this has the effect of shortening the opening and closing ramps. This could lead to serious shock loads in the valve train. Therefore the clearance should not be increased by more than 0.005 in unless the cam grinder says otherwise. Keep in mind that the valve float limit will now be lowered, so be careful.

If, on the other hand, you find you need more top end power on the night, you can decrease the lash, but this is only feasable for short distance events such as drags, hillclimbs or speedway sprints. Remember, decreasing the lash will increase valve temperatures, so always maintain 75% of the recommended clearance. Also, if you know the valves and seats are getting a bit rough or the guides are shot, do not decrease the clearance at all; you could easily wreck the motor. An increase in valve temperatures, under competition conditions, could cause pre-ignition or detonation. Both are piston and engine breakers.

You must maintain a valve to piston clearance of 0.080 in and 0.100 in respectively for the inlet and exhaust valves. Therefore it will be necessary to set the pistons up with adequate valve cut-outs before you attempt to change the valve clearance or change the cam phasing.

It is surprising how many enthusiasts have little idea of setting valve clearances accurately. Firstly, let me point out that it is impossible to do much of a job if the contact face of the rocker or valve stem tip has a dip worn into it. The feeler blade will be too wide to fit into the dip, so we will not be able to take this wear into account. When we measure the clearance we want to have the lifter fairly close to the centre of the base circle. With most ohc engines it is possible to see when the lifter is on the base circle, but with other types we have to use another method.

The simplest method for in-line engines is visually to divide the engine in half. All the rockers in the front half we number from 1 to 4 (or 1 to 6 if it's a 6 cylinder) and we do likewise for the rear half but this time we start No 1 from the extreme rear of the engine. In this way we have both No 1 rockers at opposite ends of the head, and both No 4 (or No 6) rockers in the middle, alongside each other. As we turn the motor over we always adjust the valve partner to the one that is fully open. Therefore if No 1 at the rear of the motor is fully open, we adjust its partner No 1 at the front of the motor. If No 3 at the front is fully open, we adjust No 3 at the rear, and so on.

With flat and vee motors, the safest way is to turn the motor over and adjust the inlet and exhaust rocker for each cylinder together, midway between the inlet closing point and the exhaust opening point. ie. with the piston at TDC at the end of the compression stroke. If you adjust each cylinder in turn according to the firing order, it will save time turning the motor over unnecessarily.

When adjusting clearances on ohc motors, I have found it simpler and more accurate to adjust the clearance by inserting the feeler strip between the cam and rocker rather than at the valve stem. However, when using this method it is necessary to reduce the clearance because of the effect of the rocker arm ratio. Therefore if the clearance at the valve is normally 0.013 in and the rocker arm ratio is 1.45:1, then the clearance at the cam lobe will be $0.013 \div 1.45 = 0.009$ in.

# Chapter 6
# The Bottom End

ENTHUSIASTS associate high performance with cams, carburettors and exhaust modifications. However, many hidden horsepower can be found by proper attention to blueprinting the bottom end of a motor. An additional consideration is the added reliability we can expect when things are done properly to an exacting specification.

Logically, the place to start is the cylinder block, because it is the home for everything else in or on the engine. First, inspect the water passages for rust or scale. If any is present it will be necessary to have the block boiled in a chemical bath for cleaning. This should be done with all the welch plugs (freeze or core plugs) and oil gallery plugs removed.

A mildly dirty block can be steam cleaned or washed with solvent. At the same time the oilways should be carefully cleaned, using brushes designed for this task. Stud holes, and particularly head and main bearing cap stud holes, deserve the same treatment. Finally high pressure air must be used to clean and dry off everything. Even brand new (green) blocks should be cleaned as outlined, with particular attention to ensure no casting sand has been left in the water passages.

With the block perfectly dry, it can be visually inspected for cracks. A competition block should be crack tested. Next take a plug tap and clean the head stud and main bearing cap threads of dirt or burrs. This is important to get a true stud tension reading. Any stud holes that have not been chamfered should be, to prevent threads pulling up. A pulled head stud thread can cause head gasket sealing problems. A pulled main bearing cap thread can allow a bearing to turn. Finally, check the depth of each hole to be certain the stud will not bottom.

To avoid cuts to yourself and possible engine damage, carefully grind away any casting slag. The main area for concern is around the main bearing webs, the sump pan deck, and in vee motors, around the oil drain back holes and the rest of the valley area.

The next operations involve 'squaring' the block. A check must be made to ensure that the main bearing bores are perfectly aligned. Any misalignment will wreck the bearings and possibly even the crank. It will also soak up a lot of power as the frictional losses are greater. I have found new blocks with up to 0.007 in misalignment, so do not assume that the alignment is correct. Any mis-alignment can be corrected by line-boring. When main bearing caps are replaced by heavy duty items, line-boring will also be necessary. To ensure that alignment is maintained, the main bearing caps should be numbered and have the front position marked. This will assist in fitting each cap in its correct location each time the motor is rebuilt.

With the main bearing bores true, the block should be checked at each corner to guarantee that the distances between the top of the block (the deck) and the crankshaft centreline are identical. If the block is out of true, milling will be required. Even if the deck is true, we may decide to have it decked to reduce the distance between the top of the piston and the top of the block, to increase the compression ratio.

The cylinder bores must be true at $90^0$ to the crank centreline (ie. across the motor) to keep the frictional losses low and maintain good ring sealing. If the bore is canted slightly to the front or the rear, the piston pin will hammer out, so a check must also be made in line (ie. at $180^0$) with the crank. There must not be any steps or taper from the top to the bottom of the bore. (FIGURE 6.1)

Boring and honing should be carried out by a firm with precision equipment able to maintain a tolerance of 0.0003 in. Forget about garages using small boring machines that bolt onto the block as the tolerance can be as bad as 0.002 in.

There are definite limits as to how far a cylinder can be over-bored. If the cylinder walls become too thin, they will warp due to the pressure and heat. A situation like this will allow blow-by past the rings, resulting in lost power. Another problem not often recognised is also due to thin cylinder walls. In a racing motor, or when a long stroke crank is used, the main bearing webs can actually break away from the bottom of the cylinders.

Generally, 0.060 in oversize is about the limit. Some of the English motors will go to 0.150 in oversize, but care must be exercised. Many American motors are limited to plus 0.030 in due to thin wall casting techniques. It is possible to obtain special thick wall racing blocks for some engines. As a bonus these are generally stronger and less prone to flexing, due to the use of a special grade of cast iron.

Motorcycle cylinders are restricted to 0.120 - 0.160 in oversize, depending on the thickness of the steel liners. By boring out the original liners and pressing in new sleeves we can at times go to 0.400 in. This, however, is limited by the bore centres and block rigidity.

Remember there is no benefit to be gained if an increase in bore size will induce cylinder warping or block flexing. Both conditions will rob us of power and lead to reliability troubles. Also to be avoided is the common practice of dry sleeving cylinders to compensate for thin walls or to eliminate water seepage. What generally happens is that the sleeve shifts due to the very thin walls. This may allow water into the sump or result in a blown head gasket. Many tuners feel that sleeving is a good thing as the sleeve always has enough wall thickness not to warp. They forget that a sleeve must be adequately supported.

Even when an engine is not excessively over-bored there is no guarantee you will achieve a massive increase in power. I think most people understand that a 10% increase in cylinder displacement will not yield a corresponding rise of 10% in maximum horsepower. However, few tuners realise just how ill-advised large capacity increases can be in some situations. The point to be remembered is this; it is of no use giving the engine big lungs if the induction system (ie. carburettor, manifold, ports and valves) does not have the capability, or the potential capability, to flow sufficient air to fill those big lungs.

A situation like this is not really a problem if the engine is running in a street car, but in a road race vehicle and particularly in a rally car, this type of over-modification must be avoided because of the disasterous effect it has of compressing the power band. True, the 145 increase in mid-range power is a very important plus in favour of a displacement increase, but if the engine does not have the breathing ability to be able to rev as hard as previously, the increased number of gears changes now necessary may easily reduce the performance level of the car/engine/driver combination to what it was before the capacity jump.

In TABLE 6.1 you can see how the power range was affected on an ohc Vauxhall rally motor when the capacity was raised from 2279 cc to 2496 cc. about a 10% increase. The smaller motor makes good power between 4500 rpm and 7500 rpm, and if need be it can be lugged down to 4000 rpm which gives a very nice 3500 rpm operating range. The 2.5 litre engine is working very well at 4000 rpm (15 hp increase over the 2.3 litre engine) but it runs out of steam at around 6500 rpm, which means that the power band has been narrowed down by 1000 rpm. You will note too that there is only a difference of 1 hp in maximum power between both engines.

In its present form the 2.5 litre motor would not be any better than the smaller engine in a rally car. However, with a lot of development the big motor could prove to be marginally superior. A wilder camshaft raised maximum power to almost 209 hp and enabled the motor to run to 7000 rpm (192 hp) but the mid-range was so badly affected that the power band was narrowed to even worse than before.

After this a 16 valve Lotus head was tried to determine what effect better breathing would have (TABLE 6.2). The small engine has a 3250 rpm power range extending from 5000 rpm to 8250 rpm, while the 2.5 litre motor is best between 4750 and 7500 rpm, a 2750 rpm spread. When a wilder inlet camshaft was fitted (no other changes) this motor ran much better at 7500 rpm (239 hp) and it made 230 hp at 7750 rpm with just a small decrease in mid-range (190 hp at 5000 rpm). Maximum power went up to 253 hp.

Obviously in this instance the 2496 cc motor should be superior, but since that time the Lotus head has been outlawed and the 16 valve Vauxhall head will not, at this stage of development at any rate, perform anywhere near as well (ie. 20 hp less for the 2.3 litre motor.)

Of course not every type of competition machine requires an engine with a good wide spread of power, so large increases in displacement can be made without adversely affecting performance. Therefore if you are involved in rallycross or $\frac{1}{4}$ mile dirt speedway the 2.5 litre Vauxhall in either 8 valve or 16 valve form should prove superior. However, as you can see from both tables, there is no significant increase in maximum power, so to gain any benefit from the big motor the suspension will have to be capable of getting those extra 15-20 mid-

### TABLE 6.1    Dyno test of Vauxhall ohc rally engine

| rpm | 2279 cc engine | | 2496 cc engine | |
| | hp | torque (lbf ft) | hp | torque (lbf ft) |
|---|---|---|---|---|
| 3250 | 100 | 161.6 | 103 | 166.4 |
| 3500 | 108 | 162.1 | 118 | 177.1 |
| 4000 | 127 | 166.7 | 142 | 186.4 |
| 4500 | 136 | 158.7 | 163 | 190.2 |
| 5000 | 170 | 178.5 | 183 | 192.2 |
| 5500 | 185 | 176.6 | 194 | 185.2 |
| 6000 | 199 | 174.2 | 206 | 180.3 |
| 6500 | 202 | 163.2 | 200 | 161.6 |
| 7000 | 205 | 153.8 | 178 | 132.6 |
| 7500 | 197 | 137.9 | | |

range horsepower down onto the track to accelerate the car faster.

During the boring and honing operations, a boring plate should be fitted, along with the head gasket, and tensioned to normal head stud tension. This operation is necessary on racing engines to guarantee perfect bores. The pull of head studs can cause a certain degree of cylinder distortion. When a boring plate is fitted at the specified head tension, the block is distorted during the boring and honing procedure. Therefore the bores will be true when the head is fitted. The main bearing caps, when tensioned, also distort the cylinders, so these should be fitted as well.

I prefer to bore the cylinders to within 0.005 in of the finished size and then hone each cylinder to fit a particular piston. In this way I can keep piston clearances to a tolerance of about 0.0003 in.

The cross-hatch pattern the hone leaves on the cylinder walls is critical. It must be just right if the piston rings are to bed-in quickly and have a long life. I prefer a 45° cross-hatch with a finish of 10 - 12 micro-inches. This type of finish makes it necessary to run the rings in, but they last for a long time and seldom leak. A finish any smoother will not hold enough oil and will allow a glaze to form on the ring face and bore wall. Oil consumption will be a problem and power will be lost, due to blow-by. A rougher finish will usually eliminate the need to bed in the rings; however ring life is greatly reduced. Keep in mind too that glazing can again be a real problem but not due to lack of lubrication. A rough finish acts like a file on the rings; the added friction increases their temperature and allows glazing to form.

The upper and lower lip of each cylinder should be chamfered lightly to remove the sharp edge produced by boring. A smooth cut half-round file will do the job but take care not to let it slip and nick the cylinder wall. While you have the file at hand, lightly dress the sharp edges of the main bearing caps and webs.

Finally, check the mating face on the back and front of the block. They should be square to the crankshaft centre-line.

Two more inspections are necessary for racing engines. The camshaft bearing bores must be in line and each tappet bore must be of the correct diameter and perpendicular to the centre-line of the camshaft. A tappet tipped off centre may easily dig into the lobe of a racing cam, causing premature wear and/or breakage.

About the only other parts of the block we have to give consideration to are the main bearing caps and studs. I use aircraft quality high tensile studs when these are available. Main bearing studs should not be reused on racing engines, and the same applies to big end

### TABLE 6.2   Dyno test of Vauxhall twin cam 16 valve rally engine

| rpm | 2279 cc engine | | 2496 cc engine | |
| | hp | torque (lbf ft) | hp | torque (lbf ft) |
| --- | --- | --- | --- | --- |
| 4250 | | | 139 | 171.8 |
| 4500 | 134 | 156.4 | 154 | 179.7 |
| 5000 | 173 | 181.7 | 195 | 204.8 |
| 5500 | 188 | 179.5 | 212 | 202.4 |
| 6000 | 216 | 189.1 | 236 | 206.8 |
| 6500 | 231 | 186.6 | 251 | 202.8 |
| 7000 | 240 | 180.1 | 244 | 183.1 |
| 7500 | 244 | 170.8 | 234 | 164.2 |
| 8000 | 238 | 156.2 | | |
| 8250 | 232 | 147.7 | | |

bolts. Usually, the standard cast iron main bearing caps are acceptable for medium performance but engines in semi-race tune and hotter require steel caps for reliability. In the very hottest motors I use a main bearing support saddle. This is a one-piece device that supports all the main bearings, taking the place of the individual main bearing caps. It extends out to the oil pan deck and transfers the bearing load, so that it is shared by the outside of the block as well as the main bearing webs.

After all the machining work has been completed, the block should be thoroughly washed with hot, soapy water. Be sure to get all traces of honing grit scrubbed out of the cylinders, using a bristle scrubbing brush. Blow the block dry, using compressed air, and spray all the cylinders, tappet bores and bearing bores with a water dispersant such as WD-40. To assist oil flow back into the oil pan I recommend that the inside of the block be painted with a suitable oil resistant engine paint and sealer.

With the block prepared, we now turn our attention to the crankshaft. The majority of engines use cast nodular iron crankshafts which are suitable for use up to semi-race tune, when balanced. Engines with a higher output will require a Tuftrided cast iron, forged steel, forged nitrided steel, or a billet steel crank, Tuftrided or nitrided in that order of ascending merit.

Assuming the standard crank is suitable, we must have it crack tested before doing any work on it. If it is free from flaws, a check should be made to determine its straightness. Cranks can be straightened but generally it is a waste of time as the pressures of combustion and inertia loads will reverse the straightening process. Because a bent crankshaft increases bearing loads, it must be discarded if bent by more than 0.002 in.

Next measure each main bearing and crank pin journal. Remembering that crank journals wear oval, measure the diameter at several angles around the journal. Also measure at each end and in the middle of every journal, as wear can vary along the journal. Ovality and taper should be less than 0.0003 in in a high performance or racing crank. If the wear is greater than this, grinding the journals undersize will be necessary. However, grinding weakens the crankshaft, so a crank replacement may be necessary in high horsepower and high rpm engines. When the crankshaft is machined, instruct the grinder to pay close attention to maintaining the fillet radii specified by the manufacturer (FIGURE 6.2). Any reduction in the fillet radius will weaken the crankshaft. On the other hand an increased radius serves to strengthen the shaft. This should not be overdone or we can arrive at a situation where the big end or main bearings are locking on to the fillet.

Any casting slag should be ground off the crank and the area dressed. These slag spots can become a stress raiser or future failure point.

To assist in the smooth operation of the motor and reduce bearing inertia loading, the crankshaft should be dynamically balanced. Balancing will increase the life of the crankshaft as a result of a reduction in the shock loading and vibration to which any imbalance would give rise.

Some manufacturers list Tuftrided replacement crankshafts. They are excellent for high performance road and rally engines. These can be used in racing motors but I would suggest a strict eye be kept on rpm limits and that they be crack tested each 300 miles.

Standard cast iron cranks can be Tuftrided but there is quite a deal of risk involved. Any ferrous metal object can be Tuftrided, but as the process requires immersion in a chemical bath at a temperature of 1060°F for 180 minutes, internal stress can lead to deformation. Cast iron crankshafts are susceptible to bending and changes in the journal diameters. Ford and British Leyland scrap 40% of their Tuftrided cranks so I feel it a better

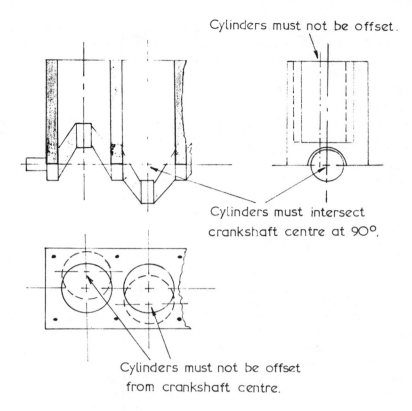

Cylinders must not be offset.

Cylinders must intersect
crankshaft centre at 90°.

Cylinders must not be offset
from crankshaft centre.

Fig. 6.1 Cylinders must be accurately bored.

proposition to buy a pretreated crank as in general they are not very much more expensive than a standard cast iron shaft.

To check whether a crank has been Tuftrided, use an ordinary medium cut file and attempt to file metal off one of the webs. If this presents no difficulty, the metal has not been specially treated. If, on the other hand, the file does not easily bite into the crank, but instead tends to skate across the surface, then it is probable that the crankshaft has been Tuftrided. A treated crank will not be harmed, so should a salesman refuse to let you carry out this test, shop elsewhere.

There is a good deal of misunderstanding about the Tuftriding process so I will explain the benefits that it will impart to a treated object. Contrary to popular opinion, it does not increase the core strength of the component. The Tuftride bath, composed primarily of cyanide and cyanate compounds, releases specific quantities of carbon and nitrogen in the presence of ferrous materials such as cast iron and alloy steel. Nitrogen is more soluble than carbon in these metals and diffuses into the component while the carbon forms iron-carbide particles at or near the surface. These particles act as a nuclei, precipitating some of the diffused nitrogen to form a tough compound zone of carbon-bearing epsilon iron nitride.

The compound zone, (0.0003 - 0.0005 in deep in treated cast-iron) is tough and very resistant to wear, galling, seizing and corrosion. The nitrogen diffusion zone (0.0008 - 0.014 in deep in treated cast iron) underlying the tough compound zone is responsible for the 149 improved fatigue properties. This fatigue resistance is the most important value of the Tuftride process in the racing engine. The nitrogen in solid solution prevents incipient cracks from becoming fatique failures, so the endurance limit of a cast iron crankshaft can be increases by 20 - 60.

Forged cranks are more suitable for higher output rally and racing engines, but this will depend on the type of steel in them. Forging increases the density of the component as the metal is literally squeezed into the required shape and compacted. This results in a stronger core and better fatigue resistance. Many American manufacturers have used forged cranks in their high performance models and petrol truck engines over the years, and these are available at moderate cost.

Forged nitrided steel and Tuftrided billet steel cranks are the best money can buy. In England, forged nitrided EN40B crankshafts are available for racing applications. In America, billet steel 4340 crankshafts are preferred.

The nitriding process can only be applied to special nitriding alloy steels. For crankshafts, a steel with a high core strength, such as EN40B, is used. Nitriding adds a tough wear resistant skin. The crankshaft is maintained at a temperature of $1000^{0}F$ for between 40 and 100 hours in a gas-tight chamber through which ammonia gas is circulated. Nitrogen is absorbed into the surface, forming extremely hard iron nitride, and nitrides of the chromium, molybdenum and aluminium present in the steel.

4340 steel has similar core properties to EN40B and when tuftrided exhibits good wear resistance. My personal preference is for a crankshaft fully machined from a hammer-forged billet of EN25 steel, followed by Tuftriding. This steel machines freely, leaving a smooth surface. Core properties are marginally superior to 4340.

Machining a crankshaft from a bar of steel is a time consuming and costly operation. However, the finished component is superior to the forged alternative. The fatigue strength (endurance limit) of a heat-treated alloy steel bar is improved about 60% by machining its surface clean. A ground or polished surface will raise the fatigue strength a further 40%. Fatigue strength is a very important consideration in a racing engine as it has a large bearing on component life and failure resistance. Forged crankshafts can be polished (very expensive) but this must be followed by shot peening to restore the tough skin formed as a by-product of forging.

Full counterbalancing is necessary on the racing crank, to reduce bearing loads. All cranks are counterbalanced overall, but not on each crank pin. As a result, the individual throws are subject to forces which, in combination, tend to make the crank whip and flex. The way to overcome this is by counterbalancing each throw. This does not change the overall crank balance, but achieves an internal balance for each throw.

To prevent main bearing failure or case stretching in the VW engine, fit a fully counterbalanced crank. Even in a very mild state of tune this is good insurance against engine damage. The standard crank will whip and pound the case, allowing the centre main to turn and wreck the engine. If you can't afford a fully counterweighted crank for your VW then have weights welded onto the standard crank.

In the high rpm engine, crankshaft modifications are in order to prevent main bearing failure due to lack of lubricant. Looking at FIGURE 6.3 you will see how the straight oilways in the crankshaft act as a centrifuge, pumping oil away from the main bearings. The scheme to overcome this is to cross-drill oil holes to break out at the sides of the pins. Great care is necessary to ensure that the new hole breaks fully into the existing one, otherwise oil flow will be reduced. The original hole must be tapped and have a threaded plug Loctited in

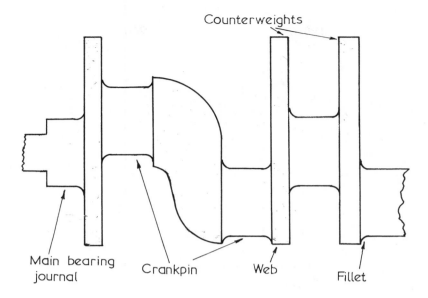

Counterweights

Main bearing
journal

Crankpin

Web

Fillet

Fig. 6. 2   B.M.C.   crankshaft.

to block it off. In engines where one main bearing supplies two crankpins, this modification is necessary in the very early stages of tune if it is intended to run the engine at high rpm.

The crankshaft journal oil feed holes should be chamfered, to improve oil flow and disperse fatigue stress loads.

Thus far we have only considered the crankshaft from the aspect of engine reliability, but it can also affect overall engine performance. Theoretically, crank throws should be of equal length and correctly indexed (phased). Slight differences in the stroke from cylinder to cylinder will not have a profound effect on performance. However, incorrect phasing will knock power. A four cylinder engine should have a piston at top dead centre every $180^0$, a six every $120^0$, an eight every $90^0$ ($180^0$ with single plane crank.) If any cylinder has a crank throw out of phase by $5^0$ this will have the same effect on performance as an ignition timing error of $5^0$ or a camshaft timing error of $5^0$. An expensive racing crank should have perfect phasing, but make a check to be sure.

Welding to increase the stroke of a crankshaft is not a practice to be recommended. The welding of the crankpins will cause a structural change in the crystaline structure of the underlying steel. The affected area then becomes a stress point, likely to fail. When the pin is ground on the new centre, much of the original core material is destroyed, further weakening the beam. Additional to these considerations, give some thought to the higher inertia loads generated by the longer throw.

At times, manufacturers increase the crankpin diameter in later model engines and in these instances it is possible to gain a small increase in stroke by grinding the crankpin to the original small diameter on a different centre (FIGURE 6.4). This modification reduces the crank beam strength and increases bearing loads, but on the plus side a useful increase in engine capacity is gained along with reduced frictional losses due to the reduced crankpin diameter. In lower stressed engines for sprint type speedway and hillclimb events, and moderate duty road engines, this modification is useful, but there are definite limitations.  151

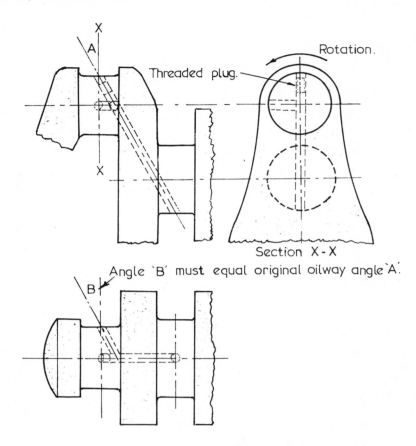

X

A

Rotation.

Threaded plug.

X

Section X-X

Angle 'B' must equal original oilway angle 'A'.

B

Fig. 6.3 Crankshaft oilway modification.

Specially-manufactured billet steel or forged cranks can be obtained with a stroke up to $\frac{1}{2}$ in more than stock. The strength of the crankshaft is not of primary concern here; it is block rigidity that matters. If the motor is to be used in sprint type competition, a standard, crack-free block with heavy duty main bearing caps and rods will be adequate. However, if the motor is expected to live for a minimum of 300 miles and more between rebuilds, then a special heavy-duty racing block should be considered. At times, a stronger, more suitable block, may be available from another model vehicle by the same manufacturer.

When a long stroke crank is fitted, some grinding may be necessary inside the block for connecting rod clearance. The clearance slots at the bottom of the bores will probably require enlarging. The camshaft also may need clearance slots but do not machine the cam all the way around as this will weaken the shaft excessively and lead to flexing and inaccurate valve timing. Do not forget to check the sump pan clearance.

The connecting rod provides the mechanical link between piston and crankshaft. It is subjected to alternating compression and tensile loads. It is true to say that the connecting rods in an engine have a tougher job to do than any other component. So it is not surprising that a large number of failures in high performance and racing engines are caused by the rods letting go.

The highest load is reached when the piston is at TDC on the exhaust stroke. This tension load can range from a few thousand pounds in a small low rev engine to well over 15,000 lb in larger, high rev engines. Interestingly, this maximum load occurs on the non-firing stroke and is caused by the inertia of the reciprocating assembly comprising the small end, piston and pin. At TDC the piston is suddenly stopped and then reversed. It is this sudden change that produces the high tensile load.

On the compression stroke the load is not as high (up to 11,500 lb) as compression builds up slowly, and soon after TDC, when combustion has finished, the load changes from tension to a light compression load.

It is not only the fact that stresses are high in a rod, but more important that they are applied and reversed each time the engine completes a cycle. This pulsing is much worse than if the loads were constant and applied continually, and it is this that leads to eventual fatigue and failure. A rod has to survive millions of stress cycles during a lifetime so it has to be tough and thoroughly prepared.

Most rods are forged from carbon steel, but they may also be made of cast iron (eg. American Motors), aluminium or titanium.

Cast iron rods have no place in a modified engine and should not be used. Titanium is prohibitively expensive and is used only in small, high speed (15,000 - 20,000 rpm) motorcycle engines. Aluminium rods are light and reasonably strong, but fatigue quickly, so they should be used only in drag race and sprint-type speedway engines where frequent replacement is possible. Chevrolet has recently released some information on connecting rod fatigue testing that they have carried out. Some aluminium rods failed after 150,000 cycles. The heavy duty small block rod, polished and shot peened, survived 1 to 2 million cycles at the equivalent of 7500 rpm. The Chevy K rod survived a minimum of 10 million cycles at 8000 rpm. When it is considered that the average race engine is required to stay together for 300 to 500 miles between rebuilds, the equivalent of 1 to 1½ million cycles, it is evident that care is needed, firstly in selecting the correct rod, and secondly in regular crack testing and replacement.

Connecting rods designed for the most stressful conditions are usually forged or machined from 4340 steel. I prefer rods fully machined from a hammer-forged billet of EN25 steel, dressed along the beams and shot peened.

Many heavy duty rods are more massive than the standard component, so there are a few things that must be considered during installation. As they are physically heavier, the crankshaft counterweighting will have to be rebalanced. Since the big end of the rod is larger, care must be taken to verify that it, and also the rod bolts, clear the block and camshaft.

Rod cap bolts have to be designed to withstand a considerable force, to stop the cap from breaking away from the rod. At times it is necessary to fit bolts of a larger diameter than standard. Whatever the diameter, the tensile strength of the bolts should be 185,000 psi minimum. Big end bolts should never be reused.

If you intend to retain the standard con rods, they must be carefully, and individually, hand picked. Rods with any forging irregularities or indentations should be avoided. Bumps standing proud of the rod can be removed, but indentations are stress points, likely to cause failure. The small end eye should be in the centre with an even thickness of material around the eye. Again the big end should be well formed and symmetrical. Select rods that are reasonably equal in weight. A heavy rod may be excessively weakened when material is ground off to balance it with the lighter rods. If they are not already numbered, number 153 each rod and cap, using a number punch, to ensure that they are never mismatched.

Standard connecting rod preparation must always include a check to ensure that the rod is not twisted or bent. Either condition will wreck the piston and/or big end bearings. Also necessary is resizing to bring the rods to an equal length. At the same time the big end inside diameter should be checked for size and concentricity with the bearings fitted and the bolts torqued to specification. The small end bush should be honed to give the correct piston pin fit.

The failure point for many rods is at the corner formed by the flat machined for the rod bolt and nut seat. These corners must be radiused to avoid stress concentration in this area. Every con rod will require some modification here (FIGURE 6.5).

The tough skin formed on the con rod by forging gives the rod much of its strength and fatigue resistance. Therefore the rod should never be polished unless it is followed by shot peening, to create another work toughened and compressed skin. It is a waste of time polishing the entire rod and then having it shot peened. If you have a look at the shank of a rod you will see, along its edges, a rough band where metal appears to have been sawn away. That is where the excess metal, called flash, was squeezed out from between the forging dies when the rod was being made. Later, most of the flash is trimmed off but a bead is left, as you can see. Of course, there is no hard skin along this ridge, in fact its roughness is a stress raiser, so this ridge should be removed on a sanding belt. Give the entire beam a polish with fine emery cloth and then follow up with buffing and shot peening.

The shot peening process has a very useful place in connecting rod preparation. Fatigue failure almost always starts at the surface due to a combination of two things. Firstly, under most forms of loading, maximum stress is at the surface, and secondly, surface imperfections are stress raisers. By bombarding the surface with steel shot the surface layer is compressed and unified. This means that when the component is under load, any tensile stresses at the surface will be reduced and any compressive stresses will be increased. Because peening can seal over surface cracks, all crack testing must be done first. Also any straightening should be carried out before peening, or this will remove the effect of peening. After peening, check the component dimensionally, as there will be some growth and if the peening has been done incorrectly, bending may occur.

The relationship betwen con rod length and the crankshaft stroke, called the con rod ratio (con rod length ÷ crank stroke = con rod ratio), is of importance in the high performance and racing engine. Most rod ratios range from 1.5 to 2:1; 1.65 to 1.75 is average.

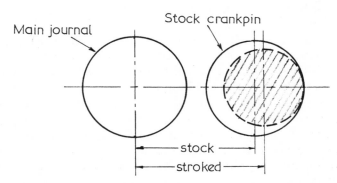

Fig. 6. 4 Crankshaft stroking by crankpin dia. reduction.

The length of the rod directly affects the performance of an engine. Basically, a long rod will improve top end performance and also reduce piston and cylinder wear. A short rod picks up bottom end performance but increases piston and cylinder wear.

The long rod will cause the piston to dwell at TDC longer and to move away from TDC more slowly. This is at a time when piston velocity is critical for good cylinder filling. If the inlet valve is opening too soon or too quickly, or if the ports are too large, mixture velocity and power will be lost at lower engine speeds. Therefore to pick up bottom end power with a long rod it will be necessary to change the valve opening characteristics of the cam and also reduce the valve and port sizes.

A short rod will accelerate the piston quickly from TDC, filling the cylinder completely at lower engine speeds, at the expense of high speed performance. This means that intake valve opening can be more rapid and larger valves and ports can be used to take advantage of the higher piston velocity to aid cylinder filling at higher speeds. With this understanding it is possible to compensate and make any engine perform equally, regardless of whether it has a long or a short rod (forgetting about wear for the moment). On the other hand if we want top power for a long, fast circuit, we can use a long rod, or if we need low end power for a short slow circuit, we use a short rod.

With shorter rods, engine wear is a problem, and for this reason I do not like rod ratios below 1.65:1. This is worth thinking about before you fit a long stroke crank as the tendency for the piston to rock in the bore is increased as the rod length to stroke ratio is reduced. Shorter pistons with a reduced compression height must be used when a stroker crank is fitted, otherwise they would pop out the top of the cylinder. Short pistons rock more than standard pistons, accelerating the wear problem.

Bearings in a high power engine, as well as providing a low friction wearing surface, also have to absorb tremendous shock loads. Therefore only top quality trimetal bearings should be used for the mains and big ends. White metal bearings are satisfactory for carrying the camshaft.

I use only Vandervell lead-indium and TRW Clevite CL-77 bearings because of their special features. Both types are able to stand up to the worst competition loads when correctly installed. These bearings are steel backed, with a copper-lead intermediate layer. This layer gives the bearing good fatigue strength and load carrying capacity, also resistance to hydraulic break out. The running surface for the Vandervell bearing is a precision overlay of lead-indium while the CL-77 overlay is lead-tin.

Correct bearing clearance is an obvious necessity. Excessive clearance will promote knocking and pounding and allow excessive oil throw off into the cylinder bores. This will cause higher frictional losses in the cylinder and increase oil consumption. Excessive clearance at the big ends will lead to oil starvation at the main bearings, with resultant bearing failure. Insufficient clearance will cause rapid bearing deterioration as a result of the increased temperatures that come about due to insufficient oil flow or a thin oil film (TABLE 6.3). Con rod side clearance (end-float) also affects bearing lubrication, so this should be checked on every big end to ensure proper oil control.

There are just a few simple rules to follow for correct bearing installation. Accurately measure and record the inside diameter of every main bearing and big end housing (without bearings fitted). Now do the same with the crankshaft main and crankpin journals. Unwrap all the bearings and carefully wash them in clean solvent, to remove the protective film. Measure the bearing shell thickness. The difference between the shaft and housing diameters is the space left for the bearing shell, plus the running clearance. When you sit  155 down to work out the clearances, don't forget to double the bearing shell thickness as there is a shell on each side of the shaft. If the clearances are too tight, the offending journals will need a light lapping.

### TABLE 6.3   Bearing clearances for trimetal copper lead bearings

| Diameter of shaft (in) | Clearance between shaft and bearing | Side clearance |
|---|---|---|
| 1.5 | 0.0012-0.0017 | 0.004-0.006 |
| 2.0 | 0.0015-0.002 | 0.005-0.007 |
| 2.25 | 0.0018-0.0025 | 0.005-0.007 |
| 2.5 | 0.0022-0.0027 | 0.005-0.007 |
| 2.75 | 0.0024-0.0028 | 0.006-0.008 |
| 3.0 | 0.0025-0.0028 | 0.007-0.009 |
| 3.25 | 0.0025-0.003 | 0.007-0.009 |

*Note: In engines where two con rods share a common crankpin (eg a V8) multiply side clearance by 3 for steel rods, and by 4 for aluminium rods.*

After ensuring that all the bearing housings and bearing shells are perfectly clean and dry, fit the shells and check oil hole alignment. Any misalignment should be corrected, using a small round key file. After filing, carefully dress the steel back of the shell to remove any metal fraze. Next coat all the bearings with engine oil and fit the crankshaft. Do not use a 50 - 50 mixture of oil and any substance like STP. Fit the main bearing caps in their correct order with arrows facing the front of the block and gradually tighten them down. Before final tightening, the crank should be tapped to each side with a soft hammer in order to line up the bearing caps. Now check the crankshaft end float. It should be within 0.004 - 0.006 in with a cast iron block. If the clearance is more than this, fit thicker thrust washers.

When it comes to fitting the big end bearings follow the same procedure as for the fitting of the main bearings. There are still a few engines around using lock tabs on the big end bolts. Throw these away, as they crush and give a false bolt tension reading. Use Loctite on the threads and you won't have any problems with loose bolts.

Moving further up in the block, the next components for consideration are the pistons, piston rings and piston pin. Firstly, you must decide whether the standard piston is up to the job. If the motor is in sports tune, it is quite probable that the standard cast and slotted pistons will be satisfactory. Higher states of tune will demand unslotted cast pistons, and in racing tune unslotted forged pistons will be necessary.

Most production engines use cast pistons, because this type is easy to produce and shape as required. Some high performance engines will be fitted with high quality forged or cast pistons right from the factory eg. Cosworth Vega, Lotus/Ford Twin Cam. By looking inside the piston you will be able to see whether it is cast or forged. Cast pistons have quite intricate under-crown shapes around the gudgeon pin boss. Forged pistons are machined smooth inside and lack intricate struts and braces.

The cast piston has a relatively low material density. Forged pistons are much denser and consequently have a higher tensile strength. They are capable of withstanding higher pressure and heat loads than the cast piston. Due to their high density, thermal conductivity is improved such that a piston crown temperature reduction of $100^\circ$F is usual.

Additional to these advantages, the forged piston can be machined to have a much thinner crown and skirt, and can therefore be much lighter and still stronger than a cast item.

The worst feature of production pistons is the slot for oil drainage behind the oil control ring. This usually extends almost from one boss around to the other boss, on both sides of the piston. To make the situation worse, expansion control slots cut into the piston skirt usually break into the oil drain slot. Slots weaken the piston considerably, allowing the skirt to break away from the top of the piston. In standard production engines this can be a problem, so you can imagine what you are up against if slotted pistons are retained in a high performance unit. Pistons suitable for high performance use (either cast or forged) do not have any slots for expansion control or oil drain back. Instead, small holes are drilled right the way around the oil control ring groove, for oil drainage. Extra piston clearance and special design take care of expansion.

Racing pistons may be of either the full skirt or the slipper variety. Many American pistons are a cross between both designs, having a skirt extending to below the pin boss, but cut back to the thrust faces below this point. Generally, I prefer the full skirt or the American design for best expansion control and scuff resistance.

We tend to think of pistons as being round, but actually the skirt is cam ground an oval shape. The piston also tapers from bottom to top. Both ovality and taper are necessary to prevent seizure. The top of the piston is almost twice as hot as the bottom of the skirt, so it expands more. Due to the extra metal around the pin bosses, more heat is directed to this area, elongating the piston across the piston pin axis. To compensate, the piston skirt is ground oval. Most pistons are from 0.005 - 0.012 in less in diameter across the pin axis than across the thrust faces. Be careful to measure piston clearance only on the thrust faces, and at the bottom of the skirt.

Accidentally dropping a piston may damage the skirt and lead to eventual seizure, due to skirt distortion. Never bang a piston pin out with a hammer and drift. This is a sure way to push the skirt out of shape. If the pin will not push out easily, heat the piston in boiling water or oil and then gently tap it out with the con rod secured in a vice to prevent any pressure at all on the piston.

For better lubrication, and to allow for extra piston expansion, high performance engines must have more piston to cylinder clearance than models off the showroom floor. I prefer 0.0013 - 0.0015 in clearance per inch of bore for road and rally engines. Race engines require 0.0018 - 0.0025 in clearance per inch of bore. There should be a maximum of 0.0005 in difference in clearance between the tightest and sloppiest cylinders. If the tolerance is greater than this, try swapping the pistons around in different cylinders. When it is finally decided which piston goes where, number each piston inside the skirt, using a suitable marking pen. Do not mark the crown as this may be machined later to give the correct deck height.

As the majority of motors have heads with inclined or canted valves, some thought must be given to providing adequate valve to piston clearance. There should be a minimum of 0.060 in vertical clearance, although I prefer 0.080 in for the inlets and 0.100 in for the exhaust. The cut out diameter for safety is 0.120 in greater than the valve head diameter.

There are two basic ways to go about checking the safe valve working clearance, but both methods involve quite a deal of work. Either technique requires that the motor be almost totally assembled. The cam must be installed and accurately timed, and the head and head gasket need to be fitted.

The first way involves the use of a piece of modelling clay pressed down on the top of a 157 piston. After the clay has been smoothed out, spray it and also the valves in the cylinder being checked with a light coating of WD-40. This will help prevent the clay sticking to the valves later, when the clearance check is made. Fit the head and head gasket, tension it down and adjust the valve clearances. Now very carefully turn the motor over two complete turns to completely open and close both the inlet and exhaust valve. Remove the head and measure the thickness of the clay over both valve cutouts. Next cut the clay, using a sharp, wet knife, to check the clearance around the periphery of the valve head.

The other method is accurate only if the valve cutouts are central under the valve, as there is no provision for a check to be made on the clearance between the edge of the valve head and the edge of the cutout. In this instance light checking springs need to be fitted instead of valve springs. The head and head gasket are tensioned down as before and the valve clearances adjusted. Next, set up a dial gauge on the inlet valve and turn the motor over until the valve is fully open. Zero the dial gauge and push the valve open as far as it will go. The dial gauge reading gives the clearance. Measure the exhaust valve clearance similarly.

To assist in equalising compression and combustion pressures, the crown of every piston must rise to the same point in each cylinder. This is called the deck height of the piston. In a racing engine we would want to be running minimum deck clearance to assist cylinder scavenging, and to up the compression ratio. A good solid motor with steel rods can run with a minimum of 0.040 in clearance between the piston crown (not the compression lump) and the squish area of the head. Therefore if the head gasket is 0.030 in thick when compressed we could run a minimum deck clearance of 0.040 - 0.030 = 0.010 in. This means that the pistons would all be machined so that they are 0.010 in from the top of the block at TDC. If one piston is 0.015 in down the bore then it will be necessary to machine all the other pistons so that they are also 0.015 in from the block deck at TDC. To restore the compression we would then need to machine 0.015 - 0.010 = 0.005 in from the block deck.

Aluminium connecting rods stretch more at high revs and aluminium has a greater coefficient of expansion than steel, so we would need at least 0.070 in piston to head clearance. Engines that have steel rods but suffer block flex or crankshaft whip eg. VW, will require 0.060 in clearance. Most American V8s are more rigid and can run 0.045 in given the full treatment of steel crank and rods and heavy duty block. If a standard block and crank are retained, increase the clearance to 0.050 in.

As I mentioned right in the beginning of this book, the top of the piston is a part of the combustion chamber, and those high compression lumps on the top of your pistons can add to, or detract from, the complete combustion of fuel inducted into the engine. They may retard flame travel after ignition and upset complete cylinder scavenging during the exhaust cycle. On the intake stroke, the dome can restrict the critical initial fuel flow and then disrupt final mixture homogenisation before ignition.

To improve fuel flow into the cylinder at low valve lift, the intake valve pocket must be layed back to reduce valve shrouding (FIGURE 6.6). As the initial flow is along the floor of the port and around the short radius toward the squish area of the head, this modification will assist in cylinder filling. Many tuners worry about removing metal from the piston dome because of the slight drop in compression ratio; however the improved flow and better combustion will far exceed the slight power losses due to the drop in compression ratio.

After ignition, we want the flame to travel smoothly across the piston dome and back
toward the squish area. Any abrupt edge on the compression lump will disrupt the flame

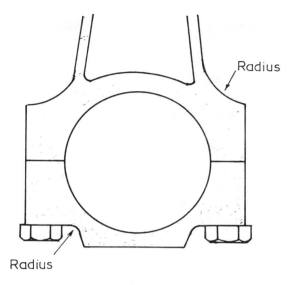

Fig. 6. 5 Connecting rod modification.

front as it moves across the piston, leaving pockets of mixture that are either unburned or only partially ignited. Rounding and smoothing the top and sides of the dome does much to reduce this problem.

The exhaust valve cutout must not be layed back as this is usually not advantageous. The sharpness of the exhaust valve pocket does cause some flame disruption but exhaust flow and cylinder scavenging is usually superior when the exhaust valve is shrouded by the cutout.

After the engine has been run for a time, a careful study should be made of piston dome colouration. This is a surprisingly accurate means of investigating combustion completeness. Keep in mind that combustion begins before the piston reaches TDC and continues well past TDC. If at any time something happens to cause the flame to stop, the piston colour will indicate where the dome is causing the flame to stop.

All motors with bathtub or wedge chamber heads will show an area of no carbon buildup on both the piston and cylinder head. This is in the squish (or quench) area where no combustion takes place due to the closeness of the flat face of the head and piston. Any other areas on the piston dome where there is little or no carbon buildup likewise indicate that the dome is coming too close to the combustion chamber and this is retarding the ignition flame at and around TDC.

The approach is to lightly machine the compression domes until the carbon buildup is more even in quantity and colour. Because the flame moves from the spark plug out across the combustion chamber you will need to keep in mind the direction of flame travel when you come to remove any metal from the dome. Generally, it will not be necessary to machine the entire uncoloured area as it is usually the area immediately in front of and around the beginning of the uncoloured area, relative to the direction of flame travel, where the dome is coming too close to the combustion chamber wall and creating a pocket of unburned fuel. The place of least flame activity is usually around the high side of the 159

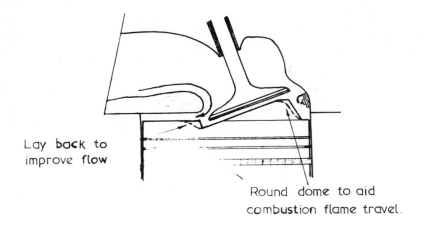

Lay back to improve flow

Round dome to aid combustion flame travel.

Fig. 6. 6  Piston dome modification.

piston dome in the area of the intake valve cutout, close to the cylinder wall. If you can modify the dome to colour evenly in this area, you are well on the way to achieving good combustion.

Engines that are to be supercharged or turbocharged may require a low compression ratio to avoid detonation. To achieve this, dished top pistons should be used for best combustion control. Some feel that flat top pistons that have a lower than standard compression height for use with stroker cranks can be used, but this is not so. If a flat top piston were used with a deck clearance of, say, 0.150 in to reduce the compression ratio to 7:1, then the top of the piston would be so far away from the squish area of the head that combustion would be upset due to lack of squish. A dished top piston has a flat band around the outside of the crown that will come into close contact with the head and provide the required squish for good burning.

The piston pin is retained by a variety of means in the production engine, the most common being by either an interference press fit in the connecting rod, or by flat circlips. If circlips are used, they should be coated with Loctite. Ensure that the circlip grooves are clean and undamaged so that each circlip can seat securely. The interference press fit (0.0015 - 0.0025 in) is suitable for racing engines, but care must be taken to assemble and remove the piston from the rod without causing any piston damage.

As racing engine speeds are now moving past 8000 rpm, many engine builders are experiencing problems with circlips (either flat or round wire). At very high rpm they may close up, due to the forces exerted on them, and drop out of the piston into the bore. To overcome this it is necessary to employ another means of pin retention. Some have reverted to the old method of pinch-bolts but generally I prefer to use Spirolox or in extreme instances an interference press fit.

The fit of the pin in the piston exercises more control over piston dimension than is often appreciated. The additional clearance given a piston by cam grinding is nullified if the piston is unable to expand correctly due to a tight pin. The pin clearance (pin to piston and pin to rod) in the high performance and racing engine must be greater to compensate for forces the standard production engine is unlikely to experience. At high engine speeds 160 crankshaft whip and con rod distortion can severely load the piston pin and if the pin fit is too tight, piston to cylinder scuffing or seizure may result. In extreme instances the pin will push the side out of the piston.

For most engines I set pin to rod clearance at 0.0008 - 0.0015 in and pin to piston clearance a little tighter at 0.0005 - 0.0008 in. This will alleviate any binding between rod and pin or between pin and piston that could lead to piston damage. However, no matter how free the pin is, any con rod misalignment could wreck the piston, so have the rods checked to ensure that they are not bent, twisted or offset.

The piston ring, as it slides up and down the cylinder wall, has to function like a bearing, and as well it has to seal off the combustion chamber to keep the gases from escaping past the piston into the crankcase. Most engines use either two or three rings per piston.

The first or top ring is called the compression ring. Its purpose is to contain the combustion pressure so that maximum power can be obtained. This ring also has the burden of dissipating most of the piston crown heat (about 80) to the cylinder wall.

Some racing engines do not use a second compression ring, but if yours does, it has the task of backing up the top ring in sealing off the combustion charge. Additionally, the second ring may support the oil ring in scraping excess oil off the cylinder wall.

The bottom ring is the oil scraper or oil control ring. Its job is to scrape oil from the cylinder wall, and ensure that enough oil remains behind to lubricate the upper rings and assist in sealing.

Let's take a closer look to see what goes on when the compression ring seals off the combustion chamber. Many feel that it is the ring's inherent radial tension that holds it against the cylinder wall. Radial tension does help, but it is gas pressure behind the back of the ring that forces the ring face against the wall.

There is a detrimental phenomenon that may occur in a high rpm engine to reduce the ring's sealing ability. This is ring float or flutter. As the piston approaches TDC it is slowed down by the connecting rod, but the rings try to keep on moving and if they have enough weight they will leave contact with the lower side of their grooves and bang into the top of the groove. When this happens, the ring seals off the gas pressure in the combustion chamber so that the gas cannot get behind the back of the ring and force it against the bore wall. Any gas pressure that may have been behind the ring quickly leaks into the crankcase and combustion pressure forces the ring to collapse inwardly. Immediately the ring breaks contact with the bore wall, the combustion gases blow-by into the crankcase.

Radial tension in the ring is unable to prevent blow-by caused by ring flutter. However a certain degree of radial tension is necessary for good sealing, otherwise the pressure at the back of the ring would only be equal to the pressure trying to force the ring off the cylinder wall. This would allow blow-by and it is this type we normally see occuring when the rings are old and have lost their tension.

Ring flutter allows blow-by but it can also wreck engines. When the ring loses contact with the bore wall it is unable to transfer heat from the piston to the water jacket. The end result can be melted pistons or severe detonation, due to increased combustion temperature.

The wider a ring for a given radial depth, the lower the speed at which this effect commences. This is one reason why thin rings are used in racing engines. Assuming the radial depth is $1/26$th of the bore diameter, the maximum allowable acceleration for a ring $1/16$ in wide is 80,000 ft/sec$^2$, with other widths in proportion ie. 125,000 for 0.040 in rings, 100,000 for 0.050 in and 64,000 for $5/64$ in rings.

161

Piston acceleration at TDC is found by the formula:

$$\text{Acceleration} = 0.000457 \times N^2 \times S \times \left(1 + \frac{S}{2L}\right) \text{ ft/sec}^2$$

N = rpm
S = stroke in inches
L = connecting rod length

For many years I positioned the rings accurately so as to reduce gas leakage through the ring gap. Then it was pointed out to me that rings do, in fact, rotate so I was wasting my time staggering the gaps. It has been proven that the ratio of ring rotation to crank rotation is about 1:1000. In other words a motor operating at 7000 rpm will have the compression rings rotating at 7 rpm.

Leakage through the ring gaps and blow-by (not flutter-induced blow-by) is more of a problem at low rpm, simply because there is more time for the gases to find their way through the ring gaps. This is why slow rev truck engines use three and even four compression rings. It is also why very high rev engines usually require only one compression ring, providing the oil control ring can look after oil control without the assistance of a second compression/scraper ring.

These days ring breakage is rare and usually can be attributed to worn piston ring grooves that allow the ring to flop around and break, or excessive taper of the bore which causes radial flutter and subsequent ring breakage. If new rings are fitted to a worn bore, and a ridge is present at the top of the bore, the new rings will bang into the ridge and break. Excessive piston to bore clearance can lead to ring failure due to the piston rocking and twisting the rings as it passes TDC.

Generally, a racing engine should be set up with very tight groove clearances of 0.001-0.0015 in. Certainly there should not be more than 0.002 in side clearance between the ring and ring groove. A road motor should ideally have the same groove clearance as a racing unit, but up to 0.0035 in clearance is acceptable.

Another cause of ring breakage is insufficient ring gap, allowing the ring ends to crash together. I like to set my engines up with 0.005 in gap per inch of bore. The current trend in racing circles is to reduce ring gap, and some are down to 0.0035 in per inch of bore.

Ring material is usually cast iron; either plain, chrome plated or moly-filled. For road and rally use, the chrome ring is hard to beat as it can extend the intervals between ring replacement considerably, and is available at reasonable cost. Chrome has a lower coefficient of friction than cast iron, so bore wear and frictional losses are reduced. Chrome rings are a little harder to bed-in than other types but if the running-in procedure outlined is adhered to, you should have no problems.

For racing I prefer Sealed Power/Speed Pro moly-filled nodular cast iron rings. Nodular iron has almost three times the strength of conventional grey cast iron. It is ductile rather than brittle and can be bent without breaking. Molybdenum belongs to the same chemical family as chrome; however it has a lower coefficient of friction and higher resistance to abrasion. Its thermal conductivity is several times greater than that of either cast iron or chrome plated cast iron. The porosity of molybdenum acts as an oil reservoir, reducing scuffing and cylinder wear.

The humble plain cast iron ring is suitable for racing or road use. It will not last as long as the other types, but it beds in quickly and seals effectively.

For oil control I like the multi-piece pressure back type for road engines, where low oil consumption for many thousands of miles is important. This type of ring is unsuitable for high speed race and rally engines due to the very high radial pressures exerted on the bore. The idea with these engines is to keep frictional losses to the very minimum and at the same time maintain adequate oil control. Therefore only low tension type oil control rings should be used for race engines. The most common low tension types are the old one piece cast iron scraper ring and two piece Hepolite MSO ring. The American Sealed Power/Speed Pro low tension oil ring is excellent in this type of application.

When rings are being fitted, care is needed to avoid fitting them the wrong way up and to prevent damage by incorrect installation. Compression rings can be permanently twisted if they are fitted in the groove at one end and then gradually screwed around until the entire ring is in place. Instead, they should be expanded sufficiently to fit over the piston and then allowed to drop into the groove. Special expander tools are available for this purpose but I prefer two 0.015 in feeler blades placed between the ring and piston. The blades provide a bearing surface and prevent the ring digging into the piston.

Taper face rings are marked TOP and should be fitted this side up. This provides the greater diameter or contacting edge on the lower face of the ring.

The unbalanced section or torsional twist ring is fitted with the inner chamfered edge uppermost. This causes a slight dish in the ring face and provides the same characteristics as the taper face ring, such that the lower edge makes a high pressure contact with the cylinder wall. Whereas the taper face ring eventually wears parallel, the torsional twist ring retains its characteristics.

The 'Multo-Seal' type ring is fitted with the serrations in the ring face downwards.

All multi-piece oil control rings should be fitted in accordance with the packaged instructions. Always double check that the ends of the expander ring have not been lapped over.

Before fitting the assembled pistons in the engine, dip each entire piston in engine oil and oil the walls of each cylinder. Some feel that the oil should be fortified with some additive like STP; some even paint straight STP onto the cylinder walls and pistons. This is wrong. Piston rings are not designed to cut through an additive like this; the end result could be glazed rings and bores.

The initial bed-in of rings is achieved by giving the car a full throttle burst for a few seconds, followed by snapping the throttle shut and coasting for a few more seconds. This should be repeated at least twelve to fifteen times with the engine at normal operating temperature. Accelerate the vehicle in top gear from the slowest speed it will pull in that gear.

By giving the engine full power, the high gas pressures force the rings out against the bore wall. Snapping the throttle shut causes a vacuum in the cylinder which draws up extra oil. This and low engine speed minimises the risk of glazing and allows the ring face and cylinder wall to cool.

After the rings are initially bed-in, the engine can be operated at up to 80% of its rev/power potential, but constantly vary the speed. If this is not done, the rings may still glaze. After about half an hour of this on the dyno or the race circuit, the rings can be considered as being run-in. A road engine with chrome rings should be run in for around 200 miles, preferably in one session. Again, constantly vary the engine speed and include heavy acceleration for short bursts as for initial bedding in. Avoid constant high speed until the engine has done 500 - 700 miles.

I prefer to break in my engines on the dyno, carefully controlling the engine speed and  163 load to ensure long engine life and maximum power. This takes 2 - 3 hours for most brands of engines. When the engine cools, the tappets are adjusted and the head is retensioned. Then, following a warm-up to bring the water and oil up to temperature, full load power tests are made to determine ignition advance, fuel jet sizes etc. By the end of the tests the engine is fully run-in, having spent at least four hours running on the dyno (TABLE 6.4).

Some feel it is preferable to run an engine on the dyno from some external power source. Theoretically this should smooth out the differences in fit and surface finish but this solves only part of the problem. Internal temperatures influence the fit and shape of parts. To further complicate matters, clearances will alter with mechanical loads as well as with temperatures. It follows then that the engine must be run- in under its own power, initially unloaded and then progressively loaded to produce the required running surface.

The pulley or harmonic balancer attached to the nose of the crankshaft has its part to play in the durability of an engine, and the surrounding environment. Most four cylinder engines use a pressed metal drive pulley, spot welded or riveted to a hub. At higher engine speeds, ie. 6000 rpm plus, a pulley of this construction is liable to fly apart, wrecking anything in its path. To avoid this, a cast or machined component should be used.

The harmonic balancer is fitted to six and eight cylinder engines to dampen crankshaft torsional vibrations that could, if not controlled, wreck the crankshaft. At times the balancer and pulley may be one piece, or a separate pulley may be bolted to the harmonic balancer. Again, if this pulley is a pressed metal component, scrap it to avoid problems.

The actual harmonic balancer is made of three parts bonded together. A rubber belt is bonded between the outer inertia ring and the hub. Failure is normally caused by the inertia ring losing its bond with the rubber. If this occurs at high engine speed you can be assured of spectacular and expensive results. To prevent this, the harmonic dampener must be carefully inspected on a regular basis. If you race, do it after each race meeting. To assist in your inspection you should mark a distinct, common line between the hub and inertia ring. If the two marks move out of line, it indicates the ring is moving on the hub, so scrap it. Under no circumstances should you try to repair the balancer by bolting the inertia ring to the hub. This will wreck your crankshaft just as surely as running 2000 rpm over the limit. The inertia ring must be able to move, within limits, to dampen crankshaft vibration.

There is little that can be done to improve the reliability of the harmonic balancer except to check it for runout before fitting. The other modification necessary, if a fully counterbalanced crank is fitted, is to machine away the counterweight cast as part of the hub.

Before you fit the harmonic balancer (or pulley) to the engine, paint it black. After

### TABLE 6.4   Standard break-in procedure on an engine dyno

| rpm | Engine load (torque lbf ft) | Time (mins) |
|---|---|---|
| 3500 | 40 | 10 |
| 4000 | 50 | 30 |
| 4500 | 70 | 30 |
| 5000 | 85 | 30 |
| 5500 | 100 | 30 |

*Note: This is the procedure used for all race and rally Ford BDA engines of 1600 - 2000 cc producing maximum torque of 135 - 165 lbf ft. Other engines require a different run in load according to their displacement and torque output.*

fitting, accurately find TDC and file a good groove into it, to align with the TDC mark on the engine timing case. Paint the groove with silver or white paint. If you also paint black the area around the timing marks on the engine timing case, and the TDC and ignition timing marks or pointer silver, the ignition timing will be much easier to adjust later on. To adjust the timing accurately you must be able to see the timing marks easily, so anything that you can do to make them stand out must help.

The flywheel is attached to the other end of the crankshaft. To ensure that it remains attached, two good dowels ($\frac{3}{8}$ in) and retaining bolts that have been coated with Loctite and correctly torqued provide good insurance. Manufacturers, to cut costs, seldom fit dowels, so it will be necessary to machine the flywheel and crank to fit these.

Many place a lot of importance on flywheel lightening, thinking that this will improve the acceleration of the car because the inertia is reduced. All a light flywheel does is allow the engine, when it is not driving the car (ie. in neutral), to pick up or lose revs more quickly. Firstly, this makes for quick gear changes. Secondly, it reduces an undesirable twisting load on the end of the crankshaft.

A high power engine is able to accelerate a lightweight car quickly, therefore the crankshaft is also accelerating at a fast rate. However, a heavy flywheel may tend to lag behind the crankshaft, inducing a twisting force on the end of the crank. This will happen in reverse when the engine is slowed quickly; the heavy flywheel will attempt to turn the crankshaft.

A very light flywheel is undesirable for a road vehicle as it can produce a lumpy engine idle. The reason manufacturers use a relatively heavy flywheel in the first place is to absorb the uneven torsional impulses coming through the crankshaft and keep the engine turning smoothly at low engine revs. A fairly hot engine with a relatively heavy flywheel is much more pleasant to drive on the road than one with an overly light one.

If you decide to use a lighter flywheel it is not always necessary to buy a new lightweight version or even have your old flywheel turned down. Some manufacturers have, over the years, built many engines of various capacities around the same basic design. Therefore the flywheel fitted in production to the 1000 cc version may also fit the 1500 cc derivative and save possibly 5 - 7 lbs. If you have the 1500 cc engine in mind for modification, you can use the lighter flywheel from the smaller engine.

Lightening should only be done near the outside of the flywheel. Removing metal from the centre is fatal and likely to lead to failure. When metal is removed from the outside this makes life easier on the centre of the flywheel as the inertia loads are reduced. This is important as some flywheels are none too strong. To prevent distortion from heat, do not machine away so much of the clutch side of the flywheel that there is only a thin ribbon of metal left, just wide enough to provide a seat for the clutch plate friction material. If the clutch is subjected to severe usage, that thin ribbon may distort, due to localised heating, and allow clutch slip.

# Chapter 7
# Ignition

INTERNAL combustion engines (of the type being considered here) rely on an electric spark to start combustion of the fuel charge in each cylinder. If these engines are to run efficiently, that spark must be delivered at precisely the right moment in relation to the position of the piston and the rotational speed of the crankshaft. Also, the spark must be of sufficient intensity to fire the fuel/air mixture even at high compression pressure and high rpm.

The most common ignition system relies on a points type distributor to time and distribute the spark, and a coil to provide the spark (FIGURE 7.1).

The distributor has two switches, the contact breaker points and the rotor, and also an advance mechanism to vary the time at which the points open and close.

The switching of the primary (low tension) circuit is accomplished by the contact breaker points which are opened and closed by the distributor cam. When the points are closed, electric current flows through the coil primary winding, and then through the points, to earth. The current in the low tension winding produces a magnetic field which surrounds the secondary or high tension winding. As soon as the points open, current flow through the primary stops and the magnetic field collapses, causing a current to be induced in the secondary winding. This creates a high voltage current (up to 25,000 volts) capable of jumping across the spark plug gap, to fire the fuel mixture.

The high voltage current flows from the coil to the centre of the distributor cap and through the carbon brush to the rotor button. The turning rotor then directs the current back to the distributor cap and to the individual cylinders.

At normal engine speeds and low compression pressures, this conventional system works very reliably, with just periodic maintenance required to replace the points. However, when an engine is modified, the ignition system has to work much more efficiently under adverse conditions.

Because we live in an electronic age, many people right away think that the conventional ignition is best scrapped and replaced with a transistorised or capacitor discharge unit. I'm not going to say that all electronic ignition systems are no good, but I will say that relatively few are able to perform better than a modified conventional breaker points system. Even the best electronic systems can be unreliable (especially when wide plug gaps are used) which is why you will often see two 'black boxes' wired up with a change over switch on cars involved in races longer than 150 miles.

Many of the electronic units on the market merely replace the points with a magnetic sensor or light sensitive trigger to control primary current flow, while the remainder of the system stays basically the same as standard. In fact you will find quite a few units that are just a slip-in replacement for the points.

Some of the car manufacturers are changing over to electronic ignition, but this is not in the interests of high performance in most instances. Usually the reason is to reduce maintenance by eliminating the breaker points and to reduce exhaust emissions as the average motorist isn't interested in keeping the point gap/cam dwell correct or the timing spot on. When points are used, the timing and dwell will change due to wear and this increases the emissions.

With the conventional system, as the engine speed increases the time the points are closed between each opening is decreased. This means that the coil has less time to build up a full magnetic field between plug firings, so the voltage available to fire the plugs is reduced. A high speed misfire results unless a high performance coil is used.

A standard coil will supply 18,000 strong sparks per minute. This corresponds to 9000 rpm for a four cylinder engine, 6000 rpm for a six and only 4500 for an eight. High performance coils have a higher spark rate and high speed voltage is much improved.

When mounting the coil, ensure that it is in the coolest possible location, but never more than 18 in from the distributor. High temperatures badly affect a coil's efficiency so never mount it on the engine or close to the exhaust. If you cannot find a suitable cool location close to the distributor, then you will need an air duct directing cool air onto the coil.

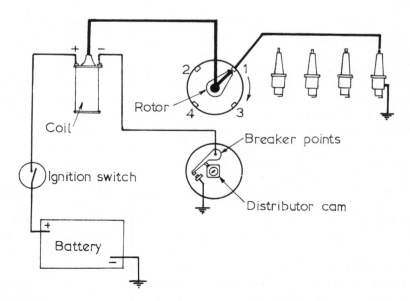

Fig. 7.1  Conventional negative earth ignition system.

If a coil is wired with reverse polarity there is a 40% loss of energy, so always be sure to attach the correct wires to the low tension terminals. The wire from the coil to the points should be connected to the coil terminal with the same polarity as the earth terminal of the battery ie. if the negative (—) battery terminal is earthed then the wire running between the coil and the points should be connected to the negative (—) coil terminal.

Where available, I recommend the use of the Accel Super Coil (No. 14001). It has the highest energy output of any coil intended for use with a points ignition system. To reduce the point current from 2.5 amps to 0.025 amps and increase their life, the Accel Ignition Amplifier (No. 35355) can be used in conjunction with the Super Coil.

To ensure that the coil is given sufficient saturation time to produce a good fat spark at high rpm, the point dwell angle must be correct. Decreasing the point gap increases the amount of time the points remain closed, consequently the coil is given a longer saturation time. However, if the point gap is set too close, a whole new set of problems arise. Most manufacturers state that the dwell angle should be within a certain range eg. $57^0$ to $63^0$. Usually it is best to adjust the dwell to the midway angle, in this example $60^0$, for best power.

Accel dual point distributors are available for many V8 engines and Mallory make a variety of dual point breaker plate conversions that you can fit to your standard distributor. These are a good investment for six and eight cylinder engines as coil saturation time, and hence spark intensity, is increased.

The standard dual point Accel distributor is suitable for 6500 - 7000 rpm V8 engines, and the racing distributor is good for 8500 rpm. The latter uses needle bearings and is available with mechanical tachometer drive.

The dual points increase the coil saturation time by being wired into the primary circuit in such a way that battery current flows through the coil when either set of points is closed. Their position in relation to the distributor cam is staggered so that one set opens before the other, but the spark isn't fired until the second set opens to break the primary circuit. As the spark is fired, the first set of points are already on their way closed, many degrees sooner than the set that actually broke the primary circuit to produce the spark. This increases the total dwell angle over that of a single point distributor, which results in better coil saturation and a hotter high rpm spark.

Mallory and a few other manufacturers also make three and four lobe dual point distributors for dual coil installations on six and eight cylinder engines. With this type of design point flutter is virtually eliminated and because of the dual coil setup, coil saturation time is increased to give a strong spark even at 10,000 rpm with a V8.

Earlier, I mentioned that a standard coil could supply enough sparks to allow a four cylinder engine to run at 9000 rpm. This figure is drastically reduced on some four cylinder engines such as the crossflow English Fords and the 2000 ohc Pinto, using an Autolite, Motorcraft or Fo Mo Co distributor.

These distributors have a cam grind that requires a point gap of 0.025 in (to prevent point bounce) which gives a cam dwell angle of only $39^0$. Such a short dwell angle reduces coil saturation and limits engine rpm. As the above mentioned distributors are of poor design, they are best replaced by an equivalent Lucas unit if you intend regularly to use more than 6000 rpm. The Lucas distributors are easy to obtain as Ford use Lucas units as well as their own brand distributors in these engines during production.

For the past 10 - 15 years many auto manufacturers have fitted a ballast resistor into the primary ignition circuit to improve coil saturation at high rpm. The resistor is fitted between the ignition switch and the coil but it may not look any different to regular electrical wire. Some manufacturers fit a resistor mounted in a ceramic insulator block. This is the type that I prefer for performance engines.

A ballast resistor is, in reality, a thermal resistor. This means that as the resistor gets cooler it allows a higher voltage in the ignition system. At low engine speed, when there is ample time for full coil saturation, the resistor heats up and reduces the voltage to about 8 volts. As an 8 volt coil is used with a ballast resistor the spark plugs still receive a full 25,000 volts. With an increase in engine speed there is less time for current flow through the coil so the resistor cools down and finally allows a full 12 volts to the 8 volt coil. This increases coil saturation and improves the spark rate and spark intensity at high rpm.

There is a side benefit of this system during engine starting. When the engine is being cranked on the starter, the resistor is by-passed and a full 12 volts is delivered at the coil to produce a hot spark. As full voltage is going to the 8 volt coil for only a short time, no damage results.

The condenser is included in the primary ignition circuit, not to stop the points burning as many believe, but to quickly drain off electrical energy from the coil primary. This speeds up the collapse of the magnetic field when the points open and increases the high voltage spark intensity. Without the condenser there would not be any spark.

The condenser is a very reliable component but I suggest that only a high quality brand such as Accel be used in performance applications. The better condensers are welded to their mounting strap. This is important as a poor earth between the condenser case and mounting strap reduces the condenser's effectiveness in quickly collapsing the coil's magnetic field. Quality condensers also have good internal electrical connections and high quality insulation to ensure top performance.

The other problem that limits the high speed capabilities of points type distributors is point bounce. This causes erratic firing due to the point rubbing block losing contact with the cam. To increase the speed at which point flutter occurs, high performance points with a stronger spring tension must be used. If points with a higher spring tension are not available, a double spring point set can be made by using a spring from an old set of points clipped inside the existing single spring.

High performance points have a spring tension of 32 - 45 oz. This allows engines to run to very high rpm without being troubled by point bounce. The limit depends on the shape of the distributor cam lobes and the number of lobes. Four cylinder engines with a 4 lobe cam and 32 oz points will run to 9000 rpm, and eight cylinder engines with an 8 lobe racing distributor and 42 oz points will run to 8500 rpm. Four cylinder motorcycles and other engines using a single lobe cam will run to 12,000 rpm without problems.

When points are being fitted, the distributor cam must be lightly lubricated with a high temperature moly distributor grease to reduce wear on the point's rubbing block. This is very important in high rpm applications, otherwise the block will wear rapidly, changing the spark timing and dwell angle.

Also check that the point contact faces are correctly aligned. (If one piece points are used, this can be done before the points are fitted.) If the alignment is not good, carefully bend the fixed contact.

Often the contact centres are also out of alignment. This cannot be corrected with one piece points, but when two piece points are used, the moving contact can be raised or lowered by using insulating washers of different thicknesses at the base of the pivot pin.

When points are pitted, do not file them with an ordinary points file as the finish is too rough for good conductivity. Instead, use either a fine diamond points file (very expensive) 169 or a small carborundum oil stone to give a smooth finish. When finished, wash the points in a non-oily solvent to remove any traces of oil and grease or tungsten grit.

Although I believe very firmly that the breaker points type ignition system will work well on most high performance and racing engines, there are certain applications where a good electronic or magneto ignition will raise the performance level, especially at very high rpm. I have never found any electronic system to be as reliable as the conventional system, but this problem is being overcome by some manufacturers.

Unless you consider fiddling with points to be a hassle, then I cannot see any reason to fit capacitor discharge or transistorised ignition to a street machine. If the car already has factory fitted electronic ignition then it may be in your interests to switch to a better electronic system. For example, the transistorised reluctor type ignition fitted by Chrysler, American Motors and Ford (and it will probably be used by other manufacturers as it is cheap) causes starting problems as the low speed spark is very weak. Once the engine has been modified, this trouble can be compounded; also the high speed spark output is poor.

Once your engine speed reaches 8000 rpm for a four cylinder engine, 7500 rpm for a six cylinder or 7000 rpm for a V8, you have just about reached the outer limits for a single coil, breaker points type ignition. The engine will run to more rpm with this sytem, but you will be losing out on power due to weakening spark intensity.

As I pointed out earlier, changing to an electronic ignition is not a guarantee that you will have a fatter spark at high rpm. Most transistorised ignitions and quite a number of capacitor discharge systems do not give a good high speed spark, in spite of advertising claims.

I have not had the opportunity to test all of the electronic ignitions around, but many that were tested proved disappointing. The Lucas 'OPUS', Accel BEI, and Allison CD all give good high rpm ignition, and are relatively reliable in service.

The Lucas 'OPUS' (oscillating pick-up system) ignition has been used on Formula 1 cars since 1967. It will produce a good spark at 11,000 rpm on the Cosworth-Ford V8, as the output signal from the magnetic pick-up does not vary with speed.

In the distributor the cam and points have been replaced by a non-metallic drum carrying small ferrite rods (one for each cylinder), and a pick-up head mounted in epoxy resin. As the drum rotates, the ferrite rods pass by the pick-up head, producing a signal in the output windings of the pick-ups.

This signal is then amplified electronically and used to switch off the high voltage transistor, thus breaking the coil primary circuit and producing a high voltage in the coil secondary windings. The high voltage from the coil is distributed by a conventional rotor button and distributor cap to each cylinder.

The advance mechanism is the usual centrifugal type, located within the distributor body. Some units are available with centrifugal and vacuum advance for road cars.

The Allison Opto XR-700 CD ignition is a very good system. It is actually a conversion kit designed to replace the breaker points with a light emitting diode (LED) and pick-up. Naturally your distributor must be in good condition, with no shaft play and a properly functioning advance mechanism.

Each Allison kit contains a light control rotor and detector block to control primary circuit switching, and a 'black box' control module.

This system is triggered by a tiny infra-red light beam passing across a gap between a LED and a photo transistor. A slotted rotor interrupts the light beam to produce the switching signal, which is transmitted to the control module for amplification. The amplified signal then breaks the primary circuit, at which time the capacitor releases its stored up energy to the coils primary winding, to produce a high energy spark.

To help combat the unreliability problem, the Allison control module contains as many standby components as it does working components. This means if one semi-conductor should fail, the standby takes its place to allow continued running.

It also contains a special protection system to prevent damage to the electronic components should a plug wire come off when the engine is running. This would normally damage most CD ignitions as they are not able to withstand the electrical stress caused when the stored up energy cannot quickly be discharged to earth (Spinning the engine on the starter to do a compression check, with the plugs not earthed, or with the CD unit left connected also will often cause 'black box' failure).

The Allison people developed their CD ignition on a Formual Atlantic open wheeler racing car, and from the results it seems that they have done their homework.

The Accel BEI (Breakerless Electronic Ignition) capacitor discharge ignition is available for most American V8's. It is a complete system with a high quality needle bearing distributor guaranteed to $\frac{1}{4}^0$ timing accuracy from 0 - 15,000 rpm.

Like the Allison unit, the Accel uses a LED timing device to release the stored up capacitor energy to the coil primary. The 370 - 400 primary volts generate a high energy 41,000 volt spark in extremely quick time.

Rise time for a conventional ignition is 75 - 125 micro-seconds, and reluctor transistorised systems are even slower. The CD system has a rise time of only 20 microseconds, which enables it to fire badly fouled or wet plugs. With other systems the rise time is so slow that a fouled plug will bleed off the voltage across the fouled insulator, causing a misfire, or at best produce a spark of low intensity. A CD ignition, however, delivers full voltage, as the 35,000 - 40,000 volts is produced so quickly that it jumps the plug gap before it has time to bleed off.

The CD voltage is high (both in primary and secondary) but this does not damage the coil as it is of such short duration. However, because the spark duration is only about $\frac{1}{6}$th that of a conventional system, the fuel/air mixture must be relatively rich or a misfire will result. For this reason I do not recommend an ordinary CD ignition on an emissions engine where the mixture is very lean. Multi-spark CD systems that produce sparks through $20^0$ of crank rotation are being developed for these engines.

Whenever a CD ignition is fitted, be sure to mount the control box away from heat, preferably in a cool air stream. Heat is a killer of electronic components, which is why they are mounted on a heat sink. However, remember that as well as dissipating heat, a heat sink can also absorb huge quantities of heat, if mounted in a hot environment.

The Scintilla Vertex magneto is probably the most reliable, maintenance free, high performance ignition system available anywhere today. The mere fact that it was in use 50 years ago supplying the spark for aeroplane engines should tell you something about the Vertex magneto.

The basic magneto unit is adaptable to any engine, by changing the drive gear and shaft, points cam, and cap. It is a fully self-contained ignition system without the need for an external power source (battery) as it generates its own primary current.

A magneto can save a lot of weight on a push-start racing machine. The battery, coil, starter, alternator, voltage regulator and cables can all be done away with. However, there are more important reasons for using a Vertex mag. It is not worried by coil saturation time or point burning and pitting (points last 60,000 miles plus.) As the engine speed increases, 171 the spark intensity increases up to a maximum of 40,000 volts.

In the magneto the primary current is produced in a similar way to that of an alternator. The alternating current (ac) is not rectified to direct current (dc), but passes through the points unchanged. This contributes to good point life as there is little possibility of pitting if the points are kept free of oil and grease.

When the points are closed, the primary current passes through the internal magneto coil to produce a strong magnetic field, which surrounds the coil's secondary windings. The magnetic field collapses when the points open, inducing a high voltage to fire the plugs. In this respect the magneto is very similar to the conventional breaker points and coil type ignition.

However, because the magneto primary voltage is not regulated, the primary voltage increases proportionately with the engine speed. This feature of the magneto ensures that the coil is fully energised (saturated) between each plug firing, regardless of how fast the engine is spinning. Also, because the primary voltage increases with an increase in engine rpm, the secondary voltage does likewise, to produce a proportionately bigger spark.

The rise time for a magneto ignition is about 35-40 microseconds, which means that it will fire all but the most badly fouled plugs.

Installation of a Vertex mag is very simple, providing that you have purchased a unit with the correct drive gear, points cam, advance curve etc, tailored to your engine. First check the shaft end play, and then recheck the play after the mag has been tightened down. 'Vee' engines with milled heads and manifolds may mesh the drive gears too tightly and cause serious shaft bind that could wreck the unit.

The numbered buttons on the mag cap show the magneto firing sequence, therefore if you were fitting the Vertex to a Chevy speedway sprint car with a 1-8-4-3-6-5-7-2 firing order you would insert the No. 1 plug wire in the No. 1 hole, No. 8 plug wire in the No. 2 hole, and so on. The cap must be inverted to determine which hole corresponds to which number on the cap. The plug leads are secured in the cap with small screws, which will break if you use too much force.

When fitting the cap be very careful not to damage the tall red pole protruding from the magneto case. This pole fits into a hole in the cap, so line the cap up correctly before attempting to fit it.

The 'P' terminal on the side of the magneto case is an earth post, which should be connected to earth via a kill switch. When the switch is closed (off) the engine is shut off. Remember that the engine will not start with the kill switch in the off position as the primary current will go straight to earth, rather than through the coil. Never connect a live wire to this 'P' terminal or your expensive Vertex will be ruined. Also don't spin the engine (or magneto) when any plug wires are removed, unless the kill switch is closed, as the unit could be damaged by an internal electrical flash-over.

To prevent demagnetising the magneto when any arc welding is being carried out, the kill switch must be in the open (on) position. Take care that the welding cables do not come in contact with the magneto case, as this could also demagnetise the unit.

Within any distributor some type of mechanism is employed to advance the spark as the engine speed increases. At idle the plugs will fire around $5^0$-$10^0$ before the piston reaches top dead centre (TDC) but at maximum speed the distributor will automatically advance the timing so that the plugs spark at, say, $35^0$ before TDC. This extra advance is necessary to allow the fuel/air mixture the correct amount of time to burn properly.

172        Obviously at 3000 rpm the piston is taking a lot less time to move from $10^0$ before TDC

to TDC than it is at 800 rpm. At 3000 rpm the combustion flame has to have progressed just as far as it would have at 800 rpm by the time the piston passes TDC, therefore we have to start the flame burning earlier to make up for the time deficit.

Probably you are wondering why different engines need a different amount of advance, even though using the same fuel which should burn at a set rate? Beside the type of fuel being combusted there are many other factors that influence the flame speed. The first one is the fuel/air ratio. Very lean and rich mixtures both burn slowly, hence the need for more spark lead. A mixture close to full power lean burns the hottest and requires the least advance.

An increase in the compression ratio increases the density of the compressed mixture and also its temperature. This increases the combustion rate; likewise an improvement in volumetric efficiency has a similar effect.

As the engine speed increases, fuel atomisation improves. Small fuel particles have a proportionately larger surface area; therefore they burn more rapidly. This partly explains why spark advance is not increased proportionately with engine speed.

The size of the combustion space and the location of the spark plug in that space also influences the amount of advance required. Obviously the further the flame has to travel (as in a big combustion chamber), the longer it will take to burn the mixture completely. Also the closer the spark plug to the centre of the chamber, the quicker the combustion time.

As mentioned in other chapters, the shape of the chamber and piston crown, the amount of exhaust gas left unscavenged and the squish (or quench) effect also influence the rate of combustion.

Right away you can see that once your engine is modified some, or all, of these factors will be changed from what they were in the stock engine. Hence you will possibly have to reset the initial advance and modify the distributor to change the total advance, and also the rate of advance.

The initial advance is the amount of advance which is supplied to the engine when it is first started and perhaps up to 450 - 1000 rpm, before the distributor automatically starts to increase the advance. It is controlled by the position of the distributor in the engine. Rotating the distributor body in the direction of rotation of the rotor button decreases the initial advance and turning it in the opposite direction increases the advance.

The initial advance can be set using either a strobe timing light with the engine idling, or a lamp connected through the points to the battery, with the engine stopped. The engine must be turned over by hand and when the light goes out (indicating the points have opened, breaking the circuit), check the timing angle off the crank pulley or flywheel and adjust the position of the distributor until the angle is correct. When the latter method is used, this is referred to as the static timing.

When a wilder camshaft and extra carburation is used, it is generally necessary to increase the initial advance. However, if there has been an increase in the compression ratio this will tend to offset the amount of extra advance required.

The total advance is the total amount of spark lead automatically added by the various systems in the distributor, plus the initial advance angle. If the engine has $10^0$ initial advance and $35^0$ total advance, it means that the distributor automatically advances $35^0 - 10^0 = 25^0$ crankshaft degrees or $12\frac{1}{2}^0$ distributor degrees. (The distributor turns at half engine speed).

Most high performance engines use a system of centrifugal advance, controlled relative to engine speed by revolving bob weights and springs. Increasing the weight of the weights or decreasing the spring tension changes the advance rate, so that the engine reaches 173 full advance more quickly. The amount the distributor can advance is controlled by a stop peg which allows the distributor cam to move a fixed amount.

Some cars, notably early model six cylinder American Fords and late model VWs, use a simple vacuum advance distributor. These should be thrown out as they are not acceptable, even on the standard engine.

Generally, production engines use a combined centrifugal/vacuum advance system. The centrifugal system works as described earlier and the vacuum system backs it up to further increase the advance. The vacuum unit receives its signal either from below the carburettor throttle plate (manifold vacuum) or from above the throttle plate (spark ported vacuum). The manifold vacuum advance unit is added to improve low-speed fuel economy by increasing the advance when the throttle is almost closed during light load cruising. The spark ported vacuum system is purely an emissions device designed to improve the spark advance rate and performance on emissions engines.

Either vacuum system will work acceptably when combined with the centrifugal system in cars modified for slightly above-standard performance. However, once the limits of sports tune are approached, the vacuum advance mechanism reduces performance by upsetting the spark timing.

If you check the plate on which the points are mounted (the breaker plate) in a vacuum/centrifugal advance distributor you will find that it can be wriggled up and down and all over the place. You will also note that the points open and close as the plate is moved up and down. At higher engine speeds the movement of the points opening and closing causes the breaker plate to move about in a similar way and this makes the spark timing erratic.

When this type of distributor is used, the vacuum hose should be disconnected (block up the vacuum hole) and the breaker plate stabilised. Usually it is possible to silver solder the plate halves together in a few places; if not, try bolting the top and bottom half together. Some distributor manufacturers make a non-vacuum type breaker plate that can be used as a bolt-in replacement.

Most performance engines require less total advance than standard, due to the improved fuel/air density at higher engine speeds, but the rate of advance must be increased so that full advance is reached at 2500-3000 rpm, instead of the more usual 4000-5000 rpm.

The amount of total advance required will vary, but generally an engine of up to 1600cc in semi-race tune will want $25^0$-$30^0$, which equals $7.5^0$-$10^0$ distributor advance if the initial advance is $10^0$.

As the cylinder displacement increases, so the total advance required increases. Assuming the use of petrol (gasoline), a 350 cubic inch V8 breathing nicely will possibly need $38^0$ - $42^0$ total advance. If the initial advance required is $16^0$ then the distributor advance will be $11^0$ - $13^0$ at 2800 rpm (1400 distributor rpm).

It may seem a little confusing switching the engine and distributor degrees of advance and rpm around but it is necessary. When the distributor is being set up on a distributor test bench, you have to remember that the machine is turning the distributor at half engine speed and it is recording the advance angle on the instrument panel at half the crankshaft angle.

Top quality racing distributors have an adjustment to set the amount of distributor advance but as the stock unit is used in many applications we will consider the modifications necessary to limit the advance to the angle that we require for best performance.

All distributors limit the amount of centrifugal advance by using a slotted plate or lever

that comes up against a stop peg (often one of the pegs to which a bob weight spring is attached) to prevent the distributor cam moving any further forward, relative to the direction of rotation.

To investigate how the advance mechanism works in your particular distributor you will probably have to remove the breaker plate (the points and condenser are mounted on the breaker plate) as the bob weights and springs etc. are usually concealed in the internals of the distributor. Once you can see inside, hold the distributor drive gear to prevent the shaft turning and then attempt to turn the distributor cam forward (you will get a better grip if you leave the rotor in place and turn it). In most instances the cam will rotate a few degrees until it comes against the stop mentioned earlier.

If the cam won't move at all, you can assume that it is seized onto the drive shaft due to a lack of lubrication, in which case you will have to dismantle the cam from the drive shaft. To do this, lift off the rotor and remove the screw or wire circlip in the top of the cam. Then disconnect any springs etc. and pull the cam off the distributor drive shaft. Remove the accumulation of rust from the bore of the cam and the drive shaft and reassemble them, using engine oil to lubricate the shaft.

When you get the cam moving forward without the drive gear turning, you will be able to determine the means used to prevent it turning any further. Then work out what to do to reduce the number of degrees the cam is able to advance.

To give you an example of what is required we will assume that we are modifying a distributor for a 2000 cc. ohc Ford Pinto engine in semi-race tune. The Ford brand distributor has been tossed out and we have obtained a Lucas unit out of a wrecked 2000.

It is estimated that the engine will require $10^0$ initial advance and $32^0$ total advance. This means that we want $32^0 - 10^0 = 22^0$ crank degrees or $11^0$ distributor degrees centrifugal advance (Note - the vacuum has been disconnected and the breaker plate silver soldered).

According to Ford's specifications, the standard Lucas distributor starts to advance at 425 rpm (distributor rpm). At 900 rpm the advance is $11^0$ and at 2500 rpm maximum centrifugal advance is $13.5^0$

We want the distributor to be fully advanced at 1200 - 1300 rpm (distributor) so a slightly heavier set of governor springs will have to be fitted.

FIGURE 7.2 illustrates the type of arm attached to the cam and the stop pin that limits the advance. Measure the distance between the nose of the arm and the pin. This distance, say 0.153 in, equals approximately $13.5^0$ advance (the advance may vary from $12.5^0$ to $14.5^0$ due to production tolerances). Therefore a distance equal to $11 \div 13.5 \times 0.153 \, (0.125 \, in)$ will restrict the advance to $11^0$.

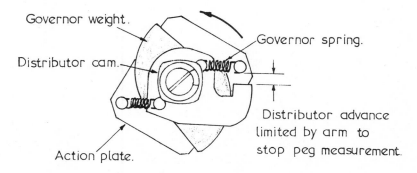

Fig. 7. 2  Distributor advance mechanism.

To reduce the measurement to 0.125 in you can weld up the nose of the arm and then file it back to give the correct measurement. When you refit the cam to the distributor drive shaft be sure always to check the distance from the nose of the arm to the same stop pin. There are two pins on the drive plate and the cam can be fitted to come against either one. The problem is that the pins are usually not $180^0$ apart, therefore the distance from the nose of the cam arm to one pin will be different if the cam is moved around $180^0$ (relative to the drive plate) to stop against the opposite pin. Until I made this discovery many years ago I was puzzled as to why my measurements seemed to be jumping about all over the place.

While the distributor is partly dismantled check that the drive shaft bearing is not worn and allowing the shaft to wriggle. If play is excessive, a new bush will be required.

Next check the distributor shaft end float. This should preferably be 0.003 in and not more than 0.006 in. When a helical drive gear is fitted, excessive end float can cause the timing to change erratically. Use shims between the gear and the distributor body to reduce the end play.

When the drive gear has been refitted, check that it is properly pinned and unable to move at all on the shaft. If any play is evident, peen the pin to tighten the gear on the shaft. A loose gear will also upset the timing.

Completely assemble the distributor and take it to an auto-electrical repair shop with an accurate distributor tester capable of spinning to half your maximum engine speed. Check the dwell variation for the four firing points. This should be less than $\pm \frac{1}{2}^0$. Then check and record the amount of advance at various distributor rpm and change the governor spring tension until the advance curve is what you want (FIGURE 7.3).

Curve 'A' is the ideal advance curve that we think should work best with this particular engine. If the advance turns out like curve 'B' we are over-advancing due to production tolerances, so we will have to add more weld to the nose of the arm. In this example the distributor is advancing $12^0$. As the distance between the arm and pin is 0.125 in we are going to have to reduce it to $11 \div 12 \times 0.125$ in (0.116 in) to reduce the advance to $11^0$.

Curve 'C' illustrates the distributor advancing the correct amount. However, the

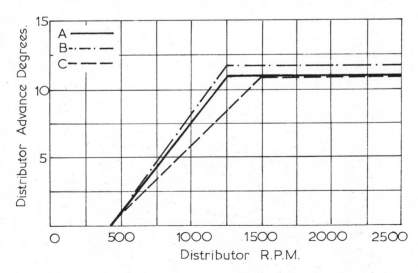

Fig. 7.3 Distributor advance curves.

governor springs are too strong and full advance is not being reached until 1500 rpm.

The only really accurate way to check if the advance curve of the modified distributor is compatible with the engine is to run it and check the power throughout the range on an engine dyno. If the spark is under or over advanced at any engine speed, this will be indicated by a loss in power at that particular rpm.

The total advance required for the best performance can be tested on the road or drag strip by timing the acceleration from 50 to 100 mph in top gear. The amount of advance that produces the quickest time will also give best power. However, this test does not take into consideration the best initial advance setting or the best rate of advance for peak performance.

If you found that the Pinto engine in this example produced the quickest 50 - 100 mph acceleration with $32^0$ total advance, as we had estimated, this would not necessarily prove that the engine is working at its best. Maybe $10^0$ initial advance is not enough to launch the car from a standing start; perhaps $13^0$ is required. In that case the distributor advance would have to be cut back to $9\frac{1}{2}^0$ to keep the total advance at $32^0$.

It could be that our estimated $10^0$ initial advance and $32^0$ total advance figures are both correct, but the engine is reaching full advance too quickly. If the engine pinged at 2000 rpm in every gear or maybe just in 3rd and top gear when accelerating hard, this would indicate that the rate of advance needs to be slowed down so that full advance is reached at 2800 rpm instead of 2400 rpm.

There are many variables so a lot of time is always involved getting the timing and the advance curve spot on just by road testing alone. Many enthusiasts have a tendency to over-advance the timing in an effort to pick up every last fraction of performance. My advice is use the least amount of advance conducive to peak performance. Usually you will find that once you reach a certain point the engine will not perform any better with just a $1^0$ or $2^0$ degree increase in advance. Instead, it seems to respond only to a $4^0$ or $5^0$ increase. When you reach the stage that the engine becomes insensitive to a small amount of additional advance then you have gone far enough, or maybe even a degree or two too far. In drag racing you may pick up a little extra performance going the extra $4^0$ or $5^0$ degrees but this is not so for other types of competition if you wish to avoid holed pistons.

How much initial advance you give a road motor has to be watched, not so much to avoid engine damage, but because the amount of initial advance that produces the best low speed responsiveness often causes starter motor kick back. This can wreck the starter or ring gear very quickly.

If you run very close to the maximum total advance that the engine will tolerate, without going into high speed detonation, then you must be very careful to compensate for changes in the atmospheric conditions. A 7 - 10% increase in the relative air density (RAD) could result in a fuel/air mixture lean enough to produce a set of melted pistons, if you do not richen the mixture accordingly.

Detonation and pre-ignition are both engine wreckers. Pre-ignition is self-ignition of the fuel caused by a hot spot within the combustion chamber, or due to the fuel becoming unstable because of excessive pressure or heat. Detonation is a violent burning of the fuel (almost an explosion) caused by colliding flame fronts after the spark plug has fired.

When engine damage results from either condition, the culprit usually can be identified after an examination of the pistons and spark plugs.

Pre-ignition damage is caused by extreme combustion temperatures melting the top of the piston and possibly also the ring lands. If a hole is present in the piston crown, it will 177 appear to have been burned through with a welding torch. The metal around the hole will have a melted appearance.

Spark plugs exposed to sustained pre-ignition quite often have the centre electrode melted away and in extreme cases the insulator nose also may be fused.

Usually, pre-ignition can be traced to combustion chamber or exhaust valve deposits becoming incandescent, but it may also be due to blocked water jackets creating a hot spot. A spark plug with a heat range too hot for the engine may glow and initiate pre-ignition.

In a few cases pre-ignition can be traced to an overheated piston providing the hot spot necessary for self-ignition. The piston may overheat due to inadequate lubrication, improper clearance or a broken ring.

A piston damaged by detonation will show signs of pitting on the crown. In extreme examples the piston crown may be holed. The hole will appear to have been punched through, with radial cracks and a depressed area around the hole. A spark plug subjected to detonation will usually show signs of cracking at the insulator nose.

When detonation occurs, a portion of the fuel/air change will begin to burn spontaneously due to excessive heat and pressure after normal ignition takes place. The two flame fronts ultimately collide and the resulting explosion hammers the engine's internal components.

Detonation can be attributed to excessive spark advance and/or lean fuel/air mixtures. In supercharged and turbocharged engines, excessive intake charge temperatures can also lead to this condition.

Due to increased combustion temperatures in a modified engine, consideration must be given to finding a spark plug with the correct heat range. A hot plug transfers combustion heat slowly and is used to avoid fouling in engines with relatively low combustion chamber or cylinder head temperatures; ie in a relatively low horsepower motor. A cold plug on the other hand, transfers heat rapidly from the firing end and is used to avoid overheating where temperatures are high, as in a racing engine.

The length of the insulator nose and the electrode alloy composition are the primary factors in establishing the heat rating of a particular plug. Hot plugs have long insulator noses, and therefore a long heat transfer path. Cold plugs have shorter nose lengths to transfer heat more rapidly from the insulator tip to the water jacket, via the metal spark plug body.

Motors in sports tune will probably require a standard plug or one not more than a couple of steps colder than standard. Semi-race engines cause us more problems as two plug types may be needed to cope with city driving and high speed running. A plug two or three grades colder than standard should be tried for everyday street use and short full throttle bursts. The plug selected must be able to resist low speed fouling and pre-ignition at a constant 80 mph. The second plug type would be used under competition conditions or sustained high speed driving.

Race engines also require two plug heat ranges, one for engine warm-up and one for racing. If there is sufficient space in the combustion chamber, projected nose or regular gap plugs are best used for warm-up, otherwise use the hottest retracted gap racing plug available. Whenever warm-up plugs are fitted, tag the tacho or steering wheel as the engine could be destroyed if, in the heat of the moment, your memory lets you down and you race with hot plugs fitted.

After you have decided what plug you think should be of the correct heat range, you must test to ensure that your choice is the right one. Providing the engine is in good condition and the carburettor is correctly tuned, reading the nose of the plug will indicate if it has the correct heat range.

So that you do not end up with engine damage it is always advisable to begin testing with plugs that are too cold or else test the machine at moderate load and speed, then check the plugs before you engage in any full power running.

For the plug reading to be accurate it will be necessary to run the engine at full throttle and maximum speed on the track (or road) and then cut the engine dead. If you allow the engine to keep running as you bring the vehicle to a stop, the plug reading will be useless.

As I pointed out in an earlier chapter, it is not just the colour of the insulator nose that we are interested in. Some fuels will not colour a plug, and it takes miles for many types to colour the insulator. Therefore all of the plug firing end exposed to the combustion flame must be examined and read. The signs to look for are indicated in TABLE 7.1

Of course, spark plug heat range must be tailored to each race circuit, for those

### TABLE 7.1  Spark plug reading for correct heat range and other conditions

| Spark plug condition | Indications |
| --- | --- |
| *Normal* — correct heat range. | Insulator nose white or very light tan to rust brown. Little or no cement boil where the centre electrode protrudes through the insulator nose. The electrodes are not discoloured or eroded. |
| *Too cold* — use hotter plug. | Insulator nose dark grey or black. Steel plug shell end covered with dry, black soot deposit that will rub off easily. |
| *Too hot* — use colder plug. | Insulator nose chalky white or may have a satin sheen. Excessive cement boil where centre electrode protrudes through the insulator nose. Cement may be milk white or meringue-like. Centre electrode may 'blue' and be rounded off at the edges. Earth electrode may be badly eroded or have a molten appearance. |
| *Preignition* — use colder plug & remove combustion chamber deposits. | Insulator nose blistered. Centre electrode and side electrode burned or melted away. |
| *Detonation* — retard ignition and richen mixture. | Fractured insulator nose in sustained or extreme cases. Insulator nose covered in tiny pepper specks or even tiny beads of aluminium leaving the piston. Excessive cement boil where centre electrode protrudes through insulator nose. Specks on plug shell end. |
| *Insulator glazing* — replace with plugs of same heat range. If condition reoccurs fit plugs one grade colder. | Shiny yellow, green or tan deposit on the insulator nose, particularly close to the centre electrode. |
| *Ash fouled* — clean or replace with plugs of the same heat range. | Thick yellow, white or light brown deposit on insulator, centre and side electrode. |

involved in road racing or long and short course speedway racing. Tracks with long straights or high speed banked turns usually require a colder plug than a circuit with short straights, and many esses and hairpin corners.

When the fuel blend is changed, the plug heat range will have to be changed accordingly. In unsupercharged applications, the plug probably will have to be one grade colder for each 10 - 15% of nitro added.

Once you have determined the correct plug heat range don't swap over to another brand with an 'equivalent' heat range. Heat range conversion charts should be used as a guide only when you swap from one plug brand to another, as different plug manufacturers use different methods of determining the heat range of their plugs. If you cross-referenced the conversion charts from all the plug manufacturers, you will find that they disagree with each other, due to different test procedures.

Even spark plugs with the same number from a particular manufacturer can have a wide heat range tolerance. This is why some mechanics are very particular about the brand of plug that they use in their engines. They claim that one particular brand gives a more consistent heat range, therefore they don't have to test dozens of plugs with the same number to find a set that have the same heat range.

As well as the heat range, the gap style of the plug must also be considered to obtain the best performance, and in some instances to avoid mechanical engine damage. (FIGURE 7.4)

The best plug to use in most engines, where there is sufficient physical room between the tip of the plug and valves and piston crown, is the projecting nose type. It has a very wide heat range to resist both fouling and preignition. At high speeds the long insulator nose is cooled by the incoming fuel charge to increase its cold heat range. At low speeds the long tip runs hotter, to prevent fouling.

If you change from a regular or retracted gap plug to a projecting nose type it may be necessary to retard the advance slightly. The projecting nose starts the ignition flame burning physically deeper in the combustion chamber and this reduces the length of flame travel within the chamber. Often, projecting nose plugs will raise the power output of the engine right through the power range because of improved combustion.

Projecting nose plugs are not recommended for highly supercharged engines or those using more than 20% nitro fuel. Generally, they are not available in a heat range cold enough for radically modified racing engines.

The conventional gap plug is next preferred after the projecting nose type. It can be used in engines not able physically to accommodate projecting nose plugs. This style has a wider heat range than a retracted gap plug and provides superior ignition flame propagation.

The retracted gap racing plug is necessary in highly modified, supercharged, or high percentage nitro-fuelled racing engines. It may also be used in racing engines where there is insufficient clearance between the spark plug and valves or piston to use either a projecting nose or regular gap design. A plug of this type should be used only when absolutely necessary. It has very little resistance to fouling and generates a poor ignition flame front.

The fine wire plug (eg. Champion Gold Palladium) has some use in semi and full race engines. It was originally developed for racing two-stroke engines but can be used in four-stroke applications requiring a wide heat range (similar to projecting core plugs) in the colder grades.

These plugs are expensive, due to the use of a fine semi-precious metal electrode, but they perform very well in high performance and racing engines requiring a cold plug relatively resistant to low speed fouling. They are not recommended for highly supercharged or high percentage nitro-burning engines.

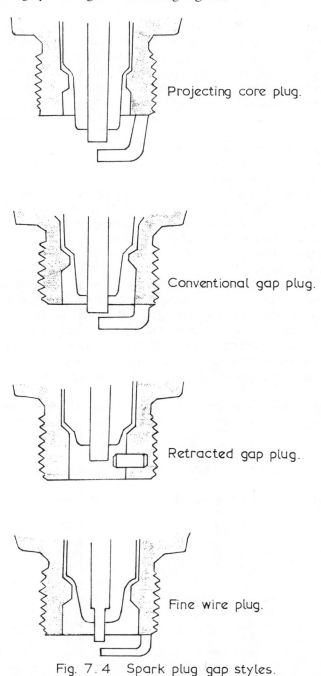

Projecting core plug.

Conventional gap plug.

Retracted gap plug.

Fine wire plug.

Fig. 7.4  Spark plug gap styles.

Whenever a cylinder head with larger valves, modified combustion chamber, or relocated spark plug is used, or pistons with a non-standard crown are fitted, always check that the spark plug is of the correct reach and gap style to avoid mechanical damage to the engine.

With the head removed, check that the plug reach (ie. the length from the plug seat to the end of the thread) is neither too long nor too short. A plug that does not extend the full threaded length of the plug boss in the head will reduce performance by masking the ignition flame and invite hot spots from carbon build up in the unused thread. A plug that is too long (ie. has exposed threads in the combustion chamber) can cause damage and stripping of the plug boss threads in the head as carbon build up on the exposed plug threads makes plug removal very difficult. Also the exposed threads can become a hot spot to initiate pre-ignition.

In some instances a change to another plug reach may be in order, but in most cases the use of a single solid copper gasket on each plug will ensure the proper depth fit. The range of Champion gaskets is listed in TABLE 7.2.

With the head fitted, check that sufficient clearance exists between the plug and piston. To allow for rod stretch the normal plug gap should be increased by 0.025 in. Turn the engine over by hand and then remove the plugs and inspect them for closed gaps. When carrying out this check remember that a hot projecting nose plug extends further into the combustion chamber than a colder one, so be sure to make the check using the hottest plug that will be used in the engine.

The width of the spark plug gap for best performance depends primarily on the compression pressure of the fuel/air mixture, the engine speed and the coil saturation time. Increasing the first two factors and decreasing the latter calls for a decrease in plug gap. It is safe to say that all modified engines require a plug gap narrower than stock.

Manufacturers stipulate a relatively wide gap as this improves the engine idle and low speed performance. The ignition spark from a wide gap is much larger than that from one much narrower, hence a larger initial combustion flame is generated, assisting low rpm running.

At high engine speeds and compression pressures the coil is not able to supply electrical energy of sufficient intensity to jump the spark gap. Accordingly, the gap must be reduced

### TABLE 7.2    Champion spark plug gaskets

| Plug diameter (mm) | Gasket thickness (in) | Part No |
|---|---|---|
| 10 | 0.045 | Y - 674 |
|  | 0.055/.045 | Y - 678 |
| 12 | 0.057 | P - 674 |
|  | 0.070/.052 | P - 678 |
|  | 0.095 | P - 677 |
| 14 | 0.057 | N - 675 |
|  | 0.135 | N - 677 |
|  | 0.070/.052 | N - 678 |
|  | 0.080 | N - 673X1 |
| 18 | 0.080 | A - 675 |
|  | 0.065/.050 | A - 676 |
|  | 0.075/.055 | A - 678 |

to avoid a high speed misfire, or the possible breakdown of the high voltage system insulation.

From experience, I would recommend that any high performance engine using a conventional points type ignition should not use a plug gap exceeding 0.028 in. Semi and full race engines may need a gap as small as 0.018 - 0.022 in with conventional plugs, and down to 0.014 in when using retracted gap racing plugs.

Engines with a capacitor discharge ignition can pick up some power with wider plug gaps as this type of ignition is relatively insensitive to high engine rpm. In this instance the plug gap should be set to the ignition manufacturer's specifications for short distance events and ordinary road use.

Those involved in long distance racing and rallying or constant high speed road driving should not use a gap exceeding 0.035 in, as any weakness developed in the CD unit during a race could lead to total ignition failure. A closer plug gap reduces the load on the 'black box', minimising the chance of any weakness developing, and if some trouble does arise, the system may have just enough reserve to finish the event.

Always check to be sure that your coil polarity is correct before you try experimenting to determine what plug gap gives the best performance. Earlier I mentioned that you lose the equivalent of 40% coil energy when the polarity is reversed, now I will explain why this is so.

The spark should always jump from the centre electrode of the plug to the side electrode as this considerably decreases the voltage required for ignition. Due to the centre electrode being at a much higher temperature than the side electrode, less voltage is needed to produce a spark, as electrons will leave the hotter surface at a lower voltage. This is why it can be difficult to get a cold motor started. Because the plug centre electrode is cold, a much higher voltage is required to produce a spark.

The coil polarity can be checked as previously explained, or by using an oscilloscope. The trace pattern will be upside down if the polarity is not correct. A dished or eroded spark plug side electrode also indicates wrong polarity. The dish at the end of the electrode is caused by metal leaving the electrode each time a spark jumps across to the centre electrode.

The life of a spark plug is not as short as many would suppose. Some drag racers have the idea that a new set of plugs is required for each $\frac{1}{4}$ mile trip; but cars involved in 500 mile speedway races and 12 and 24 hour road events go the full distance without a plug change. A road machine should not require a plug replacement more frequently than 7000 - 10,000 miles, and racing plugs will easily last 300 miles with proper care, or about 50 trips down the drag strip for unsupercharged petrol or methanol burners.

A road vehicle should have the plugs filed, gapped and tested every 3,000 miles, and a race machine after each event. Retracted gap plugs cannot be filed, and fine wire electrode plugs should not be filed.

Projecting nose and conventional gap plugs should have the earth electrode bent back far enough to permit filing of the sparking surfaces shown in FIGURE 7.5. A point file can be used to file a flat surface with sharp edges on both the centre and side electrode. This lowers the voltage requirement to fire the plug, firstly because electricity prefers to jump across sharp edges, and secondly because the electrical conductivity of the electrodes is improved. The heat and pressure of combustion tends to oxidise and break up the electrode firing surfaces, increasing the electrical resistance. Filing removes this 'dead' metal and exposes new highly conductive material.

Spark plugs should never be cleaned with a wire brush as metallic deposits will 183

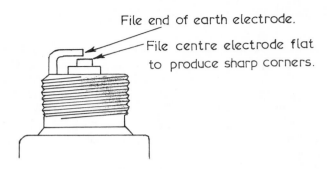

File end of earth electrode.

File centre electrode flat
to produce sharp corners.

Fig. 7.5 Spark plug electrode filing.

impregnate the insulator and short out the plug. I also do not recommend cleaning with a plug cleaner as some abrasive material always seems to become wedged between the insulator and plug shell. If this cannot be probed out with a scriber, it will drop out in the engine and possibly cause some damage. If you choose to have your plugs abrasive blasted, be sure to remove all abrasive grit from inside the plug nose and from the threads.

Personally, I prefer to leave plugs uncleaned. If they are fuel or oil fouled I clean them with a tooth brush and ether, or some other non-oily solvent. If the insulation is breaking down due to leaded fuel deposits, I throw the plug away.

The spark plug leads provide the electrical connection between the distributor cap and plugs, and also an effective insulating barrier to prevent the ignition current tracking to earth. Most cars use radio suppression cables with a powdered carbon impregnated rayon cord to conduct the high voltage current. With age, the electrical resistance of this cable increases, and in some instances it won't conduct electricity at all. Therefore suppression cables should be tossed out and replaced by high quality copper cored cable. To cut out radio interference on road cars resistors can be fitted to each spark plug. (Some high performance cars have copper leads and resistors fitted by the makers.)

The high voltage cables need to have spark plug and distributor cap boots to prevent HV track over or arcing. Many high speed and full acceleration misfires can be attributed to the spark jumping from an exposed spark plug top to a nearby earth, usually the head or an exhaust pipe.

To be able to withstand the high underbonnet temperatures usually experienced with high performance cars, the cables and boots should be of top quality silicone. I recommend Accel 'Yellow Jacket' 7 mm wire for the majority of applications, and Accel 'Fat Stuff II' 9 mm wire for racing V8 and V6 engines, where the plug wires pass very close to the exhaust headers.

Cross fire (induction leakage) will occur whenever high voltage wires are grouped closely together and run in parallel for any distance. This causes the engine to run roughly, and can result in serious preignition or detonation.

This problem is not due to poor plug lead insulation, but rather to magnetic induction. A magnetic field surrounds any high tension conductor, and the lead which is carrying high voltage at any instance induces voltage into an adjacent plug lead.

A cross fire that will give us trouble is most likely to occur between consecutive firing cylinders when these are located alongside each other in the engine. The way around the problem is either to separate the leads involved so that they are about 3 in apart and not running parallel with each other, or they should be routed to cross over once. I prefer this latter method as crossing the wires once inverts the magnetic field in the second wire and effectively cuts out any induction. Remember never to tape HV wires together or run them through steel clips or other steel fittings.

If the engine has a 1 - 8 - 4 - 3 - 6 - 5 - 7 - 2 firing order (common to most V8 engines), the plug leads to No. 5 and No. 7 should be crossed or well separated. The Ford V8 firing order of 1 - 5 - 4 - 2 - 6 - 3 - 7 - 8 calls for leads No. 7 and No. 8 to be crossed or parted.

Beside the plug leads, the distributor cap, rotor button and coil tower can also be high voltage leakage, or flashover, areas. These parts must be free of accumulated dust, moisture, cracks and carbon tracks to ensure that full voltage is reaching the plugs. Therefore a periodic check must be made to ensure that none of these conditions exist.

Unknowingly, some tuners bring trouble upon themselves by removing carbon from the distributor cap terminals and the rotor button contact. Actually carbon in these areas assists electrical conduction. The real problem is that quite often the knife or screwdriver being used to scrape the carbon from the distributor cap terminals slips and scratches the glaze inside the cap. This drastically reduces the dielectric strength and can lead to a carbon track forming during wet conditions. Often a piece of abrasive paper is used to polish the rotor button contact. This cuts straight through the insulating glaze and results in voltage leakage to earth.

When high voltage ignition systems are used, particular attention must be paid to keeping all the insulating mediums clean, otherwise less voltage will be available to fire the plugs than when the standard ignition system was fitted. Actually, when a high output ignition is fitted, only top quality distributor caps and rotors, made of alkyd material, should be used. This material is resistant to carbon tracking, even when cracked.

# Chapter 8
# Lubrication and Cooling

THE MECHANICAL well-being of an engine is utterly dependent on good lubrication and adequate cooling. A minor breakdown in either system could well mean the destruction of the engine, particularly under competition conditions. In standard tune, the stock lubrication and cooling system will, if in good condition, be able to cope with the demands you may place on the engine. However, as higher states of tune are sought, inadequacies will become readily apparent.

The lubrication system has to provide a supply of oil to all moving parts, to prevent metal to metal contact and carry away heat from high temperature areas such as the engine bearings and valve springs. However, if the wrong oil is used, lubrication could still break down, regardless of the efficiency of the oil supply system. For this reason we need to have a good understanding of oil and how it functions.

The viscosity of oil is a measure of its ability to flow through a graduated hole at an established temperature. High viscosity oils are thick and offer more resistance to flow. Low viscosity oils flow more easily and so offer less resistance to the engine turning over.

A viscous (high viscosity) oil leaves a physically thicker oil film under any condition than does a non-viscous (low viscosity) oil. This fact influences both engine wear and blow-by. Obviously if an oil film is so thin that it cannot keep moving parts from contacting one another, wear results. Realising that gases in the combustion chamber are at a high pressure following ignition and that the oil film between rings, piston and cylinder wall is assisting in sealing, we know that the oil film must be viscous enough to withstand this pressure.

If too heavy an oil is selected, it will fail to get between closely fitting parts in sufficient quantities to lubricate or conduct heat away. Tests on viscous oils in the 60 and 70 grades have given poor results due to temperature buildup at the bearings and the inability of the oil to lubricate in tight areas. Added to this, these oils have been found to hold heat rather than dissipate it and to trap air, so de-aeration is a problem.

Many drivers use a thick oil to give a good oil pressure reading, this apparently imparting to them some sense of confidence in the engine holding together. However, the reluctance of the viscous oil to pass through the bearings creates a wiping action, which actually promotes wear and a substantial decrease in power due to the cranking and pumping resistance of thick oils.

All oils thin when hot and thicken when cold, but they do not all react to temperature change in the same way. For example, two 40 grade oils which possess the same viscosity at $100^0$C may have radically different viscosities at higher and lower temperatures. The oil which thins the most at high temperatures will also thicken the most at low temperatures. The oil showing the least change in viscosity is the most desirable one to use. Such an oil is said to have a high viscosity index while the one most affected is regarded as a low VI oil. An oil with a high VI is most desirable for racing engines, provided the high rating has not been obtained by using additives.

VI improvers, referred to as polymers, have enabled the development of multi-grade or multi-viscosity oils. Polymers are molecules which expand and thicken the oil as the temperature increases, and reduce in size and thin the oil as it cools. Therefore an oil such as 20W-50 will have the characteristics of 20W oil at low temperatures and of 50 SAE at high temperatures. These oils are fine for road vehicles in the highest state of modification, but they should not be used in a highly modified race or rally engine.

Large advances have been made in polymer chemistry but these VI improvers are still not completely shear stable at high loads. During shock periods they tend to lose their structure momentarily and collapse, so a 20W-50 oil would only be offering the protection of a 20W oil under those conditions. This loss of structure is particularly likely to occur at heavily loaded areas such as at the bearings and the tappets. You will find that most camshaft grinders recommend that their cams be run-in using a straight 30 or 40 grade oil for this very reason.

Beside polymers, an oil may contain an anti-oxidant, a detergent and a foam suppressant.

Oxidation occurs due to the presence of oxygen and combustion by-products in the oil and due to the temperature of the oil itself. As the oil temperature increases past $100^0$C, the rate of oxidation accelerates and the anti-oxidant becomes less effective.

The by-product of oxidation and combustion is sludge. To keep this in suspension, rather than allow a build-up inside the engine, detergent is added. Racing oils, however, contain very little detergent and for this reason they should not be used in road vehicles.

To counter aeration, a foam suppressant is added. The foam suppressant will prevent the formation of foam under the conditions for which the oil is designed to be used, but it cannot eliminate the foam resulting from the presence of water in the oil or from air sucked into the oiling system either through a fractured pick up or due to oil surge which would allow the oil pump to pump air.

There are basically three types of oils:- mineral oil derived from crude oil; vegetable oil from the castor oil plant; and synthetic oil which is man-made and used straight or blended with mineral or vegetable oil.

Most engines use mineral oil, which is able to provide adequate lubrication under normal circumstances. For high performance road engines I prefer to use Castrol GTX or BP Corse Plus. Either oil should be changed every 60 days or 3000 miles. If a good deal of stop-start city driving is engaged in, this should be reduced to a 30 day oil change period for best wear protection and to resist sludge build-up.

I realise that many car manufacturers recommend an oil change period longer than this, but remember that the average engine does not have the high bearing and tappet loads of the high performance unit. Also a real problem with the high performance engine is oil dilution due to blow-by and the presence of raw fuel on the cylinder walls. Because it is modified to work best at higher engine speeds, fuel vaporisation is poor at lower speeds. Some of the raw fuel inducted into the engine at low rpm will remain clinging to the cylinder walls, eventually finding its way into the sump to dilute the oil. The build-up of raw fuel and combustion by-products (which increase with an increase in fuel consumption) reduce the oil's lubricating ability. The only way around the problem is to use a high performance oil and change it more frequently, and let's face it, oil is relatively inexpensive.

Before changing the oil, take the vehicle for a good run to bring it to normal operating temperature. This ensures that any sediment and sludge will be well mixed, and will drain out in the oil. The oil will be very hot so take care or you could be badly burned.

For road motorcycles I recommend Castrol Grand Prix, with the above stated oil change period.

BP Corse 30, 40 or 50 is a mineral oil suitable for racing or rally use. These oils were originally developed for the Grand Prix Maserati racing engines to combat camshaft/tappet wear. As for any racing oil, Corse should be changed after each race meeting.

For the most highly stressed rally engines and all my racing engines I specify Castrol R40 castor oil. This oil provides the best anti-wear protection of any that I know. Many tuners do not like castor oil or blended castor/synthetic because of some problems associated with the use of an oil of this type.

Some claim that castor oil gums up the rings and causes ring sticking, but I have never found this problem, even in my two-stroke racing engines. There is one area for concern; due to castor-based oils being hygroscopic, they will absorb moisture from the atmosphere. Therefore once a container is opened, its entire contents should be used, or if oil is left over this should be poured into a smaller container so that there is no air space left above the oil from which it may absorb moisture.

Some feel that they can gain some added protection through the use of oil additives or the use of oil qualified to meet diesel engine specification. In the main, oil additives appear to be based on polymers, which means they thicken the oil as the temperature increases. Other additives contain solids in suspension such as graphite and molybdenum disulphide, both of which offer a degree of anti-wear protection. Diesel engine oil is made to combat the by-products of combustion of diesel fuel. While most oil companies have diesel oils that meet the latest SE specification for petrol engines, these oils are developed for fleet operators with both petrol and diesel-engined vehicles. They are good enough for an SE specification and for use in standard vehicles, but they do not provide the protection of the high performance oils, which far exceed the requirements of SE classification in most instances.

No matter how good your oil is it must be maintained at the correct temperature to lubricate effectively. A good deal of engine wear takes place because engines are operated with cold oil and/or water. An engine should never be driven hard until the oil reaches $50^0$C. The ideal operating temperature is 80 - $90^0$C. It can go as high as $130^0$C for short periods but oil breakdown and excessive oxidation will take place above this temperature.

To maintain the oil at 80 - $90^0$C, an oil cooler will be necessary for a competition vehicle. This should be painted matt black to aid heat radiation. The oil lines connecting the oil system to the oil cooler should be of at least $\frac{1}{2}$ in, and preferably $\frac{5}{8}$ - $\frac{3}{4}$ in bore, so as not to restrict oil flow. Some oil cooler take-off sandwich blocks which fit between the oil pump and filter are particularly bad in this respect. I have seen sandwich blocks for the English

Fords that require the oil to travel through two 90⁰ bends. If you must use a sandwich block, pattern it after the one fitted to the Twin Cam Escorts.

In hotter climates, high performance road vehicles may also need an oil cooler. It is always a worry recommending an oil cooler for a road car or bike because for a good deal of the time the oil will be over-cooled, particularly during winter. Cold oil promotes engine wear and sludge build-up so be sure to fit a shutter or blind in front of the oil cooler to prevent air passing through it when driving and/or weather conditions are not conducive to a high oil temperature.

Before you decide on an oil cooler for a road machine, be sure you really need one. Fit an oil temperature gauge and determine your oil operating temperature in mid-summer. If under normal driving conditions your oil temperature is in excess of $110^0$C, fit an oil cooler. However, if it stays around 100 - $110^0$C and climbs to $120^0$C only when you run at full throttle for quite a few miles, you will be wasting your time and causing yourself unnecessary trouble by fitting an oil cooler.

Air-cooled car engines almost always require additional oil cooling capacity when modified for more power. However, as these are usually rear engined vehicles, the extra oil radiator should be placed in a more direct air stream, preferably at the front of the car. The plumbing required makes this quite an involved operation, and you will need a two-stage oil pump, one stage to circulate the oil through the engine and the other to pump it to the oil cooler and back to the sump.

A less radical conversion for the VW is to adapt the Porsche 356 oil cooler and fit a deep well oil sump with both internal and external finning. The internal fins increase the heat absorbancy rate from the oil to the sump. The external surface must be painted matt black to obtain peak radiation efficiency.

Air-cooled road bikes can generally do without additional oil cooling if of wet sump design, by painting the oil filter canister and sump matt black. Bikes using a dry sump system, if ridden hard for long periods, almost always require an oil radiator. When an oil cooler is fitted, be sure to mount it high up on the frame down tubes. Overheating of the cylinder head could result if the oil cooler restricts air flow to the head. Any air that does reach the head would be preheated after passing through the oil cooler so its cooling value is minimal.

The next requirement of an efficient lubrication system is adequately filtered oil. Any solid material in the oil will act as an abrasive, wearing away at bearings, crank journals, tappets and cam lobes etc. The oil filter must remove the majority of this type of material from the oil. Very few lubrication systems are unfiltered these days, but if yours isn't (eg. VW) remember that long engine life is at least partly dependant on clean oil, so steps must be taken to install a filtering unit.

The term 'Micron Rating' is often misused in filtration technology. The important figure is the one that indicates the smallest particle totally removed by the filter. For example, a filter may have to stop all particles over 40 microns from passing through, but 5% of particles of 20 - 30 microns size are allowed through. A system suitable for a racing engine should remove all particles, but this ideal is not possible at present.

A micron is one millionth of a metre. A human hair is about 50 microns thick. The larger the particles circulating in an engine's oil, the more likelihood there is of abrasive wear. The challenge facing filter manufacturers is to stop all of these abrasive particles, with a filter that has an acceptable service life. You can do your part by changing the filter regularly, as specified by the manufacturer, and by re-installing the new filter correctly. If 189 the type fitted to your engine has a replaceable element, be sure to remove all traces of sludge from inside the canister before fitting a new element.

A race or rally engine with thousands of dollars invested in it requires a higher level of filtration than that offered by over-the-counter spin-on or replaceable element filters. The standard type of oil filter may have a by-pass in case it becomes clogged up with sludge and other material. This is done for the benefit of the motorist who doesn't bother having his filter changed regularly and also to prevent the filter element rupturing when the oil is cold and viscous. Once the by-pass opens, due to excessive pressure, unfiltered oil is allowed to circulate through the engine. It can easily be seen that the area where the by-pass is located is where much of the sediment material from the oil collects. When the by-pass opens this rubbish is then flushed through your engine (FIGURE 8.1).

A racing oil filter must not contain any by-pass and consequently must be burst proof at oil pressures up to 200 lb. It must also be fine enough to stop abrasive particles from circulating with the oil without reducing oil flow to a dangerous level, particularly during cold starting. Very few oil filters are able to meet this specification. The only type that I know of are produced by the Mecca Corporation in America.

Many engine tuners cut open their oil filters to judge engine condition; however, I believe in a better system — oil analysis. For a small fee, specialised laboratories and oil companies will analyse oil for the presence of wear metals (indicating filtration effectiveness and/or engine wear), for dilution and sludge (indicating excessive blow-by, incorrect oil type or incorrect oil change period), and other potential problems.

As engine tune is increased and bearing clearances become greater, the need to investigate the flow potential of an engine's oiling system grows in importance. In lower stages of tune the standard oil pump, if in good condition (check manufacturer's specifications for gear clearances etc.) will usually be acceptable. It may be possible to increase the oil pressure and oil flow a small amount by fitting a stronger relief valve spring or by fitting a spacer under the existing spring. A common modification with the four cylinder English Fords is to increase oil pressure to 45 lb with a spacer or to 60 lb by using a stronger spring.

Once the engine reaches semi-race tune, a higher capacity oil pump, which utilises wider gears, will become necessary to keep sufficient oil passing through the engine. At times it may be necessary to change the oil pump drive due to the standard drive not being able to cope with the additional oil pump load.

Some engines suffer oil starvation because of restrictive oil passages. The German Capri V6 and Buick V6 are both good examples of this type of problem. The Capri has an oil passage in the block about 40% smaller than the oil pump outlet. In the very early stages of tune this passage must be enlarged to match the pump outlet, if bearing failure is to be avoided.

The V6 Buick has a passage for oil pickup running from the middle of the block to the oil pump located at the front of the engine. This passage is about 25% too small to flow enough oil for a racing engine. After the oil leaves the oil pump, it encounters another restriction, a 90° bend. Following this, the oil is fed into the right lifter gallery, which supplies the right bank lifters, the cam bearings and finally the mains and big ends. Additionally, the front cam journal bleeds off oil for the left lifter bank. All of this bleed-off to the valve gear, combined with the oilway restrictions, reduces the oil flow to the crankshaft bearings. An early modification in the development of this engine must include enlarging the pickup gallery and eliminating the 90° bend after the oil pump. This engine is a

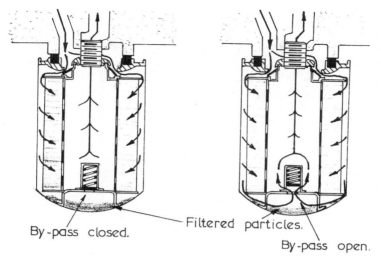

By-pass closed.

Filtered particles.

By-pass open.

Fig. 8.1   By-pass type spin-on oil filter.

good candidate for an external oil plumbing system that supplies oil directly to the main bearings.

Many engines, in fact, bleed too much oil for the lubrication of the cam and the lifters. To limit the bleed-off, restrictor plugs should be fitted. If you have switched from hydraulic to solid lifters, oil flow to the lifters should be restricted by reaming the lifter bores and fitting a lifter sleeve kit.

Some tuners, in an endeavour to supply oil in sufficient quantities to the main bearings, increase oil pressure to 100-120 psi. This should never be necessary if the lubrication system is properly modified. In fact if an engine is experiencing any failures at 60-70 psi it usually indicates that work is required to open up oilways and/or restrict bleed-off to the cam and lifters. The power required to pump oil through an engine is considerable so do not increase the power drain to ancillary equipment by unnecessarily increasing the oil pressure.

Oil surge can be a serious problem, and hard to overcome in some engines (eg. VW). Any vehicle with a wet sump (ie. oil reservoir in the sump) will be prone to oil surge unless the manufacturer has taken preventative measures during production (very unusual). Oil surge is caused by braking, acceleration or cornering forces surging the oil away from the oil pickup, allowing air to be pumped to the bearings. If allowed to go unchecked, bearing failure is imminent.

The trend to reduce surge is to fit vertical baffles in the sump, but these have little effect as the oil will rise over them during hard acceleration or braking. Instead a flat, horizontal baffle should be fitted in the sump about ¼ to ½ an inch above the full oil level.

Check first that at this height the rods will not hit the baffle. The baffle should cover the entire oil reservoir area in the sump. A hole just large enough for the oil pickup to fit through should be cut. Around the hole a ½ to ¾ in turned down lip is required, to discourage oil surging up through the hole. This hole for the pickup will also take care of oil drain back into the reservoir. Don't forget to cut a hole for the dipstick (FIGURE 8.2).

To ensure that the baffle is working and to keep a check on the oil pressure, a reliable capillary type (not electric) oil pressure gauge is required. A sudden drop to zero will 191 indicate surge or a low oil level; a small pressure decrease indicates bearing failure or a blocked oil filter.

During the heat of the moment, gauge readings can be missed, particularly cornering force induced surge readings. For this reason I also fit an electric oil pressure switch, adjusted to operate at 30 - 45 psi. I wire this switch to a three inch stop/tail light mounted on the dash and fitted with a 21 watt lamp. If the light flashes on, low oil pressure is indicated. A vehicle driven at night will also need a change-over switch to connect with a five watt lamp in the light, otherwise you could be momentarily blinded if the 21W lamp is flashed on in the dark.

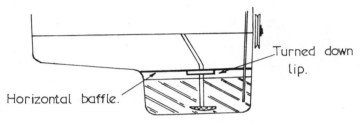

Turned down lip.

Horizontal baffle.

Fig. 8.2   Wet sump anti-surge baffle.

The dry sump system virtually eliminates oil surge, but creates a few other problems. This sytem uses a large capacity oil reservoir (two gallons for 1600 - 2000 cc) mounted in a convenient position. The oil pump is a three stage unit; one stage pumps oil from the oil tank through the oil cooler and the engine, the other two stages draw oil and a large quantity of air from the engine oil pan and pump this back to the oil tank.

The beneficial aspects of this type of system are obvious. The absence of oil surge helps increase engine life and reduces the risk of bearing failure. The vehicle can be lower without the risk of sump damage, as a shallow oil pan without a reservoir is used. Oil leakage from the engine is reduced as the two scavenge pumps reduce pressure (caused by blow-by) within the crankcase.

A benefit not so obvious, which I will explain later, is a rise in power of the order of 3 - 4%, in spite of the dry sump oil pump requiring around 7 hp more to drive, in a 5 litre motor, than a conventional pump.

The disadvantages of the system are these. The oil tank requires an air space almost as large as the oil capacity, so a two-gallon system will use a three and a half gallon tank. The tank must have an efficient system of vents and baffles to allow efficient de-aeration of the oil, without allowing any oil loss through the escape of oil mist to the atmosphere. If aerated oil is pumped back through the motor, bearing failure could result.

A better system which at least solves a major part of the problem of de-aeration is to pipe the oil from the scavenge pumps to a centrifuge and then to the oil tank. The centrifuge will remove perhaps 70% of the air from the oil and allow a decrease in the size of the oil tank. More importantly, the quality of lubrication will be improved, due to the air content of the oil being reduced from 7% to around 2 - 3%.

In recent years the lubrication system has been carefully scrutinised in the search for more power. It should be obvious that a crankshaft rotating at 8000 rpm and banging into the gallons of oil draining from the camshaft, lifters and rockers etc. will be experiencing a certain degree of drag. Maybe not as much drag as you experience when you drive into a puddle of water at high speed, but there will be drag none the less. This drag consumes a lot of power and results in oil frothing (aeration), and due to the friction involved and energy being expended, heating of the oil as well. 'V' type push-rod engines are the worst offenders in this respect as they dump all the oil from the cam and lifters onto the crankshaft.

You learned at school during physics classes that fast moving air creates a low pressure zone, which is why aeroplanes fly etc. A crankshaft spinning at 8000 rpm is also moving the air at quite a speed, and this too creates a low pressure region in the area through which the crank and rods are moving. Now the rest of the crankcase may be experiencing a pressure of 2 - 5 psi depending on the effectiveness of the breathing system on your engine.

Let us assume that there is a difference in pressure of 5 psi between the high pressure and the low pressure zones in this engine. What will tend to happen is that the oil pouring through the engine bearings will continue to cling to the crankshaft, because the centrifugal force of the crank is unable to overcome the pressure differential within the crankcase. Of course part of this mass of oil must continually be released, but in a big V8 there may be three pints of oil clinging to the crank, and being carried around by it to cause fluid drag additional to that being caused by oil drain-back from the cam and lifters.

An effective dry sump system can help with this problem in the following way. If large scavenge pumps are used, the air pressure in the sump pan can be brought to almost zero or close to being equal to the low pressure zone surrounding the crankshaft. This will allow the force of gravity to have its way and pull a considerable amount of oil away from the crank. Basically, this explains the power increase shown in dry sump engines.

The dry sump system can't get all the oil away from the crank and for this reason we need a system of screens and scrapers to assist (FIGURE 8.3.). The screen should be of rigid 16 - 20 gauge steel mesh running the full length of the crankshaft and positioned, as shown, in close proximity with it. The idea behind the screen is to prevent oil splashing back onto the crank after it has been flung onto the floor and sides of the oil pan. The screen effectively dissipates much of the oil's energy on the way through, so there is less energy available for splash back when the oil hits the pan.

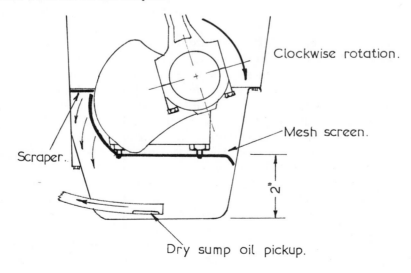

Fig. 8.3   Oil screen & scraper.

A rigid 22 gauge steel scraper positioned along the side of the oil pan deck will scrape oil from the crank and rods if machined to extend to within just a few thousandths of an inch of these.

To improve the oil drain off from the scraper, the side of the oil pan should be extended out an inch if possible. With these modifications you can expect a further 3 - 4% power increase over and above that possible with just dry sumping.

Don't despair if you cannot afford a dry sump system because the screen and scraper set-up can be adapted to work almost as effectively with a wet sump. There are two ways to approach the problem; if ground clearance is not a consideration, deepen the sump to give $1\frac{1}{2}$ inches clearance between the screen and the horizontal anti-surge baffle. For improved oil drain from the scraper, move out the side of the sump one inch, the same as for the dry sump oil pan.

If ground clearance is a problem, the only alternative is to widen the sump to lower the oil level. Again there should be $1\frac{1}{2}$ to 2 inches clearance between the screen and the horizontal baffle.

Having considered the foregoing information it should be obvious that the sump should never be overfilled. Overfill the sump and you are sure to have the crank and rods dipping into the oil every revolution. If that isn't bad enough you end up in a situation where too much oil is being thrown up the cylinders. The rings have to drag it off the walls and that consumes power. If the rings can't cope with this additional oil load you will have combustion chamber and plug oiling problems which will affect combustion and rob you of performance.

Oil leaks can be a problem with modified motors due mainly to pressure buildup in the crankcase forcing oil out past crankshaft oil seals. Most engines in standard tune rely on a single $\frac{1}{2}$ or $\frac{5}{8}$ in hose connected to the air filter or inlet manifold, to vent crankcase pressure. Any high performance engine should have at least a 1 in hose connected into each rocker cover and another hose (1 in) connected into the block. Take care when connecting breathers into the motor that oil is not going to be splashed up the breather pipe by a rocker arm or a con-rod. If such is the case, steps will have to be taken to fit a suitable deflector at the breather inlet.

A competition engine should be fitted with an evacuator breather system, such as that manufactured by Moroso and Edelbrock. The breather pipes are connected into the exhaust header at the collector and rely on the vacuum created in the exhaust to scavenge crankcase pressure. The evacuator operates at 1 to $1\frac{1}{2}$ psi negative pressure. Wet sump engines usually respond with a 1 - 2% power increase when an evacuator is fitted.

Your engine may be air-or water-cooled but either way you directly or indirectly rely on a flow of air to stabilise the temperature of the cylinder head and the cylinders. The cooling system of every internal combustion engine performs a vital function; the dissipation of heat in order to maintain normal engine operation.

The heat engine relies on the conversion of fuel into heat, and then into mechanical energy to produce power at the crankshaft. Only about one third of this heat is converted into power; another third is eliminated through the cooling system.

If your engine is air-cooled there is not a great deal that you can do to increase the engine cooling capacity to cope with higher power outputs. Therefore it is essential to ensure that the cooling system provided by the vehicle's manufacturer is operating at 100% capacity.

Heat radiation from the cooling fins is retarded by the presence of oil and mud, so ensure that the fins are clear. Fins that are silver coloured can have their radiating capacity improved by a coat of matt black paint.

Anything that is obstructing air flow onto the head and cylinders should, if possible, be moved to another location. I am amazed by the number of bikers who persist in fixing lights, air horns and oil coolers in front of the engine. The idea should be to encourage air flow over the motor, not restrict it.

Air-cooled cars rely on a fan to circulate cooling air over the head and cylinder. Think carefully before you decide to modify a cooling system of this type as there are several arrangements in service from the various manufacturers. Without a proper understanding of the system any modification could spell disaster for the engine.

The first consideration is whether the air inlet or outlet is ducted, because it is important to keep the inlet and outlet separated. If the inlet is taking in hot air that has just been expelled through the outlet, overheating and even a blow up could result.

On the VW Beetle the outlet is ducted (FIGURE 8.4). The fan intake is open inside the engine compartment and the hot air is exhausted beneath the engine tray. Therefore hot air from under the car must not be allowed to enter the engine compartment. Ensure that all the tinware is properly fitted and sealed with Silastic. Check the rubbers around the spark plug caps; hot air escaping through there will be recirculated. Badly planned body modifications may also allow the entry of hot air into the engine compartment, so look into this as well.

The Type 3 and 4 VW use a ducted intake. The outlet is open and the space between the engine and body is not sealed. In this instance you must ensure that the inlet duct remains sealed and that any modifications do not bring the inlet and outlet so close that hot air will be recirculated.

Most air-cooled cars have their air intake in a low air pressure area which reduces the amount of air available for cooling. Never, ever, fit a different pulley to slow the fan. Some claim that this gives better cooling because the fan is more efficient at lower speeds. Also they feel because less power is being used to drive the fan, performance will increase. I have found the opposite to be true; slow up the fan and blow up the engine.

Water-or liquid-cooling is usually thought to be more straight forward than air-cooling, and to a degree this is so. For instance, it is easy to accommodate a large power increase from a liquid-cooled motor and avoid overheating; you simply use a larger radiator. Other aspects of water cooling are, however, not so elementary.

The two major deterrents to proper heat transfer from the combustion chamber and cylinder to the cooling medium (usually water) are deposits and air in the cooling system.

Metallic oxides (eg. iron oxide-rust) are formed in the water passages. A deposit twelve thousandths of an inch thick will cut heat transfer up to 40%. In order to maintain optimum heat transfer within the engine, the cooling system should be chemically cleaned in a bath when the engine is stripped down, and the sytem should contain an inhibitor that will keep water jacket surfaces clean and free of deposits.

There are two basic types of inhibitors; chromates and non-chromates. Sodium chromate and potassium dichromate are two of the best and most commonly used water-cooling system corrosion inhibitors. These chemicals are toxic, so handle them carefully.

Non-chromate inhibitors (borates, nitrates, nitrites) provide protection in either water or water and permanent anti-freeze systems. Chromates must not be used in systems protected by anti-freeze.

When freeze protection is required, a permanent type anti-freeze must be used. If a solution, 30% by volume anti-freeze is used, additional inhibitor protection will not be 195

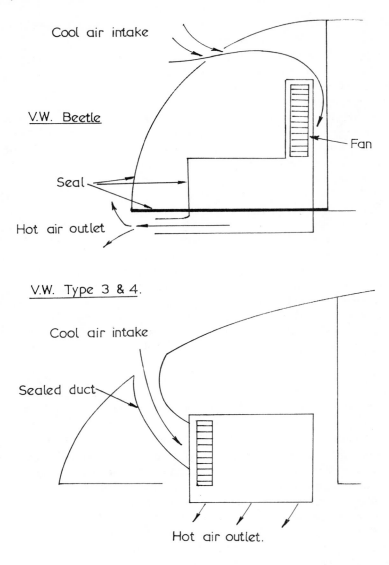

Fig. 8.4   V.W. Cooling systems.

required. Solutions of less than 30% concentration do not provide sufficient corrosion protection, so a non-chromate type inhibitor should be added. Concentrations over 67% adversely affect heat transfer and should not be used in high performance or rally vehicles.

Ethylene glycol base anti-freeze is recommended for use in all high performance engines. Methyl alcohol base anti-freeze should not be used because of its effect on water pump seals and radiator hoses, and because of its low boiling point.

Anti-freeze containing cooling system sealer additives must not be used due to the possibility of sealer plugging the radiator core tubes and various other areas in the cooling system. In fact a sealer or stop leak of any description is not to be recommended, except in an emergency to get you home or to finish the race. Then, as soon as possible, it should be flushed out of the cooling system by a cooling specialist, using high pressure air and water.

Petroleum-derived products such as soluble oil, often used as a water pump lubricant and rust inhibitor, should never be used in the cooling system. A 2% concentration of soluble oil will raise the cylinder head deck temperature by around 10%, due to the reduced heat transfer efficiency of the coolant. One popular radiator stop leak contains a high proportion of soluble oil, which is another reason for keeping clear of radiator sealers. Soluble oil turns water a milky colour when added.

The presence of air bubbles in the coolant reduces water pump efficiency and the heat transfer capacity of the coolant. Air can be sucked into the system through a leaking hose or gasket and gas bubbles can form in the system due to localised boiling.

In the first instance air can be kept out by ensuring that the system is free of air or water leaks, and by maintaining the coolant at the correct level.

In the second instance gas bubbles or steam pockets are prevented by pressurising the system to the degree necessary to prevent the coolant boiling. Many wonder why it is that we pressurise the cooling system. The boiling point of water is $100^0$C (at sea level) so why is it necessary to increase the boiling point by pressurising the system when most cars operate at around $90^0$C and most competition vehicles operate at a lower temperature, usually $70^0$ - $75^0$C?

Firstly, the system is pressurised to prevent boiling after the engine is turned off. Once the coolant stops circulating, its temperature climbs rapidly from its normal $90^0$C to something like $110^0$C, way past the boiling point of water at sea level pressure (14.7 psi). If the water boiled each time the engine were stopped, a considerable amount of coolant would be lost.

Secondly, regardless of what the temperature gauge is reading, the temperature is very high in the water passage around the combustion chamber, particularly close to the exhaust valve. Remember that the temperature gauge is only giving a reading of the circulating water temperature, not the temperature of the water around the exhaust valve seat. The temperature here is well above the boiling point of water, so to prevent the water around the combustion chamber from boiling and forming a steam pocket, the cooling system has to be pressurised. If the coolant were allowed to boil here, localised heating of the metal would occur, creating thermal stress points that would lead to cracking of the metal.

By pressurising the system to 14 psi the boiling point is raised to approximately $125^0$C at sea level. Normally the water around the combustion chamber should not reach this temperature, but this allows a margin of safety, to allow operation at altitudes above sea level.

To maintain the cooling system at the required pressure it will be necessary regularly to inspect the radiator pressure cap seal for deterioration and also check the cap 'blow-off' pressure.

The actual heat exchange between the coolant and air takes place at the radiator. Bugs and debris that restrict air flow through the core should be cleaned out to maintain cooling efficiency. The radiating efficiency will be improved if the radiator is regularly re-painted with matt black paint. This will serve to increase the life of the core as well, by reducing the effects of external corrosion.

Besides contributing to the mechanical well-being of the motor, the liquid cooling system can be modified to release more power from it.

A high temperature thermostat which maintains the water temperature at $88^0$-$90^0$C is usually fitted to production cars, but this is not the temperature for best power. The $88^0$C thermostat is fine if you want good heater efficiency in winter and the higher temperature compensates partly for the stock manifold and carburettor being unable to vaporise the fuel properly, but apart from that there is no reason for its use.

Some feel the higher the engine temperature the less the cylinder wear, but that assumption is true only up to a point. I have found a water temperature of $70^0$C to be ideal, from the aspect of best power and lowest bore wear. A side benefit of lowering the water temperature is lower oil temperature, which can mean the difference between requiring or not requiring an oil cooler.

Generally, I have realised a power increase of $2\frac{1}{2}\%$ right through the range, and sometimes up to $3\frac{1}{2}\%$, by lowering the water temperature from $88^0$C to $70^0$C.

The water temperature can be lowered to $70^0$C by fitting a $70^0$C thermostat, providing the radiator is large enough. Do not have the engine operating at below $70^0$C as engine wear accelerates quickly below this temperature. A road or rally vehicle should never be run without a thermostat if you want good engine life. An engine will take much longer to warm up, and will not get hot enough for best fuel vaporisation. The result; increased engine wear, less power and diluted engine oil.

A thermostat may cause undue restriction to water flow in a racing engine, so if this is the case a restrictor plate with a suitable size orifice to maintain the water temperature at $70^0$C will have to be made up to fit in place of the thermostat. Actually, a selection of restrictors will be required, to allow for climatic and seasonal changes.

I am very careful to reduce engine wear to a minimum, consequently I advocate warming a cold engine for a minimum of three minutes at 2000 - 2500 rpm before driving off, then I keep engine revs reasonably low until the oil and water temperatures approach normal. High performance motors cost a lot of money and this type of care pays good dividends.

The fan fitted to most cars consumes a good deal of power which can be used beneficially to improve performance or reduce fuel consumption. Generally, a road speed of 25 mph and above will provide sufficient moving air to cool the engine. Therefore a fan will not be required in competition vehicles. I have never had one fitted to my road car, although I would recommend that a fan be retained if you engage in peak hour city driving.

If a fan is required it would be of benefit to fit an electric unit. One of these can be an engine saver on rally and dirt speedway vehicles. You never know when you are likely to be bogged or when you are going to come up against a greasy half mile climb in a rally; either occurrence would probably cause coolant boiling in the absence of a cooling fan. Speedway cars are, at times, required to circulate for what seems like an eternity, at a crawl under yellow lights; an ideal situation for coolant boiling and engine damage.

Liquid-cooled vehicles with rear-mounted radiators (eg. Imp, Renault) or side-mounted radiators (eg. Mini) will almost certainly require a larger cooling fan and also a separate expansion tank connected to the radiator, if modified for more performance. Some engines have a tendency to overheat if the radiator header tank is not completely full to give proper water flow down through the radiator core. An expansion tank ensures that the top tank is always full.

If a front-mounted radiator is installed, the fan can be removed and you can be sure of maintaining the correct coolant temperature under competition conditions. This is a simple modification on the Mini, particularly if of the Clubman body design.

The Hillman Imp and Renaults require a duct in the boot (FIGURE 8.5) and this can pose a problem in rally cars where boot space is precious for an extra fuel tank. Be sure to run $1\frac{1}{4}$ in i/d aluminium or copper tube through the car, so as to ensure good water flow from the engine to the radiator.

Many large engines, being designed to operate at low rpm, have water pumps which circulate the water too quickly for good cooling at high engine speed. These can be modified, with good results, by machining the impeller to reduce its diameter. As an example of this, consider the 351 Cleveland Ford. If fitted with the Boss 302 cast-iron impeller pump, an engine producing 600 hp will pick up an extra 5 hp, and achieve better cooling by reducing the o/d of the impeller by about a $\frac{1}{2}$ inch.

To keep a check on engine temperature, an accurate temperature gauge should be fitted, not one just showing C - N - H, but a gauge giving a reading of the actual coolant temperature.

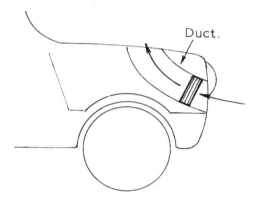

Fig. 8.5 Hillman Imp front mounted radiator.

Before you even think about modifying a fan-air cooled engine (eg. VW) be sure to fit a cylinder head temperature gauge; it could save you a lot of money. The liquid surrounding the combusion chamber of a water-cooled motor tends to act as a heat sink and stabilises the combustion chamber temperature. An air-cooled head has very little in reserve to take away a sudden increase in heat. Therefore the combustion chamber and piston temperature could take a sudden and unexpected rise, large enough, perhaps, to melt the pistons. For this reason the head temperature must be continually monitored when engaging in high speed motoring.

What is the maximum safe head temperature? That depends on where you measure it and on the quality of the pistons. If pistons suitable for competition are being used and the temperature is being recorded from a thermocouple washer at the base of the spark plug, I would suggest throttling back once the temperature exceeds 220°C. If the thermocouple is attached elsewhere on the head, I would advise the same action be taken on a 200°C readout.

# Chapter 9

# Power Measurements and Tuning

MANY RACERS spend vast amounts of money building an engine, but never concern themselves with fine tuning on an engine dynamometer. No matter how much we may try to fool ourselves, there is no way an engine can make top performance tuned by ear and/or experience. Even when you build a number of engines to identical specifications, each one will have to be set up differently for best power. I have found that I pick up at least 5 more horsepower by fine tuning on the dyno. If it is a motor with which I have not had a lot of experience, more often than not I gain something like 10.

There are two basic types of dynamometers, the engine dyno and the rolling road or chassis dyno. The rolling road is very convenient as you just drive the car on to a set of rollers and run the engine to find the power and torque output. However, this type is a waste of time for engine development or fine tuning. All you will determine is if the engine is developing good power. For example, if a car fully developed for rally work usually produces around 145 - 150 hp at the wheels and yours is turning out 148 hp then you are on a good thing. On the other hand if it showed 135 hp then you can be sure something is amiss. The engine dyno is very sensitive and will give a clear indication of precisely what size carburettor jets and ignition timing the engine prefers for best power. We can also check the effect of a change in the dwell angle, or a change in spark plug gap. The cam can be advanced or retarded and the change in power noted. We can note the results of any changes in carburettor venturi size or air horn design. In fact anything that it is possible to twiddle with should be twiddled and the results accurately recorded so that you will know exactly how to set the engine up to perform at its best on any circuit. This all takes time, but at the end of the session you will know exactly what to do to get the best low end power when you need it. You will know what combination gives best overall power and if you need maximum power you will know what magic to perform to achieve that too. Remember to keep accurate notes; do not leave anything to memory.

Now don't get me wrong; engine dynos are definitely not the 'be all and end all' of engine tuning. There are clearly definable limits to their usefulness due to the static nature of the load applied to the engine. You can't, for instance, check how crisply an engine will accelerate or what its throttle response will be like. This can only be done on the race circuit (or road) and fine tuning adjustments will have to be made accordingly.

Usually the areas where you will get caught out are those of carburation and ignition timing. There are many combinations of different brand manifolds and carburettors which, on the dyno, give seemingly identical performance, but on the race circuit there generally will be one set-up that is superior to the rest, allowing improved lap times or maybe better performance in race traffic if you have to drive through the field, as in speedway racing.

There are several types of engine dynos in use and while all do a good job in enabling a motor to be set up correctly do not take a lot of notice of the power figures. Variations of up to 10% from one dyno to another are not uncommon. The reason for this is that tuning companies do not have the money to outlay on the latest, most accurate dynos. Instead, in many cases they make do with older or new, less sophisticated types. This in itself is not such a bad thing providing all the tuning is done on the same dyno. Otherwise you may try out some new trick bit and find it gives you 8% more power on a dyno on the other side of town, when in actual fact you had lost power with that trick. It was just that the dyno was reading higher than the one on which the motor was originally tuned (TABLE 9.1).

Another trap may also result from these older dynos still being around. Within the trade it is generally well known whose dyno gives the highest, most distorted power outputs. To sell an engine or even go-quicker bits, some have resorted to testing their motor or equipment on such a dyno to make it appear from the dyno test sheets that the motor is much hotter than it really is. Before you buy a motor or equipment on the pretext of it being more powerful, or more something, be sure you know on which dyno it was tested and make enquiries as to the fidelity of the power readings on that dyno. Also ensure the engine number is quoted on the dyno sheet and check that it corresponds with the motor you are buying, otherwise you could be taken for a ride at considerable expense.

While we are on the subject, keep in mind that there is no guarantee a company does top quality work just because some big names use their engines or equipment. What you buy and what the top name buys (or is given) are not necessarily of the same standard. This is unfortunate, but it is a fact of life. Power figures get thrown around rather carelessly by some firms. I refer to them as 'paper horse power' the same as I refer to car manufacturers' figures.

To cite an instance of this, I remember a top engine builder advertising his particular engine to produce in excess of 200 hp. This was surprising as most comparative engines were

### TABLE 9.1  Dynamometer comparison using 350 cu in Chevy test engine

| rpm | Dyno A | | | Dyno B | | |
| | hp | Torque (lbf ft) | | hp | Torque (lbf ft) |
|------|-------|-----------------|--|-------|-----------------|
| 5500 | 472   | 450.7 | | 477.7 | 456.2 |
| 6000 | 505.3 | 442.3 | | 532.7 | 466.3 |
| 6500 | 567.6 | 458.6 | | 560.5 | 452.9 |
| 7000 | 601.4 | 451.2 | | 582   | 436.7 |
| 7250 | 606.3 | 439.2 | | 582.8 | 422.2 |
| 7500 | 611.8 | 428.4 | | 584.8 | 409.5 |
| 7750 | 622   | 421.5 | | 551.4 | 373.7 |

*Note: This motor was not altered in any way between tests. The hp and torque figures have been corrected to compensate for changes in air density.*

producing around 15 hp less. A couple of these trick engines were bought for evaluation and one produced 186 hp and the other 193 hp. Now these were guaranteed to produce a minimum of 200 hp. About the same time a top name driver ran two engines identical to these and on the same dyno they did indeed produce in excess of 200 hp. The two dud engines were stripped and deck heights were found to be all over the place; combustion chamber volumes had not been equalised, the valve seats were not concentric or of equal width, and inlet ports were not of the same configuration. A pair of replica engines were built up using the same design features, but with everything done correctly, and these produced 208 and 209 hp. That must prove something about doing things the correct way. It also proves you don't get the best just because you pay for it. To get the best in many instances you will have to tidy up the loose ends.

Top firms have their problems with outside suppliers too, so it is not always entirely the fault of the engine builder when things go wrong. Obviously he must bear some responsibility if he has not made an adequate check to ensure the outside work is up to standard. Just a few years back a Formula 1 engine constructor was having a series of crankshaft problems. When an investigation was made, it was found that the supplier had made a machining error during manufacture, due to an improperly dressed grinding wheel. A whole batch of cranks was affected and those that had not been used were scrapped. You can appreciate how much harder it is for a private individual to get top quality work when a World Championship engine constructor can't always get it.

Getting back to horsepower figures again, few realise that they do not tell the whole story about engine performance or even how well a motor has been modified. Of much greater value are the torque and brake mean effective pressure (bmep) figures. These indicate much more to us and show where we are heading with our modifications.

Torque is the ability of the engine to do work, measured in pounds force per feet (lbf ft). This is a measure of the work an engine will do regardless of whether it is 1000 cc or 8000 cc. If an engine is producing torque of 100 lbf ft it means that it will lift a load of 100 lb with a lever 1 ft long connected to the crankshaft. If the lever was 2 ft long the same motor would lift 200 lb, or 300 lb if 3 ft long. This is why we have a gearbox, namely to multiply the torque output of an engine. If this engine with 100 lb ft torque were operating in a vehicle with a low gear ratio of 12:1, we would have a twisting force of 1200 lbf ft on the rear axles ($100 \times 12 = 1200$).

Power is the rate at which work is done,

$$\text{Power} = \frac{\text{work (or torque)}}{\text{time}}$$

In the Imperial system, power is measured in pounds/feet per minute. However, these units are very small, so the unit we know as horsepower (hp) is the one used today. One horsepower equals 33,000 lb/ft per minute. This was worked out as a result of experiments carried out by James Watt, using strong dray horses. It is obvious, realising power is the rate at which work is done, that two motors both producing 100 lbf ft torque could have differing power outputs. In fact if one motor lifted its 100 lb load twice as quickly as the other, then it must be twice as powerful or have double the horsepower. Engine speed is measured in revolutions per minute and this is the time unit we use in calculating horsepower, so

$$\text{hp} = \frac{\text{torque} \times \text{rpm}}{5252}$$

Remember that I said horsepower figures can be very deceptive when we go about assessing how well a motor has been modified. We can end up with a nice big power figure because the motor will turn a lot of rpm, but in actual fact the motor will not do any more work than it did previously as the torque output has remained the same. For this reason we have a measure called brake mean effective pressure (bmep). This gives a true indication of how effectively the motor is operating regardless of its capacity or its operating rpm. It is, in fact, a measure of the average cylinder pressures generated during all four engine strokes. We calculate bmep using the formula:

$$\text{bmep} = \frac{\text{hp} \times 13,000}{\text{L} \times \text{rpm}}$$

L = engine capacity in litres

The highest bmep will occur at the point of maximum torque. In fact this formula gives the true bmep only at that point. At other places on the horsepower or torque curves it is not exactly true, but very close so do not let this worry you.

The average motor runs at a bmep of around 130 - 145 psi. A good road motor should run at 165 - 185 psi. Rally engines will generally be in the 175 - 195 bracket and racing motors from 185 - 210 psi. A few exceptional motors will run up to 220 psi, naturally aspirated.

In standard form, motors such as the Alfa Romeo double overhead cam, the Lotus/Ford Twin Cam and the Ford BDA operate at around 170 psi, but few motorcycles approach this figure (generally around 145 psi) even though claiming power outputs of 80 - 100 hp from 1000 cc.

On paper, 175 hp from a 1300 cc Ford BDA looks impressive, but when you work it all out it is rather pathetic. This motor was a fully modified racing unit using two 45 DCOE Weber carbs and Cosworth Formula 1 cams. It produced 102 lbf ft torque at 7200 rpm and 175 hp at 9500 rpm. The rev limit was 10,500 rpm. The bmep is 194 psi. A properly modified motor should have produced 207 - 210 psi considering that the motor has four valves per cylinder, good porting, good combustion chamber for a proper burn etc. In fact a well tuned Mini 1300 using the old five port head will run a 195 psi brake mean effective pressure and so will the 355 cubic inch Grand National speedway V8 motors — and on a single four barrel carburettor at that.

Another measure we use to analyse combustion efficiency is called brake specific fuel (bsf). This is worked out by dividing the engine's fuel flow (lb of fuel per hour) by its horsepower output. If the engine was consuming 174 lb of fuel per hour at 5000 rpm and the power output at that rpm was 424 hp then bsf would be $174 \div 424 = 0.410$. Obviously the less fuel the engine is using for each horsepower produced, the more efficient combustion must be. As the numerical value of the bsf decreases, combustion efficiency improves, up to the point where subsequent reduction in the bsf causes reductions in horsepower.

When a motor is run on the engine dyno, a record is made of its output each 500 rpm over its operating range. These figures must then be 'corrected' to keep them standard, otherwise they would be of no real value for comparison on another occasion. At frequent intervals throughout the dyno session a check is made of the barometer reading and also of the wet and dry bulb air temperature readings, as atmospheric conditions affect the power output of an engine. It stands to reason, the denser and cooler the air, the more oxygen and fuel you can cram into the cylinder, which produces more power. To compensate for this during the test session, and to give a true comparison with earlier tests and also subsequent tests, a correction factor is introduced.

With the dyno session over and all the twiddling completed, don't go home and file away the dyno sheets. The next thing you must do is work out your gear change points for maximum acceleration. In TABLE 9.2 I have listed the figures for a modified 1700 cc Lotus/Ford Twin Cam. I call this a 'Clubman' motor as it has a wide power spread making it suitable for a road car, but it is also hot enough to make its presence felt at club level race and rally events. Although it will run to 7800 rpm, this is a bit above the capabilities of the special Ford tuftrided and cross-drilled cast iron crankshaft. The standard connecting rods, although polished along the beams and shot peened, are really only good for 7300 rpm. If steel Cosworth rods were fitted, we could raise the limit to 7500 rpm. You will note that the motor makes a big jump in power and torque between 5000 and 5500 rpm so we would want to operate above 5500 rpm, if possible. Using the following formula, we can work out what rear axle ratio we must use to obtain our desired top speed.

$$\text{Road speed} = \frac{\text{rpm} \times \text{tc}}{\text{gr} \times 1050}$$

tc = tire circumference (diameter $\times \pi$ ) in inches
gr = overall gear ratio

As this vehicle will be a dual purpose family car and rally machine, a compromise must be struck, so a 4.7:1 axle ratio is chosen. On the other hand if its life was going to be spent purely in the forests, a 5.14:1 would be ideal. Of course a race circuit car would have to be geared according to the circuit. A road car would use a 4.125:1 diff.

TABLE 9.3 indicates three gear sets we could use. Most clubman-type vehicles would use the standard gearbox with semi-close ratios. Some may have the special Ford race/rally 'Rocket' gear set and a few would use the special Ford race/ultra close ratio 'Bullet' set.

### TABLE 9.2    Dyno test of 1700 cc Lotus/Ford Twin Cam

| rpm | hp | Torque (lbf ft) | |
|---|---|---|---|
| 4000 | 89.7 | 117.8 | |
| 4500 | 102 | 119 | |
| 5000 | 114.3 | 120 | |
| 5500 | 135 | 128.9 | |
| 5750 | 143 | 130.6 | BMEP 190.2 psi |
| 6000 | 147.5 | 129.1 | |
| 6500 | 153.5 | 124 | |
| 6800 | 155.3 | 119.9 | |
| 7000 | 156 | 117 | |
| 7300 | 154.7 | 111.3 | |
| 7500 | 146.6 | 102.7 | |
| 7800 | 121 | 81.5 | |

### TABLE 9.3    Gear ratios using 4.7 : 1 diff

| Gear set | 1st | 2nd | 3rd | 4th | 5th |
|---|---|---|---|---|---|
| Standard Escort T/C | 13.97:1 | 9.45:1 | 6.57:1 | 4.7:1 | |
| Rocket box | 11.94:1 | 7.83:1 | 5.90:1 | 4.7:1 | |
| Bullet box | 10.8:1 | 7.98:1 | 6.01:1 | 4.7:1 | |
| Peter Hollinger box | 12.55:1 | 8.37:1 | 6.58:1 | 5.73:1 | 4.7:1 |

Keeping in mind my earlier remarks regarding torque multiplication, we should prepare a table such as TABLE 9.4. This gives us an indication of torque at the axles at various engine rpm in all gears. Remember the higher the twisting force (torque), the faster the vehicle is going to accelerate. Some drivers change up a gear when the engine reaches maximum hp revs, but if the engine can be safely wound past that point, then it generally should be for best acceleration.

Looking at TABLE 9.4 you will notice that the road speed at maximum horsepower rpm (7000 rpm) in low gear is 35 mph. Rear axle torque is 1634 lbf ft. If the car is then changed into 2nd gear, engine rpm are going to drop to approximately 4500 and rear axle torque is now 1125 lbf ft. However, if the engine had been taken to 7300 rpm the rear axle torque would be 1555 lbf ft and on the change to 2nd gear it would be 1134 lbf ft at 5000 rpm, so the car would be accelerating faster. Checking through, you will find the gears should be changed up at 7300 rpm (or 7500 rpm with Cosworth rods) and changed down at 5000 rpm for the best performance. If the car was coming out of a corner at 48 mph in 3rd gear, the axle torque would be 782 lbf ft, but if it was in 2nd gear the torque would have been more than 1172 lbf ft.

**TABLE 9.4    Rear axle torque and road speed using 4.7 diff and Escort T/C gearbox**

| rpm | 1st gear 13.97 | | 2nd gear 9.45 | | 3rd gear 6.57 | | 4th gear 4.7 | |
|------|--------|-------|--------|-------|--------|-------|--------|-------|
|      | *torque* | *speed* | *torque* | *speed* | *torque* | *speed* | *torque* | *speed* |
| 4000 | 1646 | 20 | 1113 | 30 | 774 | 43 | 554 | 60 |
| 4500 | 1662 | 23 | 1125 | 34 | 782 | 48 | 559 | 68 |
| 5000 | 1676 | 25 | 1134 | 37 | 788 | 54 | 564 | 75 |
| 5500 | 1801 | 28 | 1218 | 41 | 847 | 59 | 606 | 83 |
| 5750 | 1824 | 29 | 1234 | 43 | 858 | 62 | 614 | 86 |
| 6000 | 1804 | 30 | 1220 | 45 | 848 | 65 | 607 | 90 |
| 6500 | 1732 | 33 | 1172 | 49 | 815 | 70 | 583 | 98 |
| 6800 | 1675 | 34 | 1133 | 51 | 788 | 73 | 564 | 102 |
| 7000 | 1634 | 35 | 1106 | 52 | 769 | 75 | 550 | 105 |
| 7300 | 1555 | 37 | 1052 | 55 | 731 | 79 | 523 | 110 |
| 7500 | 1435 | 38 | 971 | 56 | 675 | 81 | 483 | 113 |
| 7800 | 1138 | 39 | 770 | 59 | 535 | 84 | 383 | 117 |

Moving to TABLE 9.5 you will note that the gears are 'gathered', meaning there is a smaller gap between 3rd and 4th than between 2nd and 3rd or between 1st and 2nd. Again the change up speed would be 7300 rpm (7500 with Cosworth rods) but the change down speed would be 5900 rpm in top gear, 5500 rpm in 3rd gear, and 4800 rpm in 2nd gear.

The Bullet set (TABLE 9.6) are evenly spaced except for 3rd to 4th. The change up speed would be 7300 rpm (7500 with Cosworth rods). The change down speed should be 5750 rpm in top, and 5500 rpm in the other gears. Both the Rocket and Bullet gear sets allow this motor to operate in the ideal upper section of the power band, ie. above 5500 rpm. The Rocket box would be more at home on the race circuit than in forests due to the large gap between 1st and 2nd gear. The Bullet set is right for a rally car, giving a good gear for any corner.

In virtually every instance you would, in fact, reduce acceleration by revving this motor to 7800 rpm. Beside the mechanical aspect of risking a blown motor, it is obvious that 205

### TABLE 9.5    Rear axle torque and road speed using 4.7 diff and Rocket box

|  | 1st gear 11.94 | | 2nd gear 7.83 | | 3rd gear 5.90 | | 4th gear 4.7 | |
| rpm | torque | speed | torque | speed | torque | speed | torque | speed |
|---|---|---|---|---|---|---|---|---|
| 4000 | 1407 | 24 | 922 | 36 | 695 | 48 | 554 | 60 |
| 4500 | 1421 | 27 | 932 | 41 | 702 | 54 | 559 | 68 |
| 5000 | 1433 | 30 | 940 | 45 | 708 | 60 | 564 | 75 |
| 5500 | 1539 | 32 | 1009 | 50 | 761 | 66 | 606 | 83 |
| 5750 | 1559 | 34 | 1023 | 52 | 771 | 69 | 614 | 86 |
| 6000 | 1541 | 35 | 1011 | 54 | 762 | 72 | 607 | 90 |
| 6500 | 1481 | 38 | 971 | 59 | 732 | 78 | 583 | 98 |
| 6800 | 1432 | 40 | 939 | 61 | 707 | 81 | 564 | 102 |
| 7000 | 1397 | 41 | 916 | 63 | 690 | 84 | 550 | 105 |
| 7300 | 1329 | 43 | 871 | 66 | 657 | 87 | 523 | 110 |
| 7500 | 1226 | 44 | 804 | 68 | 606 | 90 | 483 | 113 |
| 7800 | 973 | 46 | 638 | 70 | 481 | 93 | 383 | 117 |

### TABLE 9.6    Rear axle torque and road speed using 4.7 diff and Bullet box

|  | 1st gear 10.8 | | 2nd gear 7. 98 | | 3rd gear 6.01 | | 4th gear 4.7 | |
| rpm | torque | speed | torque | speed | torque | speed | torque | speed |
|---|---|---|---|---|---|---|---|---|
| 4000 | 1271 | 26 | 940 | 35 | 708 | 47 | 554 | 60 |
| 4500 | 1285 | 29 | 950 | 40 | 715 | 53 | 559 | 68 |
| 5000 | 1296 | 33 | 958 | 44 | 721 | 59 | 564 | 75 |
| 5500 | 1392 | 36 | 1029 | 49 | 775 | 65 | 606 | 83 |
| 5750 | 1410 | 38 | 1042 | 51 | 785 | 67 | 614 | 86 |
| 6000 | 1394 | 39 | 1030 | 53 | 776 | 70 | 607 | 90 |
| 6500 | 1339 | 42 | 990 | 57 | 745 | 76 | 583 | 98 |
| 6800 | 1295 | 44 | 957 | 60 | 721 | 80 | 564 | 102 |
| 7000 | 1264 | 46 | 934 | 62 | 703 | 83 | 550 | 105 |
| 7300 | 1202 | 48 | 888 | 65 | 669 | 86 | 523 | 110 |
| 7500 | 1109 | 49 | 820 | 66 | 617 | 88 | 483 | 113 |
| 7800 | 880 | 51 | 650 | 69 | 490 | 92 | 383 | 117 |

we are losing torque so fast that we would have much better axle torque in a higher gear.

Look again at TABLE 9.4 and notice how big the step is in axle torque between each gear with a change up at 7300 rpm. In the change from 1st to 2nd gear we are dropping from 1555 lbf ft to approximately 1134 lbf ft, a gap of over 400 lbf ft. From 2nd to 3rd we lose about 250 lbf ft torque (1052 - 788). From 3rd to 4th we drop about 150 lbf ft (731 - approximately 584). These large 'holes' between gears are acceptable because of the wide power band of the 'Clubman' motor. However, better performance would be possible with closer gear ratios.

Ideally, there should be little or no loss of axle torque in the change from one gear to the next. You can see how the close ratio four-speed boxes almost achieve this, and the five-speed box produced by the Australian gearbox wizard Peter Hollinger gives us the ideal with this particular motor. From this you should realize how necessary close ratio gears are, and remember, the more highly tuned the motor is, the closer the gears must be. Engine tune must therefore be kept compatible with available gearbox and diff ratios.

From TABLE 9.9 note how the standard Escort Twin Cam gearbox could be

### TABLE 9.7 Rear axle torque and road speed using 4.7 diff and Peter Hollinger box

| rpm | 1st gear 12.55 | | 2nd gear 8.37 | | 3rd gear 6.58 | | 4th gear 5.73 | | 5th gear 4.7 | |
|------|--------|-------|--------|-------|--------|-------|--------|-------|--------|-------|
| | *torque* | *speed* | *torque* | *speed* | *torque* | *speed* | *torque* | *speed* | *torque* | *speed* |
| 4000 | 1478 | 22 | 986 | 34 | 775 | 43 | 675 | 49 | 554 | 60 |
| 4500 | 1493 | 25 | 996 | 38 | 783 | 48 | 682 | 55 | 559 | 68 |
| 5000 | 1506 | 28 | 1004 | 42 | 790 | 53 | 688 | 62 | 564 | 75 |
| 5500 | 1618 | 31 | 1079 | 46 | 848 | 59 | 739 | 68 | 606 | 83 |
| 5750 | 1639 | 32 | 1093 | 48 | 859 | 62 | 748 | 71 | 614 | 86 |
| 6000 | 1620 | 34 | 1081 | 50 | 849 | 64 | 740 | 74 | 607 | 90 |
| 6500 | 1556 | 37 | 1038 | 55 | 816 | 70 | 711 | 80 | 583 | 98 |
| 6800 | 1505 | 38 | 1004 | 57 | 789 | 73 | 687 | 84 | 564 | 102 |
| 7000 | 1468 | 39 | 979 | 59 | 770 | 75 | 670 | 86 | 550 | 105 |
| 7300 | 1397 | 41 | 932 | 62 | 732 | 78 | 638 | 90 | 523 | 110 |
| 7500 | 1289 | 42 | 860 | 63 | 676 | 80 | 588 | 92 | 483 | 113 |
| 7800 | 1023 | 44 | 682 | 66 | 536 | 84 | 467 | 96 | 383 | 117 |

### TABLE 9.8 Dyno test of blueprinted 1560 cc Lotus/Ford Twin Cam

| rpm | hp | Torque | |
|------|------|--------|------|
| 4000 | 78.0 | 102.5 | |
| 4500 | 89.6 | 104.6 | BMEP 165.9 psi |
| 5000 | 96.0 | 100.8 | |
| 5500 | 102.2 | 97.6 | |
| 6000 | 108.0 | 94.5 | |
| 6500 | 103.7 | 83.8 | |
| 7000 | 92.5 | 69.4 | |

### TABLE 9.9 Rear axle torque and road speed using 4.7 diff and Escort T/C gearbox

| rpm | 1st gear 13.97 | | 2nd gear 9.45 | | 3rd gear 6.57 | | 4th gear 4.7 | |
|------|--------|-------|--------|-------|--------|-------|--------|-------|
| | *torque* | *speed* | *torque* | *speed* | *torque* | *speed* | *torque* | *speed* |
| 4000 | 1432 | 20 | 969 | 30 | 673 | 43 | 482 | 60 |
| 4500 | 1461 | 23 | 988 | 34 | 687 | 48 | 492 | 68 |
| 5000 | 1408 | 25 | 953 | 37 | 662 | 54 | 474 | 75 |
| 5500 | 1363 | 28 | 922 | 41 | 641 | 59 | 459 | 83 |
| 6000 | 1320 | 30 | 893 | 45 | 621 | 65 | 444 | 90 |
| 6500 | 1171 | 33 | 792 | 49 | 551 | 70 | 394 | 98 |
| 7000 | 970 | 35 | 656 | 52 | 456 | 75 | 326 | 105 |

considered as a good thing when mated with the standard Lotus/Ford Twin Cam motor. There are no gaps in torque between gears, so we cannot ask for more than that. However, as is evidenced by TABLE 9.4, when the motor is modified, gaps do indeed open up between gears.

Of course all of the above calculations will be wasted if your tachometer is inaccurate, so have it checked and recalibrated. Only then can you be sure that you are operating in the power band. Unfortunately, many have been led to believe that the tacho reading is infallible 207 and beyond question; in general I have found electronic units to read, on average, around 700 rpm fast. Those units fitted as standard equipment to showroom models are sometimes even more inaccurate; one I remember being 2100 rpm fast.

Only by taking the time to have a good think about gearing and gear change points can you expect to get the best out of a motor. If you find the steps between gears are so large that the motor is dropping out of the power band then you should do something to improve mid-range power. You can achieve this by using smaller carbs (or change to smaller chokes in Webers) and advancing the cam. If that doesn't fix it, change to a softer cam grind.

You are probably wondering just how fast it is safe to rev a motor, but of course there is no definite answer. The number of variables involved means that you must use an educated guess, or what is generally known as a rule of thumb. You must remember that engine wear increases dramatically at higher rpm so a road motor should not be subjected to peak rpm operation continuously, unless you have the time and money for a rebuild every 2000 - 3000 miles.

The same type of reasoning applies in the case of the other types of motors where the rpm limit rule is applied. A rally motor operating at or close to the limit will require a rebuild at 1200 - 1500 miles; a road race engine every 300 - 500 miles; and a drag race motor every 1 - 4 meetings. The rebuild must include not only the replacement of worn parts, but also careful crack testing of components likely to suffer fatigue failure.

The rule of thumb we work to revolves around the mean piston speed in feet per minute. Many people feel that piston speed is of no consequence because of the large advances that have been made in modern day metallurgy. In years gone by, this figure was used as a measure of an engine's likely wear rate; ie. the higher the piston speed the faster the engine would wear out. I have found working to an engine's piston speed is a surprisingly accurate means of avoiding blow-ups and general unreliability.

Mean piston speed is calculated using the formula:-

$$\text{Piston speed} = s \times \text{rpm} \times 0.166 \text{ feet per minute}$$

Where  s = stroke in inches

After you have calculated the rpm limit from TABLE 9.10 and the above formula you

### TABLE 9.10   Mean piston speed (fpm)

| | Road | Rally | Road race | Drags |
|---|---|---|---|---|
| Standard cast iron crank and rods | 3500 | 3500 | 3650 | 3800B |
| Standard forged crank and rods (A) | 3650 | 3650 | 3800 | 4000B |
| Standard cast iron crank, special rods and heavy duty main bearing caps | 3650 | 3650 | 3800 | 4000B |
| Special forged crank , heavy duty rods and main bearing caps (C) | 3800 | 3900 | 4200 | 5000 |
| | -4000 | -4000 | -4400 | -6000 |

*Note:* **A** *Applies to some standard high performance American V8 engines and some standard European sports car engines.*

   **B** *Applies to street machines used for occasional drag racing.*

   **C** *Most standard motorcycle engines also fit into this category due to the use of heavy duty components in standard tune.*

   *It is assumed that the engines in every category have balanced crank, rods and pistons and that either forged or top quality unslotted cast pistons are fitted.*

may find that the limit imposed by the valve gear is lower. If this is the case, do not exceed the rpm limit of the valve train.

Actual tuning on the race track or road is also necessary even after a tuning session on the dyno. This is because the load applied on the dyno may be just a flash loading; ie. just long enough to get a power reading. Such a brief run at full load may not allow sufficient heat build-up in the metal of the piston crown, combustion chamber or exhaust valve to cause detonation. However, under normal running conditions, where full load may be applied for a much longer period, detonation may occur due to the mixture being just a fraction lean or in some instances the ignition advance may be a little early.

The testing will have to be carried out in a convenient place. If it is being done on the road, be sure that you choose an isolated location where you will not annoy the local inhabitants and where they are not likely to get in your way and slow down your testing. So that driving inconsistency is not going to cloud the results, I would suggest that the test road be an uphill section with easy turns and about $\frac{1}{2}$ - 1 mile long. Prominent markers should be placed where you intend to start and stop the stop watch.

The test runs should be started far enough back from the starting marker so that you pass the marker at a pre-determined speed. I usually choose 60 - 80 mph. For accurate timing you will have to change gears at exactly the same engine rpm so that the acceleration rate will not distort the results.

As a further guard against inaccuracy, you should make 3 - 5 runs and then take an average figure for that test. To save time or possible engine damage it would be advisable if the engine began to detonate, or to run very rich on the first run, to discontinue that test and try an alternate ignition setting or jet size. You will probably find that you get faster after the first few runs so I suggest that you disregard the first test and then repeat it.

If you take a look at TABLE 9.11 you can see that there is a lot of work involved in road testing for peak performance but at the end of this test there was an overall performance gain of 8%.

This test involved a bike, which explains the column for needle position. If a car is being tuned, an extra column will be required to note the accelerator pump jet, and if a Holley carb is fitted, you will also need to record the power valve size.

The time is taken at both full and half throttle as this gives us more clues on what to try for the next test. On the drag strip, performance at half throttle is not of much concern, but on the road or the race circuit good running at half throttle is essential for crisp throttle response.

Throughout the test you should make one change at a time. This is the only way that you are going to find out to what the engine is responding. With just one variable introduced with each test it is often difficult to know what to try next, so you will appreciate that the introduction of two or more variables will make it virtually impossible to know where you are heading in your tuning.

At the start, this type of tuning can be very frustrating because you seem to be heading up so many dead end streets. If you look back to TABLE 9.11 you can see that the first five tests lead virtually nowhere. In most instances there was a loss of performance compared with how the engine had been set-up originally. (This motor had not been tuned on the dyno). After test five one could have been tempted to give up, but right from that point on it became evident that the engine was a touch rich and that clue provided the basis on which the rest of the testing was done.

The same procedure is used to test road race or drag race cars, but as the consistency of 209

## TABLE 9.11   Tuning diary

| Temp 82° | | Pressure 30 in | | Humidity 53% | | RAD 94% | | Date   17/3/74 |
|---|---|---|---|---|---|---|---|---|
| *Main jet* | *Idle jet* | *Needle position* | *Initial timing* | *Spark plug* | *Plug reading* | *Time full* | *half* | *Remarks* |
| 230 | 70 | 3 | 10° | N7Y | OK | 27.3 | 38.7 | Repeat test |
| 240 | | | | | OK | 28.0 | 39.1 | |
| | | | 12° | | OK | 27.4 | 38.3 | |
| 230 | | 1 | | | warm | 27.0 | 37.8 | |
| | | 4 | | | OK | 27.8 | 38.1 | Sounds rich at full |
| 220 | | | | | OK | 27.0 | 36.9 | throttle |
| | | 3 | | | hot | 26.6 | 36.7 | |
| | | | 10° | | OK | 26.3 | 36.0 | |
| | | 2 | | | OK | 25.7 | 35.8 | |
| 210 | | | | | hot | 25.8 | 35.4 | |
| | | 3 | | | hot | 25.4 | 35.3 | |
| | | | | N6Y | OK | 25.2 | 35.4 | Overall gain 7.7% and 8.5% |

the driver is also tested on the race circuit or drag strip, an experienced driver should preferably do the driving.


*Conclusion:*

Having read this book you will now have a better understanding of how your engine works, and how you can work with and use some of the basic laws of physics to improve its performance.

However, this knowledge is not enough to ensure the modifications you carry out will be a success. Successful tuning depends also on careful and thoughtful planning, and then skilful execution of that plan. Do not let over-enthusiasm cause you to rush through the job. Take your time and make absolutely certain that it has been done correctly.

Engine assembly work should be carried out under ideal conditions. You need good lighting and a clean, tidy, dust-free workshop. Every effort must be made to keep dirt out of the motor. Wash all parts in clean solvent and then immediately cover them with plastic sheeting (not cotton) to keep off the dust. Keep your tools and your hands clean.

Remember that the time you spend on initial preparation and cleanliness contributes immensely to the success of all engine work, in terms of both horsepower and reliability.

Good tuning.

# Appendix

## Appendix 1

### Car engine specifications and modifications

#### Alfa Romeo Twin Cam four

| | | |
|---|---|---|
| **Standard bore and stroke –** | *1300* | 74mm × 75 mm |
| | | rebore to 74.25 mm = 1299 cc |
| | *1600* | 78 mm × 82 mm |
| | | rebore to 78.75 mm = 1598 cc |
| | | rebore to 84 mm = 1818 cc |
| | | destroke to 72 mm = 1596 cc |
| | *1750* | 80 mm × 88.5 mm |
| | | rebore to 84 mm = 1962 cc |
| | | rebore to 84.55 mm = 1988 cc |
| | *2000* | 84 mm × 88.5 mm |
| | | rebore to 84.55 mm = 1988 cc |

| | | | |
|---|---|---|---|
| **Standard valves –** | *1300* | 1.457 in inlet | oversize 1.614 in |
| | | 1.339 in exhaust | |
| | *1600 and 1750* | 1.614 in inlet | oversize 1.673 in or 1.693 in |
| | | 1.457 in exhaust | |
| | *2000* | 1.732 in inlet | oversize 1.81 in |
| | | 1.575 in exhaust | |

*Note: Use oversize valves in racing engines only. Standard exhaust valves are sodium filled.*

#### Alfa Romeo Alfasud

| | |
|---|---|
| **Standard bore and stroke –** | 80 mm × 59 mm |
| **Standard valves –** | 1.457 in inlet |
| | 1.339 in exhaust |

211

## American Motors V8 (1966 and later)

| | | | |
|---|---|---|---|
| **Standard bore and stroke -** | *290* | 3.75 in × 3.28 in | max rebore 3.875 in |
| | *304* | 3.75 in × 3.44 in | 3.875 in |
| | *343* | 4.08 in × 3.28 in | 4.125 in |
| | *360* | 4.08 in × 3.44 in | 4.125 in |
| | *390* | 4.165 in × 3.58 in | 4.1875 in |
| | *401* | 4.165 in × 3.68 in | 4.1875 in |
| **Standard valves -** | *290-304* | 1.79 in inlet | oversize 2.025 in |
| | | 1.4 in exhaust | 1.68 in |
| | *343-401* | 2.025 in inlet | |
| | | 1.68 in exhaust | |

*Note: The 290-360 engines (except the 290 and 343 Trans-Am) use malleable iron con rods which break easily. The 390-401 engines have forged rods and cranks which makes them more suitable for modification.*

## BMC - British Leyland 'A' series

| | | |
|---|---|---|
| **Standard bore and stroke -** | *850* | 62.916 mm × 68.26 mm |
| | | rebore to 66.5 mm = 948 cc |
| | *997* | 62.421 mm × 81.28 mm |
| | | rebore to 66.5 mm = 1129 cc |
| | *998* | 64.567 mm × 76.2 mm |
| | | rebore to 66.5 mm = 1059 cc |
| | *1098* | 64.567 mm × 83.72 mm |
| | | rebore to 66.5 mm = 1163 cc |
| | *970 'S'* | 70.612 mm × 61.91 mm |
| | | rebore to 71.628 mm = 998 cc |
| | | rebore to 73.5 mm = 1051 cc |
| | | destroke to 58.8 mm = 998 cc |
| | | destroke to 50 mm = 849 cc |
| | *1070 'S'* | 70.612 mm × 68.26 mm |
| | | rebore to 71.628 mm = 1100 cc |
| | | rebore to 73.5 mm = 1159 cc |
| | | destroke to 64.7 mm = 1098 cc |
| | *1275 'S'* | 70.612 mm × 81.28 mm |
| | | rebore to 71.12 mm = 1292 cc |
| | | rebore to 72.136 mm = 1328 cc |
| | | rebore to 73.5 mm = 1379 cc |
| | | stroke to 84 mm = 1426 cc |
| | | stroke to 87 mm = 1477 cc |
| | | destroke to 76.5 mm = 1298 cc |

*Note: The 997 and 1098 cranks are weak; limit engine to 6500 rpm.*
*The 1300 block without side covers is more rigid and is recommended for racing engines over 1328 cc. When stroked, the standard 1275 'S' crank is only recommended for speedway or hillclimb racing; the later 1100 'S' and 1300 engines and 1275 'S' changed from 1.625 in diameter crankpins to 1.750 in crankpins, so these can be stroked by grinding the crankpin to 1.625 in on a new centre and fitting the small diameter bearings and con rods from the early motors - do not supercharge. Steel cranks stroked to 87 mm are only recommended for speedway and rallycross engines.*

| | | | |
|---|---|---|---|
| **Standard valves -** | *850-998* | 1.093 in inlet | oversize 1.312 in |
| | | 1 in exhaust | 1.093 in |
| | *997 Cooper* | 1.156 in inlet | oversize 1.312 in |
| | *and 1098* | 1 in exhaust | 1.093 in |

| | | |
|---|---|---|
| *998 Cooper* | 1.213 in inlet | oversize 1.312 in |
| | 1 in exhaust | 1.093 in |
| *Cooper 'S'* | 1.402 in inlet | oversize 1.48 in |
| | 1.214 in exhaust | 1.14 in |
| | (smaller exhaust must be used) | |
| *Leyland ST 8 port* | 1.402 in inlet | oversize 1.48 in |
| | 1.214 in exhaust | 1.14 in |
| | (smaller exhaust must be used) | |

*Note: The best head for non-'S' engines is the 998 Cooper/1100 MG head, casting No. 12G295. When larger 1.093 in exhaust valves are fitted, the block must be relieved for clearance.*
*1.535 in inlet and 1.22 in exhaust valves may be used in Cooper 'S' heads if the valves are offset 0.070 in for clearance.*

## BMC - British Leyland 'B' series

| Standard bore and stroke - | *1800* | 80.25 mm × 88.9 mm | |
|---|---|---|---|
| | | rebore to 81.8 mm = 1869 cc | |
| | | rebore to 82.28 mm = 1892 cc | |
| Standard valves - | *MK1* | 1  1.565 in inlet | oversize 1.65 in or 1.725 in |
| | | 1.345 in exhaust | 1.425 in or 1.475 in |
| | *MKII* | 1.625 in inlet | oversize 1.65 in or 1.725 in |
| | | 1.345 in exhaust | 1.425 in or 1.475 in |

*Note: Block must be relieved 0.100 in when large exhaust valves or high lift cams are used.*

## Buick V6

| Standard bore and stroke - | 3.8 litre | 3.8 in × 3.4 in | |
|---|---|---|---|
| | 4.1 litre | 3.975 in × 3.4 in. | |
| Standard valves - | | 1.63 in inlet | oversize 1.71 in or 1.75 in |
| | | 1.42 in exhaust | 1.5 in |

*Note: The standard cylinder heads up to 1978 flowed very poorly. The later revised heavy duty head flows very well and is recommended for all performance applications. This revised head will not fit the early block (casting no. 1249432).*

## Buick 455 V8

| Standard bore and stroke - | 4.312 in × 3.9 in | |
|---|---|---|
| Standard valves - | 2 in inlet | oversize 2.125 in exhaust |
| | 1.625 in | 1.75 in exhaust |

*Note: Stock 'stage 1' engines have the larger valves already fitted.*

## Chevrolet V6

| Standard bore and stroke - | *200* | 3.5 in × 3.48 in | rebore to 3.56 in |
|---|---|---|---|
| | *173* | 3.5 in × 3 in | rebore to 3.56 in |
| Standard valves - | | 1.6 in inlet | oversize 1.72 in |
| | | 1.38 in exhaust | 1.5 in  213 |

## Chevrolet V8 small block (emissions engines)

**Standard bore and stroke -**

| | | |
|---|---|---|
| *262* | 3.671 in × 3.10 in | |
| | rebore to 3.731 in = 271 cu in | |
| *267* | 3.50 in × 3.48 in | |
| | rebore to 3.56 in = 277 cu in | |
| *305* | 3.74 in × 3.48 in | |
| | rebore to 3.80 in = 316 cu in | |

**Standard valves -**

1.725 in inlet
1.505 in exhaust

*Note: The 262 and 267 engines use a special head casting with small ports which makes them unsuitable for modification. Therefore use 307-283 heads with 1.94 in inlet and 1.505 ex. valves. The 303 engine uses heads the same as the standard 307-283. These should be fitted with 1.94 inlet valves.*

## Chevrolet V8 small block

**Standard bore and stroke -**

| | | |
|---|---|---|
| *283* | 3.875 in × 3 in | |
| | rebore to 3.935 in = 292 cu in | |
| *302* | 4.00 in × 3 in | |
| | rebore to 4.060 in = 311 cu in | |
| *307* | 3.875 in × 3.25 in | |
| | rebore to 3.935 in = 316 cu in | |
| *327* | 4.00 in × 3.25 in | |
| | rebore to 4.060 in = 337 cu in | |
| *350* | 4.00 in × 3.48 in | |
| | rebore to 4.060 in = 360 cu in | |
| | stroke to 3.75 in = 388 cu in | |
| *400* | 4.126 in × 3.75 in | |
| | rebore to 4.186 = 413 cu in | |
| | stroke to 4 in = 440 cu in | |

*Note: The 400 motor is not recommended for modification unless the short (5.565 in) con rods are replaced by rods at least 6 in long. The stroked 400 motor is for racing only - use Chevy heavy duty block No. 0382318 or No. 3970010. The 3 in, 3.25 in and 3.48 in cranks can be used in the 400 block to give 321, 348 and 372 cu in respectively - if bored to 4.186 in the displacement is 330, 358 and 383 in. When the shorter stroke cranks are used with the 400 block, it is necessary to use special TRW thick wall main bearings as the 400 crank has 2.65 in diameter mains - the other cranks have 2.45 in mains.*

**Standard valves -**

| | | |
|---|---|---|
| *early heads* | 1.725 in inlet | |
| | 1.505 in exhaust | |
| *later heads* | 1.94 in inlet | |
| | 1.505 in exhaust | |
| *high performance heads* | 2.02 in inlet | |
| | 1.6 in exhaust | |

*Note: Best performance heads to use are the 461, 492 and 292 - identified by casting number, usually on bottom of one of the intake runners.*

214   *'461' (Part No. 3928445) early fuel injection head - best for street engines. Use TRW or Manley 1.94*

*in and 1.5 in valves up to 350 cu in - 2.02 in and 1.6 in for larger engines.*

*'492' (Part No. 3987376) late straight plug fuel injection head and (Part No. 336746) angle plug LT-1 head - best for road racing and short speedway. Use TRW or Manley 1.94 in and 1.5 in valves up to 292 in, 2.02 in and 1.6 in valves up to 327 ins and 2.05 in and 1.6 in valves for larger engines.*

*'292' (Part No. 3965784) turbo head - best for drag, super speedway and boat racing motors above 330 ins (otherwise use 492 head). Use TRW or Manley 2.05 in and 1.6 in valves up to 360 cu ins, 2.075 in and 1.625 in valves for larger engines. When larger 2.075 in valves are used, the exhaust valve guides must be offset 0.040 in for clearance between valve heads.*

*Special Note: If your class of racing permits the use of special heads then the Brownfield aluminium heads should be considered. Out of the box, with just minor cleaning up of the ports and combustion chambers, these heads will give almost as much power as the most radically modified '492' and '292' heads. Standard they produce about 46 hp more than lightly modified '292' heads on a 372 cu in sprint car speedway engine. The Brownfield heads accept standard Chevy parts, so are a much cheaper power route than the Weslake four valve heads. Standard valve size is 2.02 in inlet and 1.6 in exhaust. Oversize 2.05 in inlet valves may be fitted. Care should be exercised that these heads are not radically ported as this could cause cracking. The exhaust ports should not be recontoured as they already flow at their peak.*

## Chevrolet V8 big block

**Standard bore and stroke-**

| | | |
|---|---|---|
| *396* | 4.094 in × 3.76 in | |
| | rebore to 4.154 in = 408 cu in | |
| *402* | 4.125 in × 3.76 in | |
| | rebore to 4.185 in = 414 cu in | |
| *427* | 4.251 in × 3.76 in | |
| | rebore to 4.311 in = 439 cu in | |
| *454* | 4.251 in × 4 in | |
| | rebore to 4.311 in = 467 cu in | |
| | stroke to 4.25 in = 496 cu in | |

*Note: 6.405 in long Can-Am rods should be used for racing with 4 in and 4.25 in stroke cranks. The tall truck block (0.400 in taller) should be used with the 4.25 in stroker crank.*

**Standard valves -**

| | |
|---|---|
| 2.065 in inlet | oversize 2.19 in or 2.3 in |
| 1.72 in exhaust | 1.88 in or 1.94 in |

*Note: For sports and medium semi-race tune the standard closed chamber oval port heads give the best performance. Use standard size TRW or Manley valves in the 396-402, and 2.19 in and 1.88 in in the 427-454.*

*For hot semi-race tune, road racing and short speedway racing use the closed chamber rectangular port heads. Use 2.19 in and 1.88 in TRW or Manley valves in all the hot semi-race motors and 396-402 race motors. Use 2.3 in and 1.94 in valves in race motors over 415 cu ins.*

*The open chamber rectangular port heads should only be used for drag and boat racing. Use 2.19 in and 1.88 in valves in the 396-402, and 2.3 in and 1.94 in valves in larger motors.*

*Very powerful big block engines tend to have head gasket leakage problems where the extra head stud should be (but isn't because that is where the inlet port is) on cylinders 2, 6, 3 and 7. This problem can be overcome by 'O' ringing the block, but a less expensive modification is to fit four additional head bolts. First a hole must be drilled from the face of the head through the water jacket and into the inlet port floor. This hole is then tapped and plugged (be sure to seal the plug). Then the plug is drilled to accept a 5/16 in NC countersunk allen head bolt. An access hole must be drilled and fitted with a plug in the top of the port. Fit the heads to the block and drill the block and head gaskets. Be sure to machine the plugs flush with the face of the head. Then fit the bolts and tension them to 18-20 lbf ft.* 215

# Chevrolet straight 6

Standard bore and stroke -

*230*   3.875 in × 3.25 in
rebore to 3.935 in = 237 cu in

*250*   3.875 in × 3.53 in
rebore to 3.935 in = 258 cu in

*292*   3.875 in × 4.125 in
rebore to 3.935 in = 301 cu in

Standard valves -

1.72 in inlet          oversize 1.94 in or 2.02 in
1.5 in exhaust                              1.6 in

# Chevrolet Vega ohc four

Standard bore and stroke -          3.501 in × 3.625 in
Standard valves -          1.6 in inlet          oversize 1.67 in
1.375 in exhaust

*Note: For reasonable performance the combustion chambers must be welded up to give a squish area opposite the spark plug. The stock head has no squish area at all.*

# Chevrolet II 4 cylinder

Standard bore and stroke -          3.875 in × 3.25 in
rebore to 3.895 in  = 155 cu in
rebore to 3.935 in  = 158 cu in

Standard valves -          1.72 in inlet          oversize 1.94 in or 2.02 in
1.5 in exhaust                              1.6 in

*Note: If your class of racing permits the use of special cylinder heads then the aluminum head designed by Frank Duggan and produced by Arias Pistons should be considered. It features round inlet ports inclined at 45⁰ and can be fitted with 1.97 in inlet and 1.585 in exhaust valves. With just minor port work a 155 cu in midget speedway engine will produce 265 hp with one of these heads.*

# Chevrolet Vega Cosworth 4 valve

Standard bore and stroke -          3.501 in × 3.160 in
rebore to 3.531 in  = 2028 cc
stroke to 3.625 in  = 2327 cc

Standard valves -          1.4 in inlet
1.2 in exhaust

# Chrysler slant 6

Standard bore and stroke -          3.4 in × 4.12 in
rebore to 3.5 in = 238 cu in

Standard valves -          1.625 in inlet          oversize 1.725 in
1.365 in exhaust                              1.45 in

# Chrysler Hemi 6 (Aust)

Standard bore and stroke -

*215*   3.25 in × 3.68 in
*245*   3.76 in × 3.68 in
*265*   3.91 in × 3.68 in

Standard valves -          *215-245*   1.84 in inlet

1.5 in exhaust
265    1.96 in inlet
1.6 in exhaust

## Chrysler Hemi V8

**Standard bore and stroke -**      426    4.25 in × 3.75 in
rebore to 4.310 in = 438 cu in
stroke to 4.25 in = 496 cu in
**Standard valves -**      2.25 in inlet
1.94 in exhaust

## Chrysler V8 'A' block

**Standard bore and stroke -**      273    3.63 in × 3.31 in
rebore to 3.69 in = 283 cu in
318    3.91 in × 3.31 in
rebore to 3.97 in = 328 cu in
340    4.04 in × 3.31 in
rebore to 4.10 in = 350 cu in
360    4.00 in × 3.58 in
rebore to 4.060 in = 371 cu in
**Standard valves -**    273-318    1.78 in inlet        oversize 1.88 in
1.5 in exhaust
340    2.02 in inlet
1.6 in exhaust
360    1.88 in inlet        oversize 2.02 in
1.6 in exhaust
*High performance*    2.02 in inlet        oversize 2.08 in
*W-2 heads*    1.6 in exhaust

*Note: The W-2 heads are recommended for all performance engines in semi-race or full race tune.*

## Chrysler V8 'B' block

**Standard bore and stroke -**      383    4.25 in × 3.38 in
rebore to 4.31 in = 394 cu in
400    4.34 in × 3.38 in
rebore to 4.37 in = 406 cu in
413    4.19 in × 3.75 in
rebore to 4.25 in = 426 cu in
426    4.25 in × 3.75 in
rebore to 4.31 in = 438 cu in
440    4.32 in × 3.75 in
rebore to 4.35 in = 446 cu in
stroke to 4.25 in = 505 cu in
**Standard valves -**      2.08 in inlet        oversize 2.14 in
1.74 in exhaust

## Chrysler Lotus Talbot Twin Cam 16 valve

**Standard bore and stroke-**      95.25 mm × 76.2 mm        217

## Chrysler Lotus Talbot Twin Cam 16 Valve - continued

| | |
|---|---|
| **Standard valves -** | 1.40 in inlet |
| | 1.215 in exhaust |

# Chrysler Mitsubishi four (Galant/Lancer)

| | | |
|---|---|---|
| **Standard bore and stroke -** | *1300* | 73 mm × 77 mm |
| | *1400* | 73 mm × 86 mm |
| | *1500* | 74.5 mm × 86 mm |
| | *1600* | 76.9 mm × 86 mm |
| | | rebore to 79.25 mm = 1697 cc |

| | | | |
|---|---|---|---|
| **Standard valves -** | | 1.496 in inlet | oversize 1.578 in |
| | | 1.22 in exhaust | 1.28 in |

# Chrysler Sunbeam and Avenger 4 cylinder

| | | |
|---|---|---|
| **Standard bore and stroke -** | *1300* | 78.6 mm × 66.67 mm |
| | *1500* | 86.12 mm × 64.3 mm |
| | *1600* | 87.335 mm × 66.67 mm |
| | *1800* | 86.12 mm × 77.19 mm |
| | *1800 GT* | 87.335 mm × 77.19 mm |
| | *2000* | 90 mm × 77.19 mm |
| | | rebore to 90.5 mm = 1986 cc |

*Note: The 1800 GT and 2000 motors are Group 1 homologated, available from Chrysler (Talbot) Competitions Dept.*

| | | | |
|---|---|---|---|
| **Standard valves -** | *1300* | 1.448 in inlet | |
| | | 1.228 in exhaust | |
| | *1500 sc* | 1.448 in inlet | oversize 1.55 in |
| | | 1.228 in exhaust | 1.34 in |
| | *1500 twin carburettor* | 1.498 in inlet | oversize 1.55 in |
| | | 1.228 in exhaust | 1.34 in |
| | *1600* | 1.498 in inlet | oversize 1.65 in |
| | | 1.228 in exhaust | 1.42 in |
| | *1800 GT* | 1.65 in inlet | |
| | | 1.42 in exhaust | |
| | *2000 early* | 1.65 in inlet | |
| | | 1.42 in exhaust | |
| | *2000 late* | 1.8 in inlet | |
| | | 1.5 in exhaust | |

# Cosworth DFV Formula 1

| | |
|---|---|
| **Standard bore and stroke -** | 85.72 mm × 64.77 mm |
| **Standard valves -** | 1.32 in inlet |
| | 1.14 in exhaust |

# Cosworth FVA Formula 2

| | |
|---|---|
| **Standard bore and stroke -** | 85.72 mm × 69.09 mm |
| | stroke to 80 mm = 1847 cc |
| **Standard valves -** | 1.32 in inlet |
| | 1.14 in exhaust |

# Cosworth Ford BDA 4 valve race engines

*BDB rally engine*
**Standard bore and stroke -**        83.5 mm × 77.62 mm
       stroke to 82 mm = 1796 cc
**Standard valves -**        1.275 in inlet       oversize 1.325 in
       1.075 in exhaust       1.145 in

*Note: Use oversize valves in 1796 cc motor only.*

*BDC race engine*
**Standard bore and stroke -**        83.5 mm × 77.62 mm
       stroke to 82 mm = 1796 cc
**Standard valves -**        1.325 in inlet       oversize 1.36 in
       1.145 in exhaust

*Note: Use oversize valves in 1796 cc motor only*

*BDD Formula Atlantic race engine*
**Standard bore and stroke -**        81 mm × 77.62 mm
**Standard valves -**        1.22 in inlet
       1.0 in exhaust

*BDE race engine*
**Standard bore and stroke -**        85.725 mm × 77.62 mm
       stroke to 82 mm = 1893 cc

*Note: Some BDE blocks will rebore to 87 mm giving 1846 cc with standard crank and 1950 cc with 82 mm crank.*
**Standard valves -**        1.36 in inlet
       1.145 in exhaust

*BDF race engine*
**Standard bore and stroke -**        88.9 mm × 77.62 mm
**Standard valves -**        1.36 in inlet
       1.145 in exhaust

*BDG race engine*
**Standard bore and stroke -**        90 mm × 77.62 mm
**Standard valves -**        1.36 in or 1.4 in inlet
       1.145 in or 1.2 in exhaust

*BDH race engine*
**Standard bore and stroke -**        81 mm × 63 mm
**Standard valves -**        1.275 in inlet
       1.0 in exhaust

*BDJ race engine*
**Standard bore and stroke -**        81 mm × 55.34 mm
**Standard valves -**        1.22 in inlet
       1.0 in exhaust

*BDM race engine*
**Standard bore and stroke -**        81 mm × 77.62 mm
**Standard valves -**        1.325 in inlet
       1.145 in exhaust

# Datsun 1200

| | | |
|---|---|---|
| **Standard bore and stroke -** | 73 mm × 70 mm | |
| | rebore to 76.85 mm = 1299 cc | |
| **Standard valves -** | 1.38 in inlet | oversize 1.496 in |
| | 1.14 in exhaust | 1.26 in |

*Note: Block must be relieved for clearance when large exhaust valve is used.*

# Datsun ohc four

| | | | |
|---|---|---|---|
| **Standard bore and stroke -** | *1600* | 83 mm × 73.3 mm | |
| | | rebore to 86 mm = 1703 cc | |
| | *1800* | 85 mm × 78 mm | |
| | | rebore to 87.8 mm = 1889 cc | |
| | *2000* | 85 mm × 86 mm | |
| | | rebore to 86 mm = 1998 cc | |
| | | rebore to 87.8 mm = 2083 cc | |
| **Standard valves -** | *1600* | 1.654 in inlet | |
| | | 1.3 in exhaust | oversize 1.378 in |
| | *1800 and 2000* | 1.654 in inlet | oversize 1.772 in |
| | | 1.378 in exhaust | |

# Datsun ohc six

| | | | |
|---|---|---|---|
| **Standard bore and stroke -** | *2400* | 83 mm × 73.7 mm | |
| | | rebore to 86 mm = 2569 cc | |
| | *2600* | 83 mm × 79 mm | |
| | | rebore to 86 mm = 2753 cc | |
| | | rebore to 87.25 mm = 2834 cc | |
| | *2800* | 86 mm × 79 mm | |
| **Standard valves -** | | 1.654 in inlet | oversize 1.72 in or 1.772 in |
| | | 1.378 in exhaust | |

*Note: Oversize 1.72 in valve for circuit racing engines over 2700 cc.*
*Oversize 1.772 in valve for drag race engines only.*

# Fiat 1600 Twin Cam

| | |
|---|---|
| **Standard bore and stroke -** | 80 mm × 80 mm |
| **Standard valves -** | 1.63 in inlet |
| | 1.42 in exhaust |

# American Ford 2300 ohc four

| | |
|---|---|
| **Standard bore and stroke -** | 96.04 mm × 79.4 mm |
| | rebore to 96.79 mm = 2337 cc |
| | stroke to 85 mm = 2502 cc |
| **Standard valves -** | 1.735 in inlet |
| | 1.5 in exhaust |

*Note: To get the best out of this engine the hydraulic tappet must be replaced with mechanical units and a mechanical cam fitted. To effect this, remove the hydraulic adjuster bodies and mill the top of the adjuster boss down 0.200 in. Machine eight press-in steel sleeves 1.7 in long to replace the hydraulic adjusters. Drill and tap the centre of each sleeve to suit 2000 Pinto adjusters. Press the sleeves into the head and secure them by pinning. Then fit the 2000 cc Pinto adjusters, lock nuts and rocker stabiliser springs.*

220

## American Ford six

| | | |
|---|---|---|
| **Standard bore and stroke-** | *200* | 3.683 in × 3.126 in |
| | *250* | 3.683 in × 3.91 in |
| **Standard valves -** | | 1.65 in inlet — oversize 1.173 in |
| | | 1.4 in exhaust — 1.5 in |

## Ford V8 Windsor

| | | |
|---|---|---|
| **Standard bore and stroke -** | *289* | 4.002 in × 2.875 in |
| | *302* | 4.002 in × 3.0 in |
| | | rebore to 4.032 in = 306 cu in |
| | *351* | 4.002 in × 3.5 in |
| | | rebore to 4.032 in = 358 cu in |
| **Standard valves -** | *289-302* | 1.78 in inlet — oversize 1.938 in |
| | | 1.45 in exhaust — 1.688 in |
| | *351* | 1.84 in inlet — oversize 1.938 in |
| | | 1.45 in exhaust — 1.688 in |

*Note: The 351-W heads are best to use on all motors as the ports and valves are larger. These heads will fit the low block motors, but 351-W inlet manifold gaskets must be used. Also fit heavy washers under the head studs as the bolt holes are $\frac{1}{16}$ in larger diameter. To raise the compression, use high compression pistons or skim 0.050 in off the 351 heads.*

## Ford V8 Cleveland

| | | |
|---|---|---|
| **Standard bore and stroke -** | *Boss 302* | 4.002 in × 3.0 in |
| | *351* | 4.002 in × 3.5 in |
| | *400* | 4.0 in × 4.0 in |

*Note: The heavy duty 'Australian' block should be used for endurance racing.*

| | | |
|---|---|---|
| **Standard valves -** | *Boss 302-351* | 2.19 in inlet |
| | | 1.71 in exhaust |
| | *Standard 351-400* | 2.04 in inlet — oversize 2.19 in |
| | | 1.65 in exhaust — 1.71 in |

*Note: The open head chamber should be replaced by a closed chamber head for best performance.*

## Ford V8 big block ('FE' series)

| | | |
|---|---|---|
| **Standard bore and stroke -** | *390* | 4.05 in × 3.78 in |
| | | rebore to 4.110 in = 401 cu in |
| | *427* | 4.234 in × 3.78 in |
| | | rebore to 4.264 in = 432 cu in |
| | *428* | 4.130 in × 3.99 in |
| | | rebore to 4.160 in = 434 cu in |

*Note: The crankpins can be reduced from 2.5 in to 2.38 in diameter to reduce bearing friction and pick up 20-30 hp; the journals must also be widened and Chrysler 'B' block con rods fitted. The 427 can be stroked to 456 cu in by fitting the 428 crankshaft.*

| | | |
|---|---|---|
| **Standard valves -** | *390-428* | 2.03 in inlet — oversize 2.093 in or 2.19 in |
| | | 1.546 in exhaust — 1.653 in or 1.78 in |
| | *427* | 2.093 in inlet — oversize 2.19 in |
| | | 1.653 in exhaust — 1.78 in |

## Ford V8 big block ('385' series)

| | | |
|---|---|---|
| **Standard bore and stroke -** | *429 Boss and wedge* | 4.36 in × 3.59 in |
| | | rebore to 4.4 in = 437 cu in |
| | | rebore to 4.44 in = 445 cu in |
| | | rebore to 4.52 in = 461 cu in |

221

### Ford V8 big block ('385'series) - continued

|  | *460 wedge* | 4.36 in × 3.85 in |
|--|--|--|
|  |  | rebore to 4.4 in = 468 cu in |
|  |  | rebore to 4.44 in = 477 cu in |
|  |  | rebore to 4.52 in = 494 cu in |

*Note: Most pre-1971 model blocks will rebore 4.44 in without any problems, but later blocks tend to have thinner walls. Some pre-1971 model blocks and all the special Boss 429 blocks will rebore to 4.48 in.*

*Some Boss 429 blocks will rebore to 4.52 in. The standard crankshaft can be stroked 0.18 in and 0.3 in respectively if the crankpins are offset ground to reduce their diameter from 2.5 in to 2.38 in (Chrysler rod size) or 2.2 in (big block Chevy rod size). This modification also serves to increase power due to reduced bearing friction. When the special high nickel content Boss 429 block is used, steel cranks of up to 4.65 in stroke may be used with 2.38 in diameter crankpins. The 460 crank may be fitted to the 429 block.*

| **Standard valves -** | *429-460 wedge* | 2.078 in inlet | oversize 2.25 in |
|--|--|--|--|
|  |  | 1.656 in exhaust | 1.75 in |
|  | *429 Boss hemi* | 2.4 in inlet |  |
|  |  | 1.9 in exhaust |  |

*Note: The standard small port pre-1971 model wedge heads are better than the large port Cobra Jet and Super Cobra Jet heads for all street engines and racing engines less than 500 cubic inches.*

## Ford 427 ohc Hemi

| **Standard bore and stroke -** | 4.234 in × 3.78 in |
|--|--|
|  | rebore to 4.264 in = 432 cu in |
|  | stroke to 3.99 in = 456 cu in |
| **Standard valves -** | 2.25 in inlet |
|  | 1.9 in exhaust |

## English Ford 3 bearing four cylinder

| **Standard bore and stroke -** | *997* | 81 mm × 48.4 mm |
|--|--|--|
|  |  | rebore to 83.5 mm = 1060 cc |
|  | *1198* | 81 mm × 58.339 mm |
|  |  | rebore to 83.5 mm = 1278 cc |
|  | *1340* | 81 mm × 65.088 mm |
|  |  | rebore to 83.5 mm = 1426 cc |

*Note: It is not recommended that these motors be bored to 85 mm even though this is a common practice. The smaller motors can be stroked by fitting the crank and rods from the larger motors.*

| **Standard valves -** | *997* | 1.267 in inlet | oversize 1.375 in or 1.42 in |
|--|--|--|--|
|  |  | 1.188 in exhaust | 1.2 in or 1.25 in |
|  | *1198* | 1.267 in inlet | oversize 1.4 in |
|  |  | 1.188 in exhaust | 1.25 in |
|  | *1340* | 1.267 in inlet | oversize 1.4 in |
|  |  | 1.188 in exhaust | 1.25 in |

*Note: It is suggested that the 997 cc 105E head be used on all motors to increase the compression ratio without skimming. 1.42 in inlet and 1.25 in ex valves should only be used in 5 bearing 997 cc racing engines running at 10,000 rpm.*

## English Ford 5 bearing four cylinder pre-crossflow

| **Standard bore and stroke -** | *1297* | 81 mm × 62.99 mm |
|--|--|--|
|  |  | rebore to 83.5 mm = 1380 cc |
|  | *1498* | 81 mm × 72.626 mm |
|  |  | rebore to 83.5 mm = 1591 cc |

|  | *1500* | 81 mm × 72.822 mm |  |
|  |  | rebore to 83.5 mm = 1595 cc |  |

*Note: The 1297 cc motor can be stroked using the 1498-1500 crank and rods. All motors can be stroked using the 1600 crossflow crank, rods and special pistons. Only rebore to 85 mm if the block is thick enough to accept this bore without requiring sleeves.*

| **Standard valves -** | *1279* | 1.267 in inlet | oversize 1.4 in or 1.5 in |
|  |  | 1.188 in exhaust | 1.25 in or 1.31 in |
|  | *1498-1500* | 1.438 in inlet | oversize 1.5 in or 1.625 in |
|  |  | 1.188 in exhaust | 1.31 in or 1.35 in |
|  | *1500 GT* | 1.41 in inlet | oversize 1.5 in or 1.625 in |
|  |  | 1.245 in exhaust | 1.31 in or 1.35 in |

*Note: The 997 cc 105E head is recommended for all engines up to 1500 cc. Oversize 1.625 in inlet and 1.35 in ex valves may also be used in 1297 cc racing engines running at 9,500 rpm.*

## English Ford crossflow 4 cylinder

| **Standard bore and stroke -** | *1098* | 81 mm × 53.29 mm |
|  |  | rebore to 83.5 mm = 1167 cc |
|  | *1298* | 81 mm × 62.99 mm |
|  |  | rebore to 83.5 mm = 1380 cc |
|  | *1598* | 81 mm × 77.62 mm |
|  |  | rebore to 83.5 mm = 1700 cc |

*Note: The 1098 cc motor can be stroked using the 1298 crank and rods. Maximum safe bore for standard block is 84 mm*

| **Standard valves -** | *1098* | 1.41 in inlet |  |
|  |  | 1.25 in exhaust |  |
|  | *1298* | 1.41 in inlet | oversize 1.5 in |
|  |  | 1.25 in exhaust | 1.31 in |
|  | *1298 GT* | 1.5 in inlet | oversize 1.56 in |
|  |  | 1.25 in exhaust | 1.31 in |
|  | *1598 and GT* | 1.5 in inlet | oversize 1.625 in |
|  |  | 1.25 in exhaust | 1.35 in |
|  | *Kent 1598 and GT* | 1.54 in inlet | oversize 1.625 in |
|  |  | 1.34 in exhaust | 1.35 in |

*Note: Crossflow heads with shallow combustion chambers should not be used unless the head is machined down until only the outline of the chamber remains.*
*Oversize 1.625 in inlet and 1.35 in exhaust valves may also be used in 1298 cc race and rally engines running at 9000 rpm.*
*1600 race and rally engines bored to 83.5 mm (and larger) may use 1.71 in inlet and 1.375 in exhaust valves if the valves are offset 0.040 in for clearance.*

## English Ford V6

| **Standard bore and stroke –** |  | 93.65 mm × 72.39 mm |  |
|  |  | rebore to 97.15 mm = 3090 |  |
|  |  | stroke to 82 mm = 3500 cc |  |

*Note: This motor can be stroked to 85 mm for speedway or hillclimb use.*

| **Standard valves –** |  | 1.605 in inlet | oversize 1.79 in |
|  |  | 1.453 in exhaust | 1.5 in |

*Note: The standard head flows very poorly and is best replaced by an alloy version with combustion chambers.*

## Ford Cosworth BDA 4 valve

**Standard bore and stroke –**    81 mm × 77.62 mm

The BDA can be bored and stroked (or de-stroked) to the capacities as follows:

| | | | | Bore mm | |
|---|---|---|---|---|---|
| **Stroke mm** | *81* | *83.5* | *84* | *85.72* | *87* |
| 77.62 | | 1700 | 1721 | 1792 | 1846 |
| 80 | | 1752 | 1773 | 1847 | 1902 |
| 82 | | 1796 | 1818 | 1893 | 1950 |
| 84 | | 1840 | 1862 | 1939 | 1997 |
| 63 | 1299 | | | | |

*Note: BDA blocks should not be sleeved to obtain an 85 mm (or larger) bore unless the sleeves are vacuum welded to the block.*

*The special siamese cylinder thick wall Ford competition block is required for a rebore to 85.72 mm - a few of these will bore to 87 mm - minimum acceptable wall thickness is 2 mm.*

*The 84 mm crank is only recommended for speedway or hillclimb motors - the 87.6 mm crank available from some tuners should not be used.*

**Standard valves –**    1.22 in inlet    oversize 1.32 in or 1.358 in

1.00 in exhaust    1.142 in

*Note: Use standard 1.22 in inlet and 1.00 in exhaust valves in engines de-stroked to 1300 cc for lightweight racing cars. Heavier sedans (ie. over 1200 lbs) should use 1.156 in inlet valves.*

## Ford Cosworth RS 1800 BDA 4 valve

**Standard bore and stroke –**    86.75 mm × 77.62 mm

*Note: Ford produce a special replacement block for this motor. The sleeves are pressed out of the alloy block, which is then bored and chromed back to 90 mm. The latest blocks have a 90.4 mm bore giving 1992 cc with the standard crank; or 2157 cc with an 84 mm stroke crankshaft. This crank should not be used in road race or rally engines.*

**Standard valves –**    1.32 in inlet    oversize 1.37 in

1.15 in exhaust

## Ford Lotus Twin Cam

**Standard bore and stroke -**    82.55 mm × 72.82 mm

The Twin Cam can be bored and stroked (or de-stroked) to the capacities as follows:

| | | | Bore mm | | | |
|---|---|---|---|---|---|---|
| **Stroke mm** | *83.5* | *84* | *85* | *85.72* | *87* | *90* |
| 72.82 | 1595 | 1614 | 1653 | 1681 | 1732 | 1853 |
| 77.62 | 1700 | 1721 | 1762 | 1792 | 1846 | 1975 |
| 80 | 1752 | 1773 | 1816 | 1847 | 1902 | 2036 |
| 82 | 1796 | 1818 | 1861 | 1893 | 1950 | 2087 |
| 84 | 1840 | 1862 | 1907 | 1939 | 1997 | 2138 |
| 59.2 | 1297 | | | | | |

*Note: Some Twin Cam blocks will not bore to 85 mm sucessfully - minimum acceptable wall thickness is 2mm. Twin Cam blocks should not be sleeved to obtain an 85 mm (or larger) bore unless the sleeves are vacuum welded to the block (very expensive).*

*The special siamese cylinder thick wall Ford competition block is required for a rebore to 85.72 mm – a few of these will bore to 87 mm.*

*The Ford alloy block is required for a 90 mm bore.*

*The 1600 crossflow Ford crank and rods can be used to obtain 77.62 mm stroke - special pistons with more compression height are required, alternatively the 1600 block will require about 0.220 in*

*machined from the deck. The 84 mm crank is only recommended for speedway or hillclimb motors - the 87.6 mm crank available from some tuners should not be used.*

| | | |
|---|---|---|
| **Standard valves -** | 1.53 in inlet | oversize 1.625 in or 1.687 in |
| | 1.325 in exhaust | 1.42 in or 1.375 in |

*Note: When using 1.625 in inlet and 1.42 exhaust, or 1.687 in inlet and 1.375 in exhaust valve combinations be very careful to check for clearance between the valve heads when the hottest racing cams are used. Racing engines destroked to 1297 cc and running at 9500 rpm may use 1.625 in inlet and 1.375 in exhaust valves.*

## German Ford Pinto

| | | |
|---|---|---|
| **Standard bore and stroke –** | 90.8 mm × 76.96 mm | |
| | rebore to 91.55 mm = 2026 cc | |
| | stroke to 82 mm = 2159 cc | |
| | stroke to 85 mm = 2239 cc | |
| **Standard valves –** | 1.654 in inlet | oversize 1.75 in or 1.792 in |
| | 1.417 in exhaust | 1.496 in |

## German Ford V4

| | | | |
|---|---|---|---|
| **Standard bore and stroke-** | *1500* | 90.0 mm × 58.86 mm | |
| | | rebore to 91.5 mm = 1548 cc | |
| | | rebore to 93 mm = 1599 cc | |
| | *1700* | 90.0 mm × 66.8 mm | |
| | | rebore to 91.5 mm = 1757 cc | |
| | | rebore to 93 mm = 1815 cc | |
| **Standard valves -** | | 1.457 in inlet | oversize 1.653 in or 1.732 in |
| | | 1.25 in exhaust | 1.378 in or 1.457 in |

*Note: Use 1.732 in inlet valves in 1815 cc engines, and 1.653 in in smaller engines.*

## German Ford V6

| | | | |
|---|---|---|---|
| **Standard bore and stroke –** | *2800* | 92.96 mm × 68.58 mm | |
| | | rebore to 94.96 mm = 2914 cc | |
| **Standard valves –** | | 1.57 in inlet | oversize 1.65 in |
| | | 1.27 in exhaust | 1.33 in |

## Hillman Chrysler Imp

| | | | |
|---|---|---|---|
| **Standard bore and stroke –** | | 68 mm × 60.375 mm | |
| | | rebore to 68.75 mm = 896 cc | |
| | | resleeve and bore to 72.5 mm = 997 cc | |
| **Standard valves –** | *Mk1* | 1.064 in inlet | oversize 1.202 in |
| | | 1.01 in exhaust | 1.064 in |
| | *Mk II* | 1.202 in inlet | oversize 1.276 in |
| | | 1.064 in exhaust | |
| | *Sport* | 1.276 in inlet | oversize 1.312 in or 1.34 in |
| | | 1.064 in exhaust | 1.125 in or 1.156 in |

*Note: The Sport head is the best head to modify. Inlet valves larger than 1.312 in will hit the block if the bore is less than 72.5 mm.*

# Hillman Hunter

| | | |
|---|---|---|
| **Standard bore and stroke -** | 81.54 mm × 82.55 mm | |
| | rebore to 82.556 mm = 1768 cc | |
| **Standard valves -** | 1.473 in inlet | oversize 1.55 in |
| | 1.174 in exhaust | 1.312 in |
| *GT* | 1.503 in inlet | oversize 1.55 in |
| | 1.204 in exhaust | 1.312 in |

# Holden 1.9 litre 4 cylinder

| | | |
|---|---|---|
| **Standard bore and stroke -** | 88.9 mm × 76.2 mm | |
| | rebore to 90.42 mm = 1957 cc | |
| **Standard valves -** | 1.49 in inlet | oversize 1.65 in or 1.75 in |
| | 1.275 in exhaust | 1.4 in or 1.5 in |

# Holden Gemini/Isuzu Bellet ohc 4 cylinder

| | | | |
|---|---|---|---|
| **Standard bore and stroke -** | *1600* | 82 mm × 75 mm | |
| | *1800* | 84 mm × 82 mm | |
| **Standard valves -** | | 1.67 in inlet | oversize 1.772 in |
| | | 1.34 in exhaust | 1.4 in or 1.457 in |

*Note: Use 1.772 in inlet and 1.457 in exhaust valves in 1800 engines only.*

# Holden six

| | | | |
|---|---|---|---|
| **Standard bore and stroke -** | *179* | 3.562 in × 3 in | |
| | | rebore to 3.622 in = 185 cu in | |
| | *186* | 3.625 in × 3 in | |
| | | rebore to 3.685 in = 192 cu in | |
| | *202* | 3.625 in × 3.25 in | |
| | | rebore to 3.685 in = 208 cu in | |
| **Standard valves -** | | 1.49 inlet | oversize 1.65 in or 1.75 in |
| | | 1.275 in exhaust | 1.4 in or 1.5 in |

*Note: If your class of racing permits the use of special heads then the Perfectune Yella Terra special aluminium head developed by Phil Irving should be considered. Out of the box with just minor port work, these heads enable the Holden motor to produce around 90 hp per litre. Standard valve size is 1.72 in inlet and 1.41 in exhaust. The round inlet ports are inclined at $45^0$ and the exhaust ports tilt upward at $10^0$. These heads are available with either 55 cc or 60 cc combustion chamber volumes.*

# Holden V8

| | | | |
|---|---|---|---|
| **Standard bore and stroke -** | *253* | 3.625 in × 3.063 in | |
| | *308* | 4.00 in × 3.063 in | |
| **Standard valves -** | | 1.76 in inlet | oversize 2.02 in |
| | | 1.48 in exhaust | 1.625 in |

# Jaguar

| | | |
|---|---|---|
| **Standard bore and stroke -** | *3.4* | 83 mm × 106 mm |
| | *3.8* | 87 mm × 106 mm |
| | *4.2* | 92.07 mm × 106 mm |

| Standard valves - | 1.75 in inlet | oversize 2 in |
| | 1.625 in exhaust | 1.687 in |

## Lancia Beta 4 valve Twin Cam (Group 5 Turbo)

**Standard bore and stroke -** 82 mm × 67.5 mm
**Group 5 valves -** 1.339 in inlet
1.063 in exhaust

## Lancia Stratos V6 Twin Cam (Group 4)

**Standard bore and stroke -** 92.5 mm × 60 mm
**Group 4 valves -** 1.673 in inlet
1.449 in exhaust

## Mazda 626 ohc four

**Standard bore and stroke -** 80.0 mm × 98.0 mm
rebore to 80.5 mm = 1995 cc

| **Standard valves -** | 1.653 in inlet | oversize 1.732 in |
| | 1.299 in exhaust | 1.378 in |

## Oldsmobile small-block V8

**Standard bore and stroke -**

| | *260* | 3.5 in × 3.385 in |
| | | rebore to 3.54 in = 267 cu in |
| | *330* | 3.937 in × 3.385 in |
| | | rebore to 3.977 in = 336 cu in |
| | *350* | 4.057 in × 3.385 in |
| | | rebore to 4.097 in = 357 cu in |
| | *403* | 4.351 in × 3.385 in |
| | | rebore to 4.391 in = 410 cu in |
| | | stroke to 3.5 in = 424 cu in |

**Standard valves -**

| | *330/350* | 1.875 in inlet | oversize 2 in or 2.072 in |
| | | 1.562 in exhaust | 1.625 in |
| | *403* | 2 in inlet | oversize 2.072 in |
| | | 1.562 in exhaust | 1.625 in |
| | *W-31* | 2 in inlet | oversize 2.072 in |
| | | 1.625 in exhaust | |

*Note: The high performance W-31 heads are recommended for all engines smaller than 403 cu in. Big block 455 heads used as standard on Toronados, 4-4-2s and Police engines are recommended only for 403 cu in (and larger) engines (a special Holley inlet manifold is required).*

## Oldsmobile big-block V8

**Standard bore and stroke -**

| | *400 early* | 4.0 in × 3.975 in |
| | | rebore to 4.030 in = 406 cu in |
| | *400 late* | 3.875 in × 4.25 in |
| | *425* | 4.125 in × 3.975 in |
| | | rebore to 4.185 in = 437 cu in |

### Oldsmobile big-block V8 - continued

|  |  |  |  |  |
|---|---|---|---|---|
|  | **455** | 4.125 in × 4.25 in |  |  |
|  |  | rebore to 4.185 in = 468 cu in |  |  |
| **Standard valves -** | *low performance* | 1.875 in inlet | oversize 2 in or 2.072 in |  |
|  |  | 1.625 in exhaust |  |  |
|  | *medium performance* | 2.0 in inlet | oversize 2.072 in |  |
|  |  | 1.625 in exhaust |  |  |
|  | *high performance* | 2.072 in inlet |  |  |
|  |  | 1.625 in exhaust |  |  |
|  | *W-30* | 2.072 in inlet |  |  |
|  |  | 1.63 in exhaust |  |  |

*Note: The best performance heads are the W-30 (casting No. 400370), but these are no longer available. The next best are the 455 high performance heads used on Toranados, 4-4-2s and Police engines (Part No. 231473). These are often sold as W-30 heads.*

## Opel ohc four

|  |  |  |
|---|---|---|
| **Standard bore and stroke -** | *1.9* | 93 mm × 69.85 mm |
|  |  | rebore to 95 mm = 1980 cc |
|  |  | stroke to 82 mm = 2325 cc |
|  | *2.0* | 95 mm × 69.85 mm |
|  |  | rebore to 95.25 mm = 1991 cc |
|  |  | rebore to 96.25 mm = 2033 cc |
|  |  | stroke to 82 mm = 2378 cc |
| **Standard valves -** |  | 1.574 in inlet |
|  |  | 1.338 in exhaust |

*Note: For best performance the Opel alloy crossflow head should be used, fitted with 1.93 in inlet and 1.614 in exhaust valves.*

## Pontiac V8

|  |  |  |  |  |
|---|---|---|---|---|
| **Standard bore and stroke -** | *350* | 3.88 in × 3.75 in |  |  |
|  |  | rebore to 3.94 in = 366 cu in |  |  |
|  | *400* | 4.12 in × 3.75 in |  |  |
|  |  | rebore to 4.18 in = 412 cu in |  |  |
|  | *428* | 4.121 in × 4.01 in |  |  |
|  |  | rebore to 4.181 in = 440 cu in |  |  |
|  | *455* | 4.151 in × 4.21 in |  |  |
|  |  | rebore to 4.181 in = 462 cu in |  |  |
| **Standard valves -** | *350* | 1.96 in inlet | oversize 2.11 in |  |
|  |  | 1.66 in exhaust | 1.77 in |  |
|  | *400 4V* | 2.11 in inlet |  |  |
|  |  | 1.66 in exhaust | oversize 1.77 in |  |
|  | *428* | 2.11 in inlet |  |  |
|  |  | 1.77 in exhaust |  |  |
|  | *455* | 2.11 in inlet |  |  |
|  |  | 1.66 in exhaust | oversize 1.77 in |  |
|  | *455 SD* | 2.11 in inlet |  |  |
|  |  | 1.77 in exhaust |  |  |

## Porsche 356 - 912 flat four

|  |  |
|---|---|
| **Standard bore and stroke -** | 82.5 mm × 75 mm |
|  | 86 mm barrels = 1743 cc |

| Standard valves - | | | |
|---|---|---|---|
| | *356-912* | 1.496 in inlet | oversize 1.575 in or 1.653 in |
| | | 1.34 in exhaust | |
| | *Super 90* | 1.575 in inlet | oversize 1.653 in |
| | | 1.34 exhaust | |

*Note: Standard exhaust valves are special sodium-filled items.*

## Porsche 911 flat six

| Standard bore and stroke - | | |
|---|---|---|
| | *2.0* | 80 mm × 66 mm |
| | *2.2* | 84 mm × 66 mm |
| | *2.4* | 84 mm × 70.4 mm |
| | *2.7* | 90 mm × 70.4 mm |
| | *2.8* | 92 mm × 70.4 mm |
| | *3.0* | 95 mm × 70.4 mm |

| Standard valves - | | |
|---|---|---|
| | *2.0* | 1.535 in inlet |
| | | 1.378 in exhaust |
| | *2.0 'S' '67* | 1.654 in inlet |
| | | 1.457 in exhaust |
| | *2.0'S' and Carrera '69* | 1.77 in inlet |
| | | 1.535 in exhaust |
| | *2.2-2.8* | 1.81 in inlet |
| | | 1.575 in exhaust |

*Note: Road racing 911 engines should have dual spark plugs fitted. Power will not increase, but acceleration and response out of corners is better.*

## Renault

| Standard bore and stroke - | | |
|---|---|---|
| | *1470* | 76 mm × 81 mm |
| | *1565* | 77 mm × 84 mm |
| Standard valves - | *1470 and 1565* | 1.378 in inlet |
| | | 1.22 in exhaust |
| | *R16TS 1565* | 1.575 in inlet |
| | | 1.392 in exhaust |

*Note: R16 TS head uses hemi-chambers, the others are wedge chambers.*

## Toyota Corolla

| Standard bore and stroke - | | | |
|---|---|---|---|
| | *1077* | 75 mm × 61 mm | |
| | | rebore to 75.75 mm = 1099 cc | |
| | *1166* | 75 mm × 66 mm | |
| | | rebore to 79 mm = 1294 cc | |
| Standard valves - | | 1.417 in inlet | oversize 1.496 in or 1.535 in |
| | | 1.142 in exhaust | 1.26 in |

## Toyota Celica/Corolla pushrod hemi

| Standard bore and stroke - | | |
|---|---|---|
| | *1600* | 85 mm × 70 mm |
| | | rebore to 85.25 mm = 1598 cc |
| | | rebore to 89 mm = 1742 cc |
| | *1800* | 85 mm × 78 mm |

229

### Toyota Celica/Corolla pushrod hemi - continued

|  |  |  |
|---|---|---|
|  | rebore to 89 mm = 1941 cc |  |
| **Standard valves -** | 1.614 in inlet | oversize 1.654 in or 1.693 in |
|  | 1.417 in exhaust |  |

*Note: Use 1.693 in valves in engines over 1700 cc only.*

## Toyota 2000 ohc 4

|  |  |  |
|---|---|---|
| **Standard bore and stroke -** | 88.5 mm × 80 mm |  |
|  | rebore to 89 mm = 1991 cc |  |
| **Standard valves -** | 1.614 in inlet | oversize 1.732 in |
|  | 1.417 in exhaust |  |

## Triumph Dolomite Sprint 4 valve

| **Standard bore and stroke -** | 90.3 mm × 78 mm |
|---|---|
| **Standard valves -** | 1.38 in inlet |
|  | 1.21 in exhaust |

## Triumph TR4 and TR4A

|  |  |  |
|---|---|---|
| **Standard bore and stroke -** | 86 mm × 92 mm |  |
|  | rebore to 87 mm = 2188 cc |  |
| **Standard valves -** | 1.53 in inlet | oversize 1.575 in |
|  | 1.187 in exhaust | 1.312 in |

## Triumph 2500

|  |  |  |
|---|---|---|
| **Standard bore and stroke -** | 74.7 mm × 95 mm |  |
|  | rebore to 75.716 mm = 2566 cc |  |
| **Standard valves -** | 1.437 in inlet | oversize 1.45 in |
|  | 1.187 in exhaust |  |

## Vauxhall Viva/Firenza/Magnum/Chevette ohc 4

|  |  |  |  |
|---|---|---|---|
| **Standard bore and stroke -** | *2000* | 95.25 mm × 69.24 mm |  |
|  |  | rebore to 95.76 mm = 1995 cc |  |
|  | *2300* | 97.54 mm × 76.2 mm |  |
|  |  | stroke to 83.5 mm = 2496 cc |  |
| **Standard valves -** | *2000* | 1.67 in inlet | oversize 1.8 in |
|  |  | 1.41 in exhaust | 1.5 in |
|  | *2300* | 1.67 in inlet | oversize 1.85 in or 1.89 in |
|  |  | 1.41 in exhaust | 1.6 in |

## Vauxhall Chevette HS2300 Twin Cam 16 valve

| **Standard bore and stroke -** | 97.54 mm × 76.2 mm |
|---|---|
|  | stroke to 83.5 mm = 2496 cc |
| **Standard valves -** | 1.40 in inlet |
|  | 1.18 in exhaust |

*Note: If your class of racing permits the use of special cylinder heads then the 16 valve Lotus head should be considered as it will give an additional 20 - 25 hp.*

# VW Type I, II, III

**Standard bore and stroke -**

| | | |
|---|---|---|
| *1200* | 77 mm × 64 mm |
| *1300* | 77 mm × 69 mm |
| *1500* | 83 mm × 69 mm |
| *1600* | 85.5 mm × 69 mm |

*Note: The 1200 can be enlarged to 1390 cc by fitting 1500 barrels, and to 1493 cc by fitting the 1500 69 mm crank. The 1300 and 1500 can be enlarged to 1584 cc by fitting 1600 barrels. The 1300 heads must be machined to accept the 1600 barrels. Special cranks and barrels are available as follows:*

| Bore (mm) | Stroke (mm) | | | | |
|---|---|---|---|---|---|
| | *69* | *74* | *76* | *78* | *82* |
| 87 | 1641 | 1760 | 1807 | 1855 | 1950 |
| 88 | 1679 | 1800 | 1849 | 1897 | 1995 |
| 90.5 | 1775 | 1904 | 1956 | 2007 | 2110 |
| 92 | 1835 | 1968 | 2020 | 2074 | 2180 |

*Note: the 88 × 76 or 90.5 × 74 combination is the most reliable for road or rally use. The crankcase must be machined to accept 90.5 or 92 mm barrels. This weakens the case and can cause cracking behind No 3 cylinder unless the case is carefully welded for additional strength. Engines using 78 or 82 mm cranks will require clearance machining of the piston skirts and crankcase; and the camshaft thrust shoulder must be re-radiused to clear No 4 con-rod. For racing, Porsche rods should be used with 78 and 82 mm stroker cranks. Special cranks are available to suit these rods.*

**Standard valves -**

| | | |
|---|---|---|
| | | *single port heads* |
| | *1200* | 1.24 in inlet |
| | | 1.18 in exhaust |
| | *1300 and 1500* | 1.297 in inlet |
| | | 1.18 in exhaust |
| | | *twin port heads* |
| | *1500 and 1600* | 1.396 in inlet |
| | | 1.259 in exhaust |

*Note: The twin port heads are recommended for all modified engines. Oversize inlet valve sizes are 1.574 in, 1.653 in and 1.732 in. Oversize exhaust valves sizes are 1.26 in, 1.398 in and 1.457 in.*

# VW Type IV (and Porsche 914)

**Standard bore and stroke -**

| | | |
|---|---|---|
| *1700* | 90 mm × 66 mm |
| *1800* | 93 mm × 66 mm |
| *2000* | 94 mm × 71 mm |

*Note: Special barrels and cranks are available as follows:*

| Bore (mm) | Stroke (mm) | | |
|---|---|---|---|
| | 72.5 | 78 | 82 |
| 96 | 2103 | 2262 | 2378 |
| 100 | 2280 | 2451 | 2576 |
| 101.6 | 2351 | 2529 | 2659 |

*Note: 1700 and 1800 rods are suitable only with a 72.5 mm crank. 2000 rods are suitable with 72.5 and 78 mm cranks. Special Scat racing rods should be used in all racing motors and also road motors with an 82 mm crank. The heads and crankcase must be machined to accept 100 and 101.6 mm barrels.*

**Standard valves -**

| | | |
|---|---|---|
| | *1700* | 1.476 in inlet |
| | | 1.299 in exhaust |
| | *1800* | 1.546 in inlet |
| | | 1.338 in exhaust |

### VW Type IV (and Porche 914) - continued

|  |  |
|---|---|
| *2000* | 1.614 in inlet |
|  | 1.338 in exhaust |

*Note: Oversize inlet valve sizes are 1.574 in, 1.653 in and 1.732 in. Oversize exhaust valve sizes are 1.398 in, 1.457 in and 1.535 in.*


## VW single ohc four

| | | | |
|---|---|---|---|
| **Standard bore and stroke -** | *1.3* | 75 mm × 73.4 mm | |
| | *1.5* | 76.5 mm × 80 mm | |
| | *1.6* | 79.5 mm × 80 mm | |
| **Standard valves -** | | 1.339 in inlet | oversize 1.5 in or 1.61 in |
| | | 1.22 in exhaust | 1.26 in or 1.338 in |

*Note: The Oettinger modified engine has an 87 mm bore and 82.5 mm stroke, and a twin cam 16 valve head with 1.26 in inlet and 1.10 in exhaust valves.*


## Waggott 4 valve racing engines

| | | | |
|---|---|---|---|
| **Standard bore and stroke -** | *1600* | 85.72 mm × 69.3 mm | |
| | *1850* | 85.72 mm × 80.26 mm | |
| | *2000* | 88.9 mm × 80.26 mm | |
| **Standard valves -** | | 1.312 in inlet | |
| | | 1.125 in exhaust | |


## Weslake small block Chevy V8 4 valve head conversion

| | |
|---|---|
| **Standard valves -** | 1.5 in inlet |
| | 1.312 in exhaust |

*Note: Rocker arm ratio is 1.5:1, inlet and exhaust. A special camshaft is required, either flat tappet or roller tappet (available from Racer Brown or Crane Cams). Special flat top pistons with cutouts for the inlet and exhaust valves are required.*

## Appendix 2   Motorcycle engine specification and modifications

### Ducati 860/900 twins

| | |
|---|---|
| **Standard bore and stroke -** | 86 mm × 74.4 mm |
| | rebore to 88 mm = 905 cc |

*Note: For racing, the standard crankpin (36 mm) must be replaced by a 38 mm pin and larger bearing. The bore can be increased to 92 mm and the stroke increased to 86 mm, but motors larger than 905 cc are very unreliable.*

| | | |
|---|---|---|
| **Standard valves -** | 1.575 in inlet | oversize 1.653 in |
| | 1.417 in exhaust | |

### Godden 500 ohc 4 valve speedway single

| | |
|---|---|
| **Standard bore and stroke -** | 85.5 mm × 86 mm |
| **Standard valves -** | 1.319 in inlet |
| | 1.122 in exhaust |

### Harley-Davidson XR750 dirt tracker

| | | | |
|---|---|---|---|
| **Standard bore and stroke -** | | 79.375 mm × 75.692 mm | |
| **Standard valves -** | *early engine* | 1.653 in inlet | |
| | | 1.378 in exhaust | |
| | *late engine* | 1.732 in inlet | |
| | | 1.378 in exhaust | oversize 1.44 in |

### Harley-Davidson 1000 V-twin

| | |
|---|---|
| **Standard bore and stroke -** | 3.18 in × 3.8 in |
| | rebore to 3.24 in = 1027 cc |
| **Standard valves -** | 1.9 in inlet |
| | 1.635 in exhaust |
| **Sports modification:** | Fit special aluminium 'Thunderheads' designed by Gary Robinson and C.R. Axtell. These heads feature good ports and 1.74 in inlet and 1.46 in exhaust valves. Compression ratio with special 0.040 in oversize pistons supplied in the kit is 10.5:1. |
| **High performance and racing modification:** | Fit special aluminium heads and barrels designed by Alan Sputhe. The barrels have a 3.60 in bore (1268 cc) and manganese iron liner. The heads are supplied with 1.9 in inlet and 1.75 in exhaust valves. |

### Honda 250 four valve single

| | | | |
|---|---|---|---|
| **Standard bore and stroke -** | | 74 mm × 57.8 mm | |
| | | rebore to 83 mm = 313 cc | |
| **Standard valves -** | *early single port engine* | 1.12 in inlet | |
| | | 0.984 in exhaust | |
| | *late twin exhaust port engine* | 1.10 in inlet | oversize 1.142 in |
| | | 1.00 in exhaust | |

## Honda 350 four valve single

| | |
|---|---|
| **Standard bore and stroke -** | 79 mm × 71 mm<br>rebore to 85 mm = 403 cc<br>stroke to 77 mm = 437 cc |
| **Standard valves -** | 1.18 in inlet<br>1.04 in exhaust |

## Honda 400 three valve twin

| | |
|---|---|
| **Standard bore and stroke -** | 70.5 mm × 50.6 mm |
| **Standard valves -** | 1.02 in inlet<br>1.26 in exhaust |
| **Sports modification:** | Raise compression ratio from 9.3:1 to 10.3:1, modify air box to improve air flow, fit free-flow exhaust. |

## Honda 450 - 500 twin

| | | |
|---|---|---|
| **Standard bore and stroke -** | *500* | 70 mm × 64.8 mm |
| | *450* | 70 mm × 57.8 mm |
| **Standard valves -** | | 1.496 in inlet<br>1.3 in exhaust |

## Honda 500 - 550/4

| | | |
|---|---|---|
| **Standard bore and stroke -** | *550* | 58.5 mm × 50.6 mm |
| | *500* | 56 mm × 50.6 mm<br>rebore to 60 mm = 572 cc<br>rebore to 61 mm = 592 cc |
| **Standard valves -** | | 1.083 in inlet<br>0.906 in exhaust |
| **Sports modification:** | | Raise compression ratio from 9:1 to 10.5:1, remove air box and fit four K and N filters, fit free-flow 4 into 1 exhaust. |

## Honda 650/4

| | |
|---|---|
| **Standard bore and stroke -** | 59.8 mm × 55.8 mm<br>rebore to 61 mm = 652 cc |
| **Standard valves -** | 1.24 in inlet<br>1.024 in exhaust |
| **Sports modification:** | Raise compression ratio from 9:1 to 10.5:1, remove air box and fit four K and N filters, fit free-flow 4 into 1 exhaust, advance camshaft 6° to improve throttle response and performance at 4500-6500 rpm. |

## Honda 750/4

| | |
|---|---|
| **Standard bore and stroke -** | 61 mm × 63 mm<br>rebore to 64 mm = 811 cc |

rebore to 65 mm = 836 cc maximum recommended for standard con rods.
rebore to 67 mm = 888 cc racing only
rebore to 71 mm = 998 cc racing only

**Standard valves -**      *early*   1.26 in inlet                    oversize 1.312 in
1.1 in exhaust
*F/2*   1.339 in inlet
1.22 in exhaust

*Note: F/2 valves will hit with modified cam; machine inlets to 1.312 in and exhaust to 1.20in.*

**Sports modification:**      Reshape inlet ports and raise compression from 9.2:1 to 10.5:1, remove air box and fit four K and N filters, fit free-flow 4 into 1 exhaust.

## Honda 750/4 four valve

**Standard bore and stroke -**      62 mm × 62 mm
rebore to 66 mm = 848 cc
rebore to 71 mm = 982 cc racing only

**Standard valves -**      0.984 in inlet      oversize 1.024 in or 1.063 in
0.866 in exhaust                    0.886 in

*Note: Oversize valves for 982 cc racing engine only*

**Sports modification:**      Raise compression ratio from 9:1 to 10.5:1 remove air box and fit four K and N filters, fit free-flow 4 into 1 exhaust.

## Honda 900/4 four

**Standard bore and stroke -**      64.5 mm × 69 mm
rebore to 67.8 mm = 996 cc
rebore to 71 mm = 1093 cc
rebore to 73 mm = 1155 cc racing only

**Standard valves -**      1.024 in inlet                    oversize 1.063 in
0.886 in exhaust

*Note: Oversize valves for 1093 cc and 1155 cc racing engines only.*

**Sports modification:**      Raise compression ratio from 9:1 to 10.2:1, remove air box and fit four K and N filters, fit free-flow 4 into 1 exhaust.

## Honda 1000—1100 flat four

**Standard bore and stroke -**      *1000*   72 mm × 61.4 mm
*1100*   75mm × 61.4 mm

**Standard valves -**      1.496 in inlet
1.26 in exhaust

**Touring modification:**      Raise compression ratio from 9.2:1 to 10.2:1, advance cams $6^0$ to improve low speed and mid-range power (check valve to piston clearance.)

## Honda 1047/6 four valve

**Standard bore and stroke -**      64.5 mm × 53.4 mm
rebore to 68.5 mm = 1181 cc

### Honda 1047/6 four valve - continued

rebore to 71.5 mm = 1286 cc racing only
rebore to 73 mm = 1341 cc drag racing only

Standard valves -

| | |
|---|---|
| 0.984 in inlet | oversize 1.024 in |
| 0.866 in exhaust | 0.886 in |

*Note: Oversize valves for racing engines over 1200 cc only.*

## Honda 997-1084/4 four valve endurance racer

Standard bore and stroke -

997   70 mm × 64.8 mm
1084   73 mm × 64.8 mm

## Kawasaki 250 single

Standard bore and stroke -

70 mm × 64.0 mm
rebore to 73.0 mm = 268 cc
rebore to 76.0 mm = 290 cc
stroke to 70 mm = 318 cc

Standard valves -

1.457 in inlet
1.22 in exhaust

## Kawasaki 500 - 550/4

Standard bore and stroke -

500   55.0 mm × 52.4 mm
rebore to 58 mm = 554 cc
550   58.0 mm × 52.4 mm
rebore to 62 mm = 633 cc

Standard valves -

1.063 in inlet               oversize 1.18 in
0.945 in exhaust

Sports modification -

Raise compression ratio from 9.5:1 to 10.5:1, remove air box and fit four K & N filters, fit free-flow 4 into 1 exhaust.

## Kawasaki 650-750/4

Standard bore and stroke -

650   62 mm × 54 mm
rebore to 65 mm = 717 cc
750   66 mm × 54 mm

Standard valves -

650   1.299 in inlet
1.10 in exhaust
750   1.339 in inlet
1.18 in exhaust

Sports modification:

Advance exhaust cam 5⁰, raise compression ratio to 10.5:1, remove air box and fit four K and N filters, fit free-flow 4 into 1 exhaust.

*Note: If 22 mm carburettors are fitted to the 650 these may be bored out to 24 mm.*

## Kawasaki 900 - 1000/4

Standard bore and stroke -

1000   70 mm × 66 mm
900   66 mm × 66 mm
rebore to 70 mm = 1016 cc (std 1000 bore)
rebore to 73 mm = 1105 cc
rebore to 74 mm = 1135 cc

rebore to 76 mm = 1197 cc racing only

*Note: Racing engines over 1016 cc should have the pressed crankshaft welded.*

**Standard valves -**           1.417 in inlet           oversize 1.476 in
          1.18 in exhaust

**Sports modification:**           Raise compression ratio from 8.7:1 to 10:1, remove air box and fit four K and N filters, fit free-flow 4 into 1 exhaust.

*Note: For racing the Z650 style cam followers and valve caps should be used for reliability.*
*If 26 mm carburettors are fitted, these may be bored to 29 mm for more top end power.*

## Kawasaki 1300/6

**Standard bore and stroke -**       62 mm × 71 mm
**Standard valves -**           1.358 in inlet
          1.16 in exhaust

## Street dohc 4 valve Jawa 500 head conversion

**Standard bore and stroke -**       88 mm × 82 mm
**Standard valves -**           1.375 in inlet
          1.25 in exhaust

*Note: The Street head flows very poorly due to wrongly shaped over-large valves. It should be modified by moving the inlet port over to enter straight into the head. The floor of the port must be filled with epoxy. Then an oval shaped inlet manifold will have to be fabricated to suit the new port entry. The head gasket and cylinder should be machined at the edges of the inlet valves to improve flow into the cylinder, otherwise the in-flowing fuel/air mixture will bang into the ledge formed by the gasket and cylinder wall and disrupt flow.*

## Suzuki 400-450 twin

**Standard bore and stroke -**       *400*   65.0 mm × 60.0 mm
          *425*   67.0 mm × 60.0 mm
          *450*   71.0 mm × 56.6 mm
          rebore to 73 mm = 474 cc
          rebore to 74.8 mm = 497 cc
**Standard valves -**           1.417 in inlet           oversize 1.476 in
          1.18 in exhaust

*Note: Use 1.476 in valves in engines over 450 cc only.*

**Sports modification:**           Raise compression ratio from 9.0:1 to 10.2:1, remove air box and fit two K & N filters, fit free flow exhaust.

## Suzuki 750/4

**Standard bore and stroke -**       65 mm × 56.4 mm
          rebore to 70 mm = 868 cc
          rebore to 73 mm = 944 cc racing only
**Standard valves -**           1.417 in inlet           oversize 1.457 in
          1.18 in exhaust           1.22 in

*Note: Use oversize valves in 944 cc racing engines only.*

**Suzuki 750/4 - continued**

Sports modification:                    Raise compression ratio from 8.7:1 to 10:1, remove air box and fit four K and N filters, fit free-flow 4 into 1 exhaust.

## Suzuki 750/4 four valve

Standard bore and stroke -              67 mm × 53 mm
rebore to 70 mm = 816 cc
rebore to 73 mm = 887 cc racing only
stroke to 59.7 mm = 999 cc

Standard valves -                       0.906 in inlet    oversize 0.984 in and 1.024 in
0.787 in exhaust                        0.866 in

*Note: Use oversize valves in racing engines only.*

Sports modification:                    Raise compression ratio from 9.4:1 to 10.5:1, remove air box and fit four K & N filters, fit free flow 4 into 1 exhaust, replace constant velocity carbs. with 26 mm slide-type Mikunis

## Suzuki 850/4

Standard bore and stroke -              69 mm × 56.4 mm
rebore to 71 mm = 893 cc
rebore to 72 mm = 918 cc

Standard valves -                       1.417 in inlet
1.18 in exhaust

## Suzuki 1000/4

Standard bore and stroke -              70 mm × 64.8 mm
rebore to 75 mm = 1145 cc
rebore to 76 mm = 1176 cc

*Note: Racing engines over 1000 cc should have the pressed crankshaft welded.*

Standard valves -                       1.496 in inlet          oversize 1.535 in
1.26 in exhaust                         1.299 in

*Note: Use oversize valves in racing engines over 1100 cc only.*

Sports modification:                    Raise compression ratio from 9.2:1 to 10.5:1, remove air box and fit four K and N filters, bore carburettors from 26 mm to 29 mm, fit free-flow 4 into 1 exhaust.

## Suzuki 1100/4 four valve

Standard bore and stroke -              72 mm × 66 mm
rebore to 75 mm = 1166 cc
rebore to 76 mm = 1198 cc

*Note: Racing engines should have crankshaft Loctited – drag racing engines should have the crankshaft welded.*

Standard valves -                       1.063 in inlet          oversize 1.142 in
0.906 in exhaust                        0.965 in

*Note: Use oversize valves in racing engines only*

238 **Sports modification:**              Raise compression ratio from 9.5:1 to 10.5:1,

remove air box and fit four K & N filters, fit free flow 4 into 1 exhaust, replace constant velocity carbs. with 26 or 28 mm slide-type Mikunis bored to 29 mm.

## Triumph 500 twin

| | |
|---|---|
| **Standard bore and stroke -** | 69 mm × 65.5 mm |
| **Standard valves -** | 1.53 in inlet |
| | 1.312 in exhaust |

*Note: Inlet valves are too large for 500 cc engine. For racing, increase port diameter to 1.16 in, not 1.25 in, to increase gas speed.*

## Triumph 650/750 twin

| | | |
|---|---|---|
| **Standard bore and stroke -** | *650*  71 mm × 82 mm | |
| | *750*  75.974 mm × 82 mm | |
| **Standard valves -** | 1.595 in inlet | oversize 1.625 in |
| | 1.437 in exhaust | |

*Note: Use oversize valves in 750 cc racing engines only. The standard valves are too large for the 650 cc engine, therefore for racing increase the inlet port diameter to 1.23 in. not 1.31 in. to increase the gas speed.*

## Triumph Trident 750

| | |
|---|---|
| **Standard bore and stroke -** | 66.962 mm × 70 mm |
| **Standard valves -** | 1.534 in inlet |
| | 1.315 in exhaust |

*Note: Inlet valves are too large for 750 cc engine. For racing increase inlet port diameter to 1.20 in. not 1.26 in; to increase gas speed.*

## Weslake/Triumph 750 twin 4 valve dirt tracker

| | |
|---|---|
| **Standard bore and stroke -** | 76 mm × 82 mm |
| **Standard valves -** | 1.15 in inlet |
| | 1.0 in exhaust |

## Weslake 500 four valve speedway single

| | | |
|---|---|---|
| **Standard bore and stroke -** | 85.6 mm × 85.9 mm | |
| **Standard valves -** | 1.25 in inlet | oversize 1.312 in or 1.375 in |
| | 1.125 in exhaust | 1.156 in or 1.2 in |

## Yamaha 400 twin

| | |
|---|---|
| **Standard bore and stroke -** | 69 mm × 52.4 mm |
| **Standard valves -** | 1.4 in inlet |
| | 1.18 in |

### Yamaha 400 twin - continued

**Sports modification:**        Raise compression ratio from 9.2:1 to 10.2:1, modify air box to improve air flow, fit free-flow exhaust.

## Yamaha 500 single

| | |
|---|---|
| **Standard bore and stroke -** | 87 mm × 84 mm |
| | rebore to 92 mm  = 558 cc |
| | stroke to 91 mm = 605 cc |
| | rebore to 97 mm = 672 cc (91 mm stroke) |

**Standard valves -**      *dirt bike*    1.77 in inlet  oversize 1.85 in, 1.9 in or 1.95 in
                                          1.54 in exhaust
            *road bike*    1.85 in inlet           oversize 1.9 in or 1.95 in
                                          1.54 in exhaust

*Note: Use oversize valves in racing engines over 558 cc only.*

**Sports modification:**        Raise compression ratio from  9:1 to 10:5.1, (only if you are strong enough to kick it over) Raise and radius inlet port. Modify air box to improve air flow. Fit free-flow muffler. Fit 45 to 55 pilot jet in carburettor to replace standard 25 pilot jet - this allows engine to run at 2000 rpm in top gear without snatching.

## Yamaha 500 four valve twin

| | |
|---|---|
| **Standard bore and stroke -** | 73 mm × 59.6 mm |
| **Standard valves -** | 1.1 in inlet |
| | 0.95 in exhaust |

## Yamaha 650 twin

| | |
|---|---|
| **Standard bore and stroke -** | 75 mm × 74 mm |
| **Standard valves -** | 1.614 in inlet |
| | 1.378 in exhaust |

**Sports modification:**        Raise compression ratio from 8.4:1 to 10:1, modify air box to improve air flow, fit  free-flow exhaust.

## Yamaha 650/4

| | |
|---|---|
| **Standard bore and stroke -** | 63 mm × 52.4 mm |
| | rebore to 66 mm = 717 cc |
| **Standard valves -** | 1.299 in inlet |
| | 1.1 in exhaust |

**Sports modification -**        Raise compression ratio from 9.2:1 to 10.5:1, remove air box and fit four K & N filters, fit free flow 4 into 1 exhaust, advance both cams $5^0$ to improve mid-range throttle response

## Yamaha 750-850/3

| | | |
|---|---|---|
| **Standard bore and stroke -** | *750* | 68 mm × 68.6 mm |
| | *850* | 71.5 mm × 68.6 mm |
| | | rebore to 72.5 mm = 850 cc |
| | | rebore to 74.5 mm = 897 cc |
| | | rebore to 74.5 mm = 897 cc. |

**Standard valves -**

| | |
|---|---|
| 1.417 in inlet | oversize 1.496 in |
| 1.22 in exhaust | 1.26 in |

**Sports modification:** Raise compression ratio from 8.5:1 to 10:1, remove air box and fit three K and N filters, fit free-low 3 into 1 exhaust.

## Yamaha 1100/4

**Standard bore and stroke -**

71.5 mm × 68.6 mm
rebore to 74.5 mm = 1196 cc
rebore to 76 mm = 1245 cc racing only

**Standard valves -**

| | | |
|---|---|---|
| *early* | 1.417 in inlet | oversize 1.496 in |
| | 1.22 in exhaust | 1.26 in |
| *late* | 1.496 in inlet | |
| | 1.26 in exhaust | |

**Sports modification:** Raise compression ratio from 8.5:1 to 10.2:1, remove air box and fit four K and N filters, fit free-flow 4 into 1 exhaust.

## Appendix 3   Table of useful equivalents

1 inch  = 25.4 mm
1 cubic inch  = 16.387 cc
1 horsepower  = 0.7457 kilowatts
1 pound foot torque  = 1.3558 Newton metres
1 pound inch torque  = 0.11298 Newton metres

1 mm = 0.03937 in
1 litre  = 61.024 cu in or 1000 cc
1 kilowatt  = 1.341 hp

1 psi = 6.89476 kilopascals
    or 33.9 millibars
    or 2.0345 inches of mercury
    or 27.67 inches of water

$^0F = \frac{9}{5} \times (^0C + 32)$
$^0C = \frac{5}{9} \times (^0F - 32)$

1 gallon (Imperial)  = 160 fluid oz
1 gallon (US)  = 128 fluid oz

# Index